The
Straight
Path
of the
Spirit

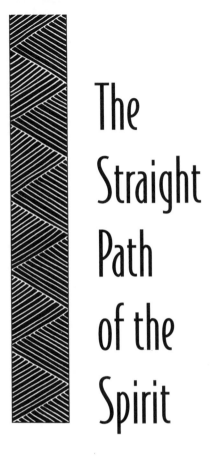

The
Straight
Path
of the
Spirit

Ancestral Wisdom and Healing Traditions in Fiji

RICHARD KATZ

Park Street Press
Rochester, Vermont

Park Street Press
One Park Street
Rochester, Vermont 05767
www.InnerTraditions.com

Park Street Press is a division of Inner Traditions International

LIBRARY OF CONGRESS CATALOGING-IN-PUBLICATION DATA

Katz, Richard, 1937–
    [Straight Path]
    The straight path of the spirit : ancestral wisdom and healing traditions in Fiji /
        Richard Katz.
        p. cm.
    Originally published: The Straight Path. Reading, Mass. : Addison-Wesley Pub. Co.,
        c1993.
    Includes bibliographical references and index.
    ISBN 0-89281-767-4 (alk. paper)
    1. Fiji—Religious life and customs.   2. Spiritual healing—Fiji.   3. Healing—Fiji—
        Religious aspects.   4. Noa, Ratu.   I. Title.
    [BL2620.F54K38   1999]   98-50340
    615.8'82'099611—dc21   CIP

Printed and bound in the United States

10   9   8   7   6   5   4   3   2   1

*To those whose gifts
remain silent*

FIJI

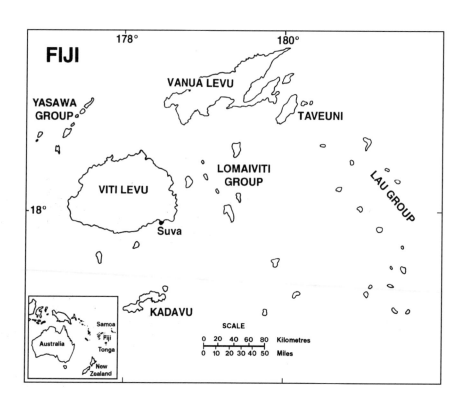

CONTENTS

Acknowledgments

Writing acknowledgments is a privilege, but like all worthy privileges it does not come easily. How can I fully describe the help I received? Or the trust and love that allowed this book to be? I can only hint at these things, hoping that my words will invite feelings that come nearer to the facts.

In the Fijian principle of exchange, from what is given there is a return, another giving. This book is part of that exchange; these acknowledgments, an honoring of some of the special recipients.

Throughout the book's story I use pseudonyms — out of respect and in accordance with people's wishes. Therefore the contributions certain persons made to the book cannot be directly acknowledged. But the intensity of their contributions remains. The people I lived and worked with in Fiji — the people on the island I call Kali, the island chain I call Bitu, in the city of Suva, and especially those in our adopted village, which I am calling Tovu — created a home with their generosity and commitment, allowing my family and me to feel like Fijians — *kai viti*. In the actual conduct of the research, Ratu Noa, Sitiveni, Inoke, and Tevita (the names are all pseudonyms) were the inner heart of the work. From their spirit came direction. Help also came with an open heart from Joseph Cagilevu, Ron Crocombe, Ratu Lala, John Lum On, G. Fred Lyons, Sereana Naivota, Tevita Nawadra, Asesela Ravuvu, Vula Saumaiwai, Chris Saumaiwai, Suliana Siwatibau, and Ateca Williams.

The Fijian government, especially the Ministry of Fijian Affairs, granted permission for the research and sensitively supported my efforts, as did the Fiji Museum, the Fijian Dictionary Project, and the Institute of Pacific Studies, University of the South Pacific.

The writing itself drew on many sources of strength and insight, especially Ratu Noa and Sitiveni. Others who offered careful and caring readings of various drafts included Beth Cuthand, Robbie Davis-Floyd, Jackie Gusaas, Eber Hampton, Mary Hampton, Paul Jacoby, David Miller, Danny Musqua, Asesela Ravuvu, Verna St. Denis, and Bob Williamson. With dedication and insight, Merloyd Lawrence took in the manuscript and helped craft it into a book. In the process she helped clarify my larger aims in writing.

The earliest stages of writing emerged within several fertile contexts: an informal writing group in Cambridge, Massachusetts, whose members were Mel Bucholtz, Steve Gallegos, and Laura Chasin; a conference on discourse in the South Pacific organized by Geoff White and Karen Watson-Gegeo at the Claremont Colleges; an article I coauthored with Linda Kilner on the "straight path"; and classes taught at Harvard University, the University of Alaska–Fairbanks, and the Saskatchewan Indian Federated College, where students enriched the material I presented with their open listening and honest response.

Harvard University, the University of Alaska–Fairbanks, and the Saskatchewan Indian Federated College provided financial and logistical support in the preparation of the manuscript. The Saskatchewan Indian Federated College, where I now teach, was especially generous, offering support from the heart. With care and dedication, Louise McCallum typed the manuscript, Dave Geary made the drawings and map, Grant Kernan produced prints, Paul Thivierge reproduced slides, and Pat Jalbert expertly guided the complex production process.

I would not have gone to Fiji, and certainly not have survived there, without my family. My ex-wife, Mary Maxwell West, my daughter Laurel Katz, and my son Alex Katz were my bedrock there. Each tried to keep me straight in what I saw and said — and continue to see and say.

As I write now, far from Fiji, I want to speak of my new family. My wife, Verna St. Denis, teaches me about honesty, respect, humility, and the struggle to be without the aid of entitlements. She offers these gifts to the writing of the book. Laurel and Alex bring new light to my writing task as I reflect on their beautifully emerging maturities. And now there are two new lives, our son Adam, whose smile penetrates to the heart, and our daughter Hannah, whose grace encircles us. Their energy makes my writing time more precious.

I hope this book expresses the yearnings of those who took part in its creation, and that in my struggle to follow the "straight path," I will be able to return their gifts.

— Saskatoon, Saskatchewan, 1993

Royalties received by the author from the sale of this book will be shared with those in Fiji who made it possible for me to learn about the "straight path."

The
Straight
Path
of the
Spirit

Coming In:
Exchange and
Responsibility

"**Y**ou must tell the story of our healing. As that story educates your people in our ancient ways, it will help us appreciate more who we are and who we must remain." Ratu Noa[1] spoke calmly, looking firmly into my eyes. I listened carefully to this traditional Fijian healer I had worked with closely for nearly two years. He continued: "Sometimes our story must be told by one of us — from the inside; sometimes by one of you — from the outside. The times determine which version of the story will be believed, and therefore which version should be put forth.

"Today our story must be told by someone like you. And I'm happy about that because you know our story. You look like one of them, but you're really one of us!" Ratu Noa smiled. "It's an exchange," he observed. "We've taught you, and now you must teach others what you've learned."

Ratu Noa's words are more than a request; they are a charge; they create more than a responsibility; they create an obligation. They strengthen similar words spoken by other Fijians with whom I worked. This book is my attempt to share what I learned — and am learning; to deepen my responsibility so that a true exchange becomes more possible, expanding the process of learning from Fijian healers to include a concrete giving back to those who are my teachers.

Yet I remain clear about the limits of this exchange. A voice from the outside can indeed become eloquent at a certain point in time *just because* it is from the outside. And spiritual families do form, bringing one within the heartbeat of another culture. I believe that happened with me in Fiji. But I can never forget that as a white person raised in the middle class, I am also forever and fundamentally different from the Fijian people I worked with. It is only by respecting the boundaries of difference, *while* stretching across them emotionally and spiritually, that I can hope to tell an accurate story — always realizing that it is just one version or one part of the story.

How did I come to meet this Ratu Noa? The enduring gray skies and commitment to the mentality of cold which shaped my Cambridge, Massachusetts world in those days had little connection with the warm

---

[1]Like all the Fijian names in the book, this is a pseudonym. See *Names That Make the Story*, p. 372, for a discussion of this use of pseudonyms.

flow of air and thriving green vegetation of the tropical world of Fiji. Yet, motivated by my long-standing involvement in traditional, spiritual healing, I found myself in Fiji, with Ratu Noa.

Planning for the trip began when my then wife, Mary Maxwell (Max) West, a doctoral student in child development, was awarded a grant to do field research — anywhere in the world. Together we sought a place where her research interests and mine could both be realized. We considered returning to the Kalahari Desert, where I had worked earlier with Zhu/twa (or !Kung) healers. But with two small children, we decided that the desert site was too remote from medical assistance.

Max wished to focus on Fijian child-rearing practices, I on the tradition of spiritual healing. The government believed such research served the needs of the nation and granted us permission to work in Fiji; Max's work on child development could suggest ways of understanding how parents influence the cognitive development of their children, whereas mine on spiritual healing could help build bridges between traditional and Western health care.

In January 1977 we arrived in Fiji — my wife, then 35, my daughter, then 9, my son, then 6, and I, then 39. It was not long before we shed our cold-protecting postures and walked with the languid, open step of the tropics. For the next twenty-two months we lived and worked there, conducting our research, of course, but also as time went on becoming another family in Fiji, even at times a Fijian family. On my second visit to Fiji, in 1985, I was alone, but this family foundation remained.

I knew that knowledge about Fijian healing, with its strong spiritual core, is never shared with someone merely for the asking. You earn the privilege of learning. I also understood that though my doctoral degree from Harvard University in clinical psychology, as well as my training in anthropology, would legitimize my research, it would rarely deal with the inner substance of that research. Yet with sixteen years' experience in various aspects of psychological and spiritual healing, including fieldwork with traditional healers, I felt prepared to begin.

The research began, however, with many false and hesitating starts. Though it was painful to admit, it became apparent that I was not ready to work with Ratu Noa. In time yes, but not right away. Being prepared had nothing to do with who I had been or what I knew. It had everything to do with who I was and what I could learn and put into practice *at that time*. I learned something about humility, and this became central to the fabric of the connection between Ratu Noa and me as it evolved. Ratu Noa became my teacher; his teachings are the inner core of the book.

Ratu Noa's words remain clear. Addressing me by my Fijian name, he said, "Rusiate, a good healer never exaggerates what he knows, he never emphasizes his own personal contribution to the healing." As always in our conversations, when Ratu Noa talked about healing, he talked about what he tried to do in his own healing work and what he wished for me, as a person who had the promise of becoming a healer.

"The words we speak are powerful," Ratu Noa continued. "They have their own power. When we treat words with respect and use them respect-fully, they can help and heal us. If we abuse them — use them dishonestly or without care — they can do serious harm to ourselves and others."

I now realize anew what always struck me when Ratu Noa expressed these thoughts. Here I am, a university professor, a person whose job thrives on words, yet all the academic training I received did not give me sufficient respect for words and their power. It would have been easy to feel inadequate to the task of writing.

But Ratu Noa's words are still alive, helping turn my sense of inade-quacy into one of humility: "If you speak from the heart, and say only what you know to be true, you never have to worry about what you're going to say or how you'll say it." When he spoke, he demonstrated this way of communicating.

Writing from the heart, I learned, means *being* prepared, emotionally and spiritually as well as intellectually. It is not a matter of techniques and procedures. Writing from the heart is simpler, but far more demanding.

Toward the end of my initial two-year stay in Fiji, I spoke at length with Ratu Noa about my return to the United States. We discussed what I should say or write about what I'd learned, and what was best to remain silent about.

Ratu Noa offered more guidance when we parted: "Your responsibility is to tell the truth about our healing work and in that to help others learn.

Tell only what you know, and that will always be enough. Tell more than you know, and that is too much; it would only exaggerate your own importance. You must also put what you know into practice.

"You have been here almost two years. We have stayed close to the healing work. Trust yourself and be straight. You are on the straight path (*gaunisala dodonu*), and if you keep following that path, you will know what to say and what not to say. Because if after all this time you have not learned what to say and what not to say, just talk about whatever you please because your speech will have no value anyway."

Trying to follow the "straight path" is the way I learn about it — just as Fijian healers do. The straight path becomes known as one struggles to find and stay on it. For Fijians, it is a powerful metaphor for the way all persons should live, and healers especially are expected to make the arduous journey it requires. The path deals with varying textures of ordinary life situations and how their challenges should be met. To travel the straight path demands attributes such as honesty, respect, service, and humility.

Ratu Noa's advice helped me decide what to write about and what form my writing should take. Six years later I completed a rough first draft of this book.

Six years is a long time. Was it a sign, I wondered, that I was trying to complete what should be left undone? Yet I needed that time, and the book needed that time. Like the sculpted figure Inuit carvers say emerges from soapstone, the book had to dwell inside me, growing beyond my understanding, in order to emerge more with its own meaning. But I was at an impasse. I had to speak again with Ratu Noa and others in Fiji about the book.

I returned to Fiji in the summer of 1985. I had only four weeks, but that proved to be enough. I returned to visit, to see my relatives and friends, and I brought the draft manuscript.

Ratu Noa was the first person I talked with. He was the central figure in my experience in Fiji; he is the central figure in the book. In many ways, it is his book. When I asked him to be co-author, however, he refused. "This book," he said, "must come from your hand. It is your story to tell. That way we Fijians can best be served. All the help you need in writing the book, I will offer. But I don't want you to use my name or include my photograph. If my healing work is to continue, it cannot become known in a public way."

"This writing job hasn't been easy," I told him. "I've tried to stay with your advice. I've tried to follow the straight path so I can write honestly, so that the book will be of service to people. But things are not always clear…and I often struggle. I need your help."

Ratu Noa leaned forward, pressing into me, and caught my eyes within his. He spoke quietly, passionately:

"Rusiate, you must try, try, and try. You must keep trying.

"This book is very important," Ratu Noa added. "It will help in the revival of traditional Fijian culture because it will reveal what is missing today in our own lives. What is missing is our traditional ways of life (*vakavanua*); that is what is needed to lead us in the present day.

"Rusiate, we have spent many, many hours together. I've established the truth of what you are writing about, including our conversations and the events you describe. All that remains is your own truthfulness in the writing — and I know that you are being truthful as you are struggling to follow the straight path. This book is good and correct, Ratu Rusiate. You have my total support, and my blessing. Let us be very simple about this. The book must be written."

It is now 1999. Fourteen years have passed since my second visit to Fiji. The words of Ratu Noa and other Fijian healers are before you. I hope they will guide you so that you too can be preparing as you read. Maybe we can all use whatever little knowledge we have as a foundation for understanding rather than as a barrier.

This book brings us full cycle, moving my obligation as a storyteller toward you, the reader, asking you to take up the responsibilities entailed in this story of Fijian healing. The fullness of that cycle celebrates the principle of exchange which is so central to Fijians' lives. As we learn from them, we honor their exchange of knowledge with us. And we must go one step further. As we recognize the value of their knowledge in our lives, we must affirm the dignity and value of the land and people from which that knowledge grows.

PART ONE

HEALING IN FIJIAN CULTURE

CHAPTER 1

Vanua:
The Land,
the People,
the Culture

Ratu Maibula is the old God, the Mighty One. Below him, like his angels, are the *Vu* [the ancestral gods]. Ratu Maibula and the *Vu* live on a mountain in the province of Ra, God's place. Ratu Maibula has authority over all things. He is God of Gods, King of Kings, Lord of Lords. He is the most supreme.

Ratu Maibula cannot be seen by anyone, only heard. Once he was married, but his wife could not see him; she could only hear what he said. He did not live with his wife — yet his wife got pregnant. Together they had two children. Ratu Maibula also planted a banana tree. He allowed no one to eat the bananas until the first fruits were offered to him, as a sign of respect. After that offering was made, people could eat the bananas.

One day Ratu Maibula's wife saw some ripe bananas. She felt Ratu Maibula would not be angry if she gave her children bananas to eat because he was their father. So she plucked the bananas and gave them to the children, who then ate them.

When Ratu Maibula heard of this, he became furious. He called for his companion, his helper who lived with him on the mountain. "Go kill my wife and my children," he ordered his companion. The companion went out to find them and saw them hiding under a tree root. When he later returned to the tree in order to kill them, they were not there. They had escaped.

Years later the children appeared at Toorak, a place in Turkey, where the children, now adults, multiplied, and from where their children and the generations that followed went to Persia, then to Africa, and finally returned to Fiji. There they multiplied further and lived on the land.

From this we know that Fiji was originally settled by Indigenous Fijians, who later, through their progeny, resettled in Fiji.

To tell you the facts, Fiji is God's residence. It is the place where *mana* is stored. Fiji is where all the *Vu* live — the *Vu* for whites, the *Vu* for Indians, all the *Vu* are here.

This story of the founding of the Fijian people, told to me by my teacher Ratu Noa, who is a respected storyteller, would be classified by some as an "origin myth." The word "myth" implies that the story is inferior to the "actual" or "true" story, one taking into account, say, archeological or linguistic evidence. But the story's reality, based on lived experience, has its own truth, as does the reality based on archeological data. Neither approach to reality has a lock on scientific method. Recognized traditional storytellers are charged with maintaining the life of their ancient stories. They are disciplined scientists, committed to truth, in particular the true rendition of what they were told and know from their own experience (Wolfe, 1989). Rigorous, specialized training in memory and communication skills makes them better able to meet their commitments (Knight, 1990). Meanwhile evidence continues to mount as to the role of "myth" in the development of Western sciences, as well as the influence of personal, political, and cultural biases (Clifford and Marcus, 1986; Gould, 1981; Hollway, 1989).

These two views of reality need not be seen as unrelated. Traditional elders are often heard to advise young people about how to meet the encroachments of Western culture: "Take what is useful from the

11

European way. Take it and blend it into our own way. But never forget who you are as an Indigenous person." In writing this book, I have tried to follow this advice about blending yet remaining true to oneself.

In this chapter and the next I provide a background for understanding traditional Fijian healing, relying on numerous ethnographies and articles about Fiji to address those elements best described by a trained outsider.[1] But the basis of and final filter for material presented in these two chapters will be the words and views of the Fijian people themselves.[2]

FIJI AND THE FIJIANS

In the southwest Pacific Ocean, Fiji stretches out across nearly one hundred inhabited islands, with most of the population of about 750,000 (600,000 at the time of my stay in 1977–78) concentrated in cities, towns, and villages on the two largest islands, Viti Levu and Vanua Levu. The many smaller outer-island communities are typically rural villages ranging in size from about one hundred to four hundred people. At the crossroads between the geocultural areas of Melanesia and Polynesia, Fiji is located at the southeastern end of the Melanesian chain of high volcanic islands that extends from Papua New Guinea through the Solomon Islands and Vanuatu. To the east is Samoa and to the southeast Tonga, both Polynesian

---

[1]These articles and ethnographies include Arno, 1980, 1992; Basow, 1984, 1986; Belshaw, 1964; Brewster, 1922; Derrick, 1950; Herr, 1981; Hickson, 1986; Hocart, 1929, 1952; Kaplan, 1988, 1989; M. M. W. Katz, 1981, 1984; Kelly, 1988; Knapman and Walter, 1980; Lal, 1983, 1989; Lasaqa, 1984; Quain, 1948; Roth, 1953; Rutz, 1978; Sahlins, 1962, 1985; Spencer, 1937, 1941; Stewart, 1982a, 1982b, 1984; B. Thompson, 1908; L. Thompson, 1940a, 1940b; J. W. Turner, 1984, 1986, 1987; Watters, 1969; West, 1988; Williams and Calvert, 1859). Since I use these sources mostly for general background and corroboration, I do not cite particular references except in instances where one source alone makes a specific point.

[2]These words and views are drawn largely from my two years of fieldwork in Fiji and from several especially valuable books written by Fijians, including Rusiate Nayacakalou's *Tradition and Change in the Fijian Village* and *Leadership in Fiji*, Asesela Ravuvu's *The Fijian Way of Life*, and Saimoni Vatu's *Talking About Oral Traditions*.

island nations. Fiji lies 1,930 kilometers (1,200 miles) south of the equator; its climate is tropical, with temperatures usually ranging from sixteen to thirty-two degrees Celsius (sixty to ninety degrees Fahrenheit), and the islands receive heavy rainfall on the windward side.

Indigenous Fijians from the central and western regions were traditionally considered more Melanesian; but in the eastern islands, such as those in the Lau group, a strong Polynesian influence is also apparent. By the mid-nineteenth century, missionary and trade contact had reduced regional differences, and today a distinctly Fijian culture, resulting from the blending of Melanesian and Polynesian elements, can be said to exist alongside more characteristically Melanesian or Polynesian culture areas.

From 1874 until 1970, Fiji was a British colony, and during the late nineteenth and early twentieth centuries, the British brought indentured laborers from India to work on the large sugarcane plantations. The descendants of those workers, as well as subsequent immigrants from India, now make up 49 percent of the population of Fiji; Indigenous Fijians account for 46 percent; and persons of European descent (especially New Zealanders and Australians), other Pacific Islanders, and people of other cultures, such as Chinese, total no more than 5 percent. This population mix raises profound and complex problems, especially between Indigenous Fijians and those of Indian ancestry.

Through their system of communal landholding, which does not permit property to be sold, Indigenous Fijians own more than 80 percent of the land. But the land that is presently most capable of producing income, including urban sites for commercial establishments and hotels, is primarily owned or operated on long-term leases by others. The commercial lifeline of Fiji is in the hands of either outside interests, especially from New Zealand and Australia, or Fijians of Indian ancestry, who are especially dominant in smaller commercial enterprises.

Indigenous Fijians blame their exclusion from the contemporary wealth of their nation on Fijians of Indian ancestry. The conflict between these two groups is intense, and sometimes violent. As one Indigenous Fijian elder put it when speaking of Fijians of Indian descent:

Village farmer[3]

"Everything we Fijians believe in, they destroy. Where we share, they hoard; where we are quiet, they are loud; where we are respectful, they are aggressive; and where we are humble, they are arrogant. We can't live with them in our place."

From Fijians of Indian ancestry there are also complaints. For them the "sharing" of Indigenous Fijians shows a lack of good business sense; Indigenous Fijians' "quietness" and "humility" are interpreted as timidity

---

[3]Individuals in these photographs are not named for the same reason that pseudonyms are used in the text. This decision should not be confused with the absence of names in many earlier anthropological photographs of Indigenous people. In those photographs, identities were denied through lack of respect rather than protected out of respect.

Adolescent and child

and passivity. With the values of each transmuted by the other into an eerie negative reflection, the gulf between the two cultures seems insurmountable.

Indigenous Fijians have applied constant pressure to solidify their political control of the nation even as they drop in number below a majority of the population. In 1977, for example, a political party that emerged with surprising strength took as its motto "Fiji for Fijians," a not-so-polite way of saying that Fijians of Indian ancestry should leave Fiji. The recent coups of 1987 were a more dramatic attempt to ensure Indigenous Fijian control.

This book is about Indigenous Fijians, who call themselves simply Fijians (*kai viti*, literally "from Fiji").[4] And Fijian is the word I will use.

▲ TRADITIONAL FIJIAN HEALING

In providing the background for Fijian healing practices, I concentrate on traditional ceremonies, religious beliefs, and values as well as social structure rather than topics such as history, political structure, and detailed linguistic analysis. This choice is based on the judgment of Fijian elders, as well as my own, as to what is important to know if one is to understand traditional Fijian healing.

There are several kinds of traditional Fijian healers: this book focuses on the *dauvagunu,* or spiritual healers. I use the term "healer" or "Fijian healer" or "traditional healer" to refer to the *dauvagunu* and "traditional Fijian healing" or "Fijian healing" to refer to their work.

---

[4] I use the terms "Indigenous" and "Western" in order to compare and contrast peoples and institutions. The literature on these two terms is, of course, extensive (for example, Barnett, 1953; Bateson, 1972; Bellah, 1968; Bodley, 1989; Diamond, 1974; Fanon, 1978; Guenther, 1986; Herbert, 1982; Huizer, 1978; Lee and Hurlich, 1982; Little Bear et al., 1984; Memmi, 1965; Nayacakalou, 1978; R. Rappaport, 1978; Trainer, 1989; B. Turner, 1990). Though the issues these sources address are complex, I wish to offer a simpler understanding, using the terms as a pragmatic manner of alluding to two different but overlapping and interrelated ways of being, which are themselves each undergoing change.

I use the term "Western" to refer to people and institutions relatively affected by

16

The concept of "tradition" is not an absolute one. Here the word "traditional" refers to a healing system that in the middle to late 1970s and mid-1980s — the time of my fieldwork — was considered by Fijians to express traditional Fijian values and beliefs, especially about the spiritual realm and issues of health and sickness. Values and beliefs were seen by people as traditional to the degree that they were the same as or similar to the way "the old people" (*qase*) or the respected elders, chiefs, and ancestors valued and believed *e liu* or "in the past." But *e liu*, which is often translated as "in the olden times" and means literally "before, in time or place," does not refer to any specific time in the past.

Since tradition is an evolving body of beliefs and customs (Hobsbawm and Ranger, 1984; B. Turner, 1990), all we can say is that the healing system described in this book is more traditional than other forms of healing now available to Fijians, including Western-oriented, hospital-based health care.

But the healing system to be described is also "not like it was long ago," as one Fijian elder notes. "In the past," he says, "we had strong healers. They were close to the *Vu* [the ancestral gods]. They respected the ways of the land [*vakavanua*] and kept all the sacred taboos. But today, it's all changing. They don't respect the old ways anymore. Today we have almost nothing left." This elder's view is repeated by others many times. And so not only is the healing described more traditional than other health services currently available, but apparently it is also less traditional than it was at one time.

---

forces such as modernism, capitalism, and urbanism; the term "Indigenous" to refer to people and institutions relatively more affected by forces such as traditionalism, cooperative economics, and rural or "bush" life. The term "Western" does not refer merely to the geographical area known as the West; it is an attitude, a way of being, that appears in many parts of the world, though it may be more concentrated in places like Europe, the United States, and Canada. The term "Indigenous" refers to Aboriginal or First Nations Peoples. Indigenous peoples are descended from the first or original inhabitants of a place, and though they are relatively more traditional, they are also often influenced by the Western values of the larger nation within which they reside.

▲ LOCATION OF THE STORY

Traditional Fijian values, beliefs, and social structure are generally stronger in the rural areas than in the urban areas, though they do exist in urban areas in adapted form, often truncated and dramatized, sometimes revitalized and purified. The same can be said of traditional Fijian healing. The reason is obvious: the vast majority of adult Fijians living in the urban areas were born and raised in the rural villages. They bring with them to the city what they learned when growing up — their traditions.

The story of healing told in this book took place in both rural and urban areas; in a specific rural area, the northern end of an island chain I call Bitu, and especially in a village I call Tovu, as well as in a specific urban area, Suva.[5]

Suva, the capital city of Fiji, is located on Viti Levu, the island with the largest population. Nearly half of Suva's seventy thousand residents are Fijians of Indian descent. This cosmopolitan setting has two active daily newspapers, a regional university, many restaurants and banks, and several movie theaters. It is also a favorite stopping place for tourists, primarily from New Zealand and Australia.

In the island chain of Bitu, people live in small coastal villages of about a hundred people, usually separated by several hours' journey on foot, or a half-hour or more by motorboat. Here the population is for the most part Indigenous Fijian; the rare exception might be a central government official, teacher, or a shopkeeper of Indian or other ethnic ancestry.

My emphasis in describing Fijian values, social structure, ceremonies, and healing, is on the form they take in Bitu, although I do at times discuss practices in Suva in order to suggest the changes that are occurring. These changes are also reflected in the rural healing system, introducing a dynamic to this story of healing. The interplay between rural Bitu and urban Suva is truly reciprocal.

---

[5]With the exception of Suva, the names of places where the story primarily took place have been changed.

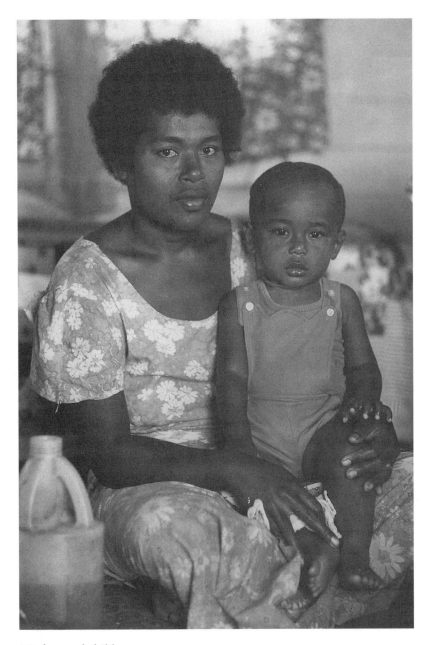

Mother and child

Just as there are similarities and differences between rural and urban Fiji, so this book is both about and not about Fiji as a nation. As mentioned earlier, Fiji is a complex nation; cultural variations, even within the Indigenous Fijian population, abound. Polynesian-influenced eastern Fiji differs from the Melanesian-influenced west, areas along coral reefs differ from mountainous ones, and coastal villages differ from upriver or inland ones. And these differences define important rules and rituals of relationship.

Persons from coastal villages, for example, see themselves as "from the water" (*kai wai*), whereas the inhabitants of inland villages see themselves as "from the land" (*kai vanua*). These identifications are assumed with pride, with the distinct implication that anyone who differs is somehow less "worthy" — not as skillful, not as smart, not as resourceful. They also create reciprocal actions of respect and ritual obligations. Meetings between persons from the land and from the water are predictable occasions for mutual joking and teasing as well as fulfilling ritual obligations of exchange. People from the water, for example, give specified foods harvested from the ocean to those from the land, while those from the land give in return foods unavailable on the coast in a complementary and enriching exchange.[6]

Despite these elegant differences, similarities exist throughout the Indigenous cultures of Fiji. Therefore, although this book focuses on a particular island chain and the Suva area, to some extent it can be generalized to other parts of Fiji.

THE VU AND MANA

It is impossible to talk about Fijian tradition without dealing with the basis of that tradition, the *Vu* — the "ancestral gods," the "spirits of dead ancestors," or more simply "the ancestors." The word *Vu* refers both to the more ancient, cosmological gods, such as Degei, who rule over all

---

[6]To make these differences more subtle, a group that is "from the water" in relation to a second group with whom it makes exchanges may consider itself to be "from the land" in relation to yet a third group that is regarded as "from the water."

Fiji, and to the spirits of dead ancestors and other relatives, who inhabit the local areas still connected with their progeny. These two groups are not disconnected; Fijians see the cosmological gods as their ancestors, their relatives, the only difference being that these gods are generations more remote in the past than recently deceased relatives.

The *Vu* are active in everyday life, and their influence penetrates into all activities. They watch over, guide, and protect their descendants, encouraging, and at times demanding, that people of today keep to and respect the old ways, the ways the *Vu* are still practicing. If people deviate from these traditions, they withhold their protection, and punishment is forthcoming. The earthly realm mirrors the spiritual realm in its values and structure, so people seek guidance from the *Vu* about how to live properly, and especially how to resolve crises. The traditional healer assumes a role of utmost importance in this search for guidance because, except for powerful chiefs, he or she has the closest and most direct link to the *Vu.*

Because of their power to bring about both good and evil in everyday life, the *Vu* are regarded with respect, fear, and awe, made the more intense by their invisibility to all but the few who like the healers can communicate with and sometimes even see them. But the presence of the *Vu* can be sensed by ordinary people, occasioning a feeling of terror, a profoundly intuitive, uncanny feeling called *rere.* The feeling of *rere* occurs most often at night, especially if one is alone and out in the bush. It may indicate that a relative has died or will soon die. Although these brushes with the spirits terrify ordinary people, who tenaciously avoid them, healers seek and accept contacts with the *Vu,* and try to extend the duration and intensity of these contacts.

The *Vu* are the source of power behind the Fijian land and people and the activities and values that connect the two. This spiritual power is called *mana. Mana* is the fundamental spiritual force that is recognized in cultures throughout the world, akin to the *n/um* of the Kalahari Zhu/twasi or the *wakan* of the Lakota people or the *chi* of the traditional Chinese. But as with these other concepts, *mana* is hard to define. "*Mana,*" said one Fijian elder paradoxically, trying to explain it, "is

21

mana." Others say *mana* is the "power to effect," or "what makes things happen." One chief likened its action to that of electricity; it is something unseen but nevertheless powerful, even devastating.

As an expression of the powers of the *Vu, mana* is meant to help and heal. But when approached disrespectfully or used improperly, it can harm or kill. Though most intense with the *Vu, mana* is also present in sacred places associated with the *Vu,* such as at ancient burial mounds and during ceremonies. Chiefs, who by virtue of their birthright are closest to the *Vu,* and healers, who learn to communicate with the *Vu,* have special access to *mana.* One chief, for instance, said that his *mana* was so powerful that whenever he bathed in a stream, the fish would die. A person fishing downstream might be overjoyed at the unexpected catch, but since the fish died from exposure to the chief's *mana,* they would now be sacred and therefore potentially dangerous, if not respect- ed. The fish would have become taboo (*tabu* or "something sacred that one is prohibited from approaching or touching"); it would be a viola- tion of the *mana* to eat them and harm would result. Unless one is qualified by birth or training to work with *mana,* one keeps one's dis- tance from it. So powerful is *mana* that close contact with it, or with anything or anyone possessing it, can be dangerous for the unprepared and even on occasion for those who are prepared as well.

The more powerful and sacred the site or person, the stronger the *mana* attached to it. *Mana* is a direct expression of the power of the *Vu* — the more powerful the *Vu,* the more powerful the *mana.* Like the *Vu, mana* permeates Fijian life in greater or lesser concentrations. Healers speak of a "*mana*-box" (*kato ni mana*), buried deep in the ocean which is the source of the *mana* throughout Fiji, and throughout the world as well.

The traditional thinking about and ways of gaining access to *mana* in rural areas undergo changes in the city. A young boxer living in Suva, for example, had had considerable success throughout the South Pacific at the time I was in Fiji. When people in Suva talked of his strength and power, the idea of *mana* often entered the conversation, though always discreetly. "I think there is something behind his boxing punch," people would say, "and I heard he goes back to his village to perform the ceremony." The "ceremony" they alluded to was a rite the young man performed to enlist the support of the *Vu* in his matches. Similar conversations might focus on an influential politician. The concept of *mana* has been adapted in urban areas to explain instances of unusual power, though people are not comfortable making that explanation overt. Their discomfort comes from their traditional respect for *mana,* which makes them both wonder whether the power of *mana* should be tapped for mundane achievements and personal gain, and also worry that maybe the person blessed with *mana* will turn its power against others.

▲ TRADITIONAL SPIRITUALITY AND CHRISTIANITY

Entering a Fijian village, one is struck by the dominance of a single large building, invariably of concrete blocks, which often sits on a hill overlooking the village, or in a prominent site near the village center. It is the Christian church. Since their arrival in the 1830s, missionaries have been singularly successful in the islands, and nearly all Indigenous Fijians are practicing Christians. Most are Methodist, though many have become Catholic. In the cities as well as in rural villages, churches are usually filled during services, and each week parishioners enthusiastically celebrate the liturgy. It is very moving to see people observe the theme of the first fruits by bringing into the church the best of their new crops and laying them proudly at the altar. In the Methodist church, the minister (*talatala*) is assisted by a pastor (*vakavuli*), a villager who helps organize the church activities of the village. There are also a number of lay preachers (*dauvunau*) in each village who take turns preaching and conducting services.

The spiritual influence in Fijian life is pervasive and dominant. The importance of the traditional ancestors, the *Vu,* in Fijian culture has today been joined and for many Fijians subsumed by Christianity. But the blend of traditional and Christian spirituality is complex. It is unlikely that anyone, especially among the older generation, fully denies belief in the traditional *Vu.* Though the Christian worldview is more often used publicly to explain experience or influence events, the *Vu* are felt to be close at hand. They are a backup source of support or a last resort for some; for many they are the foundation of spiritual reality. Lying just beneath the surface in public, often openly dominant in private settings, awareness of the *Vu* intensifies whenever there is an unexplained crisis or unexpected illness. Some turn to the *Vu* when prayer to the Christian God fails; others pray to both the *Vu* and the Christian God at the same time; still others pray first to their *Vu*, in order to "clear the ground" spiritually, then to the Christian God, more out of respect than deep belief.

Especially in urban areas and among the more educated, there is a tendency to see Christianity as the saving faith of the Indigenous Fijian people which has stamped out the "devil worship" of the old, traditional religion, the worship of the *Vu*. Carrying on the work of the original missionaries, contemporary evangelicals portray traditional Fijian religion as the work of the *tevoro*, or "devil."[7]

Referring to this evil work, the word *vakatevoro* means literally "devil-like" or "from the work of the devil." *Vakatevoro* is commonly translated as "witchcraft," but since this word is laden with pejorative connotations in the Western tradition, I use it only when speaking of others who intend such connotations.

The evangelicals' wrath is directed particularly at traditional healing, which is the most active practice of traditional religion in Fiji today. Traditional Fijian healing has become an evil to be destroyed, and healers are seen as servants of the devil whose task is to fulfill the wishes of their clients to kill or harm someone or to bring them some undeserved reward, like release from a prison sentence. Local newspapers sometimes allege the use of "sorcerers" or "witches" to influence the outcome of a sporting event, and routinely report the arrest of persons accused of practicing "witchcraft." But whereas to evangelicals the entire practice of traditional healing is *vakatevoro*, to practitioners and clients the label *vakatevoro* is reserved for those who have abandoned the healing aspect of their work.

---

[7] Fijian elders believe the word *tevoro* was imported from Tonga by Christian missionaries.

People also pray to the *Vu* during sacred nonhealing ceremonies, such as the welcoming of important visitors and the exchange of gifts for a marriage. These ceremonies are too closely linked to the political power structure to be maligned by the church. All important functions, whether at the central government or the village level, are accompanied by traditional Fijian ceremonies and therefore involve the *Vu*. Government officials are active, proud participants in these ceremonies.

Traditional healers, however, are not so firmly supported by the political power structure; their work in fact is usually done in secret, or at least privately. Healers are thus more vulnerable to the attacks of the church, and become the chosen target.

The Fijian language embodies the complexity of the connection between traditional and Christian expressions of spirituality and religion. Depending on a person's beliefs, different words are used to refer to the traditional *Vu* versus the Christian God. *Kalou* is often used to refer to the Christian God, *Kalou Vu* to the traditional ancestral gods. But those who practice Christianity to the exclusion of the traditional religion will refer to the Christian God as the *Kalou Dina* or "true God," implying thereby not only a corner on veracity but the top rank in the hierarchy. In this view, the *Vu* or *Kalou Vu* are said to serve, almost as quaint relics, below the true God. They are retained more to satisfy people's "old-fashioned" beliefs than because they possess any intrinsic power, and often these *Vu* are dismissed outright as "pagan" or "primitive."

Others with a more traditional view use the word *Kalou* to signify the "One Supreme Being" in the universe, who is worshiped by Fijians and Christians alike, and who is served by a number of powerful but lower-status gods, including the traditional *Vu* (or *Kalou Vu*) as well as Jesus Christ. This is how I use the word *Kalou*. As one healer put it: "We have no quarrel with the Christian religion. We both believe in the one supreme God. It's just that the missionaries have not actually preached the real Christianity. They are the problem. They didn't realize we already were practicing the religion they tried to give us."

The relationship between Indigenous Fijian religion and Christianity is very intricate. Fijian elders speak convincingly about Indigenous beliefs, precepts, and practices, insisting on their precontact origins; as trained storytellers their task is to carry on to the present generation the truths of the past. In some cases, these beliefs are not very different from those of Christianity, and of other world religions as well. But especially in the area of practice, there are numerous differences.[8]

▲ VANUA

The experience of *vanua*, the land and the people who live and work on it, is at the basis of Fijian life. Asesela Ravuvu, a Fijian social scientist, describes *vanua* in this way:

> *Vanua* literally means land, but also refers to the social and cultural aspects of the physical environment identified with a social group.... For a *vanua* to be recognized, it must have people living on it and supporting and defending its rights and interests. A land without people is likened to a person without soul. The people are the souls of the physical environment.... The land is the physical or geographical entity of the people, upon which their survival...depends. It is a major source of life; it provides nourishment, shelter, and protection.... Land is thus an extension of the self. Likewise the people are an extension of the land. Land becomes lifeless and useless without the people, and likewise the people are helpless and insecure without land to thrive on. (Ravuvu, 1987, p. 76)

From a structural perspective, *vanua* is a social unit identified with a particular territory. It is the largest grouping of relatives, which is then divided into increasingly smaller groups. For example, the *yavusa* is a

---

[8]Whatever intermingling has occurred will take time to sort out, and since most of the earliest written accounts of Fijian beliefs were compiled by missionaries, greater reliance must be placed on oral tradition. Likewise it may be difficult to establish whether, in any particular case, the effects of Christianity on traditional beliefs remain superficial or reach more fundamental levels.

group of people who trace their lineage on the male side to a common ancestor or ancestor god (*Vu*). Our home village of Tovu is in the same *yavusa* as its neighboring village on Bitu island.

The *yavusa* is further subdivided into clans (*mataqali*), such as chiefs (*turaga*), heralds or spokesmen of the chiefs (*mata-ni-vanua*), warriors (*bate*), priests (*bete*) and fishermen (*gone dau*). In many cases—for example, with the priestly group in contrast to the chiefs or heralds— these clans no longer serve their traditional functions on an ongoing basis, though clan functions in general are revitalized during ceremonial occasions. Other functions, such as fishing, are spread beyond the specific clan group to which they are assigned in the traditional scheme.

Contemporary Fijian healers have taken over the healing function originally assigned to the priestly clan, which also had other functions such as advising the chief about war efforts. It is said that the priests lost their power because they abused it, using *mana* to harm more than to heal, violating rather than respecting tradition.

But this structural perspective on *vanua* provides only its outlines. *Vanua* is an experience which embraces all Fijian tradition because it is the place where one's ancestors lived and died, the place where these ancestors in spirit form — the *Vu* — now live, watching over and protecting their progeny. *Vanua* exerts a spiritual force in people's lives because the *Vu* exemplify the sacred ideal of living in the old or traditional way. Close at hand, the stimulus for acting in traditional ways is strong and ever present, as are the punishments for failing to do so.

The substance of *vanua* is thus the intimate relationship between land and people, a relationship both expressed and guided by tradition. *Vanua* then becomes a dynamic statement about how to live traditionally. The terms *vakavanua* or *vakaturaga* describe this traditional lifestyle or simply "tradition." *Vakavanua* means literally having the characteristics of one who lives according to the way of the land; *vakaturaga*, having the characteristics of one who lives according to the way of the chiefs. Since chiefs embody the highest representation of the traditional way, the way of the land, the two terms can be used interchangeably.

Vakaturaga denotes not only traditional lifestyle but also the personality characteristics necessary to maintain it. To be or act in a way that befits a chief means doing so whether or not one is actually a chief by birth. Those who are *vakaturaga*, out of respect, behave toward others as if they were persons of importance, and knowing their place in the society, they fulfill their traditional obligations to those above them, below them, and at the same status level.

This portrait of one who is *vakaturaga* has dismayed some Western-trained policy analysts who advise Fiji on how to promote economic development. Such analysts see the person who is *vakaturaga* as overly compliant or complacent. "Where is the individualistic, entrepreneurial spirit?" they ask. They are further disturbed by the force of traditional kinship ties in Fiji, which encourages sharing of resources. "Where is the desire for the competitive edge?" they wonder. This kind of Western viewpoint is common in the urban areas of Fiji, which now control much of the funding that supports both urban and rural development projects.

But aside from their narrow capitalistic view of how economic development occurs, these analysts also misunderstand the concept of *vakaturaga*. There is nothing in this concept that precludes hard work; in fact, the desire to serve others can fuel individual motivation. And Fijians are constantly struggling against the more rigid and shallow interpretations of obedience which can exist. In its purest sense, *vakaturaga* connotes neither overly compliant nor overly complacent behavior. At its heart it is a way of being which emphasizes two values: respect (*vakarokoroko*) and love (*loloma*). One who is *vakaturaga* shows respect and love for all persons at all times, regardless of their social status. Such a person is truly humble.

Vakarokoroko and *loloma* are profound concepts. Though they prescribe a set of actions or manners, they are in essence descriptions of feelings. One respects the land and the people and the traditions that govern both; ultimately one's respect is for the *Vu*, since land, people, and traditions express the way and will of the *Vu*. To behave with *vakarokoroko* is to act considerately toward others, treating them as equal or superior to oneself, with deference and humility. One always recognizes others and has feelings for them, consulting with others before proceeding to take any action that might affect them. Being obedient flows from *vakarokoroko,* since one naturally listens to and follows the lead of those who have attained one's respect. In the Fijian way, then, obedience is not mere compliance, nor is it blindly pursued. *Vakarokoroko* is in behavior — speaking softly, keeping a distance from those one venerates; *vakarokoroko* is in attitude — feeling deeply for others, being humble in their presence.

Respect for others leads one to *loloma,* or the feeling of love or kindness for all others, just as the feeling of *loloma* engenders respect. One who shows *loloma* is ready to help and serve others. Dignified and composed, such an individual maintains self-respect and respect for others while exercising rightful authority during a crisis. A person having *loloma* is tolerant and serves to protect or defend others. To possess *loloma* is to recognize all persons as worthy of honor, care, and kindness. Solidarity is the aim; caring for others, the means.

Vakaturaga, then, describing how one should live traditionally, also describes the ideal Fijian way of life and the ideal Fijian personality. These cultural ideals constantly and concretely affect everyday behavior. Living in the traditional manner, Fijians achieve harmony and unity among themselves by caring for and sharing with one another, and allocating resources fairly. Only through respecting and honoring others, which is to say, through fulfilling one's duties and responsibilities toward others, is this harmony possible. Respect and honor then come back to the one who displays these qualities, while others fulfill their reciprocal responsibilities. To fail in this mutual exchange brings one shame, embarrassment, and humiliation, painful states that are assiduously avoided. To succeed brings recognition, honor, and respect, enhancing one's reputation and making one feel good, and most important, truly Fijian. But in the Fijian way, the individual does not seek or savor such recognition; humility comes first and stays to the end.

In practice, Fijians must continually face their humanity in their desire to be considered *vakaturaga.* Because they are only human, they constantly fall short of being like their ancestors, like the *Vu.* Traditional healers occupy a special place in this struggle. Like chiefs, healers are supposed to be closer to the *Vu* than ordinary persons and are therefore expected to be more committed to the struggle, if not actually more successful in it. Later we will see how healers engage in this struggle, how they seek to find and follow the straight path (*gaunisala dodonu*), the path which tells them how to be and act correctly or traditionally, and thereby how to use *mana* for healing rather than harming others.

▲ SUBSISTENCE

The basic subsistence unit of rural Fiji is the village. The population of villages in Bitu varies from about 75 to 150. Houses are constructed from a variety of materials, but their rectangular shape and general structure hardly varies. Traditional thatched *bure* are interspersed among those built in the more common style, with a sheet iron roof atop walls made of thatch or reeds, or sometimes sheet iron, lumber, or concrete blocks. The floor is the living space where, sitting crosslegged, one works, eats and visits. Mats are placed on the floor for sleeping. Houses usually have a bed and perhaps a chair, but their use is minimal, their function marginal. In houses having thatched walls, or those made entirely of thatch, floors are usually raised off the ground by a layer of crushed coral and dried coconut fronds covered by woven pandanus leaf mats. The wood floors of wooden houses are also covered with these mats. There are more chairs and other furniture in urban houses (which usually retain the same rectangular shape but are not thatched), but the floor remains the area where many activities take place.

Rural subsistence depends on the produce from gardens, which can be nearly an hour's walk away, and fish caught in the village's fishing areas. This subsistence farming and fishing

Bure

30

Men constructing the reed walls of a bure, *the traditional thatched house*

is supplemented by an occasional cash crop, such as coconuts. Cash is needed to pay children's school fees and to buy cooking utensils and household furnishings such as kerosene lamps and the occasional chair or bureau. A few persons in each village own outboard engines to power the long wooden boats that carry the people on fishing expeditions and visits to neighboring villages.

This pattern is radically different from that in Suva. Though many people still maintain gardens, the plots are much smaller than those in the villages; likewise, fishing is unavailable to most. Food is either purchased from the market or obtained from rural relatives. Housing and other basics of urban living require cash. But since job opportunities have not kept up with that demand, with well-paying jobs reserved for an elite few among Indigenous Fijians, many urban dwellers in Fiji experience hardship.

In the villages it is common for one or two groups of brothers and

Harvesting the root crop tavioka *(cassava)*

their families to form the central core, and the inhabitants are typically all related through the male line. Rural life is structured and guided by these kinship relationships and obligations; people help and are helped, they give and they get. This sharing and caring for others, the reciprocity that is both valued for itself and seen as a requirement for survival, characterize the collection and distribution of food as well as the organization of village life and ceremonies.

Meals consist of two parts: the main dish and a smaller complementary dish. The main dish (*kakana dina*, literally "real" or "true" food), which is served in abundance, consists of any one of a variety of starchy foods. Usually this is cassava (*tavioka*); taro (*dalo*), yam (*uvi*) and breadfruit (*uto*) are less common. Taro and especially yams are greatly appreciated. The product of a ritualized growing season, a nicely roasted yam is a treat after a steady diet of cassava, which is available year-round. The second part of the meal, the *coi* or the "relish," can be either flesh, such as fish, shellfish, pork, beef, or chicken, or green, leafy vegetables, such as *rourou*, taro leaves cooked in coconut milk, or *bele*, a large-leafed spinach-like plant that is gathered in the bush.

Fruits, including bananas, papayas, and mangoes, provide a delightful variety to the diet. They are not always available on the drier coral reef islands but quite abundant in the wet inland villages. Mango season is a time of plenty. As the season begins, small children are sent out at dawn to gather the few ripe mangoes that have fallen to the earth before the birds get them. Mangoes litter the ground further into the season, and people may take just a bite or two from several of the most luscious specimens, walking over fruit that is less desirable in shape or color. This time of overabundance yields to a renewed scarcity as small children are again sent out in the early morning to secure the last ripe mangoes that remain — again hoping to arrive before the hungry birds of dawn.

Coconut is a pervasive part of the diet. Many foods are cooked in coconut milk, a rich, creamy liquid made by mixing grated coconut with water. Cooked in this manner, simple foods like cassava are exquisitely tasty. Coconut oil also provides the base for the variety of oils used in skin care and for medicinal purposes.

Garden areas are usually identified as belonging to a particular family or household, and parts or all of an identified area are gardened each year by that family. But boundaries between gardens are not rigid, and the actual area cultivated depends on the energy and motivation of the

Women fishing with two-person nets

Communal fishing at the barrier reef

Women dividing the day's catch of fish into piles for each family in the village

gardener as well as his regard for the traditional patterns of cultivation of neighboring gardeners. Though the quantity and quality of root crops that come into the village may differ from one household to another, no one goes hungry when food is available.

The same rules of collection and distribution prevail in the fishing areas, which yield an incredible variety and abundance of fish and mollusks. On the coast, women fish with nets, usually two to a net close to shore, while the men go out in boats to line-fish. At certain times, especially when fish is needed for a ceremonial occasion, men and women mount large expeditions and fish together at the barrier reef surrounding the coral islands that make up Bitu. Forming a circle around a fishnet, they drive the fish toward the net by beating the water. As they move closer in a smaller and smaller circle, the fish are caught up in the net.

There is an attempt to get someone from each of the village households to participate in these expeditions. But whether a household member actually takes part or not, when the fishing party returns, every household in the village shares in the catch that is dumped on the ground. Several of the older women distribute the fish, throwing them with nonchalant skill into piles for each household. Those who provided the boat or engine or gas for the expedition, or those of chiefly status, may get a slightly larger share or more of the choice fish. And then, in following the traditional way, those so favored may give their special foods to a respected elder or chief or other people who have no one actively providing for them.

The joint ownership of the land and choice fishing areas, coupled with the emphasis on communal harvesting, ensures that sharing is the ethos of village life. Whenever family members sit down to eat, they keep their door open so that anyone walking by can see what they have on their plates and know they are not hiding or hoarding anything. More important, anyone walking by can be invited in to share the meal. The phrase *mai kana*, "come in and eat," is heard throughout the village during meal-time. In the Fijian way, just as it is proper to ask, it is also proper to decline. But though only rarely is the invitation accepted, it is sincerely meant as a sign of respect, and a commitment to reciprocity.

Food is still shared in Suva, but the exchange is less extensive, and certainly less governed by ritual and kinship obligations. Store-bought foods such as canned mackerel and tinned beef are a major part of the urban diet, and the smaller quantities and the price make sharing more difficult. While it is not only respectful to share a large catch of freshly caught fish, it is also necessary; though fish can be preserved through smoking and partial cooking, it goes bad after several days. It is not unusual for an expedition to bring in nearly forty pounds of fish, well beyond the ability of any one household, or even several households, to consume. In contrast, not only does a can of unopened mackerel keep indefinitely, but once opened, when consumption becomes necessary, there isn't a lot of fish to go around.

With cash playing a role in the food supply network, the system has taken a perverse turn. The government supports commercial fishing schemes in rural areas, usually by helping a village buy a large fishing vessel. Then what happens? With the exception of the less choice types of fish, villagers bring the bulk of their catch to Suva to sell in the urban market. With the cash from that sale, they buy the really valued fish —

canned mackerel. Tinned food, because it is a Western innovation and preferred in urban homes, as well as for its obvious storage advantages, has become the prized food in the village.

▲ SOCIAL STRUCTURE

Traditional village life is organized hierarchically. The older one is and the more senior one's position within the family, the more one is respected and obeyed; likewise, membership in the chiefly lineage group and being male bring greater respect. This hierarchical structure is neither arbitrary nor one-sided, however; it emphasizes reciprocity, responsibility, and earned respect. The chief, for example, is supposed to give as much, or more, than he receives from his people, and he must continually earn their respect. The senior member of a family is expected to respect those below him as much, or more, than they do him, and likewise earn his position by performing his responsibilities. In order to earn the respect and the devoted support of those of a lower status, those of higher status must lead the family or group, organizing its activities, especially in ceremonies, and generally looking after its welfare and protecting its interests.

Hierarchy permeates all aspects of life, in the organizing of ceremonies as well as the structure and meaning of everyday activities. Respect for those above one is shown in many ways. For example, where one is seated in a house or at a ceremony has symbolic importance. Offering someone a position toward the "high" or more private portion of a house, or at the "head" of or in the front section at a ceremony, is a sign of respect. Because the head is the most sacred part of the body, it is considered disrespectful to rise above the heads of others, either by reaching over them or standing above them, especially when they are sitting on the floor. When one must reach above someone, for instance to get something from a shelf behind the person, or stand over or walk in front of him or her, one must first excuse oneself by saying *tulou*, a word of apology, asking forgiveness for the disrespectful behavior.

Sitting cross-legged on the floor — and thereby remaining "low," inconspicuous and modest, and not, for example, pointing one's feet at others — is a prime requisite for traditional respectful behavior. This is no easy task for most European visitors, who are unaccustomed to sitting in this fashion. Such visitors frequently use chairs when they are available, thereby placing themselves above those on the floor. Also, these visitors usually walk in front of their hosts and stand above them as they go toward their chairs. Moreover, European visitors are often unaware that they should excuse their behavior by saying *tulou*. The impression created is of disregard for the values of the land, sometimes extenuated by the visitors' innocence, sometimes exacerbated by the visitors' swaggering entrance, and always muted by Fijian hosts' acceptance of the behavior, since they do not want to embarrass their visitors.

I was fortunate in having the bodily flexibility that allowed me to sit in the traditional manner for the long periods demanded by most gatherings. The people I lived with really appreciated that. For my part, I was grateful my body facilitated my showing respect.

In the villages, both men and women wear a piece of cloth wrapped around their bodies at the waist. The garment, called a *sulu*, comes down to the calves of men, and usually to the ankles of women. The *sulu* is worn by men with a shirt and by women over a dress. Though I was well practiced at wrapping the *sulu* around my waist, I never fully trusted it. Everyday activities, like carrying things, put my skill to the test. Rather than risk an unexpected exposure from some awkward movement, I usually wore a pair of shorts underneath my *sulu*, as do Fijian men themselves when engaged in particularly difficult or demanding work.

In urban areas, the *sulu* remains the standard dress worn at home and at ceremonies, though trousers for men and dresses for women have generally replaced the traditional garment during the workday. Modesty, however, remains the guiding principle in Fijian dress; respect for others, the rationale.

Meals are a daily occasion at which respect for hierarchy is displayed. Food is served to the family or group on a mat on the floor, with everyone sitting around the mat. Older men sit in the most important positions at the head or top of the mat. Served the largest and choicest pieces of food, they are given ample room in which to eat, and others of lower

The men having finished, the women and children now eat together

status are required to sit a bit apart from them. Down the mat from the older men are younger men, then children, and finally at the lowest end of the mat women who serve the food. At times the servers will not eat until the older men are fully finished with their meal. For their part, the older men, who thus enjoy special foods and large portions, are always aware of who else is eating and intentionally leave food that has been offered to them uneaten so the rest can also feed well. These customs of hierarchical deference are less closely observed in private than in public, and especially ceremonial, occasions. When the members of a family eat alone in their house, for example, all usually eat together.

As crucial as showing respect to those ranked higher than oneself is offering special treatment to those of lesser status. Likewise, it is proper for a person to graciously refuse an offer of special treatment. These actions are a demonstration of humility.

In Suva, such observances of respect and obedience within the hierarchy are more difficult to maintain. Urban criteria of respect, such as educational attainment and participation in modern commerce, have arisen, and as their influence increases, elders traditionally awarded respect are less honored, since they usually lack these credentials. It is painful to see a rural elder stand awkwardly at a city bank counter, at a loss for words, as the impatient European or Indian Fijian bank teller makes matters worse by speaking in English too rapidly for the elder to understand. Elders are often not only out of place in urban areas, but diminished by the place. Young Fijians in particular, who see their elders constantly struggle in urban settings, begin to lose their traditional regard for them.

The traditional understanding of gender differences prevails in Fijian village life. There is, for example, a division of labor according to sex, with men engaged in clearing land for gardening, building houses, and spearing fish, and women in cooking, weaving mats, baby-sitting, washing clothes, and fishing with small nets. But this division is felt by both women and men to be appropriate. One woman elder expressed it this way: "We don't want the men to get into our activities. What would a man do when we women are weaving mats together? He wouldn't know how to weave and how to participate in our women's talk. And we don't want to get into their activities. Women and men have different things to do — and that's the proper Fijian way."

Fijians value the time they spend with others of their sex, the joking and camaraderie in activities like, for women, fishing with nets close to shore and, for men, line-fishing in the ocean. The community too values the specific contributions each sex makes. Interactions in the same-sex fishing groups differ from those in the communal fishing of both men and women at the barrier reef. Fueled from both sides by jokes laced with wonderfully indirect sexual references and challenges, the mixed-sex fishing group has its own pleasures. The jokes are the more enjoyed because traditional rules limit cross-sexual contacts in public. It takes great skill and sensitivity to play along the boundaries of acceptable decency.

Though men are generally in charge of the public sphere, for example organizing and orchestrating ceremonies, women have their full say within the home and considerable influence, sometimes through their husbands, on the way public activities are arranged. It is their labor that produces many of the valued goods exchanged during ceremonies, such as woven mats and scented coconut oil. Women affect the nature of the ceremony through their collective decisions about what and how to contribute.

In Fiji, women and men function for the most part separately in ways that are meant to be relatively equal. While under the hierarchical rules of Fijian social order, where being male, as well as being older or of a high status, elicits more public displays of respect, this does not imply a disrespect for or condescension to women. When older men are seated at the head of the mat, the place of high status, and served first with the best foods, those signs of honor must, after all, be given to them by women. By showing such respect, women in turn receive respect, for among the most important traditional Fijian values for *all* people are humility, service, and obedience.

In urban areas there is a trend toward a more public and complete sharing of power between the sexes. Enrollment at the University of the South Pacific in Suva illustrates this trend: in fact, more Fijian women than men attend, a radical turn of events considering the low profile women generally assume in the village in situations of public prestige and power. But at its core, respect, whether in the village or the city, knows no gender.

CHAPTER 2

Ceremonies
and the
Work of Healing

Ceremonial life is essential in Fiji. It both celebrates the religious dimension and promotes economic and social exchange. During ceremonies, gifts are exchanged between two groups. These two groups may be the husband's and wife's people in a marriage ceremony, or the family members of someone who has died and those paying their respects during a funeral, or hosts and guests at the arrival of important visitors to a village.

Ceremonies bridge the spirit world and the everyday world. They allow the people to communicate with the *Vu*. During ceremonies, people seek clearer instructions from the *Vu* about how they should live, and plead with the *Vu* to forgive them for violating their sacred obligations. Ceremonies highlight the wish of the people to live the proper way, to show respect for others and the *Vu*. Chiefs and especially their spokesmen or heralds (*mata-ni-*

Tabua

Large ceremonial exchange: the magiti *(food) on the left, the* yau *(material goods like mats, cloth, and kerosene) on the right*

vanua) have important and difficult ceremonial responsibilities. It is their job to be sure ceremonies are performed in the proper way, precisely according to tradition; the degree of correctness observed is a sign of the degree of respect shown.

There are generally two types of gifts exchanged in ceremonies. One is called *yau*, which includes traditional items such as a *tabua* (whale's tooth), a highly valued, sacred object, and woven mats as well as recently introduced items such as bolts of cloth and drums of kerosene or gasoline. The second is called *magiti*, a ceremonial feast or gift of food, which includes traditional foods, as well as slaughtered cattle and canned foods. Through the exchange of gifts, the relationship between groups is affirmed and the identity of each group within itself strengthened. In Fiji, one is not alone; the group is one's life. Such exchanges are a way of honoring other groups and, in essence, honoring the *Vu* who stand behind these groups.

Westerners are at times mystified by this exchange of gifts and goods:

43

Ritual presentation of the tabua *(sacred whale's tooth)*

Burning hair off a pig before baking in the lovo *(underground oven) in preparation for a* magiti *(feast)*

it seems to them that each side gives the other approximately the same items. In their view, each should keep for itself what it was going to give. Each would end up with the same things, and with the need for ceremony eliminated, everybody would save time and energy. This view is more than naive; it completely misses the point. As the Fijian anthropologist Rusiate Nayacakalou (1978) puts it, "The important thing is not that Fijian exchange is not trade, but that the framework within which it takes place is primarily social, not economic. The economic relationship is brought about because of the social relationship..." (p. 40). The ceremonial exchange is a social, cultural event with sacred obligations; the material goods are the ostensible, observable medium of exchange.

An exchange requires two sides. As one side gives, the other receives; and then the other gives, and the first receives. I remember a ceremony in which a visitor asked permission to enter the village. There was only the one visitor, not enough to constitute a full side, especially in relation to the village hosts. Several of the hosts therefore joined with the visitor for the duration of the ceremony, creating two functioning sides to an exchange and thereby making proper giving and receiving possible. Ceremonial exchanges are a dynamic process. The giving and receiving are not necessarily connected in time, nor is there a discrete end to the process itself.

It sometimes seems that ceremonies are held everywhere, at any time. All major occasions of meeting, including arriving and departing, and all transition events are celebrated with ceremonies, usually complex and multifaceted. A death, for example, is observed for four days afterward, the fourth night being especially important. The ceremonial period is then extended to ten days after the death, with the tenth night particularly marked; the next period, culminating in the hundredth night, is again very important.

Much work is involved in preparing for a ceremony. The gifts to be given must be collected and decisions must be made about their distribution — what and how much goes to whom. Discussion about how a ceremony is to be conducted must work toward consensus. At times confusion and hard feelings can affect the preparations. But once the ceremony begins, each person's entire being is directed toward the sacred task. Frantic, last-minute preparations may take place inside the house, but participants leave the house calmly, bearing their gifts with pride, and walk with dignity to the ceremonial area. A rendezvous with the ancestral gods demands respectful and respectable behavior.

Healing rituals take place within this context of pervasive and intensely practiced ceremony. The healing practice is judged by standards derived from the more general ceremonial context: respectful performance, exchange, and most important, contact with the *Vu*.

▲ YAQONA

The *yaqona* plant (*Piper methysticum*) must accompany every ceremony; otherwise, the occasion is empty because the *Vu* are not present. Opening the ceremony, the exchange of *yaqona* invites the *Vu* into the peoples' lives; closing the ceremony, the *yaqona* requests permission of the *Vu* to leave. When people offer *yaqona* to the *Vu* in the correct ritual manner, communication with them is possible, and their *mana* becomes accessible. *Yaqona* is the channel to the *Vu;* it is called "the nourishment of the gods." The offering of *yaqona* thus commences the ceremonial exchange that underlies all material and social exchanges.

A tall, leafy plant that grows to about five feet in height, *yaqona* is often cultivated as a cash crop. Its long, gnarled roots are dried, pounded or pulverized, then mixed with water to form a ceremonial drink. The *yaqona* can be offered either as an entire plant, as is the case with the *yaqona* used for important formal ceremonies, or as the dried roots, or in the form of a fine powder sold in urban markets. Though *yaqona* is literally a plant, it is in essence a spiritual messenger.

The *sevusevu* ceremony is the most common way of exchanging *yaqona*. The *sevusevu* must initiate all major ceremonies, asking of the *Vu* permission to begin, and seeking their blessing on the proceedings. Whenever someone comes into a village or a home as a guest, a *sevusevu* must be performed, requesting permission to enter, to be part of the host's place or land. In return,

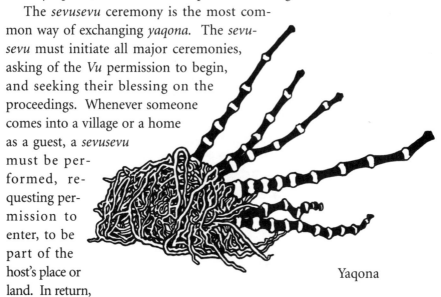

Yaqona

Ritual presentation of the yaqona

the host, by accepting the *yaqona* and at times then offering a *sevusevu* to the guest, reciprocates his respect for the land from which the guest has come. These exchanges of *yaqona* at a person's arrival in another village or home are frequent, yet often unpredictable, so Fijians make a practice of carrying *yaqona* with them when traveling to be prepared.

Though it is offered by one human being, and accepted by another, *yaqona* is actually being exchanged by the *Vu* who stand behind the human participants. The presentation and acceptance of *yaqona* is accompanied by special words, chants, and gestures, during which the atmosphere is profoundly quiet and reverent.

I remember a time when a visitor came from a neighboring village. He was no stranger to the people in our village, and was considered something of a buffoon, not taken seriously. Yet when he offered his *sevusevu,* he was treated with high regard, for he was now seen as a representative of the *Vu* of his village.

Yaqona is a central ingredient in Fijian life. It is often said that "we Fijians cannot live without *yaqona*." Mildly psychoactive, *yaqona* eventually produces a soporific effect. People become more congenial with moderate drinking; another common saying is that "without *yaqona*, we cannot have a good meeting," meaning that *yaqona* encourages people to work together. As *yaqona* drinking proceeds, people become more relaxed and mellow, eventually entering a state of utter relaxation in which talk becomes less frequent and sleepiness takes over. An animated *yaqona*-drinking session often evolves into a still, slow-moving shadow play, lasting until the *yaqona* is finished. I was told by many different people that "*yaqona* is the best sleeping pill you can take." Originally reserved for chiefs and for use in sacred ceremonies, everyone now drinks *yaqona*, and it is found not only in sacred settings but at almost every social gathering.

The sacred, ceremonial use of *yaqona* is highly ritualized, from the initial presentation

Pounding yaqona *in a hollowed-out log, readying it to be mixed with water, then served*

49

Preparing to fill the bilo *during a formal* yaqona *ceremony*

and acceptance of the *yaqona*, to the mixing with water in the large wooden serving bowl, called a *tanoa*, to the serving in *bilo*, cups made of half a coconut shell. When the *tanoa*

Tanoa

is finished, it is often then replenished with more *yaqona*, and another round is served. The phases of the ceremony are announced in a ritual fashion, and carefully delineated with signs of utmost respect, such as the *cobo*, a deep clapping of cupped hands, and low and deferential postures in front of elders. The *yaqona* is

Bilo

50

Serving yaqona *to an elder*

served to those assembled in a prescribed and invariable order, with those of highest status being served first. Only one person drinks at a time, and the round of drinking is completed when all who are supposed to drink have finished. The silence is penetrating throughout a formal *yaqona* ceremony. During less formal ceremonies, when jokes might be made after the sacred part is finished, *yaqona* can still be a channel to the *Vu*.

During purely social drinking, communication with the *Vu* can be severely undermined or even absent. The mixing and serving of *yaqona* in social gatherings is usually a truncated, often eviscerated, version of

Family drinking yaqona *with the children looking on*

the sacred *yaqona* ritual. Not all the steps in the ritual are performed; those that are are often done perfunctorily. The focus is on visiting, or even partying. Social drinking of *yaqona* is pervasive in urban areas among Fijians of Indian ancestry as well as Indigenous Fijians. In urban areas *yaqona* has become the national recreational drink.

At one gathering I attended in Suva, both *yaqona* and beer were being served. Some people drank only *yaqona*, others only beer, still others alternated between the two. Those who were drinking the *yaqona* were having a hard time keeping to any of the *yaqona* ritual. They could not, for example, serve the *yaqona* in deference to seniority because the *yaqona* drinkers were sitting among the beer drinkers, and it wasn't clear whether beer drinkers would want to participate in a round of *yaqona*. More important, since this was a beer party as well, the *yaqona* drinkers were unsure whether they should attempt to observe any of the *yaqona* ritual, since beer parties had absolutely no connection in people's minds with tradition or the *Vu.*

Interior of a concrete-block house: a tanoa *(wooden bowl for mixing* yaqona*) is leaning against the wall*

In the villages, groups made up mostly of men gather nearly every evening in one house or another to drink *yaqona*. Starting shortly after five or six, the session can go on until late evening. People then go home to eat dinner or go directly to bed. Because it occurs in the village, this nightly social drinking retains observance of the *yaqona* ritual and recognition of its connection with the *Vu*. Only after the initial part of the ceremony has been completed, during which the *yaqona* is formally announced and "opened," do people relax and joke, drinking *yaqona* while they visit. On some evenings the women, perhaps after drinking *yaqona* by themselves awhile, will join the men's *yaqona* session. The visiting then accelerates, with the joking becoming more animated and subtle sexual innuendos issuing from both men and women. It's as if a stream of fresh air has entered a stuffy room, bringing an edge of excitement, a hint of the unexpected into what was a too predictable set of conversations. But even during social drinking, abusing or insulting the *yaqona* with intentionally disrespectful behavior is forbidden, especially in rural areas. Such disrespect would inevitably bring disaster to the perpetrator, since the anger of the *Vu* would be awakened.

A final word about the phrase "drinking *yaqona*." To drink (*gunu*) *yaqona* in a traditional context — the ceremonial approach to the *Vu* — has nothing to do with Western rituals of drinking alcohol and getting drunk. Only in its more social context in Fiji is *yaqona* drinking similar to Western patterns of alcohol consumption. Especially if *yaqona* is abused, its use can result in stupor. Used traditionally, however, it increases the awareness of those taking part in the ceremony. As one elder put it, "The *Vu* speak through the *yaqona*. We must be wide awake in order to hear them."

THE HEALING CEREMONY

The traditional Fijian healing ceremony centers around exchange. The ritual exchange of *yaqona* connects the healer with the patient and, more important, with the *Vu*. Healers insist that they perform the *yaqona* ceremony in the traditional manner; in that way, they say, the *yaqona* will bring the healing *mana* to their work. In fact, urban healers especially have introduced many innovations, most of them idiosyncratic, in the traditional ceremony. These are in addition to the generic changes necessary to mark the ceremony as particularly directed to healing. Some of these elements are taken as signs of the healer's distinction and power, that the *mana* is really "with" the healer. One healer, for example, performs an impressive feat by drinking four large *bilo* of *yaqona* one right after another.

The healing ceremony typically begins when a patient comes to a healer to request help or a cure. The patient incorporates the request in a ritual presentation of *yaqona* to the healer on behalf of the ancestors. The healer accepts the *yaqona*, which may then be prepared with water and drunk by the healer and usually the patient and others in attendance, or *yaqona* already mixed in the *tanoa* may be used, or no *yaqona* may be drunk at the time. It is in the healer's acceptance of the *yaqona* that the healing itself is accomplished. In that moment, *mana* is said to become available, allowing accurate diagnosis and the selection of an effective treatment. A sacred, spiritual exchange between healer and patient has been completed. The patient returns after four days for the conclusion of the treatment or, if necessary, further treatment in the same or some new direction.

Healer

Spiritual healers vary considerably between urban and rural settings (R. Katz, 1981; unpublished data, 1977–78, 1985; Katz and Kilner, 1987). In rural areas, there is approximately one healer for every 350 people or every three villages; in urban areas, the proportion drops to one for every 1,000 people. Rural healers are almost all men and mostly over sixty. In contrast, half of the urban healers are female and urban healers in general are younger.[1] Rural healers live and work according to traditional village values. An integral part of the community, their healing practices usually continue over a long period, often more than twenty years. In contrast, urban healers often do not observe the norms of their locale, perhaps having several sexual partners, for example. The urban healer's practice can be short-lived, lasting as little as several years, and is sometimes interrupted

---

[1]Rural healers are 95 percent male; 75 percent are over sixty; 50 percent are over seventy. Of the female urban healers, 70 percent are between twenty and thirty-nine. Of male urban healers, 70 percent are between fifty and fifty-nine.

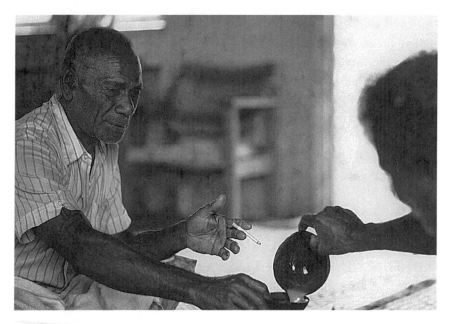

Filling the bilo *of a healer*

by periods during which no healing work is done. This is especially true of the healing practices of younger women.

Most urban healing ceremonies are dramatic, whereas in general rural ceremonies are not. Half of the women and a quarter of the men conducting ceremonies in urban areas, for instance, enter states of possession by the *Vu* behind their work. From the point of view of many rural healers, the possessed state is inappropriate. "How could a healer really become the *Vu?*" asks one rural healer. Possession is seen by these rural practitioners as an embarrassment, even a sign of charlatanism — although the state of possession still impresses them, while it evokes fear among nonhealers. It is easy to see the marketplace ethos at work as urban healers try to sell themselves and seek out new clients. For those who dwell in the city, possession is usually seen as a sign of the healer's power.

In villages, the times patients visit the healer vary, depending on the availability of the healer, who may be working in the garden or out fishing. In urban areas, healers keep more regular hours, usually during the evening, and often at these times there may be several patients waiting to be helped. Several persons might assist the healer by mixing *yaqona* or talking with patients.

In both rural and urban settings, the exchange of *yaqona* is performed in a solemn, formal manner. Complete quiet prevails during the ritual. After being treated, patients may stay on awhile, drinking *yaqona*, visiting, joking, relaxing with the healer and any others who are present (often including members of the patient's family who have accompanied him or her). Except among the evangelically-oriented Christians and some of the educated elite, there is no stigma attached to visiting a healer.

After the ritual exchange of *yaqona*, the healer usually gives the patient advice about proper behavior or advice of a more psychological nature. This is followed in about one out of four cases by the healer's giving the patient a massage or an herbal remedy. The specifics of this further treatment are based on the guidance the healer receives from the *Vu*.

The massage can be either deep or more like a light touching of the surface of the skin. Herbal remedies (*wai* or "medicines") are usually mixed by the healer or an assistant and given to the patient to take at home. The numerous herbs in the natural pharmacopoeia are derived mostly from the leaves, bark, or roots of plants. The preparation of these herbal medicines can be quite complicated, involving certain parts of the plant cut in certain ways and mixed in differing amounts. If the herb is to be drunk, it is put in a small cloth bag to be steeped in water; if it is to be applied to the body, it is mixed with coconut oil. Many of these herbs are said to be effective only if the healer picks them and thereby brings out the plant's *mana*.

Though *yaqona* is omnipresent in Fijian social life, *mana* lies dormant during ordinary social drinking. The healing ritual turns *yaqona* into a channel for *mana*. Performing the ritual is one of the healer's many functions. Healing also requires substantial interpersonal skills and social sensitivity. Helping a patient may require psychological understanding or the enhancement of belief, whereas resolving a village crisis demands skill in political negotiation with groups.

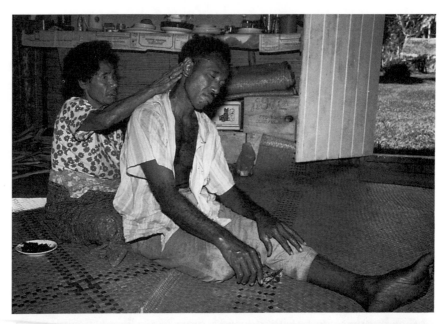

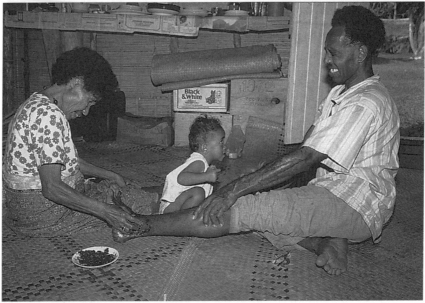

A traditional massage specialist (dauveibo) *at work*

Fijians group sickness into two major categories, depending on their etiology. The first type, natural sickness (*tauvimate dina*, literally "true" or "real sickness"), is caused by physical events; for example, one might have painful joints from having stayed in cold ocean water too long. The second type, spiritual sickness (*tauvimate vakatevoro*, "sickness caused by the work of the devil"), results either wholly or in part from spiritual factors, such as another person's *vakatevoro* or some violation of cultural norms, which is then punished by the *Vu*. Western medicine is reserved for treating natural sickness, but both natural and spiritual illnesses are brought to Fijian healers. The same pattern of symptoms can often result from either type of sickness.

The spiritual healer (the *dauvagunu*, literally, "the expert at drinking [*yaqona*]") — who is the focus of this book — is one of several other kinds of traditional healers, all of whom are called *vuniwai vakaviti*, or Fijian doctors. These other healers include seers (*daurairai*, literally, "one who is expert at seeing [into the unseen]," or "seeing spiritually"); the massage specialists (*dauveibo*, literally "one who is expert at massage"); and the herbalists (*dausoliwai*, literally "one who is expert at giving medicines"). All these healers draw their power from the *Vu*, but only the *dauvagunu* systematically uses *yaqona* to gain access to the *Vu* when a patient requests help, and the *dauvagunu* has more extensive and frequent contact with the *Vu*. The *dauvagunu* can also see into the future and give massages or herbal remedies to patients.

Because of their more intimate connection with the *Vu*, the *dauvagunu* are seen as most powerful, and they treat the broadest range of problems as well as the most severe. Sicknesses with a spiritual etiology or component, *tauvimate vakatevoro*, are their special province. Although the vast majority of sicknesses are expressed through physical complaints, such as headaches and bodily aches, physical symptoms can just as often indicate a spiritual etiology as a natural one. Sometimes both are involved, either simultaneously or sequentially (Katz and Lamb, 1983). Patients range from a boy with a swollen neck or a childless woman who wishes to become pregnant to a family seeking protection against the evil intentions of others or an entire village wanting to make amends for violating a

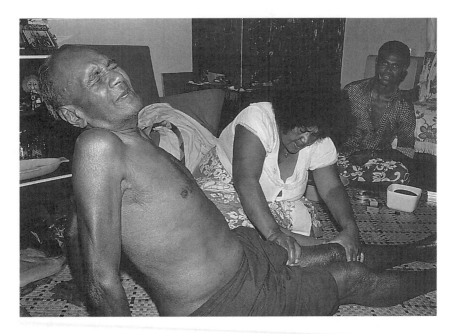

A healer at work: yaqona *having been exchanged, a massage is given (above and right)*

sacred custom. Rarely is a problem excluded from the domain of the *dau-vagunu*. But a good *dauvagunu*, after he or she has done everything possible, will refer patients elsewhere when appropriate, either to other traditional healers or to health care workers trained in Western medicine or to the hospital.

Especially in rural areas, healers are fully contributing members of society. Compared with a sample of nonhealers matched on a series of demographic variables, healers are rated as significantly more "respected," closer to the "ideal Fijian," and "harder working" (R. Katz, 1981). Healers are villagers first and foremost, but in their daily lives and especially in the performance of the healing ritual, they are expected to strive to realize Fijian ideals. Healers are to embody *vakaturaga*, the qualities of the traditional chief. They are respected to the degree that they are perceived as trying to achieve that aim.

Though it is appropriate to request from the healer only the healing influence of *mana*, some may seek to subvert the *yaqona*, using it to request *mana* to work against someone. Fijians call this latter practice *vakatevoro*, which, as mentioned in Chapter 1, means literally "something devil-like," or *draunikau*, literally "leaf of a tree" or using plants for evil magic. People do not like to talk publicly about *vakatevoro*, especially since by accusing another of it they themselves may become targets of such accusations. But the lure of *vakatevoro* makes the straight path that much more essential.

THE STRAIGHT PATH

The healing ceremony deals with resolving uncertainty and making comprehensible the unknown. It is the primary arena in which the forces of good and evil, healing and *vakatevoro*, struggle against each other. Because these forces are ever present, healers must be trained in the *gaunisala dodonu*, or the "straight path," so that they will use *mana* exclusively for healing rather than evil-doing.

The journey along the path is what enables healers to direct *mana* toward healing. Though *mana* is accessible to many, few become healers. As one healer puts it, "Few know how to begin walking on the straight path, and even fewer know how to stay on it."

Traveling the straight path means exemplifying the attributes of the ideal Fijian, the person who is *vakaturaga*, who follows traditional Fijian values and displays proper behavior — *i tovo vakaviti*, "the real Fijian way of being." Healing is possible only for a person of character, and the continuation and deepening of healing work requires the further development of character. Knowledge of healing techniques is available only to those with the proper attributes. Technical aspects of healing are significant, but the issue of character is preeminent.

The following attributes are often mentioned when prescribing the way a healer must live in order to follow the straight path. Each is described through quotations from healers about its place in the healing work (R. Katz, 1981).

> *vakadinadina* (telling and living the truth): "The amount of truth in each person determines the power of healing. You must speak to your patients only what you have been told by your guardian ancestor. If you elaborate on that and add your own opinions or try to show how much you know, you are just lying."

loloma (love for all): "In this healing work you should love everybody, whether a relative or foreigner. They are all the same for you. You must help them all because of your love."

i tovo vinaka (proper or correct behavior): "The *mana* is getting weaker in Fiji because people are not now following ancient customs. We must observe these customs, like the taboos, if our behavior is to be proper."

sega na i vukivuki (humility): "This healing work is your secret. Showing this work to everybody, even those who do not need your help, is boasting."

vakarokoroko (respect): "Everybody must be respected. Each person deserves our love and help. And the traditional ways of the land must be respected. We show our true nature by such respect."

sega ni lomaloma rua (single-mindedness): "You must firmly and fully believe in your healing work and faithfully worship your *Vu*. Once you decide about something and judge what is right, you must stick by your word and seize the moment to act. No wavering or turning back."

veiqaravi (service): "The power is to be used only for healing and serving others. You cannot use it to harm or kill others, or for your own personal gain, to get money or other things. That must be very clear. If you do, the power leaves you."

Though these attributes are linked to the healing work itself, they generally prescribe the way a healer must live. The characteristics of the ideal Fijian and those toward which the healer must aspire overlap.

It is not proper to seek the healing power prematurely or casually. Usually a person resists the healing work initially, humble before its power, unsure that he or she can meet its intense challenges on the straight path. The Fijian way is to come to the healing work slowly, carefully, "with head bowed."

Healers differ significantly from nonhealers in their attitude toward *mana* (R. Katz, 1981). Healers associate *mana* more frequently with healing than do nonhealers, respect it more, and consider it more powerful. Because they seek the experience of *mana* and are more familiar with it, healers also feel less surprised, afraid, or anxious than nonhealers when *mana* comes to them. Becoming a healer in Fiji does not bring economic rewards, increased social status, or special privileges. Healing ceremonies themselves in fact take little of a healer's time. The distinctiveness of healers lies in the character, motivations, and beliefs that prepare them for their healing work, allowing them to tap the power of *mana* for good where others cannot.

A common metaphor for the straight path is a path cut by hand with a cane knife through heavy forest underbrush. In creating the path the healer at times reaches a dead end or finds a shortcut, following both tortuously difficult passages and relatively easy ones, so that his or her movement fluctuates in rhythm and speed, sometimes circling back on itself. The Western understanding of development, including clear directions, linear progress, and success defined by levels of attainment, does not apply. "Straightness" refers not to a straight line but to a correct or "straight" attitude and motivation. As healers attempt to keep their motivation straight, they may be besieged by disequilibrium and experience transitions. The straight path does not describe an orderly process of change and achievement, in neat stages; it is instead the development of a correct attitude or motivation. Though the path itself is not straight, the way one travels it should be.

Of those healers who embark on the journey, not all continue on the straight path. Some give up working with *yaqona* entirely, finding the path too demanding and themselves unwilling or too weak to continue. This infrequent outcome typically occurs early in a healer's career, perhaps during the first phase of tests. Others may continue practicing the healing ceremony, but it becomes an empty performance since their commitment is a pretense. Such false healers can harm people by building misleading expectations, and they are particularly prone to attempt *vakatevoro*.

Straying from the straight path is deviating from cultural ideals. But what happens is that one no longer strives for these ideals rather than fails to attain them. In themselves, the ideals are not fully attainable. Traveling the straight path is living a life of special dedication to these ideals, not step-by-step achievement of them.

Healers in Fiji are not only respected but also feared. When they deviate from the straight path they become dangerous, since their power can then be used to harm others; they then cease to function as healers. Deviating from the path represents not simply falling away from ideals but also gaining power, albeit a dangerous rather than helpful power. Abandoning the path is therefore not without its rewards for certain people, who are thereby released to pursue their own interests at the expense of others. Such behavior is considered completely unbecoming, a violation of the order that is meant to govern Fijian life, and proper Fijian behavior.

Sickness or misfortune is the common manifestation of such deviation. In order to heal, the healer must stay on the straight path. Deviating from the path results not only in the loss of healing power, but usually in sickness as well. Sickness, though having particular physical or psychological symptoms, can reflect social and spiritual imbalance, disturbances created by interpersonal jealousies or improper behavior. Both sickness and health, then, reflect the degree to which individuals and communities are living within cultural ideals.

The straight path can also be seen as a means of negotiating the construction of experienced reality. Concepts of sickness and health imply patterns of meaning-making with moral implications. In following the straight path, one constructs and reconstructs reality in a culturally valued manner, creating as well new expectations for the future. Moral living results in health and makes it possible to create a more valued reality. In contrast, failing to find or follow the straight path leads to views of reality which are culturally devalued. These "mistaken" views of reality are expressed in behavior labeled as "bad" and eventually manifested in sickness or misfortune for the person and his or her relatives.

Many prospective healers work first as assistants to established healers. Approximately one third of prospective healers work with a healer who has just cured them, offering their help out of appreciation for the cure and respect for the healing power. About half of the healers have a close relationship with an experienced healer at the beginning of their careers, someone who helps the apprentice with difficult cases and provides general guidance. Through his or her behavior, the teacher demonstrates the straight path to the student. By traveling the path, the student learns how to follow it.

The straight path is characterized by transitions — moving to and from situations and states (R. Katz, 1981; Katz and Kilner, 1987; Katz and Wexler, 1990). Being "betwixt and between" is the key experience; the key dynamic is the person's ever-changing relationship to spiritual power or *mana*. Though access to power generally grows with experience, that access fluctuates. The points when the relationship to power is in flux are points of vulnerability for the healer. There are constant temptations to misuse power. But these are not merely times of danger but also opportunities for change. Traveling the straight path is a high-risk, high-gain activity.

The straight path challenges character. The education of the healer deals with subtle movements back and forth along dimensions of character, in increasingly demanding situations. This process of education releases ever more potent healing power. As one travels the path, however, living up to ideal attributes of character becomes more and more difficult. The healer is constantly tested — tempted, for example, to charge money for performing a healing ceremony, to become sexually involved with clients, and otherwise to betray the attributes that define the path. Increased power is determined by meeting severe tests of ever greater difficulty.

As healers accumulate power, they begin treating broader problems, such as hostilities between villages. Because the magnitude of power makes it harder to control, healers become more vulnerable to the temptation of practicing *vakatevoro*. Many healers who are considered very powerful are also suspected of *vakatevoro*. Testing of the healer then becomes even more important. Popular but superficial criteria for judging a healer's movement along the path include the number of clients he or she has, their responses and social status, and the degree to which the healer's cures are considered miraculous. The increasing severity of the tests faced and resolved by healers is also a measure of development, as are the nature and frequency of their visions, the number and power of the *Vu* who support the healing work, and the extent of direct communication between the healers and the *Vu*.

The criteria healers use to judge each other are important to them. These include a dedication to healing, expressed in the proper performance of the healing ceremony rather than in achieving specific cures. The healer's understanding is associated with the Fijian sense of heart rather than exclusively with the mind; the Fijian way of knowing is broadly emotional rather than narrowly cognitive. Heart, it is said, brings courage and commitment to the healer's efforts and calls for total involvement, thereby deepening understanding.

Through an act of what can be called moral exploration, the healer merges individual and sociocultural development (R. Katz, 1986; Katz and Kilner, 1987). The healer as moral explorer is sent as the community's emissary to uncharted realms of experience — areas of psychological, social, and spiritual ambiguity for the community, areas in which the meaning and structure of reality are confused or underdeveloped. On their return, healers struggle to make meaning for the community as they interpret those realms and pose new questions; in short, they offer guidance in the central issues of individual and cultural change.

The healer's journey is filled with risk — of being lost, of being wrong, of losing one's sense of place if not one's mind. The community's charge is simple: the healer must report honestly what was seen, must help clarify reality with his or her honestly made interpretations. The community's respect for healers is epitomized in its support of these moral explorations and its reliance on them.

The role of the healer as moral explorer shows us how the straight path helps to create, as well as maintain, cultural realities. The core of the Fijian healer's education is finding and staying on the straight path. The persistent struggle to do so allows the healer to gain access to *mana*, the most profound power in life, and apply that power for the good of others. Through constant interactions with the *Vu* and the realm of cultural mysteries, the healer does indeed explore moral realities. Defining reality, the healer imparts meaning and makes judgments about morality. None of these activities is predetermined. Though the straight path has existed for many before them, all healers must find and travel the path for themselves.

This moral exploration does not take the healer away from the community. The straight path unfolds in the usually mundane, concrete details and decisions of each day. It is back to this texture of daily living that we now return as we begin our story of Fijian healing.

PART TWO

THE STORY

CHAPTER 3

Healers in the City
(Suva)

The small concrete-block building lets in the already warm early morning air. There are no doors, and the top third of the walls are ornamented with large open spaces. Birds fly in and out, occasionally resting on the rafters, erasing the boundaries between inside and outside. Though my family and I are still in Nadi, the site of Fiji's main airline terminal, we have already arrived in the Fijian climate, and stand on Fijian land. Still several hours before dawn, we board a little twin-engine plane to our final destination, Suva, the capital city.

Traces of Suva's British colonial past can be seen in the latticework and arches of old government buildings, which sit on expansive, well-trimmed lawns bordered by flourishing yet neatly contained flower beds. Opening graciously onto the sea, the Grand Pacific Hotel, with its large, high-ceilinged rooms, topped with broad purring fans, and decorated with oversized caned chairs, is almost a caricature of the settings of the colonial lifestyle. The ease of these places casts a privileged air over Suva, establishing much of the city's surface impression.

Yet this ease is reserved for only a very few, most of whom are white and have either money or status or power, or all three. The other Suva consists of modest, mostly wood-frame homes in residential tracts, or shacks in bush-filled areas of less desirable land, such as ravines or low-lying swampy places. Here the rainy season turns everything into mud, and getting home can be a messy business if the planks put down to make walkways are wet or unbalanced.

The splashes of color on the carefully arranged tables of fruits and vegetables in the marketplace contrasts with the colonial elegance of Suva, especially as the crowded and noisy walkways become littered with spoiled or unsold food. Indigenous Fijians and Fijians of Indian descent sell their produce here, each group usually congregating in their own casually demarcated areas, all but ignoring their unplanned moments of contiguity.

Fijians of Indian ancestry dominate the central core of the city, especially in the actively commercial duty-free shops. Making deals with tourists is a way of life as much as a livelihood for these merchants. In the more rural outskirts of Suva, in residential areas serviced by small and scattered roadside stores and stalls, Indigenous Fijians establish the sense of place and pace — which is much softer, more patient and less time-bound. Through these more rural areas, buses roar, engines whining loudly, belching their dark exhaust. Owned and driven primarily by Fijians of Indian descent, they lace through the city and the surrounding areas, weaving physical connections among a culturally divided people.

Immersed in Suva's tropical flow of life, with its blazing heat drying everything clean after the soaking of the afternoon's torrential rains, I begin my work. It is January 1977.

There is a comforting myth that research is clearly bounded, with a "beginning" and an "end," and that ongoing events can be understood from the patterns discerned in the data collected during a thin slice of time in the field. But the work I'm about to "begin" actually starts, as such work always does, in midstream. Barely four days after my arrival in Suva, I'm thrust into a complex scene, peopled by accessible healers whose power often seems questionable, and inaccessible healers whose power is unquestionably respected. And none of these healers, of course, is waiting for my research to begin!

Fortunately, Sitiveni, a respected elder who is a fully bilingual researcher on oral traditions, agrees to bring me into this world of healers — and remain my guide. He becomes my friend and benefactor. Our enthusiasm for each other's interests fuels and defines a common aim: to seek the truth about traditional Fijian healing.

Though he is nearly sixty, Sitiveni's thin body is quick, strong, and compact. His mind flashes with insights, and his seriousness, often accompanied by a stern expression, is punctuated by a gentle lightness and occasional joking. Sitiveni is a proud man in his bearing, his attitude, his commitments, but that pride, based on his respect for his culture, never deteriorates into arrogance. Personal integrity pervades his considerable knowledge of Fijian tradition and the spiritual life that animates it.

Though Sitiveni is a longtime resident of Suva, his birthplace is Tovu, a village on Kali Island in the rural area, a ten-hour boat trip across open ocean. He remains in close contact with the village, making regular visits there. Officially the *mata-ni-vanua* (herald) for Tovu, an adviser on traditions and ceremonies, he also acts as its de facto chief, since the chiefly line is at present inactive. Tovu is Sitiveni's village; it is he who speaks on its behalf in the councils of government.

Sitiveni tells me about healers I might visit in Suva, and begins planning with me my eventual field site, which is to be in a rural village. He talks often about Tovu, bemoaning the villagers' failure to maintain traditional ways. Once or twice he alludes to the village as a good place to live; "Maybe even someone could do research there," he reflects. I've already learned enough of Fijian customs to withhold comment, but I can see an outline taking shape and wonder whether Sitiveni will invite me to work in his village — and begin to hope that he will.

Sitiveni's suggestions about traditional healers to visit in Suva always start the same way. "There's this *dauvagunu* I heard about," he would say. "I believe his name is Meli. Lives on the other side of the bus depot. You might try to see him." The particulars, of course, change for each. Eventually he suggests half a dozen healers — but always in that cryptic way, giving no further details, not even information about his own relationship with the healer, if one exists.

After I've made a visit or two to one of these healers, Sitiveni and I talk, comparing opinions. Sitiveni helps put what I see into perspective, assisting me as I try to establish the authenticity of each healer. He remains, however, spare in his discussion. I'm beginning to learn that you don't talk too much about this healing.

72

Sitiveni does another important thing for me. "I know just the person you need," he assures me. "Yes, I believe I've found you a translator." He then tells me about Inoke, a man approaching forty who is extremely intelligent, well educated, and completely bilingual. As one of the first Fijians to enter medical school, of which he completed the first two years, he has a great deal of knowledge about Western health care, which of course bears directly on my research project about traditional healing. Most important, Inoke, like Sitiveni, is a *mata-ni-vanua* who takes his function seriously. He possesses enormous knowledge of Fijian traditions and ceremonies, including healing ceremonies. Sitiveni is right — Inoke is just the person I need, a Fijian colleague who stands on a traditional base as he gains Western knowledge, just as I stand on a Western base, hoping to gain Fijian knowledge. Both of us are deeply interested in healing, walking toward each other on the same path.

There is one further part of the picture. Inoke is from Bitu, the same chain of outlying rural islands Sitiveni is from; his home village, though several hours by boat from Sitiveni's, is closely related. Inoke, Sitiveni says, knows everyone I will need to speak with throughout Bitu. Furthermore, Inoke's wife is the district nurse in Sitiveni's home village of Tovu, where both she and Inoke now live. Nasi ("Nurse"), as she is called, is, like her husband, also trained in Western methods of health care, yet she too uses traditional Fijian healing and is a firm believer in it. Nasi is also bilingual, though she is not as fluent in English as her husband. Everything seems to be coming together, and the idea of working in Sitiveni's home village of Tovu, and elsewhere in the Bitu region, grows more and more attractive.

Like Sitiveni, Inoke is also at home in the city of Suva. We travel together to visit various healers, and if he does not know them personally, he knows of them or is even related to them. As a *mata-ni-vanua* he is well versed in performing the *sevusevu*, the ceremonial exchange of *yaqona* which must precede any visit, and with which we request permission to do our work. In Suva this exchange is especially complex, since most urban healers seem to have their own requirements for the ceremony which, if not performed, pose an obstacle to subsequent communica-

73

tion. In the city, healers are constantly trying to distinguish themselves as unique, even uniquely powerful, and having their own special *sevuse-vu* has become one of their hallmarks. Inoke is able to weave his way through this maze, and his skill and persistence enable us to interview nearly all the healers we locate.

Urban healers are often difficult to find. We never get a house number, rarely a street address — in many cases, in fact, like other simple residences in Suva, their houses have no exact addresses. If their healing work is not widely known, getting directions, even when we are close to their houses, is at times problematic. Since we can rarely make appointments to meet, when we do arrive at the correct house, the healer is often not home or even has moved to a place the neighbors do not know. When we are successful in visiting a healer, we sometimes learn about when regular healing ceremonies are held — which, however, usually turn out to be distinctly irregular.

We hear about the approximate location of ten healers and have only vague information about another half dozen. Of those ten whose homes we do locate, four have moved and four are about to move. Two more move shortly after our visit.

Such moves are often necessitated by the controversial nature of the work of some healers. Neighbors' complaints about the lines that form on the sidewalk outside the house of a popular healer may account for his or her relocation. A practitioner suspected of using the rituals for negative purposes might disappear after an anonymous call to the police. Jealousy is a constant theme as healers are rumored to try to destroy successful colleagues or steal their most powerful medicines. Some healers have been charged with practicing *vakatevoro,* which is illegal in Fiji, and a few have been convicted. There are many self-appointed "investigators" in Suva — often inspired by evangelical elements in the churches — who are dedicated to wiping out the "pagan" practice of traditional healing.

Rather than risk investigation, urban healers generally keep a low profile. When their work becomes too public, or too popular, it usually becomes controversial; then it is easier to move to a new location, where they can again work quietly for a while. But more and more patients always seem to find their way to the new place. And there remain a few healers who, wherever and whenever they work, promote themselves to the public. Rather than our finding them, these healers find us.

As Inoke and I make these visits, the uniquely personal elements of each practice are highlighted within the characteristic pattern that begins to emerge. Though the healers' places of work (invariably in or next to their homes) are usually unrecognizable from the outside, inside — in the healing ceremony — high drama often prevails. The places in which a selected few healers work look distinctive from the outside; that of one woman is a traditional thatched house specially built in the style of an ancient Fijian temple (*Bure Kalou*), and filled with traditional healing paraphernalia. Since we are often taken to a healer by a client, we have the introduction of a satisfied customer. "I've been waiting for you! I knew you were coming," healer after healer greets us. "I already know who you are, and I know what you're searching for." This is disarming at the least, startling when I take such statements at face value. With some healers, I'm never entirely convinced of their foreknowledge, though with others I have little doubt.

Once trust is established on a visit, either the healer him- or herself or patients who are present tell stories documenting the healer's powers. The strength and number of the *Vu* who support the healing work are alluded to indirectly, since it is improper to speak openly about these matters. Miraculous cures or feats are described. A patient suffering from cancer who had been given up as hopeless by the best medical doctor in Suva was completely cured; a person who had lost all his belongings, including the fishing boat he needed to earn his living, was directed to a place where he found a large sum of money; an infertile woman who had tried every remedy available, including Western medical treatments, for more than fifteen years conceived immediately after visiting the healer. And then there is the list of the healer's famous patients — each seems to have at least one cabinet minister as a devoted client. Some healers even claim the prime minister as a patient, and I begin to wonder when I hear this claim from several different healers. Other feats are also recounted. One patient describes how, once filled, her healer's *tanoa* is never empty, even with continual drinking from it and without adding more *yaqona*. This magically replenished *tanoa* is likened to the biblical story of Jesus' making "many, many loaves of bread" to feed the multitude.

The dramatic detail offered in these accounts — the hopelessness of a case, the immediacy and completeness of recovery — differ from one healer to another. Some healers boastfully exaggerate for effect; others tell quieter stories, describing the ordinary problems of their patients. I am intuitively drawn toward the more modest or humble healers, rather than the ones who try to convince me that they are worth interviewing. Interestingly enough, the more modest healers often have patients present who can tell about their powers for them. But I don't avoid any healer, visiting all of them more than once.

Other issues usually come up soon after the stories of healings have been told. There is the question of healers' sharing their knowledge with others, and with me in particular. Some healers are reluctant: "Why should I talk with you?" they ask. "How do I know? Maybe you're here to steal my secrets, or pass them on to some other healer!" One healer who has already been brought to trial on charges of witchcraft fears she will be reported to the police again. With Inoke's help, I am able to communicate the sincerity of my search for knowledge. In all but one case, the healers agree, usually enthusiastically, to talk with me and to allow me to participate in their healing ceremonies.

Fijian healing is a matter of exchange. Though rarely stated explicitly, it is expected that patients give something to the healer performing the ceremony. Even though I usually am seeking only an interview rather than a healing, I always offer the kind of things that are typically given, such as a pack of cigarettes. On rare occasions, cash is the medium of exchange. Whatever is given is regarded as a gift expressing one's gratitude for help and is usually accepted at the end of the healing ritual. In the cases of some healers, however, what is given is considered a fee for services and is usually demanded before the healing or interview begins. This perversion of the traditional exchange makes me uneasy, as it does Inoke. Charging for healing is a fundamental violation of the Fijian tradition; it is appropriate only to accept a gift of appreciation.

Sitiveni is not surprised when I describe my visits to urban healers. "Yes, they do some unusual things," he says, "and not all are trustworthy. But," he continues, "it's different in our villages. There we know everybody; we've grown up with them. So we know who is a healer — and who is not! And we know what each healer can do — and cannot do. No need for them to tell us or display their powers."

Meli is the first healer I visit in Suva. A janitor at the local hospital, Meli also repairs appliances, but his repair business seems far from thriving. His yard is filled with used equipment and appliances, broken or taken apart, much of it wearing years of rust. A slight, balding man in his late fifties, Meli has four children who are all grown, though his youngest son still lives with him and his wife.

It is after six, and Inoke and I find Meli home alone. Inoke presents the *yaqona* on my behalf in the *sevusevu* ceremony as we introduce ourselves and state the purpose of our visit — to learn more about Fijian ways of helping people. Meli accepts the *yaqona* quietly, almost offhandedly.

"You're welcome to stay," he says softly. "People will not come for a while. But I'll be working tonight without Mosese, my assistant. Maybe he'll be here tomorrow night."

We talk for nearly an hour. Meli describes how he received the *mana*, how he began the healing work, the kind of cases he treats. His openness is disarming.

"I'm here every evening from six until around midnight. That way people know when they can find me." He talks like a businessman, sensitive to the needs of the consumer for regular, predictable hours.

Then Meli speaks of his assistant: "We work together. When Mosese is here, the *Vu* behind my work enters into him to do the healing. He becomes possessed [*curumi*]. You should come when he is here. That's when you'll see the full healing work."

Meli refers to Mosese as his *waqa waqa*. Leaning over toward me, Inoke explains that *waqa waqa* means a body possessed by the *Vu* for the purpose of manifesting itself.

"We should come back when Mosese is here," Inoke whispers. "That possession is something I want to see!"

77

Several patients come later that night. Meli accepts the *yaqona* that each offers and prescribes individual herbal remedies. It is a quiet night, very low-key and matter-of-fact. Meli's personality seems to be expressed in his healing ceremony.

Four days later we go to Meli's for a second visit. It's nearly seven in the evening. Again the place is quiet, though three other men and one woman are already there, patients who have already been seen by Meli. Now everyone is just sitting around, drinking *yaqona*.

Another person arrives, a tall man, thin but muscular, who is neatly dressed in slacks and a shirt. The conversation continues: still drinking *yaqona*, those gathered in the room talk about the latest government scandal, the weather, the upcoming rugby match against New Zealand.

Without warning, the tall man suddenly slumps into a heap on the floor, his body twitching violently. The twitches become so severe that as his arms and feet bang against the floor it seems as though he will break a limb. His breathing is violent; his whole body seems to grasp for air, spitting out more than he could have ever breathed in. It is a fearsome sight. No one in the room moves. Someone whispers in my ear, "The *waqa waqa* has arrived."

Mosese — or the *waqa waqa* — or the *Vu* — or some combination of those three — begins to speak.

"Greetings to all of you. Greetings. I've arrived to help the work of Meli." Mosese is now still and he is half sitting, half slouching on the floor. The violence that tore at his body is now confined to his breathing and speech. Strangled sounds come grunting out. They are difficult to decipher, yet those present listen closely and understand. The words are addressed to each of the patients in turn, prescribing additional herbal remedies and advice on rituals to perform in order to prevent sickness. All the while Meli sits quietly, unperturbed, almost nonchalant. He doesn't look at Mosese.

"Now I must return...I must return. I take leave of you good people." And with these words a final, piercing twitch slams Mosese to the floor, where he remains still, frozen like a hardened lump of melted wax. After less than a minute, his body begins to unfold and loosen. Soon Mosese is again sitting normally; only as he massages his face and rubs deeply into his eyes is there any indication of his previous state.

The conversation resumes, continuing for several more hours, and again dealing with topics of everyday life. No one speaks of the possession. Mosese leaves about an hour before the others, slipping out unobtrusively.

On a return visit to Meli's, I ask about Mosese: "Who is talking?" I can pose such a question only because I'm genuinely perplexed.

"It is the *Vu*, the ones behind my work," Meli answers calmly. He leaves to go to the outhouse.

I look at Inoke, wanting to be sure of his translation. "The *Vu*, meaning more than one *Vu*, is that what he said?" I whisper.

"He said *Vu*, meaning more than one," Inoke replies.

"Can I ask him about this kind of thing?"

"It's up to you, really — though I sure would like to know. Why not? Meli seems eager to tell us about his work."

"How many *Vu* come through Mosese?" I ask Meli when he returns.

"Three. There are three *Vu* behind my work, and there are nights when all three will visit. One after the other."

Meli goes no further; for him the answer is complete. I ask other questions, but Meli does not elaborate beyond saying, "Mosese is my *waqa waqa*. His body serves my healing work and is dedicated to the *Vu* which are behind my work."

Meli sees Mosese as an extension of his work, a vehicle through which his *Vu* can enter directly into the healing. But, Meli insists that healing occurs with or without Mosese, as the *Vu* behind the work are always on hand.

Several weeks later, I speak with Mosese alone at his house. He confirms Meli's interpretation of his role. But Mosese's words betray a slight drift toward independence.

"Sometimes I don't want to go over to Meli's. It's too hard on me. I need more time for myself."

Mosese does not remember anything about what takes place when he is in a state of possession. "I'm not the one to ask about what happens."

Less than a month after visiting Meli and his *waqa waqa*, I find myself in a situation even more difficult to comprehend. I've become friendly with Alifereti, the captain of one of the local freight and passenger boats, a forty-foot wooden vessel, engine-powered with an auxiliary sail. He makes the approximately ten-hour voyage to Sitiveni's home village of Tovu and then on to farther points, two or three times a month, depending on the weather and the amount of cargo or number of passengers wanting to make the trip. Alifereti is of the ocean; when he is inland, he gazes restlessly out to what should be a horizon. Though laconic, he's a risk taker, daring his way into strange, sometimes threatening situations. Deeply involved in traditional Fijian healing, he is also a true researcher. "I just want to know what's really going on," he says, as he describes his many visits to healers, mostly as a client. This abiding curiosity is what brings us together.

Alifereti, who is fully bilingual, takes me to some of the healers he visits in Suva. He knows a lot of them; the kind of person who shops around, he changes healers if he hears of someone better, often seeing more than one at any time. One or two we visit together seem questionable. With a darkly dramatic turn to their work and an exaggerated notion of their powers, they are, I fear, entangled with forces beyond their understanding and trying to control them for their own benefit. It is a dangerous situation, ripe for misuse and serious injury. Alifereti agrees. That's part of the reason he visits them. He likes to be on the edge of confusion and doubt. "That's where I learn," he assures me. I'm learning to learn there too. Then he takes me to Sera.

Sera's house, a small concrete-block structure on an individual plot in a residential setting, is built in the popular urban style, with no hint of the traditional Fijian *bure*. Alifereti and I enter through the front door, walking into a living room filled with Western furniture. Sera sits on a long vinyl-covered couch, motioning us to the two chairs opposite her. The floor, cut up by the bulky overgrowth of furniture towering around it, is not the arena for discourse and activity as in the typical Fijian home. Lamps are turned on everywhere, making the room seem sharply separated from the night's darkness; the blare of fluorescent lights in the ceiling fixtures generates an operating-room overbrightness.

We talk about local conditions, especially the unusually heavy rains, as well as about healing and Sera's own healing work. We talk; we visit. An ordinary situation on the surface. But Sera doesn't look ordinary, nor does she look at us in an ordinary manner. A slight, almost frail woman, her enormous hair is unkempt, loose-ended, so that the usually stately, rounded Fijian style leaps out of control. Her eyes are large, bulging containers of fright. As she sits on the edge of the sofa, her eyes seem to dash away from lurking demons. At the same time she stares piercingly into our eyes, as if she is trying to gouge something out of us. Alifereti and I are both uncomfortable, and our exchange of nervous glances deepens the tension.

Then, Sera's eyes sink into her head. She looks as though she is being pursued, a cornered, terrified animal about to be slaughtered. As her eyes roll up in their sockets, white balls now pointing at us, she slides off the couch into a fetal position on the floor. Unwinding, she begins to slither about, at first slowly, then with her outstretched body making random jerks. This creature on the floor then opens its mouth, stretching it wide, spitting out hissing sounds. Its eyes glare at us, ready to attack. Then the lights go out. And there is nobody else there who could have turned them off.

Alifereti and I are in a frenzy. The house is completely dark. We hear the horrible hissing sounds coming from the floor, first in one room, then another. We don't know what to do. At first, we run from the sounds, then cautiously approach them. Several times, we see the outlines of a slithering body in the low blue illumination from a streetlight, moving rapidly about, crawling under and behind the couch, lunging out at us. Then it is gone. We go outside, into the small backyard. The fresh air feels good. Suddenly, from a clump of bushes, Sera strikes out at us, issuing her awful sounds.

Finally her hissing becomes softer and less frequent. Soon it is quiet, though heavy breathing still comes from the living room. We go back inside. Next to the couch is Sera, curled up into a tight ball. We sit and wait.

Without warning, all the house lights come on — again unassisted. Sera is still leaning against the couch. It seems as though we've been away a long time, in a space and experience neither of us understands enough to be able to help the other out. Alifereti looks at his watch. The lights went out half an hour ago.

After several minutes, Sera slowly raises herself up and sits on the couch. She is more relaxed now; her eyes have softened, and she tucks her feet comfortably under her. She is inviting conversation.

Alifereti begins, and as usual, is direct: "What happened?"

Sera talks about her healing work and especially the force behind it, the *Vu* called Degei. Often taking the form of a snake, Degei is one of the most powerful of the traditional Fijian *Vu*.

"When you came tonight, my *Vu* decided to visit. He wanted to see you, to check you both out.· And before he left me, he told me you were okay — you were not frightened by his power, and he says that's very important. He also told me I can talk with you, that you aren't here to steal anything from my work. So now we can talk."

I feel relieved, and I see Alifereti's body loosen up also. A slight smile, even a bit of a grin, comes over his face. We look at each other as if to say, "Not frightened? You could have fooled me!"

Though Sera is willing to share her knowledge, she has little to say.

"I can't tell you anything about what happened tonight," she says several times. "I only know that there are times I begin to feel like I'm losing myself, and I get really scared. And then I black out. When I come to, I'm worn out but not scared anymore. I can remember a few things that Degei, my *Vu*, has told me. He always tells me that he was visiting me, and living in my body. And I know I become a snake, because others who've seen me tell me so.

"My *Vu* doesn't come all the time," Sera continues. "Only to check out my work, to be sure I'm doing his work the right way, and to check out some special visitors, like yourselves. You're lucky he found you were okay, otherwise I'm not sure what he would've done. It scares me just to think of it. I know that snakes can swallow people."

"Not all healers have their *Vu* visit them like you did," I comment. "What does it mean to have such visits?"

"You can tell the strength of the healer by those visits," Sera replies. "When the *Vu* comes directly into you [*curumi*], you have to be strong. Otherwise that *Vu* can rip you apart. It's especially dangerous when the *Vu* eats or devours you [*kani*]. Then it's like your insides are dissolving in acid. But when the *Vu* visits you, you know he cares about your work. You're his special partner."

As Alifereti and I leave Sera's, I turn to him. "I didn't know how far to go in there — so I just went all the way," I confide. "And then I was right in the middle of something I'd never seen before, and I still don't know what actually happened!"

"Like I said, I like living on the edge." Alifereti smiles. "I can't be sure what went on in there either — but I bet you know more about what the edge is now."

The occurrence of possession in Fijian healing is established once again. Throughout my research, however, such experiences of possession — and in particular their validity — will endure as questions. They remain experiences on the edge.

One afternoon as Sitiveni and I talk, sitting in the stream of dust-filled sunlight that cuts through his room, he says in a questioning tone, "There is this woman from back home; she's from the village just next to Tovu. I'm related to her. She moved here to Suva about ten years ago, and I hear she does the healing work. But I've never seen her. Her name is Verani." Sitiveni is requesting my help; he wants me to learn more about one of his people because he is responsible both for her welfare and the validity of her healing practice.

All along the steep, rock-strewn path to Verani's, people giving directions keep pointing up. "Up there," they say. "It's still a ways to go." It rained two days ago, and the path still is treacherous; there is no solid footing. The mud slides off the top layer of dirt and the grassy slime covering the rocks makes them slick. In places I'm going nowhere as my feet grab for traction. Several times I slip backward, into steep hard places. Soon my hands are covered with mud.

Finally a plateau comes in sight. After one last unforgiving incline, we are greeted by a wooden sign in front of a house: *Lomalagi*, "Heaven." After our climb, the sign seems purely descriptive.

"The work of *Kalou* [God] goes on here," the healer Verani later tells us, explaining the sign.

"It's really hard to get here," I comment.

"I know. I have to walk that path every day, and I'm still not used to it. It's a struggle for most people. But you know, if patients really want to come here…they climb!"

An attractive woman in her mid-thirties, Verani is slim but strong-looking. Her hands are large, almost rough, the hands of a laborer. Yet they are also healing hands: massage is one of the treatments Verani offers, in addition to herbal remedies. She is a very ordinary woman who speaks simply, even humbly, about her healing work along with her tasks as a mother and housewife, as she complains about food prices and the lack of her favorite fish, which was so plentiful back in her home village.

Sometimes two or three patients at a time wait in the main room of Verani's house. She sees them one by one in a small treatment room to the side, which is closed off by a blue curtain, guiding them into the private confines of the little room, shutting the curtain tightly after them, pulling it aside when her work is done. The *yaqona* offering from each patient is simply accepted, then put aside on a shelf. Verani's healing practice has a professional Western feel — polished, clean, efficient, discreet.

Sitiveni seems satisfied when I later describe Verani's work to him. Though he is not certain about the efficacy of her healing, he believes that she is trying her best, and for him that is enough.

One morning, as Inoke and I are planning our day, I ask him about his relative Bale, a healer whose name he mentioned when we first met and whom he sees on occasion as a patient.

"Yes, she's a good one," he says. "There's our work for today."

Walking past the hospital and up a wide street with substantial houses set back toward the edge of the cliff overlooking Suva Harbor, we come to Bale's. Large and informal, the house is in almost in disrepair. There are many rooms, and few doors are closed. We enter a big open space formed by two connecting rooms. Except for two metal chairs pushed against the wall, the area is unfurnished. In the Fijian manner, people are sitting in a circle, cross-legged on the linoleum floor. Near the center is the *tanoa*. Bale is drinking *yaqona* with three men and one woman. It is two o'clock on a Tuesday afternoon.

Bale is a short, heavy woman. Her face is round, and a smile dimples her cheeks. She commands the space she occupies, yelling out orders for more water to someone in the kitchen, laughing loudly with one of the men, gesturing expansively toward us, as if to sweep us closer to the others. Despite her heaviness, she moves swiftly, decisively. Bale engenders an atmosphere of warmth and acceptance. I immediately feel at ease, a feeling that is reinforced as Inoke and Bale exchange friendly greetings, then indulge in the teasing their kinship allows. Bale's place of healing is like a family space.

We spend three hours with her. In that time she is never alone, seeing eight different patients, all of whom visit and drink for a while before being treated, then stay at least an hour after being worked on, drinking *yaqona*. Bale usually takes the patient into a side room, whose door remains open for treatment. There, using an oil with medicinal herbs, she massages the patient's head, neck, chest, arms, and legs, ending by grasping his or her hands in her own, holding and squeezing them, then shaking out her own hands.

"It's to get rid of the bad things [*ka ca*] — their sicknesses — that I take into my hands when I massage patients," Bale explains, shaking her hands again, directing them away from people in the room. "I must shake out the patient's sickness, or else I'll get that sickness. And I have to be sure not to shake toward anyone else, or else they too could get sick." In addition to advice and instructions, Bale gives massages to all her patients.

Before we leave, Inoke asks for healing help: his stomach has been aching for more than a week. Bale gives him a massage right in the big room.

"Rusiate, I want you to see how I work," she says as she pours oil into her palms and begins working on Inoke's head. When she finishes the massage, she takes Inoke's right hand in her two hands and holds it tightly. Her hands vibrate slightly, then she releases her grip.

"I'm giving extra power to Inoke's right hand," she explains, "because that's the hand with which he greets the world."

As we start to gather up our things, Bale calls out, "Not yet, you don't. You haven't eaten any of my food!" She playfully drags us into the kitchen, sits us down, and brings over a plate piled high with taro and

85

two bowls filled with fish cooked in coconut cream. Yes, Bale's place is indeed a home.

After nearly four months in Fiji, I'm beginning to know my way around, even starting to have short, halting conversations in Fijian. But after interviews with more than twenty healers and numerous visits to their healing sessions, clarity is still elusive. My research has yielded a profuse, chaotic jumble of stories of traditional healing. Differences between healers emerge as their primary common characteristic. Some instances of possession seem staged, straining for effect. Most troublesome, the healers seem less than honest, their effectiveness questionable. At best, Fijian healers are simply human, struggling to be helpful, only sometimes succeeding. This dose of reality nevertheless feeds my desire for insight from someone who knows, someone who is both a true and a truly respected Fijian healer.

It is then that I hear about Ratu Noa. In his usual way, Sitiveni casually mentions him one day: "You know, you ought to see Ratu Noa. He's the one person who really knows. But he's hard to find, even harder to talk with. He's silent in his work." My efforts to contact Ratu Noa prove that Sitiveni's words are no exaggeration.

CHAPTER 4

Conversations with Ratu Noa (Suva)

"I'll try to help you, in any way I can
— to the limits of my knowledge."

When I finally meet Ratu Noa, I am struck by his lack of pretension. Neatly dressed in the conventional style for the Suva area, no one seeing him walk down the street would think, "Oh, there goes a traditional Fijian healer!" His house is furnished in the almost obligatory manner of a wage-earning Fijian family's home, with the sofa, chairs, table, and bed; but the Western furniture does not overwhelm the usefulness of the floor, the traditional Fijian space on which all communications and business is conducted. With Nawame, Ratu Noa's wife, working as a government nurse, and Ratu Noa himself in construction, the family could easily display more of its income, but their earnings go elsewhere, spent on helping their children and other relatives.

Ratu Noa approaches the *yaqona* without flourishes, yet with reverence. He accepts it, then mixes and serves it…slowly…carefully…weaving a partnership among those drinking with him. His seriousness allows us to reflect, even meditate on the *yaqona* and within the ceremony. Because he is a *turaga*, a high chief, he is entitled to the honor of the first *bilo*, the cup in which *yaqona* is served, but he does not call attention to this fact. When he is served the first *bilo,* he takes it humbly and gratefully. At times, over the objection of others drinking with him, who are of lower status, he succeeds in having others served first, out of respect to them. He is generous in sharing his birth-given privilege.

He makes his standards clear from the start: "Many have come to me seeking what I know. I turn them all away. They want to take information away from me and use it for their own ends. Only if one comes with the proper attitude of respect and service, and seeks to use this information for the benefit of the people, will I begin to share."

My initial conversations with Ratu Noa are indirect and elusive. Ratu Noa talks to and through Inoke, insisting that he is talking to me only *because* of Inoke. He answers my questions only because he is related to Inoke, who is serving as my translator. And much of the time Inoke and Ratu Noa simply talk to each other, reaffirming their kinship ties.

"I believe it is destined that he and I begin to talk," Ratu Noa finally says of me, still talking to Inoke. "The trail that leads from you, Inoke, to me cannot be denied, and since he is now part of that trail, having come to me with you, I cannot resist. I must hear him and respond." I remain a third party to their discussion but am now no longer excluded. Ratu Noa then looks directly at me and says, "The trail that brings you to me is strong. I am prepared to begin our conversations. I will try to answer the questions you have...as best I can."

The conversations can now begin, but the opportunities to talk remain elusive. Our meetings are fragile; each seems destined to be the last. Ratu Noa keeps the door swinging rather than open. "This could be our last talk," he will say. "We may see each other again...but I don't know how or when."

Neither do I. I have become a night traveler, going into unfamiliar territory, seeking to find the light on in Ratu Noa's house, finding instead a locked door, or a darkened house, or an apologetic response from Nawame: "Ratu Noa is not home now. He went off on the job, and I don't know when he'll be back. You might try coming here tomorrow night."

"What would be a good time?" I ask, still encased in my Western time frame. "Oh, around nine o'clock," she responds, trying to be helpful, but knowing such appointments can't be made. I come the next night at nine, only to find Ratu Noa out — again. I feel embarrassed and frustrated. It takes several missed "appointments," these "misunderstandings" about time and place, for me to realize it is more than my still inadequate Fijian and unlucky circumstances that are the obstacles.

When we do eventually reconnect, we talk…and talk. It is as if the conversations are meant to be, just as he said.

"Ask whatever you want, and I will try to answer as best I can. I will always answer only what I know, and if it's something that is beyond me, I will not give you just anything, just to make you happy. I can't tell you what I don't actually know. This work you are doing is too important for that. I now know it is a work that must be done. So, Ratu Rusiate, ask your questions — fire away!"

I don't "fire away." But Ratu Noa has opened the door, and he seems to thrive on questions. When there is a lull in the conversation, he'll lean forward and ask, "Is there anything else you want to know? Now is the time. I'm ready to answer any of your questions." But I sense that he isn't addressing my specific questions as much as my sincere wish to know. What he offers, and when, are guided by my questions; he uses them as indications of what is in my mind and heart and therefore what I am ready and worthy to hear.

The night we begin our serious, ongoing conversations, Ratu Noa lays out some of the basic principles of his work, starting with those that will guide our communication.

"I will give out information," he assures me, "if it's properly used — that is, if it's used for healing. But not if it's used improperly — that is, if someone wants to take the information away and use it for their own ends. Rusiate," he continues, "your research is meant to serve us Fijians and people throughout the world, not to ensure your own betterment. So I'll try to help you, in any way I can — to the limits of my knowledge."

It's hard for me to say anything. I look down, mumbling something about not being worthy. Then as I hear him speak again in the same vein, I am suddenly able to accept his words. It is then that I begin to work with him.

Ratu Noa seems to make a practice of repeating his main points several times. But no, "repeat" is not accurate. He treats the same point several times, each time considering it from a slightly different perspective, nesting it in a slightly different context. If I listen, really listen and hear, each somewhat different approach will guide me eventually to the same place.

Ratu Noa's words reverberate, offering me multiple chances to hear. He lets me get over my initial false humility and, as I become more truly humble, leads me to accept the responsibility he is giving me to learn about his work, to do research that truly serves others.

Ratu Noa stresses the primacy of the *Vu*, and of *Kalou*, and their hierarchical relationship in the traditional Fijian worldview. "The *Vu* set their plans, and then they carry them out. We ask and work for something, and if it's within the plan of the *Vu* for the thing to happen at a certain time, the thing will surely happen. If that thing is in the plan of the *Vu* and you don't work for it, then you won't get anything. And no matter how hard you ask or try, if you go against the plan of the *Vu*, it will be of no avail. There is a certain planned time for certain things to happen."

"All the *Vu* receive commands from *Kalou*. A certain share of everything comes from *Kalou* to your *Vu*, from your *Vu* to you and your people. You can personally meet your *Vu*; but you can't meet *Kalou*. You can personally see your *Vu*; but you can't see *Kalou*."

Before coming to Fiji, I read about *mana*, the spiritual force, and in my talks with healers in Suva would hear the word every so often. But is it too soon to raise such a fundamental topic with Ratu Noa, one that is perhaps essentially ungraspable? He said the door was open. I now risk walking in.

"I've heard some of the other healers talk about the importance of *mana* in their work." I hesitate, then speak firmly. "But I wanted to ask you about this *mana*."

Ratu Noa nods with a knowing smile, unwinding his words as if they were predestined for delivery as a whole.

"The *mana* belongs in Fiji, but it is getting weaker because we no longer observe our traditions. For example, we are violating the traditional food taboos. Now take myself. Traditionally, my people live near the shore, they are from the water. If we get fish, we must take it upriver to the inland people, the people from the land, with whom we have a traditional exchange. We give them our fish, and they give us their pig. We don't eat that fish — it is taboo; they don't eat their pig — it is taboo for them. We take that fish inland, way upriver. Even if the fish goes bad, we keep carrying it upriver, until we get to the farthest place. And then if all we have left is the basket we carried the fish in, or even just the pole we carried the basket on, we give that basket or pole to those upriver people, to show our faithfulness to the tradition. But today, people no longer follow these traditions. My people will steal the fish, and instead of taking it upriver to the rightful owner, they eat it themselves. In the past, if a coastal person stole the fish meant for the inland, upriver people, a fish bone would stick in the throat of the one who had stolen it — even if the piece of fish eaten had no bones! And then only if someone from upriver massaged the sick person's throat would he recover."

"But isn't it hard to keep observing this kind of food taboo today, living in the city?"

"People are different," Ratu Noa reflects. "It is difficult for many to keep these taboos, but I keep all of them. Practicing these traditions is a gauge of the strength of your *mana*. You must be true and straight, and to be that way you must practice the traditions. If you just talk and don't practice these things, you won't get anything. As the real Fijian life weakens, so does the *mana*."

"How do you keep to the real, traditional Fijian life with all these new things happening in Suva?" As a construction site supervisor, Ratu Noa works for a large, bureaucratic company that deals with urban planning and uses heavy, complex road-building equipment. "Isn't it hard, especially at your job, where you're always having to work according to company schedules, and supervise the operation of all that heavy equipment?"

"No, it's not hard! Being a real Fijian, faithfully observing the traditions, doesn't hinder my job; in fact, it helps me with these new things like schedules and machines.

"There are two methods for gaining the knowledge or know-how to do my work," Ratu Noa continues. "In one, you go to school for many years and get trained; in the other, the knowledge is just given to you, it is fed into you. This is true of both my healing work and my job. When we follow our traditions, knowledge is given to us. I will know beforehand that a machine on the job will have an accident, so I don't go that day to work. That is an example of given wisdom. The knowledge we learn from school [*vuku vulici*] comes to a limit, but this given knowledge [*vuku soli*] keeps going beyond that limit.

"If I want to know something or get something that is normally impossible because of my level of education, which, you know, is only second grade, then I do a special practice. I leave my home. I don't sleep with my family, I don't use any sleeping mat that is normally used at home, and I use a traditional Fijian pillow, a wooden one, not my usual pillow. In this way I'm preparing myself, and become ready to achieve what I had wished for."

"Remember, Rusiate, there are two ways we find things, two ways we learn, and there is a big difference between them. There are those who search for things and those who are given things. With me, this *mana* has always been given."

The last bus will be coming soon. Knowing Inoke and I have to leave, Ratu Noa ends our talk: "Maybe that's enough for tonight."

"Can I come tomorrow night?"

"Yes, you come here tomorrow night."

The next night Inoke and I return to Ratu Noa's. Meeting two nights in a row is unusual, and we pick up our conversation as if we paused only briefly for a breath of night air.

Tonight I have brought my nine-year-old daughter, Laurel, whose Fijian name is Lora. She is suffering from bronchial congestion and wheezing. She has a history of bronchial distress, and my wife and I hope Ratu Noa can help her. We are worried that her condition might worsen with the stress of our new environment.

Ratu Noa begins talking. "You know, Christ gives us all an example of healing power. Christ was really honest, even though the church people and priests said his work was of the devil. The amount of truth in each individual determines the power of his healing.

"Actually, I've purposely stopped healing people for quite a while now." Ratu Noa is silent a moment. "Though I *could* heal people, there is no room for me now to serve the *Vu* that gives me the power to heal; my house here is too small. Except when an emergency comes, and then I must help. Or when a patient comes who can't be helped by anyone else and I know I can help, he too I must help.

"In my old house, we had lots of rooms. I had my special room, a room for worship and work [*cakacaka ni yaqona,* "work of the *yaqona*" or healing work]. I specially prepared that room to offer my gratitude for the *mana* that was given to me. Before I go into that room, I first bathe. When I enter the room, I put on special clothes that are for that room only, throwing outside all the clothes I've been wearing. It isn't easy... You have to observe every detail. After I pray in that special room and follow all the right steps, everything will come. I'll know beforehand when a visitor is coming — I'll see him. Or if I'm preparing to operate on a case, I'll be told in detail which part will be operated on or whether an operation is even needed. These things become known to you while you do your worship.

"When I had that special room, I would see lots of patients. They came all the time."

I'm now unsure about asking Ratu Noa to help Lora. But he makes it easy. "How is Lora feeling?" he asks.

I describe her symptoms and, with an offering of *yaqona*, request his help.

Without hesitation, he asks Lora and me a series of questions about her condition — the precise symptoms, when they started, when and where they occur. "This is how I work," he says. "I ask the patient lots of questions about her condition, until the picture of her illness finally emerges."

Ratu Noa talks about the origins of Lora's condition: she was given too many sweets when she was small. He gives her an herbal medicine to take once a week for four weeks, then once every two weeks for four weeks, then once a month until our return to the United States. "By the time you get back to America, her illness will be gone and you won't have to rely on the medicine anymore."

After administering a dose of the medicine, Ratu Noa begins to give

93

Lora a massage, rapidly rubbing her chest with oil (*waiwai*), up from the rib cage and then down the center of her chest. He asks me to try, and corrects my attempt. "This is how you help her, and use this oil here, this is also Fijian medicine [*wainimate vakaviti*]."

Lora lies down on the floor beside me to rest, covering herself with her sweater.

Ratu Noa begins anew. Though he can speak some English, he uses only Fijian in our conversations. "Rusiate, the language barrier makes our work together more difficult. It is essential that the translation of my Fijian be accurate. If the translation isn't accurate, you get only half of what is meant. Fijian is a simple language, but our few words mean many things. And I have to teach you in my own language. I know Inoke is very skillful at this translating, and he is dedicated. That's good. But you try, and keep trying, to learn Fijian."

"I am...and I'll keep trying.

"I know you choose your words carefully," I add. "That's why we also tape every conversation. Then Inoke listens to the tape to hear again his translation, and make corrections when necessary."

Nawame now speaks to me in a mixture of Fijian and English, as she often does, trying to ease the difficulty of communication. "Why doesn't Lora sleep on the bed?" she asks. "It's too hard on the floor."

I answer in my own combination of English and Fijian: "Oh, she's all right where she is."

Ratu Noa looks at his wife disapprovingly. "Don't speak to Rusiate in that way, mixing in some English. He's trying to learn Fijian. And don't worry about Lora being on the floor. They have plenty of luxuries in America. They didn't come here to have luxuries, like sleeping on beds. They came to experience Fiji. Research isn't the same as tourism. They left America and left their beds there. The floor is for them!"

By the time he is finished saying this, Ratu Noa and Nawame are smiling at each other, enjoying their friendly banter. She nods in agreement, but I can tell she still thinks he is being too harsh.

"You know, Rusiate, I only went to grade two in my education. But education isn't the same as understanding. Some people go higher and

higher in their education but lack understanding. You have both education and understanding. And you and I have this understanding in common. Other researchers come to Fiji and don't know what to look for —
they remain confused."

It is late. Time to leave. Ratu Noa suggests that we set up a time to meet
— Sunday at eight. "If they ask me to report to the job on Sunday," he says,
"I'll tell them I can't come. This research work is more important."

My research in Suva is now structured around my visits to Ratu Noa.
It is important to see him whenever the opportunity offers itself —
because it is not readily, and not always, available.

When I arrive Sunday evening, Ratu Noa's son is there, just finishing
eating. Ratu Noa is in the bedroom. The son calls his father, who emerges,
rubbing his eyes; apparently he has been napping. He immediately sits
down and, after receiving my *sevusevu*, motions his son to mix the *yaqona*.

"Now we begin….What do you want to know?" he inquires with
anticipation.

Since my experiences with other healers are still fresh in my mind, I
ask Ratu Noa about those I have met. I'm seeking some standard of
authenticity, some way of judging whether a healer actually helps people.

"I met this man Meli, and have been to several of his healing sessions.
He works with Mosese, his *waqa waqa*, who is said to be possessed by not
one but several *Vu*, and in rapid succession. I have seen Mosese possessed by just one *Vu*. It's an extraordinary sight." I describe Mosese's
possessions, including the changes in his body posture and voice and the
grimacing tension and then release he would exhibit.

The description does not surprise Ratu Noa. He has, he says, heard of
many like that before. As he talks a bit about possession, it becomes clear
that he believes the *waqa waqa* is not completely truthful.

"Whenever a person is possessed by the *Vu*," he states, "it is very hard
work. Therefore I don't really believe that *waqa waqa* could be possessed
by three different *Vu*, one after another."

"You know, Meli's *waqa waqa* was one thing — but then I saw something else…and it *was* something else." I launch into a full description of
Sera and her possessed state, including the snakelike movements of her

95

writhing body and the hissing sounds that rushed from her outstretched mouth. I feel shy and nervous talking about Sera.

Ratu Noa listens patiently, his face impassive. Several times he glances up toward the ceiling.

"Being there with that Sera, while she turned into a snake, was really scary.... I was afraid. I don't know what of, but I was afraid."

A smile comes to Ratu Noa's face, and he speaks softly: "Yes, I've heard these things before.... But I bet you were all right."

"Yeah, that's what Sera's *Vu* told us — we were all right!" Ratu Noa's words lighten the atmosphere. I feel more relaxed now.

"But I didn't know what was real with Sera's experience and what was not. I want to respect whatever part of the experience may have been real." I want Ratu Noa's advice as much as to tell him about my feeling.

"Respect is always proper, Rusiate, even when you doubt the truth of what you see. We Fijians always value respect. But you must learn to see what is true [*dina*] and what is false [*lasu*], then you'll know more about respect."

"Can the *Vu* enter [*curumi*] a healer, as it seemed to happen with Sera? Or eat or devour her [*kani*], as she claimed?"

"If the *Vu* comes near to you, Rusiate, you can't just lie down. When the *Vu* comes near you, it can only make you go up! You sit suspended in the air, and you can stay up there for five minutes! But the *Vu* doesn't enter or possess you, and certainly it doesn't eat or devour you."

"Five minutes!" I know my disbelief shows, and I'm embarrassed.

Ratu Noa is tolerant. "Yes — I can do it. Five minutes is not unusual.

"The other things you describe, Rusiate, the possession things with Meli's *waqa waqa* or Sera, they are just made-up things to get you to believe in their healing strength. The Suva healers want to make money; that's why they create a dramatic style in their work, that's why they show off a lot [*levu na vukivuki*]. But those of us who know, we see that it is only a lie."

"But what about all those things they do when they say they're possessed," I continue, "like when their voices change, and tears flood into their eyes, or their bodies become rigid or convulsive?"

"The true work doesn't want that kind of display or showing off." Ratu Noa is firm and careful; as he talks of his own healing efforts, he is modest and respectful, referring to it only as "the work," *na cakacaka*. "Let me give you an example. Here we are sitting together, just telling stories. My *Vu* could come to me [*sa lako mai vei au*]. I wouldn't know it was coming, but all of a sudden I'll go up from here."

Ratu Noa smiles again, teasingly, and his voice grows bold: "But if I wanted to, I could intentionally just lie down and creep like a snake, or make snake sounds! All that is just foolishness.

"I'll tell you this, Rusiate. To hear the *Vu*; that's possible. To see the *Vu*; that's possible. But lying down, being eaten, having a little visit by one *Vu*, then after a little while by another — all these things are impossible! They've never really happened in Fiji. Maybe in another part of the world, but not here."

"Maybe in Hollywood?" I suggest. Ratu Noa's laughter prompts my own. Hollywood as the land of outlandish fantasy has made its mark in Fiji.

"This thing here is your own secret." Ratu Noa has become serious and again alludes only indirectly to the healing work, now calling it "this thing" (*na ka oqo*).

"If you show this work to all other people, it's boasting," he continues. "Only the healer who doesn't tell the truth shows off a lot. I'll give you an example. Suppose a woman patient comes to such a bad healer. That healer may say the patient's possessed by the devil when probably it's only a mental problem. That healer is only making a show to get the business. And it's a big sin to lie to a person. Don't lie. If you come to me with your troubles, and I lie to you, I'm diverting you into the wrong path, which will only cause more problems.

"Rusiate, no matter how much faith you have, if I'm lying, the healing I offer will be useless! This stuff you describe with Meli's *waqa waqa* and Sera is just like Hollywood. That stuff comes from the lips, not the heart."

"This makes it very difficult for me," I say, "because in my research I feel I have to talk to all kinds of healers, even the bad ones, the ones that seem to be lying. That way I can see the full range of healing efforts here in Fiji. But it's just like you say with some of those bad ones, it's like a movie, and people flock to see the movie. With some of those healers who show off, long lines of people wait to see them."

"I think you're wasting your time speaking to those who are just lying. What can you learn but lies?" Ratu Noa's words rip apart my "scientific" research design, which calls for interviewing a broad spectrum of Fijian healers. But Ratu Noa has a sharper insight, and I'm already beginning to waver.

"I'll tell you how you can spot a healer who is only lying." Ratu Noa makes his offer inviting. "With some healers, you ask about a certain thing, and keep asking, probing deeper and deeper. They will give lots and lots of explanations, but then they reach a point where they know no more. They cannot continue on. They were showing off all along because they can't tell the truth. If a healer speaks the truth, he can carry on and on and on."

Then Ratu Noa bores into me. "But I won't tell you the truth unless you ask me for the truth. If someone wants the truth, you tell him. That is the way we do things here.

"In this work you don't go around saying, 'I can do this,' or 'I can do that.' Keep quiet, keep these things to yourself…and just carry on with the work." Ratu Noa faces me squarely. "When someone comes up to you for help, it's far better just to say, 'I'll try.' It's no good saying, 'Oh, that's no trouble, I can do it!' If you try to help a person, and you can't, far better to advise that person to go to the hospital. Just give what is proper to give."

The *tanoa* is nearly empty; only one round of *yaqona* is left. And we all know the *tanoa* will not be filled again tonight. The evening is ending.

Ratu Noa leans forward, talking right into me, as if no translation is needed. "When I give knowledge to you, Rusiate, I give it bit by bit. If I gave you the whole thing all at once, you couldn't use it. That's the way to do it."

Ratu Noa is developing his plan. He is becoming my partner in the research, or rather, the research is being absorbed into his commitment to teach me.

"Ratu Rusi, you are seeking understanding in the correct way. Because of that I'm telling you things I have not told others. And our talks are good. But you must begin to participate in the healing, to practice. Only then will your understanding deepen. Tovu would be a good place to begin this practical part of your research. There you can work with one of my best students, Tevita. I'll let him know you're coming."

CHAPTER 5

First Visit to Tovu

As Ratu Noa encourages me to participate more fully in the healing, to practice so that I can begin to understand, I intensify my search for a field site. For more than two months, Mere and I look for a place where we can live and work, and where hopefully I can participate in a practice. I agree with Ratu Noa that, if it is to be accurate, my research must be grounded in my personal search for healing knowledge.

Our focus is on rural areas — to understand traditional Fijian healing, it will be best to live in a traditional environment. My work in Suva, where traditions are undergoing rapid change, will continue, providing an important dynamic aspect to the research.

I want to go to Tovu and meet Tevita, Ratu Noa's student, but the way is not yet open. First, there is a trip south to Beqa, known as the island of the firewalkers. Then we go west to the island of Ovalau and, ranging out from the city of Levuka, visit several villages. The right place to work has not yet emerged. And all this while, Bitu, the chain of outlying islands, and especially the village of Tovu, on the northern end of that chain, continues to attract us. Everyone who speaks of Bitu says things like "They still keep the real Fijian ways down there," or "Bitu is a gathering place for the *Vu*."

I even hear about Bitu from the local Peace Corps office. "You sure you want to go there?" asks the Peace Corps director. "That's the only place we are a bit scared about placing our volunteers. Twice in the last two years we've had to evacuate a volunteer. We called it a medivac, describing the reason as medical illness, but in both cases there was something much stranger happening that we really couldn't figure out...and certainly not talk about. Both those volunteers were convinced they were being chased out by spirits, that they were bewitched. We hear that Bitu can be a dangerous place for an outsider."

Though I don't fully accept the explanation of "witchcraft," the Peace Corps story is further evidence of the activity of traditional spiritual beliefs in Bitu. Yet an element of doubt, even fear, comes in. Maybe Bitu, because it is "really Fijian," is not the place for a white person.

Sitiveni soon eases those doubts and fears. He now clearly states his view: "Bitu is the region where your work can develop, and the village of Tovu will be the perfect place for you to live. Tovu will be the base of your research." Sitiveni's invitation to live and work in his village galvanizes our efforts. Forgoing a trip to the interior of Viti Levu, the main island of Fiji, we plan an immediate trip to several villages in Bitu, in particular, Tovu.

Now that I reflect on this decision, I wonder why it took so long to occur. So many elements point us toward Tovu. Besides Tovu's immersion in the strong traditional life of Bitu, Tovu is Sitiveni's home village, the village he serves as *mata-ni-vanua*. It is also the place where Inoke's wife, Nasi, is stationed as a rural nurse, and she and Inoke live there; Inoke's home village is also in Bitu, a bit south of Tovu. Most important, Tevita, one of Ratu Noa's most loyal and trusted students, lives and practices his healing work in Tovu, and that is where Ratu Noa has advised me to go. But it is also clear why I am only now going to Tovu. Sitiveni had to invite me — and he has only just become ready.

Before we leave for Tovu, Sitiveni confirms how appropriate it will be as a research site. "The *Vu* are fond of Bitu, and especially the village of Tovu. And lots of healers practice because the *Vu* are so near.

"But you know," he continues, "those people in Tovu don't always do the right thing. Sometimes they call on those *Vu* for evil things. It seems I'm always having to watch over them and keep them in line. I had this dream once about those Tovu people. It showed me how they were misusing the *Vu*. I had to go directly there and set things right."

101

Relating his dream, Sitiveni takes me into the more private parts of Tovu: "I arrive at a village in a Land Rover, with a European on each side of me. We see a big *bure* up on a hill. We drive along the flat sandy area below, and go up the hill, to the large *bure*. I now realize I am in Tovu.

"The *bure* has only two doors, one in the front and one on the side. I go into the *bure* and discover it is my uncle's, and then I lie down in the middle of the floor. My uncle doesn't pay attention to me, but keeps tending the fire. The two Europeans have now disappeared. I know then they are twins that the *Vu* sent to guide me. I then go out behind the *bure*. There are lots of ten-gallon biscuit tins there. I want to know what's inside them, so I open up one of the tins. It's filled with a smelly, horrible liquid, a liquid with a monstrous shape. I open up all the tins, and they are all filled with this horrible liquid.

"I go back into the *bure* and lie down again in the middle of the floor. Then I hear voices, low voices, in conversation. I can't make out what people are saying, I can't see them properly. I look out the front door but can't see them properly. I ask my uncle who these people are and he doesn't answer. Then the *yaqona* is being served; those people have come into the *bure*. The others from Tovu who have come sit in the traditional pattern for the serving of *yaqona*. The *yaqona* begins, but it is not being served properly — the order of who drinks first is not correct. This happens for several rounds of *yaqona* and each time I become more disturbed. I just sit there, quietly, but very upset. The *yaqona* continues, and the conversation goes on, but I don't really hear it. Finally I can take it no longer and I say, 'Shut up.' The conversation continues. Finally I say again, 'Shut up.' The conversation continues.

"Then I stand and take two big strides to the center of the *bure*, and with a third movement, kick over the *tanoa*. The *tanoa* overturns and the *yaqona* spills out, out the door. I speak firmly and loudly: 'Now I've knocked over your *tanoa*, your *tanoa* is overturned. Don't do this work anymore! Now all of you — get out. Get out of here.' They began to leave, first one by one, then all the others leave in a group. Then...I awake."

Sitiveni told this dream to the people of Tovu as a warning that the village should cease its *vakatevoro*. Overturning the *tanoa* that is being used to serve *yaqona* improperly, he says, means he is overturning their *vakatevoro*. As the healing work is rarely labeled explicitly, so also *vakatevoro* is often only vaguely alluded to. In Sitiveni's dream it is symbolized by the *tanoa*. The monstrous, smelly liquid he finds in it, Sitiveni tells me, is the first sign that something is wrong, and his sense that things are "out of order" is confirmed by the violation of the rules of precedence in serving *yaqona*. "They abused the *yaqona*," he laments.

"And I've had to warn the people in Tovu again," Sitiveni confides. "Just recently I told them to quit their *vakatevoro*. 'There is only one *Kalou* here,' I told them, 'and we worship him up there in the church.'"

Without another word, Sitiveni closes the topic. My question — who or what is abusing the *yaqona?* — remains unasked. For now, I can only speculate — and worry.

My family and I board the boat that is scheduled to leave for Bitu at 1:00 A.M. The actual time of departure is indefinite, but it will likely be before dawn. The journey from Suva to Tovu is an ocean trip of between eight and twelve hours, depending on the weather, which can at times make travel altogether impossible. The boat, a thirty-foot wooden trawler, is hauling a full cargo in addition to eight passengers and two crew plus the captain, my friend Alifereti.

It feels good to be on Alifereti's ship. As he goes about his preparations, we visit a bit. We inevitably talk about our time with the healer Sera and her possession. "You weren't really afraid, were you?" he teases.

"No, not really — Didn't you see how calm I was?" I reply, my bravado increasing. "You saw my courage, didn't you? You saw me without fear — as I ran into that wall to escape the hissing snake!" Although we laugh, our sense of awe of the spiritual forces that could be expressed in possession states persists.

Alifereti's voice lowers: "You're going to the right place, going to Tovu. I know that land. It's my regular route to go around the whole chain of islands in Bitu. Lots of strange things happen there." That's not exactly what I want to hear, but I'm at least reassured that I'm heading in the right direction. Alifereti confirms that: "Yes…you'll see lots of healing there."

The bunk beds inside the cabin, wooden shelves with a shallow edge that seems to mock the comfort and safety of a bed, are full, so we sleep on the deck, on top of the closed hatch over the hull. I don't know when we left; when I first wake up, we are already well outside Suva Harbor, in open ocean. It is not yet dawn, but already the sky can be seen parting from the sea — and the sea is becoming rough. As the boat climbs over the crest of one wave and enters the trough of the next, we lose sight of the horizon. All around us, up into the sky, are sea and waves. Since this is my first time at sea in such weather, and in such a small boat, I'm frightened by the endlessly immense wall of waves that confronts us, and the way they shake the boat as if it were a bathtub toy. Others on the boat, experienced travelers, also look frightened. Alifereti says it's too late to turn back to Suva Harbor, and, moreover, within an hour we should be out of this rough stretch of ocean and begin to pick up the sheltering effect of the islands. I give myself over to the ocean, trusting its still hidden protection.

At dawn, we enter calmer seas; the ocean now invites us to come through. Wrapped in the sunshine of a bright morning, the clammy sea-air of the night begins to dry out. After being on the water for more than eight hours, we can now see the northernmost tip of Bitu, several small uninhabited islands that seem sprayed out onto an endless stretch of water.

After another hour of weaving through small low-lying islands, we face a bigger island, Kali, which is crested by a ridge gently sloping into the ocean. Directly in front is a well-protected harbor, its sides fingering out into deep water, its center marked by a long stretch of golden white beach. The tide is inching out, exposing an increasing expanse of sand. We have arrived at Tovu.

Tovu's beauty strikes me forcibly; a few sounds of delight are all I can manage — no words. As we go ashore in the small powerboat lowered from the ship's deck, the village comes into focus, as do the mostly older people who line the shore, watching and waving. As I walk into the village itself, this feeling of serene beauty continues. Neat, criss-crossing footpaths decorate the smooth, lush grass, connecting the more than twenty houses. All are in the traditional rectangular style, most with thatched walls. Some are traditional thatched-roof *bure*; the rest have roofs of sheet metal. There are two relief houses, structures made of concrete blocks with sheet metal roofs, built by the government after numerous homes were destroyed in the most recent hurricane. There is one large house, also made of concrete blocks. Carefully spaced shrubs and flowers form boundaries around many of the dwellings, marking off space while still inviting one to enter.

A small creek runs through the south end of village, widening into a little delta as it meets the ocean at the west. The village houses are on the ocean side of the creek; on the other side, partially hidden by the bushes and trees, lies the school complex. Surrounding a large playing field are two classroom buildings and two dormitories, long, rectangular buildings of one story made of concrete blocks. Except for the church, they are the largest structures in Tovu. Two concrete-block buildings that serve as teachers' quarters sit just on the other side of the creek. A thin line of bushes separates them casually from the village houses close by.

Atop a hill on the east, the Methodist church, two stories high, with a sharply peaked metal roof, strives to look over the village. The dirt path up to its front door is wide and steep. Near the entrance rests the *lali*, an enormous hollowed-out log whose sides are worn down from the years of beating with thick sticks. Its deep sounds call people to church as well as announce other important gatherings and messages. Aside from the school, the church is the only place with glass windows. All other buildings have sheets of wood in the windows which are propped open with sticks.

Toward the western end of Tovu is a clinic and nurse's sleeping quarters. Both are traditional *bure,* their roofs sloping low on their sides. Along the slight ridge that curves around the south-eastern side of the village there is a fenced area protecting a growing area for young pine trees. Tovu has been selected by the government as a site for a pine-growing scheme, and the seedlings are kept in this nursery until they are ready for planting. Aside from the money that comes in from selling fish and *yaqona,* the pine scheme is peoples' only source of income. Most of this money goes to the two families that have supervisory responsibility. In the middle of the village is a store, a small, square thatched building perched on four poles. The entrance is at the top of a staircase carved out of a coconut log. Irregularly stocked with bare essentials, such as flour, kerosene, and matches, and some luxury items, like chips and soda, the store is as much a village meeting place as a shop. With the storekeeper behind a small table, the store can hold two customers at most at the same time, while others gather outside.

The land around Tovu rises up into a ridge that encloses the level ground of the village. In the southeast the incline is very steep, and a waterfall can be seen farther up the creek. From the ridge the metal water tower pipes cool water down to the twelve taps spread throughout the village. As the land rises from the village, the bush takes over, scrub and heavy forest.

Tovu is sharply set off from the bush. The grass shines as the dew begins to yield to the day's warmth. Order seems to prevail in this well-groomed settlement.

We remain in Tovu three days, living in the house that Luke, the acting chief, uses, and that Sitiveni stays in when he visits. A carefully maintained Fijian *bure* and the largest house in the village, it is situated in the middle of Tovu and most of the other houses are visible from it. All important visitors stay here. For our part, we feel awkward, especially during the long days when we struggle to communicate with our hosts, who speak no English. Inoke has not come with us. Without him to translate, the days pass slowly and with difficulty.

After school gets out at about three and throughout the evening, the situation improves. Master Jone, the head teacher at Tovu, who is bilingual, takes us in hand. Master Jone also invites our children, Lora and Alex, whose Fijian name is Eliki, to attend school so that they will be occupied during the days. The word "occupied" is mild for the excitement and challenge they feel being in school with the village children, speaking primarily Fijian.

Master Jone takes me to drink *yaqona,* at his place the first night, at Tevita's the second night. This is a new experience. We drink *yaqona* and drink *yaqona* and drink *yaqona* some more. Starting in the late afternoon, around five, we don't finish until past eleven. It's a late supper for me, as it is for most of the men in Tovu. While they sit around drinking *yaqona*, they visit, tell stories, joke — all in Fijian. I understand very little, though I am helped occasionally by Master Jone.

But I do understand one thing: I'm starting to feel different at these *yaqona* sessions. All my systems are shutting down into something like a waking sleep. I learn the word for this state: when you drink lots of *yaqona*, you become *mateni*, which is translated as "drunk." But it's not the same as being drunk from alcohol. Everyone confirms this realization: "Being *mateni* with *yaqona* is a good thing," one Tovu elder says. "It makes us feel good, makes us want to listen to each other and work together. When you're *mateni* from liquor, that's a bad thing. People can't get along then, and it always ends up in a fight."

I've now been at many *yaqona* sessions. Every time I visit a healer, in the city of Suva or elsewhere, *yaqona* is present, and it's present at most ordinary social visits as well. But this is the first time I've become *mateni*. Maybe it's because I'm just sitting, hour after hour, drinking. At Ratu Noa's, where I also spent many hours with the *yaqona*, I was also asking questions. Master Jone tells me that the *yaqona* in the village is purer and stronger than that in Suva. Certainly, I notice, it is served more frequently and in larger *bilo*. And in Fijian custom, you do not refuse a *bilo* that is offered but drink the *yaqona* down in one gulp.

Whatever the reasons for my new experience of being *mateni*, I'm faced with a dilemma. I already know from Ratu Noa that I must "stay close to the *yaqona*" if I want to learn about healing. Now I see that by staying close to it, I can also become *mateni*, and then it's hard to follow what is happening. I wonder whether that is just what is needed for me really to understand — to stop trying to "follow what is happening"? Or can one drink lots of *yaqona* without becoming *mateni*? I think about Ratu Noa. Now I have something new to ask him. How is *yaqona*, as he says, the "channel for healing," and how do I work with the *yaqona* and keep the channel clear?

The morning we leave, I pay a brief visit to Tevita. Without an interpreter present, there is very little we can say. But I do communicate greetings from his teacher. It seems Tevita has already heard from Ratu Noa about my arrival. He now wishes me well, and invites me to come back to Tovu. "Ratu Noa has told me about you," Tevita says. "He wants me to help you, and I can do that."

Tevita's words are level-headed; so is he. A muscular man in his forties, he has an easy smile and calm manner. I like him, and I sense the feeling is mutual. I look forward to working with him.

As we make our way to the beach to board the motorboat waiting to take us out to Alifereti's ship, which is now anchored in the bay, we see the entire school lined up along the beach. The schoolchildren are singing a song, a goodbye song, we are told, and they wave their handkerchiefs. Some are crying. We too begin crying. It's a goodbye song, but it ends "And we wait patiently for your return." We've been in Tovu barely four days and already we feel emotionally attached, and desire to return soon.

CHAPTER 6

Conversations with Ratu Noa (Suva)

"If you want the yaqona *to have a heavy meaning for you...
it all depends on you and how you approach the* yaqona.*"*

Since coming back from Tovu, everything has been focused on our return to set up our permanent home. Tomorrow we leave. Tonight I go to see Ratu Noa.

Many things have happened since our last talk. Ratu Noa listens to my account of the various trips looking for a place to live, and especially about the visit to Tovu.

The talk glides into late evening. Ratu Noa's son has joined us, as has a cousin, a man about Ratu Noa's age. They exchange family news. The *yaqona* drinking continues, *tanoa* after *tanoa*. Each round punctuates our presence, and reaffirms our togetherness as the *bilo* is passed in the same order and with the same gestures to each of us. In a long evening like this, one begins to take pleasure in the reassuring repetition of little idiosyncrasies of how each person takes the *bilo* and drinks. The liquid sounds fill the stillness of night, washing things clear. Water splashes into the *tanoa* as the *yaqona* is being mixed; *yaqona* cascades back into the *tanoa* from the serving *bilo* as it is stirred before serving.

There is a lull in the conversation, and Ratu Noa looks in my direction. A space has been created if I want to enter. In that stillness and with the focus on me, I realize what's been happening over the past several hours. I'm feeling something — maybe not *mateni*, but different.

"When I went to Tovu, I felt really *mateni* in their *yaqona* sessions. It was hard for me to stay with the conversation, or even to keep awake. Tonight, even though we've drunk as much *yaqona* as I did in Tovu, I don't feel that way — but I do feel different from my usual self. I feel as though we're all in a special space, talking to each other and into the night, listening really carefully, hearing really well. It's almost like there's no world outside our conversation."

Ratu Noa smiles. "You see, Rusiate, I told you that you that staying close to the *yaqona* will teach you. You're beginning to see the two kinds of *mateni*. Yes, you get *mateni* from the *yaqona*, but sometimes when you're *mateni* you can catch vital information, and sometimes you just get sleepy."

"So some *mateni* helps the [healing] work, and some doesn't?"

"Yes!" Ratu Noa is smiling again; his approval is clear. "One type of *mateni* is good for the work; with this type, you are given the *mateni* and at the same time the power is given to you. That's the good type, the type you're feeling tonight. The other type of *mateni* is more like being drunk; it's when you just want to go to sleep. It's not good for the work. And the two types are very different."

"From my stay in Tovu it seems that lots of people there know that sleepy type of *mateni!*"

"Very few people know the *mateni* that brings you power," Ratu Noa agrees. "Most people are *mateni* that other way — they just keep drinking, and drinking, and drinking, and drinking...and then they stop talking. They're asleep! But with me it's different. The more *yaqona* I drink, the better it is — the more I can talk, and the more active my mind is. When there is the slightest signal in the air, my mind acts like a magnet to attract it. This is the good *mateni*. Then I can see things that are invisible to others; I can see outside the house when we're inside. During the useless *mateni* you can't learn anything. In the good *mateni*, your eyes open up, but the useless *mateni* is just like closing your eyes."

"But the same word, *mateni*, is used to describe both of these states?" I'm now a little confused.

"It's good you asked, because I want you to be very clear about these things. With the useless type, you just drink and you're *mateni*. The other type, where you can see and hear special things, is like opening a new road for you, opening a new face to you. It isn't the same kind of *mateni*."

As Ratu Noa talks further about *mateni*, I realize that more important than understanding what Fijian word to use is being clear about the differences between the two *yaqona* experiences.

"Sometimes, Rusiate, you want to go drink *yaqona* because you're happy. If you go that way, you'll just get *mateni* and then want to sleep. But if your mind is tuned for a special target or you're thinking of some message to come when you go to drink *yaqona*, you won't get sleepy. If you go with the intention of solving a problem or doing some special work, then the good kind of *mateni* comes and you actually see and hear the answer to the problem.

"When I talk about this good kind of *mateni*," Ratu Noa continues, "it's not like the Chinese taking opium and entering their 'twilight dream.' The Chinese believed that if they dreamed in that way the answer would come. But my work is different — no sleep, no dreaming. My work is like a magnet; it catches knowledge and lets you see things.

"If you want the *yaqona* to have a heavy meaning for you, Rusiate, it all depends on you and how you approach the *yaqona*. It doesn't matter who is around you or where you are. Even if you're at a *yaqona* party where everyone is just getting sleepy, you can direct the *yaqona* for yourself to that special purpose I spoke of. When you're served your first *bilo*, you can say to yourself, under your breath, 'I want to drink this *bilo* to help me in my work.' And then that *yaqona* will help you to see. If you want to drink for fun, don't use this method. And remember, when you are doing your work and you find it difficult, call for *yaqona* to be made for your work."

Ratu Noa's use of the word *cakacaka*, "work," is an acknowledgment of the way my research and my participation in the healing work are merging. Though the usual word for research is *vakadidike*, he calls both my *cakacaka*. But now, it's clear from his gesture toward the *yaqona* that he's talking about my practice in the healing work.

I'm beginning to understand time by how much *yaqona* is left in the *tanoa*. Only a little remains, and soon I'll have to leave. The *tanoa* is more sensitive and flexible than the clock; the *yaqona* will last until the conversation has reached a fitting end.

"Is there anything special I should do in Tovu with your student Tevita?"

"Yes, I've already given him instructions," Ratu Noa responds. "Now I'll tell you the same. Every Monday night, go to Tevita's house for a few bowls of *yaqona*."

Ratu Noa has just requested that I become a regular participant in Tevita's healing work. His expression "Go...for a few bowls of *yaqona*" is characteristic of his understated way.

"Every Monday, Rusiate, you should be present because on that night Tevita does his special *yaqona*. All the *yaqona* brought to him during the week to request his healing is presented formally on that night so the healing can occur. Don't miss Mondays. If you have to be away, tell Tevita where you'll be."

"And what about the other nights?" I wonder.

"The other nights would also be good to be with Tevita," Ratu Noa says, in part to be agreeable, "but Monday is the day not to miss. Here in Fiji, Monday night is the lucky time, the special time for healing.

"If you have any difficulty at all with your research while you're in Tovu, tell Tevita," Ratu Noa adds, "and then Tevita will contact me. Tevita and I work together. Three months after the day you start working in Tovu, Tevita should contact me, and through him I'll give you a certain power to help you in your research. I'll give Tevita instructions on what to do to pass that power on to you."

"Ratu Noa, before you said there were two sides to my work, the research and the personal. Is there anything more I should be doing on the personal side?"

"Those things on the personal side will come automatically," he says firmly. "This healing work depends on the kind of person you are.

"Rusiate, you've entered the healing circle in Fiji. The *Vu* have taken your name down, and after three months your name will be sent up to the proper place where they'll decide about you. Remember all the hard work you must put into this thing — the healing is never easy! Their decision up there is based on our hard, faithful work. But don't worry. Help will be coming from my side. And stay with Tevita, because he also is in that same healing circle."

CHAPTER 7

Moving to
the Village
(Tovu)

The boat to Tovu moves once more through the night, but this time through gentler seas. My family and I are again traveling on my friend Alifereti's vessel. It is July, five months after our arrival in Fiji.

There is mostly cargo aboard: lumber for government buildings scheduled for construction in the southern end of Bitu. Along with us, a Fijian family takes up the space on deck and in the cabin. Gathered around their belongings, they are returning home to southern Bitu. The father has been hospitalized in Suva for surgery on his legs, numbed due to a circulatory problem. He remains unsteady, and is assisted around the boat by one or another of his four children. The family's possessions, mainly clothes and some pots and pans, are wrapped in traditional woven mats and tied in cloth. One large suitcase, battered but held together with a belt, stays with the father, a prized Western-style possession. Though smaller, my family has more possessions. We are surrounded by two large, still fresh-looking suitcases, a forty-horsepower outboard engine and a smaller eight-horsepower one, and mountains of cartons secured with rope which contain research tapes and film, kitchen utensils, kerosene lamps, and canned food. Not wanting to impose on others in the weeks before we can set up a domestic routine, we are bringing lots of food. The cartons are heavy — we have brought too much.

"You going to set up a store there in Tovu?" Alifereti teases.

"Well, you know these Westerners, always looking for a way to make some money," I reply with mock seriousness. "And since you're my friend, I'll only charge you half price."

"Half price? After all I've done for you! Exposing you to the snake lady, showing you the depth of your own fear...I'm more than a friend. I think you'd even call me a buddy."

"Well, for my buddy...how about ten percent off?"

"Now, that's more like it!"

Kali is in sight, but we steer to the east toward a smaller, low-lying island. The beach that rims the entire shore stings my eyes with its glaring white expanse. With coconut trees moving silently in the slight wind, it is truly like a tropical paradise.

"We'll be stopping first in Ogo," Alifereti announces.

A large carton containing a cooling unit is unloaded at Ogo. Sliding for a moment out of control, it nearly capsizes the small boat that has come out to pick it up. The young men who man the boat laugh, joking at their precarious imbalance rather than worrying about the possible loss of their cargo.

"The Ogo people have this commercial fishing scheme, supported by the government," Alifereti explains. "The government is sending them a cooling unit to keep fish fresh on the way to Suva for sale there. You'll meet the Ogo people — they're closely related to the Tovu people. And these Ogo people have lots of problems, lots of problems. They're some of Tevita's best customers."

At Tovu the tide is in. We anchor close to the shore. As our baggage is unloaded into the two boats that have come to take us ashore, I feel embarrassed — so many cartons. Each time one of the young men helping with the unloading staggers unexpectedly under the weight of a carton, I wince.

Our accommodations have already been arranged: Sitiveni has decided we should be near the school, under the guidance of Master Jone. We will live in the small *bure* that sits fifty feet from Jone's large wooden residence; it had served as the place where his guests stayed, and where he would drink *yaqona* with his friends. We soon have a small, thatched kitchen built. The large school playing field, along the sides of which are class-

115

room and dormitory buildings, lies to the south, about forty feet from our front door. Ten feet behind the *bure* is the creek; by crossing over the two coconut trees that are laid over it to serve as a bridge, we enter into the village proper. Though we are formally within the school compound, we are at its fringe; close to the village, we are on its outer edge.

Not only has Sitiveni asked Jone to look after us; in Fijian custom, we have become part of Jone's household or extended family. No one can simply move into a village without being invited and without being "adopted" in this way by a village family.

In the first week we eat many of our meals with Jone and his family. A stocky, active man who has just turned forty, Jone moves comfortably through a wide variety of situations, whether delivering the opening day talk as head of the school, drinking *yaqona* with people in the village, talking with government bureaucrats about educational development, meeting with professional colleagues in teachers' workshops, participating in the ceremonial life of the village, or acting as host to a visiting American researcher. Some attribute much of his confidence to the fact that he is of chiefly status; his father, who has since died, was an important *turaga* on Momoto, a large island to the east of Tovu. Through his Momoto lineage, he is related to people of Ogo, and that island is one of his favorite *yaqona*-drinking places.

Outgoing and generous, Jone likes being, and especially joking, with others. I'm particularly struck with how at ease he is in the village. Though as an outsider, as head of the school, and as a person of chiefly status, he does maintain a certain distance from the villagers, he is more with them than apart. They respect him and turn to him for advice.

But Jone is complex. Despite his self-assurance in different situations, he is also dissatisfied. He wonders whether being schoolmaster in Tovu is "all there is" for him. Sometimes he aspires toward a promotion that would put him in charge of a larger, urban school; at other times he reflects on the expectations of people in his home island that he take up the chiefly responsibilities of his father. At times his dissatisfaction deepens, and then his temper shortens and he can be harsh. Hard-working and intense, Jone feeds his many sides — and in the process becomes moody.

Jone's wife is also from the east, also an outsider to Tovu. Unlike her husband, however, she has no close relatives in the area. A proud woman, she sees herself as the "headmaster's wife." She visits and goes net-fishing with the wives of other schoolteachers and a few of the village women. Jone's teenage son attends the village school and blends into village life, surrounded, in typical Fijian fashion, by a tight group of age-mates. Sometimes his mother objects to the company the boy keeps, criticizing one village family or another, but Jone generally allays her fears about the "bad influence" of the village.

As we talk, Jone constantly adds more Fijian to his conversation, explaining words I do not grasp. It's a gentle way to learn, unlike the total immersion in Fijian which occurs in the village. Aside from Inoke, who has moved back to the village to help me with my research, Jone is the only person in Tovu who is truly bilingual and willing to speak in English. The assistant head of the school and Inoke's wife, Nasi, are both largely bilingual but not as comfortable speaking English, and miscommunication sometimes results. Several others, shy about their bits-and-pieces knowledge of English, will speak a word or two only under duress, when conversation in Fijian is impossible.

In the village I spend hour after hour sitting and drinking *yaqona*, listening to the talk, at times catching only a word or two and hoping no one directs a question to me. When the conversation does focus on me, I struggle to respond, initially relying primarily on a smile, a nod, or a shrug to convey that I'm trying to take part. After I begin speaking more in Fijian, it doesn't become any easier. I constantly make mistakes, mispronouncing words, substituting incorrect words, and my blunders furnish many opportunities for others to laugh at me. I keep confusing *kama*, "fire," with *kaba*, "to climb up," so that I speak of "firing up the steep hillside" or "the big climb-up that destroyed the forest." I manage to keep my perspective — mostly — and come to enjoy with those around me the humor provided by my elementary Fijian. Embarrassing as it is, that village learning makes it possible, after a year, for me to understand Fijian and speak adequately, and after a year and a half, I am speaking more fluently.

Jone demonstrates, in his aspirations if not always in his behavior, the ideal of *vakaturaga*, the quality of character worthy of being a chief. He always emphasizes respect. "Even when you disagree with someone, even if you think a person is a fool, you must show respect, and respectfully disagree or respectfully decline to follow that person's advice," he says.

As a man of the "new education" in the lineage of traditional chiefs, Jone combines a contemporary, Western attitude toward Fijian traditions — what he calls a "modern, scientific" attitude — with a deep knowledge of these traditions, and an enduring regard for their power. He criticizes villagers for, on the one hand, holding "superstitions" and, on the other, not observing the traditions "correctly," "in a way that will please the *Vu*."

When he speaks about traditional Fijian healing, he points to its shortcomings, its lack of a "scientific base," while at the same time saying that at least it "carries the message of our *mana*," unlike Western medicine.

"The most important thing," Jone stresses, "is who practices traditional healing. Too many times the healer is just doing *vakatevoro*. We're lucky here in Tovu. Tevita is a good man; he's honest in his practice."

Jone is a bit like Inoke, my research associate. Inoke lives in the nurse's quarters with Nasi, who is the government nurse in charge of Kali Island. Even more than Jone, Inoke is a man of two worlds; he has gone further in his education, completing two years of medical school, and has lived longer in urban, Westernized settings. At the same time, as a *matani-vanua*, he is an active adviser to the chief and the people about traditions, and remains an active participant in ceremonies. And much more than Jone, Inoke is deeply concerned with issues of health and the practice of both traditional and Western medicine.

The Tovu nursing station is a fascinating blend of Western and traditional practice. Within the small thatched *bure* that serves as the clinic are an outer room where the nurse works at the desk on her patients' records, and which also contains shelves lined with medicines, and an inner room, which is furnished with a bed where a patient can rest or even stay a few days if necessary. The nursing station, with its antibiotics, ointments, and basic first-aid items, is equipped to handle simple infections, burns, wounds, and broken bones. The most common complaints treated are headaches or body aches, which are usually treated with aspirin, followed by infections, such as an abscesses, and respiratory problems, both treated with antibiotics. The Tovu clinic also dispenses medicines for persons diagnosed with high blood pressure and provides prenatal care. More serious complaints are either referred to the larger rural clinic to the south, in Delana, about an hour's boat trip away, where a medical doctor is stationed, or to Suva, for more extended hospitalization and specialized treatment.

Nasi is an intelligent, kindhearted woman. Though an outsider — she is from southern Bitu — she is a welcomed member of the village. She visits often in people's homes, not only on clinic business, and participates actively in Tovu's ceremonial life. People like Nasi and believe she is a good nurse. Though she occasionally bemoans her patients' failure to understand her treatments — not taking prescribed medicines, for example, or taking them improperly — she generally likes them too.

Nasi respects Western medicine. Her nurse's training in Suva was a two-year course in which she studied fundamentals of anatomy and physiology, basic diagnostic techniques, use of medications such as antibiotics and ointments, first-aid treatment, and the principles of modern hospital care, especially the importance of antiseptics and cleanliness. But she respects traditional Fijian healing even more. Nasi works with all the Fijian healers in the Tovu area, sending patients to them when she thinks they can help, listening with care when patients describe the treatment they have already received from healers.

"I do what I can," she says, "but I can only help with those sicknesses Western medicine can treat, things like simple colds, or cuts, or burns, or infections. But there are times when these symptoms, which may seem simple, are not — there are other things behind them. Then I must turn to Fijian healers like Tevita. And other times, right away I know the sickness is not for Western medicine, it's a sickness that can't even be described with European words. Those sicknesses are also meant for our own Fijian healers."

Though Nasi doesn't talk about her belief in Fijian healing with her immediate supervisor — the doctor in Delana — people in Tovu and in the other villages on Kali know about her acceptance of the traditional way. She herself is frequently a patient of traditional healers, most often Tevita.

119

Nasi is supported in her work by Inoke, who is in effect an informal "doctor-in-residence" at Tovu. Though of course he doesn't officially practice medicine, he and Nasi continually discuss cases, and he advises her on the basis of both his medical school training and his extensive knowledge of traditional healing. Inoke knows all the Fijian healers in Bitu, and he knows their work from the inside. Though he keeps abreast of developments in Western medicine and seeks the best medical care that is available for himself and his family, he too is a frequent and dedicated user of Fijian healing, and always takes his family to such healers when it seems appropriate.

Though Inoke is formally my research associate, Nasi is also very helpful. Like Inoke, she is fascinated by the idea of researching traditional Fijian healing, believing as he does that there is tremendous power in that tradition, and that it is important to document its efficacy. They are both concerned that the central government is increasingly relegating Fijian healing to a subsidiary role, at times even threatening its extinction, as it pushes for the modernization — that is, Westernization — of health care in Fiji.

We spend many hours with Nasi and Inoke, talking, visiting, eating, fishing. Always willing to discuss the meaning of Fijian words and their usage, as outsiders in Tovu, they are also perceptive commentators on village life, able to notice things that would be obscured by the forgiving veil of kinship.

One day we talk about the healers in Tovu. Besides Tevita, who is the only *dauvagunu,* or spiritual healer who works intensively with *yaqona,* there are three others: Lilieta, who is the wife of Tevita's brother, is a healer specializing in massage; Komera, another middle-aged woman, is a healer specializing in herbal remedies; and Asenati, who at almost eighty is one of the oldest women in Tovu, practices both massage and herbal remedies. Moreover, Suliana, Tevita's wife, used to be an herbalist before she married and now assists Tevita in his work, collecting and preparing herbal remedies for him.

"There's lots to choose from here in Tovu," Nasi says. The people are lucky, because all these healers do good work."

"Tevita is basically in charge," Inoke adds. "He's the one with the most power, the one with the strongest *mana*. The others work with him and he works with them. If they can't help, they send the patient to him." Inoke pauses. "But I heard that Tevita was originally taught by Asenati, that originally she did the powerful work…but now she is old, and works only a little."

As the weeks pass, the rhythms of Tovu life reveal themselves. The weather is an intimate partner. The sun can be brutal if not monitored; the seas deadly if not respected. Winds sometimes bring on high seas, increasing the dangers of the coral reefs and outcroppings that surround the islands. Especially at low tide, the reefs can rip apart the boats of the unwary. The tide is the clock, governing where a boat can be anchored and how one can reach the harbors of other villages; that rhythm in turn influences the times for fishing, visiting, and collecting supplies across the creek, which is passable only at low tide. The children help get the firewood and water that are needed every day. The gardens must be tended, providing the daily starchy root crop. Cassava is eaten at every meal, usually boiled, sometimes roasted or baked as a pudding. At times taro is available; with good weather, some fish is added.

The government pine scheme in Tovu is just one of many such schemes throughout rural Fiji. The government plans to market the wood overseas, especially in Japan. Tevita is in charge of the Tovu operation, drawing a small salary for his work. At times, as when seeds are to be placed in little plastic packets of dirt for germination, or the seedlings planted on the hillside, the scheme employs many Tovu residents and pays them a small daily wage. Nearly every day Tevita and his assistant go up on the ridge where the seedlings are growing in the black plastic bags to water the fragile green growth. If the sun is too strong, the delicate leaves turn brown and the seedling sometimes dies, encrusted in cracked, hard soil. Planting is a joyful time. Carrying the bags containing the precious seedlings, and with lots of laughter and high spirits, people leave the village and scatter over the cleared area. Once planted, the seedlings are upright but frighteningly small against the rocky, severe terrain around them.

Also punctuating Tovu life is the rhythm created by the traditional ceremonies held to mark major life events and crises: births, marriages, deaths; visitors; the building of a house or launching of a boat. For less important events, a simple *yaqona* ceremony is sufficient. But on more important occasions, such as a visit by a high chief, gifts are given and a *meke*, or sacred dance, often performed, in addition to a chiefly *yaqona* ceremony. Women work hard weaving mats and practicing the *meke* in preparation for the ceremony; both men and women together must make a successful catch to provide fish; and everyone must help in gathering items of value to give as *yau*, "wealth," and in preparing the food offered as a *magiti*. If people can plan for the ceremony, the work is more relaxed, spread out over time, though the days before the arrival are always hectic. If the event to be celebrated is unexpected, such as the death of a high chief, preparations can become almost frenzied, consuming the entire energy of the people for days.

Whatever the ceremony, *yaqona* is always presented and drunk. On important occasions, the *yaqona* drinking can continue for days, sometimes through the nights as well. The activity of the entire village is centered at these times on the ceremony, and in particular the drinking of *yaqona*.

A more predictable rhythm emanates from the hill overlooking the village, where the church regularly calls the people with the deep voice of the *lali*. Energetically beaten by two people, the *lali* issues sounds that make the body vibrate, and insist to the heart that something important is about to happen. Each Sunday is set aside for worship. In Fiji, Friday is called *Vakaraubuka*, the "day to gather firewood"; Saturday is *Vakarauwai*, the "day to collect water"; and Sunday is *Sigatabu*, the "sacred day." With the essentials in hand, little subsistence activity is necessary on Sundays, though water is still collected. No hard work is performed, however. The village is quiet, and the day unfolds slowly.

The beat of the *lali* travels along the stillness, announcing the beginning of each of the three Sunday services: one in the early morning; another, the best attended, at about ten; and one in the evening. Everyone goes to at least one service — or else can explain the absence. The focus of the service is one or another theme that emerges in the liturgical readings for that week — the role of mothers and fathers in the family, for example, or the offering of one's first fruits to *Kalou*. During the week the *lali* beats into the night air before the meetings of various groups at the church almost every evening — the women's group, a youth rally, the Bible study group.

The first time I attend a Sunday service, Tevita is in charge. He oversees the order of the service, including readings from the prayerbook and choral singing, and, most important, he delivers the sermon. Tevita is one of half a dozen men who share that responsibility in Tovu, performing on a regular rotation. They are called *dauvunau* (lay preachers).

The people of Tovu, including all five of the traditional healers, are practicing Methodists. Traditional healing in Tovu does not conflict with Christianity, which is one of the organizing principles of Tovu life.

Soon, we are happy to learn that the canned foods we brought are valuable, as gifts or items of exchange for local foods. They help us make the transition toward our own strategies of food gathering. As often happens in our attempt to become part of the community, our children lead the way. Invited to join their Fijian age-mates in catching crabs, netting small fish near the mouth of the creek, and gathering shellfish along the shore, Lora and Eliki bring food to our kitchen. What a wonderful experience for them as well as for us! Soon the women and men are inviting us to participate in their different fishing excursions, and fresh fish becomes a frequent part of our diet. Starchy root crops — the ubiquitous cassava and occasional taro — come primarily from Jone's gardens, supplemented increasingly by others, as we establish exchange relationships in the village.

After about a month, we start a large vegetable garden next to the creek. Along with a handy water supply and constant sunlight, the hard work of preparing the soil and weeding the plants yields food. Tomatoes, cucumbers, and lettuce eventually enter our diet and that of many in the village. Such vegetables are appreciated by Tovu people to add variety to the starchy foods and fish. Our imported food dwindles to a small supply of staples, such as tinned beef, and a few specialty items, like ketchup and tamari sauce. Bland cassava jumps to life with a little ketchup or tamari!

One day I become irritated with Lora and Eliki. They are talking so fast, gesturing so dramatically — it's not like them. I wish they would calm down, and I snap at them, criticizing their enthusiastic speech. Only several days later do I realize how much we've changed in Tovu. The kids are talking like Fijians, even when they speak English, adopting the lively Fijian style of speech. I was criticizing them because they have already become what I am still struggling to be: comfortable with Fijian, comfortable in Tovu. With the continued companionship of school-mates and peers, they are nearly fluent. After that I stop trying so hard to learn Fijian and begin to speak it more. Following the lead of the children, I relax into being just a resident of Tovu; learning how to live there naturally follows.

CHAPTER 8

Tevita's Healing Work (Tovu)

Just as Ratu Noa said, my research is flourishing as my involvement in the life of Tovu deepens. We have been living here three months now.

Inoke and I work out our collaboration as we go along. It's hard to make plans with Inoke. He has many obligations of his own to attend to: family responsibilities in his home village in Delana, ceremonial duties there and farther south as one of the favorite *mata-ni-vanua* of the Bitu chiefs, and commitments in Bitu and Suva as a government consultant on health and development projects. None of these activities is full-time, but when we travel outside Tovu, our trips frequently have other purposes besides research which Inoke must fulfill. Inoke is building us a boat of our own but for now we are using his, and so I am especially obliged to accommodate his needs.

But despite the diversions from the research, Ratu Noa was right. Traveling with Inoke allows me to meet elders, chiefs, and healers all over Bitu, and through him I'm invited to participate in several important ceremonies. Inoke is related to many Bitu people and knows, or knows of, many, many more. He is never shy to ask for their cooperation in our research. Though Bitu is known, especially in Suva, as "the place where the *Vu* like to visit," people there do not talk openly about the work of *mana*, especially to strangers. Inoke opens doors. Everywhere we go, we talk with the local healers and participate in their work.

On the surface, Inoke doesn't always seem to display the Fijian ideal of humility. His main requirement of others is: "No bullshit." "If a person doesn't deserve my respect, why should I pretend to be respectful and humble before him? Above all, I want to be honest."

Sometimes Inoke embarrasses me with his demands on others. But that is more a matter of my personal preference than one of his overstepping Fijian customs. Inoke lives according to the traditional Fijian way — he only stretches that way to its limits. He takes what is rightfully his, but never hesitating to do so. Always he makes things happen sooner and more intensely rather than trying to make things take place which were not meant to be.

Inoke and I make several trips south, interviewing two healers near Delana and other healers farther south in Bitu. But most of the time I remain in Tovu, often visiting Tevita by myself, with no translator. At first I simply follow Ratu Noa's advice: "Stay with my student Tevita," he said, "and work with him." Soon I find that I also like Tevita; I want to spend time with him. He is becoming a friend, and his family and mine are growing close — going out together fishing and gathering, exchanging foods, visiting. Lora and Eliki each count among their best friends two of Tevita's children.

Spending time with Tevita involves nothing extraordinary. Good-natured and modest, he avoids flourishes, drama, and any hint of the mysterious in his healing work. A strong and industrious man, he keeps busy tending his garden, fixing things around the house, fishing, and caring for the pine scheme. We often work together, with me helping in whatever way I can. Since my Fijian is still elementary and Tevita does not speak English, our words are few when we are alone. This bothers neither of us; we can speak through silence. Even among other villagers Tevita is not a great talker; though not overly reflective, he is comfortable listening, or just sitting quietly.

Like most men in Tovu, Tevita drinks a lot of *yaqona*. Often we are together in the evening either at his house or elsewhere drinking *yaqona*, usually with many different people from the village, sometimes only with members of his family and a few others. Ratu Noa's words come back to me — "Stay close to the *yaqona*." Though there may be others in the room, drinking *yaqona* with Tevita brings me closer to him. The *yaqona* connects us both to Ratu Noa, carrying us along a spiritual network. This is not a hushed and reverent effort; we sit together as ordinary people, among others, joking, talking, and communicating in our way. Day by day we are becoming linked through the medium of commonplace activities and the bond of the *yaqona*.

One afternoon I'm sitting at Tevita's house while he is cleaning up his kerosene lamp. Nasi comes in, accompanied by Inoke, who presents a *yaqona* to Tevita on Nasi's behalf. She is sick. For the past week, she has ached all over her body and feels weak; she has dreams almost every night, dreams that make her wake up in a sweat, and she has become fearful of the dark. None of the medicines at the nursing station has made her any better. Can Tevita help?

Tevita accepts the *yaqona* on behalf of his *Vu*, saying he will do his best. He asks permission not to mix the *yaqona*: "I've been drinking too much these past few days…and also I have to check on those pines before it gets dark." Placing the *yaqona* on a shelf with several others he has recently received, he then asks Nasi some questions about her sickness: "Are the pains especially bad anywhere in particular?… What have you eaten recently?… Have you gotten cold from fishing in the ocean?" After checking with Inoke, Nasi says she can't add anything to her original complaint.

Tevita then asks her to tell him one of her dreams. Nasi describes a dream in which she is walking along a coconut tree that serves as a bridge over a swollen creek. Suddenly she is knocked over, and as she falls into the swift waters below, she wakes up.

"Do you see anyone at night?" Tevita asks.

"Nobody…but I'm still afraid."

"Can you think of anyone who might be jealous of you?"

"No."

Turning to Inoke, Tevita asks them both if there is anything they have done incorrectly, not following the traditional ways.

"No…not that we know of," they respond almost simultaneously.

Tevita feels Nasi's stomach, pressing in on it, almost kneading it, and then massages her back with an herbal remedy mixed in oil. He calls to his wife Suliana, who is sitting apart from the others, to help him find a particular herbal medicine. Though she often prepares herbs under Tevita's direction, she also mixes remedies of her own at times. At the shelf across from Tevita, she picks up some herbs tied in a small bag. Tevita gives the bag to Nasi and instructs her on how to prepare tea from it. She should drink the tea twice a day for four days. After that, she is to come back so he can see how she is. If she is not better, he can decide whether to continue the treatment or try something else.

Nasi thanks Tevita, and both she and Inoke stay awhile and visit, joking about one of the sillier old men in the village. Soon Nasi takes her leave, saying she must get back to the nursing station. Inoke follows her half an hour later.

Later I visit with Nasi and Inoke. They believe Nasi's sickness is caused by the *Vu*, a sickness Western medicine cannot cure. Inoke points out that traditional healing treatments customarily extend over four days. He invites me to go with them to Tevita's at the end of the treatment period.

On the afternoon of the fourth day, I accompany Nasi and Inoke to Tevita's. Again, Inoke presents a *yaqona* on behalf of Nasi, now requesting Tevita's help in completing the treatment.

"How do you feel?" Tevita asks Nasi.

"That herb had a good effect," Nasi replies with relief. "All my symptoms vanished on the fourth night — the aching all over my body, all that dreaming, and my fear at night. Now I'd like another four nights of the herb."

"That's okay...you can have more." Tevita's medicines are to share, to be given to others. "If you wish you can have more."

"I've given you a *wai ni vakatevoro*," Tevita says, indicating that the herbal remedy he gave her has been formulated to treat sickness caused by the *Vu*. "Whenever I give this particular mixture of herbs and the patient experiences relief from her symptoms, then I know the *Vu* are involved.

"I'm glad Nasi asked for more medicine. That's how we work," Tevita explains for my benefit. "In traditional Fijian healing you must go in pairs. For example, this one treatment for Nasi should consist of two courses of taking the herb, and there are four nights in each course. After that pair of treatments, if the patient still complains, you can change to different herbs."

Inoke and Nasi visit awhile with Tevita, who is now joined by Suliana. After a time Suliana takes her leave, going to the kitchen to prepare the evening meal. Two of Tevita's younger children come noisily into the house, and he motions them to sit quietly. That's too much for them to manage, so they leave as quickly as they entered.

The bar of sun cutting across the mat has turned reddish as it begins to slide up Tevita's body. Soon our visit will be over as the house will fill up with Tevita's six children, and the evening meal will be served. Before we go, I want to relay Ratu Noa's message to Tevita.

"Tevita, I want to tell you about my talks with Ratu Noa," I say. My announcement is a request for permission to continue.

"Yes...yes. I've been waiting to hear from him."

"Ratu Noa said to tell you that he and I are working together on my research. But he advised me that for my research to go well, I must also participate in the healing work."

Tevita nods, affirming the truth of what I'm saying. He waits for me to continue.

"Ratu Noa said, 'Try to come every Monday evening to Tevita to do the work, and if you're unable to be there, tell Tevita where you'll be.'"

"Yes, I know," Tevita responds. "...I already know. Ratu Noa and I communicate. And I agree with him. But there are problems with Monday night. That used to be our working day. All of my four helpers [*liga ni wai*] from around Kali would come here to do our work. But lots of other commitments have come up, so it's hard to keep the Monday practice regular. Before, I used to have a ceremony at the houses of each of my helpers as I traveled around the other villages of Kali. But Ratu Noa said, 'No, just one house for the ceremony.' And Ratu Noa is in charge of the work. When Monday became too busy, I changed the ceremony to Wednesday, and held it with just myself and my two Tovu helpers. But the last several months more commitments kept arising, and we couldn't hold a regular Monday or Wednesday service."

Tevita pauses, then decides. "It will be on Monday now because that's what Ratu Noa seems to want. But…but I can't promise to do the ceremony every Monday. I'll just try my best to have it here on Mondays whenever the house is free."

We sit in silence. Tevita asks his youngest son, who is now sitting beside him, to fetch some oil so he can rub it on his skin, a nightly skin care routine for Fijian people. He applies the oil to his legs as if sculpting clay, then puts the bottle away. Throughout he looks deep in thought. Turning to me, he remains pensive.

"I'm surprised Ratu Noa has allowed you to learn as much as you have." There is no judgment in his words; it is a simple statement of fact. "When other people wanted to do research on his work, Ratu Noa sent them away. With other healers it would be hard to get the facts because this is considered sacred work."

Again silence. Tevita's words still fill the air. Then, as they recede, he continues.

"Let me tell you how I use *yaqona*. I just take the *yaqona* the patient has presented to me and turn my whole mind to the idea of that *yaqona*. I concentrate on it, on what the *yaqona* is for, on what the patient wants. I don't announce the *yaqona*, as is done in the typical ceremony, when the *yaqona* is accepted on behalf of the *Vu*. No, our ceremony is different. The *yaqona* opens our practice for the night, and all my helpers and I concentrate our minds on each case."

"What is this concentration like?"

"I can't compare it to anything." Tevita does not wish to elaborate. He presses on.

"The Monday healing ceremony is a *yaqona* ceremony for opening the practice. The patients bring in their *yaqona* then, and when they are here, I make a list of all of them and their problems. Each helper gets the list. I call out the number of the patient, and my helpers and I concentrate our thoughts on giving the patient a healing. And in Suva, Ratu Noa knows exactly what goes on here on Monday nights. As we work here, he knows of our work. If I refer a patient to him that night, he's already in the know. Like I said before, we communicate.

"Monday nights, Rusiate, you're welcome. You can help us. You know, Rusiate — you're lucky...Ratu Noa turned the others away."

The following Monday, three men from Ogo come to Tevita's house with a *yaqona*. They're asking for help with the commercial fishing scheme they run. It seems that there is conflict in Ogo between the "old guard" who oppose the project and those who are in charge of it, mostly younger men. Those who oppose the scheme, including the chief, think the younger men are investing Ogo's resources in a risky proposition. The younger men maintain that the others are not "keeping up with the changing times," and lack the entrepreneurial spirit necessary to survive in today's world.

At Tevita's, one of the Ogo men, Jese, the spokesperson for the fishing project, summarizes the position of his group: "We think those older men are jealous of our fishing project. They want to control it for themselves. And their jealousy could hurt our business — especially that chief. We know him. He does the *vakatevoro*. They could turn the *Vu* against us. Tevita, we need your help. We need protection against them. We need protection for the fishing project."

Tevita takes their *yaqona* and puts it on the shelf. Then we mix some other *yaqona* and, for the next several hours, drink — socializing and joking. That is the Monday night healing ceremony. At some later time Tevita must do what is asked of him, sending protection to them. But the Monday ceremony he described to me — with his helpers present and calling out patients' numbers so all can concentrate on the healing — is not followed. In fact, Tevita's helpers are not even here.

The next day when I talk with Inoke, he tells me the background of Tevita's work with the Ogo fishing scheme. Over the years, Tevita has supported the business as the project managers regularly come to him with *yaqona*. That connection actually started with Ratu Noa, who was in on the very beginning of the project, supporting it when it was merely an idea. Inoke describes Ogo as a divided community, with the fishing project managers on one side and the rest of the community, consisting mostly of older people, on the other.

"Me, I side with the fishing scheme people," Inoke asserts. "They're the way of the future. Maybe they don't respect the old ways enough...but how else can you change things? But it's a dangerous situation," Inoke warns, "because those old people are really jealous, and they have lots of power. Especially that old chief. I don't trust him. People already suspect him of doing bad things. A guy like that could kill you!

"Those Ogo fishing project people are smart," Inoke continues. "They go to Tevita, and in Tevita they've picked the right one. That Tevita is honest; he's really good with this healing work. And he's backed up by the best, by his teacher, Ratu Noa. If they have to fight against the evil work of that old chief, then I think Tevita can help them."

For the next several weeks Tevita is very busy, and no Monday night ceremonies are held. His house is continually filled with visitors; after some pine scheme officials have left, Suliana's relatives come. But we continue to spend time together.

One afternoon, I give him a notebook, asking if he would be willing to keep a list of the patients he sees, their complaints, his treatments, and the outcome. He enthusiastically agrees.

"You know, Rusiate, I also do research. I used to keep a casebook where I listed all the patients I saw. It was up to five hundred names.... But the book was lost in a hurricane. It's important to keep a casebook. Then you can show others the work you've actually done."

Tevita begins to talk about the healing work and the *Vu* that are behind it. "The power of the *Vu* is proportional to the character of the healer. If the healer worships faithfully and hard, the *Vu* will be strong. The *Vu* are different in their grades, their strength — some are very powerful, others less so. But both the character of the healers and the strength of the *Vu* are important."

"Is serving the local *Vu* important?"

"Some of the local *Vu* have only limited power. Some of the *Vu* known throughout Fiji are more powerful. And some of the local *Vu* are served by the local people only for bad purposes.

"You know, Rusiate, there are age limits to being a healer. Sometimes a person still in school can be given the power. But those young ones usually don't last. Because once you deviate in this work, your power is cut off. There was one man to the south who was given power from Ratu Noa but lost it. And then there are ones whose character is not straight and they still practice, but their effect is nil. They just waste time. There are only three real healers here in northern Bitu; to the south is Isei, in the middle Tomasi, and up here in Kali, it's me."

"Can you tell me about the *mana* that is behind the work?"

"*Mana* is just like a gift to a person; it's not something you expect will happen to you. When you're faithful to your work, you feel a greater healing power. The *mana* of being faithful to your work, that's your healing work.

"But the healers in Fiji are divided into two groups," Tevita cautions. "*Mana* is not only used for healing; it can also be used for killing."

"What about those healers who seem to make a business of their work?"

"There is no set rule for all healers," replies Tevita. "For some healers it's a business — they are not straight. If someone brings a present, like money, it cannot be accepted as part of the healing ceremony, it is not related to that work. It is the *yaqona* that belongs to the healing ceremony. And you don't need a big *yaqona*, you don't have to spend money for lots of *yaqona*. A couple of little stems will do."

Tevita relaxes into himself, his sitting body molding more comfortably onto the floor. He turns away, reaches toward the shelf, and brings down some *yaqona*.

"Rusiate, I think we can have a little healing ceremony now, before the people come back from the bush." Though unexpected, Tevita's statement is completely sensible.

Only Inoke, who is translating, and I are present as Tevita mixes a small amount of *yaqona* in the *tanoa*. Tevita sits at the top of the room, the *tanoa* in front of him. He mixes the *yaqona* and pours a bit onto the side of the *tanoa*, in each of the four directions. After only a few words he serves the *yaqona*, first to Inoke, then to me, then to himself. We drink two rounds, and the *tanoa* is empty. Again, with only a few words, Tevita closes the *yaqona*. After less than ten minutes, the ceremony is

133

over. For those ten minutes, the room is deeply still; now Tevita changes the mood, returning to normal conversation.

"Rusiate, we won't have a session Monday night because too many people will be in Tovu for pine planting. Even though cases are waiting for healing, with all those visitors in Tovu, any ceremony I might try would be too public. People might say, 'Oh, what's this?'

"Is there anything else you wanted to ask me?" Tevita's question surprises me. He's more talkative than usual.

I can't help thinking about why Tevita's helpers are not here, and why they also weren't present the night the Ogo people came. And I realize I don't know much about his two helpers in Tovu, Eroni and Alipate.

"How are helpers chosen?" I ask.

"No one is forced to be a helper. I just ask them politely. If they agree we carry on. I only ask persons who are straight in character. But I don't want too many helpers, and I've turned down many who want to become helpers. The idea of the helpers is to give me a rest; I send instructions to them and they can do some of the healing work.

"Eroni has been helping me for a long time. Alipate is my most recent helper. He was sick and went to Suva. Ratu Noa healed him and made him a helper. But they are not always with me when I work — only if they can make it."

I still don't know why they aren't present, and remain unclear whether the reason is a complicated matter or just that they come when they can, and sometimes they're not available.

"Tevita, I heard about one Ogo man, Peniasi, who used to be your helper but had to give up his practice."

"The story is this," Tevita responds. "Peniasi was sailing in his canoe and got sick suddenly. He just snapped. Therefore it's hard to figure out the cause.... Maybe something was wrong in his practice. But even when Peniasi was normal, he was not very straight. He had a bad heart.

"Peniasi was a former patient of mine. He stayed for a while here in my house. Possibly he had turned from healing to killing, or joined the wrong company and misused his power and privilege. That man didn't have a clean heart.

"Yet...I could have misled him," Tevita reflects. "I could have misled him, because he always answered my questions by saying just 'yes'... 'yes'...'yes.' The cause of his snapping was the *Vu*. But exactly why he snapped, I don't know."

Here is another matter short of resolution. But my academic inquisitiveness, demanding definite, if not precise, answers, is fortunately resting, and hopefully in retirement. Listening patiently, I'm gradually understanding some of the complexity in the use and misuse of *mana*, the gaining and the losing of power.

In measured time, I raise a new question.

"Tevita, I'm having a little problem with the *yaqona*. Ratu Noa said I should stay close to the *yaqona*, and I try. But sometimes I get a little *mateni*, and that doesn't seem to be related to the healing work."

Tevita smiles and nods as I speak. Clearly he understands my dilemma.

"You know, Rusiate, when I drink in this house for the healing ceremony, I won't get *mateni*, no matter how much *yaqona* is served to me. Elsewhere though, I'll get *mateni*. You know that *mateni* feeling — you get groggy, your legs go numb, your sense of balance is off, you start to lose your sense of position.

"If I'm attending to a patient, the more *yaqona* I drink in the healing ceremony, the better I'm able to see the ailment and suggest a cure. In some special cases, where the patient is very sick, I request lots of *yaqona*. 'Serve me lots,' I say. 'The more *yaqona*, the more power.' There was one case I treated — Jese, who heads the fishing scheme in Ogo. Jese was carried into my house, seriously sick. I drank *yaqona* for eight days and eight nights, nonstop. At the end we declared the *yaqona* finished, and Jese got up, walked away, and went back to Ogo."

"But what explains this difference between what happens when you drink *yaqona* in the ordinary drinking times and in the healing sessions?"

"I wonder that myself, Rusiate...I wonder why I don't get drunk in my healing sessions.

"You know, Rusiate, I'm amazed at how you've been granted permission to look into this healing work. It's never happened before."

Tevita smiles at me, and continues. "In this healing work we always

135

divide things into pairs. The more cases, the longer the ceremony. But we don't have to worry because Ratu Noa is also working on these cases at the same time in Suva. All the *Vu* know the special day of the healing work; they don't have to be called. And if we have to deal with an emergency on another day, the *Vu* are called just by the special way we prepare the *yaqona*. But there is no need to announce the *yaqona* with formal ritual prayers and offerings. Just prepare it in the ordinary way I do and you communicate with the *Vu*."

Tevita, like his teacher Ratu Noa, makes it seem simple. Just be straight; or more realistically, try to follow the straight path. But I already know that that is not so simple.

CHAPTER 9

Conversations with Ratu Noa (Suva)

"Being ordinary...being simple — that's my special way."

"I'm surprised Ratu Noa has allowed you to learn as much as you have. ...It's never happened before." Tevita's words come back to me on the bus to Ratu Noa's house in Suva. After nearly three months in Tovu, I'm thinking more and more like a Tovu-person. And I feel somewhat unprepared for this visit to Ratu Noa. At the same time, I wonder how much I have actually learned. One thing is sure, however — whatever I'm learning is coming in unpretentious packages.

Seeing Ratu Noa, I feel at ease again. Though I have immense regard for his knowledge, I'm not intimidated by him. He speaks with confidence, yet diffidently; with authority, yet humbly. When he pulls out the *tanoa*, the talk and work begin without embellishment, ending the same way, as the empty *tanoa* is put to rest for the night.

Ratu Noa is generous in his instruction, forgiving the ignorance that underlies most of my questions. But my questions come more and more from the heart, which feeds his desire. I can even say I try to be straight, but I realize that there are many levels of understanding which remain hidden to me. And most important, my understanding does not easily translate into practice, which is the crux of the straight path. Take the

137

concept of humility. How deep is my understanding? Deep enough to make me a humble person? The answer is clear. No.

Living in Tovu keeps me constantly aware of my confusion about *yaqona*, and that is where I begin.

"I try to stay near the *yaqona*, like you said, but when they're just drinking *yaqona* for the fun of it, to visit and tell stories, it doesn't seem like the *yaqona* is connected any longer to the healing work."

"Only if you stay near the *yaqona* can you see the true *mana*; there is no other way but through the *yaqona*." Ratu Noa leaves no room for doubt; then he refines his statement. "The *yaqona* is like a magnet; it attracts *mana* and brings things together so you can understand them. But don't just drink *yaqona* anywhere or to excess; just two *bilo*, then you can leave. On the Monday night healing sessions, it's only the first two *bilo* that matter. You are not allowed to talk then. And they mix only enough *yaqona* for those two rounds. Then they close off that special *yaqona*. After that others may want to mix more *yaqona*, and drink it to pass the time away, to joke and tell stories — and you can stay if you like.

"Rusiate, when you drink *yaqona*, whether it's just for telling stories or not, you must keep thinking of our work — whenever you take the *bilo*. And there will come a day when you too, like me, will be able to actually see and hear the *Vu*. 'Do this,' they may say, or 'don't do that.' As we sit here now, drinking *yaqona* and talking, I'll hear comments from the *Vu*. Like right now they tell me this is a useful discussion we're having, and that the work you're doing is useful.

"Rusiate, sometimes you really want to drink *yaqona*. But remember, it's not you that wants this *yaqona*; someone else wants that *yaqona* and is making you thirsty. That other can't come and tell you, 'I want to drink *yaqona*,' or command you, 'Drink *yaqona*.' No, you'll just feel thirsty." As I gain proficiency in Fijian, I appreciate more the subtlety Ratu Noa's way of alluding to the *Vu* — these "someones" and "others" that grace his conversation.

I've been in Tovu almost three months now. The Monday night healing sessions with Tevita have been held irregularly at best. Almost predictably, something comes up to obstruct them. I can't follow Ratu Noa's advice, but I don't want to blame Tevita, nor do I want to be rigid. Yet the question remains — how important is the regularity of the Monday evenings?

"If I'm away on a Monday night," I ask, shifting the focus away from Tevita, "and can't participate in the healing session, what should I do?"

"It's okay if you have to be away. But wherever you are, whenever you take the first *bilo* of *yaqona*, always remember your work. Say to yourself, 'I take this first *bilo* to help with my work.'"

By now I am accustomed to Ratu Noa's referring to my *cakacaka*, both as a researcher and as someone learning to become a healer. It's not always clear how a particular comment may touch upon one or the other or both. That's for me to figure out — by practice. But I'm still not sure how much responsibility I should be taking for the specifics of the healing work. By participating in Tevita's healing ceremony, I'm part of the healing and responsible for it. But what about performing healing rituals — whether accepting *yaqona* from a patient, or learning to prepare medicinal herbs? And more fundamentally, what about contact with the *Vu* behind the healing work? On the other hand, from what I've already learned about the straight path, no one ritual is the essence of healing — being straight is. And in that sense, I've been given all the responsibility I could ever possibly have.

"When you take the first *bilo* in that special way," Ratu Noa warns, "don't *do* it in a special way!" Ratu Noa instantly stops my ruminations, pulling me sharply back into the conversation. "Take that first *bilo* in an ordinary manner, but concentrate your mind and say those words to yourself — 'This is to help my work.' No one must know what you're doing. Don't make it conspicuous, like taking the *bilo* slowly or holding it a long time before you drink as if saying a prayer. If you're conspicuous, others who have the *bilo* will know what you're up to and may block your work when they drink the *yaqona*. Every time you drink the special *bilo*, you must hide yourself."

Ratu Noa makes me anxious when he speaks about those who "have the *bilo*" — that is, those involved in *vakatevoro*. He and others are constantly talking about the two sides or two uses of *mana*; that is why the straight path is so necessary — to keep one on the right or straight side.

But now he's talking about how I myself can avoid the effects of those who use *yaqona* improperly. I'm part of the battle to keep straight. I'm grateful for his advice, but I'm a little scared about being so vulnerable.

There's a knock at the door. A young man enters, limping. Ratu Noa motions him to sit down. The young man hands him a *yaqona*, and without any words or gestures, Ratu Noa places it behind him, on the floor.

"Is it still painful?" Ratu Noa asks.

"Yes." The young man's voice is weak.

"That's all right," Ratu Noa assures him. Pointing to the young man's bandaged right foot, he says, "Once the fluid goes out from that abscess, it'll be less painful."

Ratu Noa gives the patient an herbal medicine, instructing him to take it the next two mornings. "This herb is to be wrapped in a leaf and heated. Put it on the abscess in the morning, covered by a bandage so the air doesn't go in, and take it off after work. This will help draw out the evil stuff in that abscess. Tomorrow you come again."

"This is a very painful injury," the young man offers with a grimace. "You know, I went to the Suva hospital, and they couldn't help. But I've been helped here!"

Ratu Noa nods almost imperceptibly. He continues his instructions: "Once the patient is healed, there is no use continuing the treatment. The type of *draunikau* ("bad medicine") which is making this patient sick is usually done only by people from the Solomon Islands. They use plants for the evil work, putting the bad medicine on the road. You can't see it. But once you step on it, it starts to make your foot itch. When you scratch, the sickness starts. If you can get the right herb to treat it, you can recover; if not, the sickness gets worse and worse."

"He's right about that," the young man volunteers. "I've had this abscess for three years. I've tried all sorts of medicines and injections, and none worked. I've come here just two days and already I've noticed a big difference."

Again Ratu Noa is more interested in explaining the case to me than spotlighting the young man's heartfelt testimonial. "It's no good for only me to know a treatment like this; far better for everyone to know how to treat a case of *vakatevoro* like this young man has. That's why I want you to know these things." Ratu Noa turns his attention directly to me. "Before you go back to America, Rusiate, you must learn these things."

I've already thought about this part of the teaching, but have despaired about its practicality. How could I administer Fijian remedies in the United States? And even if I could, would I want to practice in such a *concretely* Fijian way?

"But how can I learn about these things?" My question, optimistic rather than doubtful, simplifies these concerns.

"You can be there in America and write to me — tell me the disease you're treating, and I'll send you the herb. Fijian medicine goes right across the ocean! So when you find a disease that can't be treated by Western medicine, notify me and I'll send an herb. And most important, you must take some *yaqona* with you."

I know the *yaqona* is the vehicle for healing...and that's what worries me. Not only do I not know how to perform the *yaqona* ceremony, I'm also not sure I would be allowed to take any *yaqona* out of Fiji.

"It's very hard to take *yaqona* to America," I ask as much as say.

"That's all right, Rusiate. You don't have to mix *yaqona* every time you see a patient. Only when you meet some difficulty."

Ratu Noa's emphasis clears away some of my lingering doubts. The power of *yaqona* does not come from rigid performance of the ritual.

The young man, taking his herbs, thanks Ratu Noa and leaves.

"In which house do you see more patients?" I ask. "In this house or your old house downtown where you had the special room for healing?"

"Lots more patients went to the other place, but many also come here now," Ratu Noa replies, "even though it's a long bus ride out of town. Also, after my job each day, patients will pick me up and we'll drink *yaqona* at their place, and then that's where I do the healing. But I always return home to do my regular healing service.

"You know, Rusiate, all different races are my patients — Indians, Chinese, Westerners, as well as Fijians. But I don't want to attend to too many people because I can't get enough people to help me, and since I have a regular job to keep up with, I don't have enough time. But whenever there is a real need, I'm available. When someone wants to come, I wait. But the patient must come when they say. Once someone told me he would come at ten in the morning but didn't come until four in the afternoon. I missed a whole day of work that day. I sent that patient away and told him to come back the next day."

I know how important it is to fulfill my commitments to Ratu Noa, including coming when I say I will. Our earlier meetings — actually our "mis-meetings" — established the preciousness of each conversation.

"What are some of the differences between good healers and bad ones?" I ask.

"Some healers say that every form of complaint is connected with the devil [*tevoro*] or the *Vu*," Ratu Noa begins. "These are the bad healers. The good healers can differentiate between illnesses that come from the *Vu* and those that don't. A lot of complaints are just ordinary problems [*tauvimate dina*]; they aren't connected with *vakatevoro*. When a good healer sees something is an ordinary complaint, he takes *yaqona* from the patient only once and then usually sends the patient to the hospital. And a good healer usually doesn't tell the patient the cause of the illness; he only tries to heal him. Because if the cause is another person's evildoing, telling the cause will only intensify and multiply the ill-feeling between your patient and the one doing harm.

"Good healers are told exactly what to say to their patients by the *Vu* that support their work; and that's all they say — they don't elaborate. But bad healers add on to what the *Vu* tell them. Often they say an ordinary illness is connected to the devil, which brings them fame, but in the end it may kill the patient. Sometimes when patients hear that their illness is caused by the devil, though in fact it's just an ordinary sickness, they don't go to the hospital, and their health can go down and down. Sometimes they even die. What the false healer really wants is *yaqona* and other gifts, like tobacco. He wants them today, and tomorrow, and the next day and the next. Patients will keep coming back to those healers if they are told their illness is related to the devil.

142

"Rusiate, never add on to what you are told, to what you know. Boasting is not good. Our work is not for the proud person. You must be brief and speak the truth. Speak only what is necessary. The more you talk, the less truth there is."

"There are certainly lots of these 'talkers' here in Suva!" I observe.

"Yes, there are."

"Ratu Noa, I've heard that a good healer must treat all the cases that come to him; that the good healer feels love for all and wants to help. But what about someone who comes to you for help in escaping a prison sentence for a crime he committed, or someone who wants you to harm another person?"

"It all depends on your decision about whether to help a person or not," Ratu Noa says, "because that decision will boomerang back to you. Your decision must always be straight. You cannot help anyone who intentionally breaks the law. If it's a mistake, the first time someone's in trouble, it's okay to help. But if someone comes back a second time, having intentionally broken the law, you say, 'Now you must pay the price; I can't help you.' Once I was offered a lot of money to help someone who had stolen something to avoid a court judgment; I said no. Taking that money is just being greedy. I do receive things as a token of thanks from patients, but I never charge or demand payment. That's taboo.

"Rusiate, the thing we do is not easy. You must walk straight, and run straight. Don't do your work thinking that the patient will pay you. You just work. This healing work is the gift of *Kalou;* that means you must give life and health to others freely. If you observe this rule, the *mana* comes; if you break it, the *mana* goes."

I know these basic taboos or prohibitions: never use spiritual power to harm another; never charge for services. But there is a third taboo, regarding sex with patients, about which I heard something that upset me.

"Ratu Noa, another healer told me that though sex with a patient was taboo when one was just beginning in the healing, it became appropriate when one was very advanced, if done in a special way."

We've entered into new terrain. Maybe it's too soon.

"Rusiate, the answer is simple: you must be straight. In this kind of work, you have the power to seduce a woman, but don't use it that way. In the beginning, you're not even allowed to sleep with your wife at certain times; after you've completed your training, these restrictions are removed. But don't ever use women with your power. It's like helping someone who intentionally breaks the law."

"Is there anyone you know who no longer has the power because of having sex with a patient?"

"Yes, that's what happened to Peniasi, the man from Ogo who used to be Tevita's helper. That man tried to turn his power over to seduce women. When Peniasi diverted his power, a woman came to him unconscious and slept with him. It was just as if she lost her mind. Afterward she woke up and realized what had happened. And now Peniasi has lost his mind. That's the boomerang effect I spoke of. That mental illness is Peniasi's punishment."

In Tovu, Tevita earlier said the healing power had left Peniasi because he tried to use it to kill another, but Tevita was vague about this. Whatever the cause, Peniasi no longer practices healing, and he *is* considered mentally disturbed by the people of Ogo.

Time is on my mind now. I have to leave Ratu Noa's soon and in a few days will be returning to Tovu. I want to know whether there are any further instructions.

"Ratu Noa, it's September now, not yet five months since we've been working together. I know that's still what you called the first period of training. But I'm going back to Tovu in a couple of days and won't see you for a while. Is there something else I should be doing in Tovu, after spending three months there, as you told me to?"

I hope I'm not being too eager. But I've learned to follow Ratu Noa's advice: if there is something I want to know, I should "fire away." "Don't be shy," he keeps assuring me.

"Just attend the Monday and Wednesday sessions with Tevita," Ratu Noa replies. "If you're away from Tevita and in an ordinary *yaqona* session, try to remember your first two *bilo*. Most people don't know even this little point. In fact, remember your first *bilo* — never mind the second.

"You know, Rusiate, some healers want to perform in a special way,

144

showing off for everyone to see. But not me. When someone brings me a *yaqona*, I will announce it to my *Vu* — in my own time and in my own way. Being ordinary…being simple — that's my special way."

The evening has become still. When Ratu Noa pours *yaqona* in the *bilo* for each of us to drink, it's like a clean falling of water into cupped hands. There is nothing else to ask.

Ratu Noa breaks the silence. We talk a little more, about my impending return to Tovu, about his job. Nawame, Ratu Noa's wife, comes in the back door; she's been out visiting. She sits down, quietly listening. A smile gradually comes over her face.

"So I see your Fijian is getting better," Nawame says to me. "You stay around this house and pretty soon they won't recognize you in America anymore. This man here," she says, nodding in the direction of Ratu Noa, "he's a stubborn one. No English for him. He'll make you Fijian yet!"

"She's right," Ratu Noa says, "there is only a little left before you can understand the Fijian language. And then, it will be easy for you to talk with me. Because I know English only a little."

Ratu Noa is flattering me; my Fijian is still elementary. "Wait a minute — your English is better than my Fijian." I know Ratu Noa can understand English; I've seen him respond to my questions before they're translated. But I also know he will not speak in English. Not only is he modest, even shy, about his minimal command of spoken English; more important, he wants what he says to be conveyed accurately and in its original form.

"Remember this, Rusiate. When you come back from Tovu, every time you come back, you must come and see me."

For me, this has become a first principle.

145

CHAPTER 10

A Death
(Tovu)

The October night sparkles. Stars pierce the sky over Tovu like new spring grass, making the slim moon just another point of light. It is still, as insect-sounds surround the sleeping village.

A different sound adds to the soothing night-blanket. Not yet recognizable, it is still disturbing. My wife and I turn over in our sleep. Before we're able to rejoin our dreams, the strange sound yanks at us, forcing us to hear. It is louder and louder. Like a wailing, like a pack of wolves calling into the night air. But there are no wolves here! What could be howling like that? The sounds are not clear, but their meaning is getting clearer. People are crying; it is the beastly cry of total grief. And it comes from Master Jone's house. Yes, just up the hill from us, people — I think women — are wailing, shrieks muffled within weeping and moaning.

Almost suddenly, night yields its territory, as morning gains an edge in the east. We lie in bed, restless in uncertainty, fearing something dreadful. But staying inside is no longer possible. Coming outside into the steel-blue light, we shiver, then shudder. It is more than cold; it feels clammy. Several people pass by, hurrying to Jone's house. Now the sounds are unforgiving; no more comfort in ambiguity. There is a tragedy at Jone's.

Tevita walks by. We exchange a glance. He looks tired, shadowy in the blue light. Neither of us speaks, but I ask for help with my eyes.

"This is a bad thing that has happened," he finally mumbles — at least I think he says that. Neither of us is quite awake. "There is a bad thing here. Jone is dead. He died last night at Ogo. They were celebrating the launching of the new Ogo commercial fishing boat. In Ogo, that's where he died."

Tevita shakes his head slowly, sadly. He looks fragile. The blue light seems to take away some of his life, leaving him hollow. He turns and walks up the hill, toward Jone's house.

Jone is dead? The thought tries to escape. Maybe I misunderstood what Tevita was saying. No — no. That doesn't work. Jone is dead!

But how could that be? I just saw him yesterday afternoon. He was coming back from a meeting in the south. He stopped briefly at his house, bringing two large cabbages to his wife — gifts from people at the meeting.

"Why don't you stay home tonight and rest," she pleaded with him. "You've been going here and going there without a break for the past week. And you haven't been taking care of yourself. Look, today you haven't even eaten yet and it's already almost dinner time. All you've done is drink *yaqona* at that teachers' meeting down south. That's no meal. You'll get sick if you keep this up." Jone's wife was distressed as much as angry. She seemed to know her words would not affect her husband.

"Yes, I know," Jone responded automatically. "But I promised those Ogo people I would go to their celebration tonight. They're celebrating the first trip of their commercial fishing boat. I promised them…I promised them, and I have to go." He ended up talking into space, having already turned away from his wife. Then he started walking into the village, toward the beach and his boat.

I just saw him yesterday afternoon. Yes, he did look tired. His shoulders were rounded, and his head a little low. His normally heavy yet compact body looked overweight. But still, just yesterday!

I feel lost. Jone was our guardian. He helped my family and me settle into Tovu, gave us staples from his garden, helped both Mere and me in our research whenever a question arose. He was a friend. The loss of Jone begins to seem overwhelming.

I find myself walking to Jone's house with my family. Without knowing what to do, we enter the ceremony marking his death which is already in progress. Inside the house, people are drinking *yaqona*. His body lies at the head of the room in an open coffin. Beautifully decorated woven mats cover his body, their multicolored yarn fringes tucked under his chin, framing his head. Draped over the coffin, her arms wrapped around his body, Jone's wife weeps softly, her large body heaving rhythmically, at times convulsively. She is attended by several women from the village, who periodically give her water and fan her gently.

Around the walls sit the people of Tovu, women in one group, men in another. The women talk in low, animated voices, going over and over the details of the death. Several among them are wailing in what I now recognize as a characteristic expression of grief. As they cry out, giving breath to the air, they wipe their faces with handkerchiefs from time to time; some pound on the floor or sway in place. The men are mostly quiet. Sitting with them, I feel comfort and strength. We talk briefly about Jone and the family he left. "What a terrible thing…and he was such a good man." That theme is repeated as each new visitor arrives. My eyes become wet; often we cry together. All the while, the *yaqona* is served continuously — and it's strong.

As the hours pass, new groups keep coming to pay their respects. After making their ritual presentation of *yaqona* and gifts, they too sit to drink *yaqona,* to visit and talk. Sometimes a group of people inside will leave to make space for the newcomers; sometimes the room just becomes more crowded.

The sun's midday heat has begun to dominate the room. The air becomes stiff and thick as more and more people are gathered in the house. An old woman says, "This heat's not good for that body. Soon we'll all be driven out!" Her age and status entitle her to make a joke; afterward the atmosphere lightens, and people relax a bit. They are relieved. The conversation regains a more usual tone and volume. People are settling in.

As the afternoon proceeds, I realize my family and I are fully in the midst of the ceremony. But I know it could be no other way. We are part of things.

"We're really glad you're with us," Jone's wife says on her way out for some fresh air. "You're part of our family."

Later Inoke and his family come to pay their respects. After their *yaqona* is ritually accepted, he sits next to me.

"I can't fully understand this thing," he says, bewildered. "Jone went over to Ogo late yesterday afternoon. When he got there, the ceremony for launching their commercial fishing boat had just started. When it was over, the party began. There was lots of drinking and lots of dancing. It all took place in the old chief's house, and Jone was sitting the whole time right next to that chief. Oh, he got up to dance — he danced a lot — but he always returned to his place, sitting next to that Ogo chief. Everyone who was there said Jone seemed to be having a really good time; he was drinking and dancing and joking around. Then without any warning, he collapsed. No warning at all! He was sitting down, enjoying himself, laughing — and then he fell over dead. Everybody was shocked...and terrified. So suddenly, and without any warning! The party was over!

"You know, Rusi, it does sound like a heart attack," Inoke continues, now more speculative. "It sounds like a heart attack, but...but why there at Ogo?" Jone was overweight and tired, Inoke reflects; he was drinking and dancing all night — good conditions for a heart attack. But he was young, barely forty, and a strong, active man. "I'll tell you this, Rusi, I can't help thinking there may be more to it than that. I'm confused." His medical training tells him one thing, he explains, but as a Fijian he is certain: "Other things are at work in this case."

He says no more, but his worried look remains. But there isn't much time to ponder his words. One of the elders calls me into a side room where a small group of men sit around a *tanoa* drinking *yaqona*.

"Some of us have decided to keep the *yaqona* going through the night," he says. "We thought you'd want to be with us." I feel honored. But it is only the next morning that I know what I've agreed to. All night, hour after hour, I fight sleep, struggling to understand bits of the conversation and to keep drinking *bilo* after *bilo* without getting sick, while the cold of the darkening night keeps sucking away my resolve. As

I think about it, in the warming light of the following morning, I can only feel grateful that I made it.

Later that morning I learn that I have been involved in an important part of the ceremony for Jone's death — keeping the *yaqona* going the first night, like a death vigil. Without really knowing what to do or how, I have been guided by a wisdom in the ceremony.

The funeral ceremony continues as more groups visit and more gifts arrive. Jone's family, assisted by others, begins preparing food for the guests. My family and I help in different ways — cooking, comforting Jone's widow, taking part in the *yaqona* ceremony.

Around noon, I go back to drink *yaqona*. I meet Inoke outside Jone's house.

"There's lots of talk about Jone going on here," he confides. "People can't understand why Jone died. They all say 'he was such a good man.' I know it can be explained. Jone was run down. He hadn't taken good care of himself for a while. He was ripe for a heart attack. And some of the people here talk about that...but they still can't understand why. If he had a heart attack, why him? And why at Ogo? And that's how I feel too, though I know more of the physical explanations for why people have heart attacks."

Inoke pauses, then continues, now in a whisper. "There's lots of talk about that old chief in Ogo." He suddenly becomes indirect. "You know, that old chief has done bad things in the past. He uses the *yaqona* in the wrong way. He's known for that. And he is very jealous of the fishing scheme in Ogo.... He's been trying to wreck it. Those in charge went their own way, leaving him out. And I agree with them, because that old chief doesn't know how to run a business. Yes, people are saying it was that old chief. Because Jone was sitting right next to him the whole night. Jone was the innocent victim of that old man's evil intentions.

"Let me tell you something," Inoke says, leaning close. "The way I'm talking to you now is not what people are actually saying. They don't even mention people like that old chief by name; they only refer to him by implication. And they don't talk directly about using *yaqona* for evil; they'll say something like 'He'll do it,' and that's all they'll say. Everyone knows what is being said and who is being accused, but no one wants to state any of these things directly, in public. Of course, in private much more is said — and names are named."

"But why would Jone's death come about when the chief is actually after the fishing scheme?"

"Well, Rusi, that's the Fijian way. When someone uses *yaqona* for evil intentions, the evildoer has to give something in return. You see, if that old Ogo chief uses *yaqona* to get his *Vu* to harm the fishing project, he must then promise to give that *Vu* something in return. He performs a thanksgiving [*madrali*], thanking the *Vu* for its help; and the usual thanksgiving is to offer the life of another human being [*nai madrali bula*]. Jone was his sacrifice — even though Jone was a good man, and not part of this conflict between the chief and the leaders of the fishing scheme. And such a sacrifice is even more appreciated if the victim, like Jone, is innocent and good. Jone sat next to the chief, so he was especially vulnerable to the chief's thanksgiving pledge.

"That's what people are saying," Inoke concludes, shaking his head. "And I can see their way of thinking. I also believe that chief is responsible. Why else would Jone die in Ogo? And collapse right next to that old chief?"

Like Inoke, I too want to believe only the physical explanation. Jone was overweight and overtired, he had overexerted himself — that he died of a heart attack ought to be the natural conclusion. But I can't merely accept that conclusion and leave it there. Tovu is filled now with conversations in corners; people have worried looks. The suspicions Inoke has outlined are on everyone's mind, pulled out for reexamination whenever a new person enters the group who has perhaps another perspective on the reasons for the death. People are saying Jone's death involved foul play — and this thought frightens me. I fear the power to kill which some people are said to have. Also, with suspicions so aroused, people will look in all directions for an explanation. I myself could be blamed, or my family. After all, coming to Tovu just under three months ago, we are a new ingredient in village life. Maybe people will think our arrival somehow set in motion events leading up to Jone's death. This new thought adds to my fear: here I am thinking about being a suspect. I realize how deeply involved I am in the life of Tovu.

As Inoke turns to leave he says, "You know, Rusi, I just heard something else. Over at Tevita's, some man said that maybe those Ogo people who run the fishing scheme are to blame; maybe they didn't launch their boat properly and Jone's death is the penalty for their breaking a traditional taboo. Tevita told the man that wasn't true...but I don't know. I heard that same charge from another person."

I'm astonished at the number of suspicions emerging, and at the same time I'm relieved to hear them. "It's those Ogo people" is almost a comforting refrain.

Before I follow Inoke back into Jone's house, Votea, a good friend of Jone's, comes over. Since Jone's teaching took most of his time, Votea regularly brought food to his family. Jone was one of the few people in Tovu who earned a salary, so he could afford to hire Votea. But it was work based on friendship. It was from the food Votea brought that Jone would give my family and me whatever we needed.

Votea is shaken; he has lost a big part of his world. As he looks at me, he starts to cry — and immediately I do too. We hug each other, still without words. Then Votea speaks, in quiet bursts that are muted by his inner sobbing.

"Jone was such a good man...and now we're left alone. We must stick together, Rusiate. And I'll help you. Now that Jone is gone, I'll get food for you. I'll take care of you, just like I did for Jone. Don't worry...don't worry, Rusiate. Your family will eat well."

In a near whisper, Votea continues: "It's those Ogo people. Jone should never have gone there last night. Those people in Ogo are up to no good. People like you and me, we have to be careful." He touches my shoulder. "We're glad you and your family are living in Tovu with us. You're good people. Yes, we'll take care of you...just don't worry."

Votea's words make me feel good, protected...and very sad. I stop thinking about blame being put on my family, and allow my grief for Jone and his family its full range. He was a good man.

Late that evening, word reaches Tovu that Jone's relatives from his home island of Momoto have arrived in Ogo. They will spend the night in Ogo, resting and gathering up their ceremonial gifts. Jone's family is related to the Ogo people, so their plan makes sense. In the morning, Jone's relatives will come to Tovu. Among them are Jone's two sisters.

Before dawn, women are already preparing food. Enormous iron pots borrowed from the school kitchen straddle the large fires, and tiny bubbles shoot to the water's surface. The women sit near the pots, scraping, cleaning, and cutting up the starchy roots that will be eaten — the perennial cassava and lots of the highly valued taro. Their talk is animated, warmed by the fire. In the chill of early morning, the rest of us look longingly at the fire, but there is little room left for anyone not cooking.

But we can hear bits of their talk. The questions continue: "Why did the death happen?" "Who is responsible?" Even though Jone was tired and ill-fed, and therefore weakened, still people ask "Why?" He was so young; an active man — and a good man. "Why?"

A new theme enters the conversation. "What is it about our place?" one woman wonders. "Why should this happen to our Tovu teacher? Why us?" The question "Why us?" is picked up by others and reformulated in different ways, never becoming more specific. Just "Why us?"

The question introduces new tensions. Though "those Ogo people" remain prime suspects, certain fingers start to point, ever so carefully and indirectly, closer to home. A definite unease enters the air. Is there danger in our midst? "Not me," voices seem to imply, "but maybe someone else, right here in Tovu."

CHAPTER 11

A Second Death
(Tovu)

Jone's body remains in his house, his face, now gray, still visible at the open top of the coffin. It is the second morning after his death.

A small advance party of Jone's relatives from Momoto has just been sighted setting anchor in Tovu Harbor. In the traditional manner, they have come from Ogo to announce the wish of the full group of relatives, including Jone's two sisters, to visit Tovu and pay their respects to the deceased. Once permission has been granted, they'll return to Ogo, then bring all the relatives to Tovu.

We sit drinking *yaqona*; the liquid is cold, further chilling our bodies. Several of the elders leave to meet the advance party formally. We wait, but not for long. The word comes to us through a messenger, a Momoto man whose blank, downcast face warns us.

"We apologize for coming to your village in this manner. But we have no choice. We must bear this unfortunate task. There has been another death.... Jone's sister has died. She died suddenly while staying in the old Ogo chief's house. She was just sitting there in Ogo late last night and collapsed. Right away...she was dead."

The messenger stops; his face contorts, his shoulders droop. Now that his terrible job is done, grief fills his frame. Struggling to control his emotions, he completes his task. "We're all in mourning for this second tragedy," he continues, "but we'll be here as soon as possible. We'll come to Tovu to pay our respects to our relative Jone."

Almost before it is proper — the ritual of hearing out the messenger and sending him back is barely over — people begin expressing their shock...and their fear. At first it is only half-spoken, as an old woman mumbles to herself, "Now Jone's sister...now the sister...and what next?"

After the messenger has left and only the small Tovu group remains, people begin speaking for others to hear, though their voices remain quiet. "But how could she die?" asks another. "She was even younger than Jone — maybe thirty-five, and in good health. And why so suddenly, without warning? And why again in Ogo, and in that chief's house?"

"That's what I'm thinking," adds another. "Why in Ogo, and in that same house as Jone died in?"

The news of Jone's sister's death spreads rapidly through the village, instilling confusion and disbelief. Then fear creeps over the people, wrapping itself around their words and behavior. The very structure of the funeral celebration is threatened as people struggle to make sense of this latest event. But the ritual structure prevails, overcoming while accommodating the incessant private conversations about the two deaths. As people cast about for explanations amid the suspicions of wrongdoing, the funeral establishes renewed order. Everyone has a role. Some continue to present *yaqona* and sacred objects such as *tabua* (whale's teeth) along with food and other gifts — mats, cloth, drums of gasoline — to Jone's family and relatives. Others prepare vast quantities of food to feed the visitors as well as all of Tovu.

There are still two more days until the fourth night after Jone's death, the culmination of this stage of the mourning. These four days are of primary significance, though another period of mourning succeeds them, ending on the tenth night. These ceremonial markers will now be extended an extra two days in order to honor Jone's deceased sister. At these special times, much of what has been presented to Jone's family will be redistributed to those who have come to pay their respects and to help with the ceremonial preparations, put into piles for the various families to take.

During brief encounters going to and from the funeral events and in informal conversations at home, the rumors spread, some developing into hypotheses about the reasons for these deaths. Inoke and others have made statements that the two deaths seem to have resulted from heart attacks or were related to fatigue and stress. But these statements, though accepted by many, remain uninteresting to all — even Inoke. They are not offered as the sole or even major explanation. They explain for some how the deaths might have occurred, but leave unresolved the major question of why they occurred, and specifically who or what was behind them. To answer this question, people search for relationships gone wrong and spiritual principles violated.

The old women are the first to articulate another reason for the sister's death. "In the old days, that was our way," they say. Asenati gives more details: "When an important person died, a person like a chief, then a close relative, someone like his wife or his sister or his mother would kill herself out of respect for that chief. Jone was a chief. That sister could have died for that reason — out of respect." Though everyone accepts this explanation to some extent, especially the elders, few see it as complete. Questions remain.

Suspicions again focus on the old Ogo chief: "Two people. Both die without any warning, without any reason. And both die in that old man's house." Those in charge of the Ogo fishing scheme also come under scrutiny. It seems that the fishing boat was launched improperly. On its maiden run from Suva to Ogo, it carried a taboo cargo, namely an empty coffin that had been ordered by an Ogo family expecting a death. That transgression was exacerbated by the celebration of the boat's launching, which amounted to celebrating wrongdoing. These managers of the fishing scheme had to pay for their violation of the sacred ways. But somehow the managers' punishment was deflected to Jone, who, because he was a respected chief and a good man, became a desirable victim. His innocence made the price paid even more shocking.

A small group of us are drinking *yaqona* at Jone's house when word comes that his Momoto relatives have arrived in Tovu. We await their formal arrival at the house and the exchange of *yaqona* and *tabua* which will mark our solemn greeting.

Our talk is suddenly interrupted by a young boy who bursts into the room. Though he tries to be respectful and inconspicuous, he cannot contain himself. He goes straight to Inoke and blurts out so all can

156

hear: "Come quickly! It's Jone's other sister. She's dead. She just died. She came here with the group of Momoto relatives, and as soon as she came here, she fell down to the ground. Nasi is there with her and needs your help."

Inoke rises unsteadily; his foot is stiff from having sat for a long time, and he hasn't fully taken in what the boy said. Then he recovers his balance and bolts out the door. Another man follows close behind him.

The observance of Jone's death is again shaken to its core, and for the moment it seems that it may cease. But the rest of us remain seated, keeping the *yaqona* alive, the ceremony going.

Too stunned to talk, we all watch intently as the *yaqona* is served. The *yaqona* must protect us. When we speak again, it's not about this third and latest death. The conversation falters. We sit ready to accept the details of this new tragedy, already accustomed to our numbness.

Ten minutes later Inoke returns. "We're lucky this time," he says with a smile. "Jone's sister is okay now. But it was touch and go. She was unconscious and had no pulse. Tevita was already there, working on her. And I helped Nasi give her a shot of Adrenalin. She's up now, and feeling stronger. I don't know what happened. She probably fainted.... But when she was lying there, she had no pulse. It really scared me!"

The ceremony resumes in earnest. In the face of the many unexplained events, the ritual takes on additional responsibilities: it must prevent further tragedy and reestablish meaning as people are brought back to their *Vu*. Though rumors still abound, they do not entirely dominate village life, driven as it is by the unyielding demands of satisfying subsistence needs.

Tevita has been very busy during these past few days as people seek his explanation of what has happened. He is seen as one not implicated in these events, but with a knowledge of tradition that provides insight. His response is typically understated: "We can't really know now why these bad things have happened. We only know what we must do to give us strength and that is to stay close to the *yaqona*. Tevita speaks of the importance of *mana*. While acknowledging that it can be used to harm others, he stresses that it is meant for people's protection.

Jone's Momoto relatives leave the next day. Almost as if taking over their space, a new theme reaches tentatively toward expression. I first hear it from Asenati: "With all these deaths," she says, "there must be something wrong back in their home, in Momoto. Something must have happened back there in Jone's family, with his parents. Now the children are paying for it." Others speak in a similar way about some supposed wrongdoing in Momoto. Such talk is subdued and remains suggestive. Details are either absent or not forthcoming.

Since Ogo remains the site of the prime targets of suspicion, the arrival of the three managers of the Ogo fishing scheme in Tovu startles us. Again led by Jese, they have brought a *yaqona* to ask Tevita to protect their fishing boat from trouble or accident. "With all the recent tragedies," Jese says, "we are fearful for our fishing business. We ask you for protection."

Tevita all along has used his healing work to support the early planning of the fishing project and the securing of the boat. But today the atmosphere in Tovu is charged with fear of Ogo, and these men make up one of the more feared groups. Others would be wary of this request for help, but Tevita doesn't waver. He agrees to help the fishing scheme managers. He will perform a cleansing of the boat and try to build up a protective shield (*sasabai*) around it.

"Rusi, you can come with us," Tevita offers. At any other time his invitation would be welcome. I'm glad Tevita includes me in his work, and I've never been to a cleansing ritual. But I hesitate momentarily. What will people think of me? I wonder. Will they think I'm in cahoots with these Ogo fishing people? That I'm trying to wash away their guilt? That I'm part of their guilt? Then I look at Tevita and see his confidence. I trust his understanding and honesty and decide to go.

We move the healing ceremony from Tevita's house to the Ogo fishing boat, which is anchored close to shore now that the tide is in. Tevita pours a little *yaqona* in different parts of the boat to cleanse it and build up protection. At first I feel a little uncomfortable, thinking about those who may see us here in the harbor and assume only the worst. But I put my doubts aside and participate fully in the ceremony now under way.

Tevita ends the ceremony with words of advice to Jese and the two other managers of the fishing project: "You must be careful. People in Tovu suspect you of wrongdoing. Remain straight — straight in your actions, straight in your thoughts. Only then can I help you."

CHAPTER 12

"Lots of Dreams, Lots of Problems" (Tovu)

Rere — "fear" — is a word that has been heard frequently in Tovu over the last two months. At times it refers to an especially deep fear, the terror or dread that comes from an encounter with unknown and awful forces. It's this deep kind of fear that has seized people. Jone's death, and the death of his sister, simmer in the Tovu air.

Jone's death in particular generates *rere* in Tovu. He appears to different people, during the day as well as at night, in clearly human as well as ghostly forms, in waking states as well as in vivid dreams, through half-heard plaintive calls as well as extended conversations. The people know what these visits mean: Jone is unsettled in death, not ready yet to leave Tovu, lurking about because there is unfinished business to complete. Jone lives in the unresolved questions surrounding his death, and the web of suspicions gradually enfolding the village. Tovu is in a state of low-grade chronic tension, a state that is exacerbated by Jone's reported appearances.

Schoolchildren frequently report seeing Jone up in the hills around the playing field, and they avoid the area adjacent to the hills. If it is necessary to go there, they travel in groups, running as fast as they can, but at night they refuse entirely. Our children too have this feeling of *rere*. Though at first they tell us about how the "other kids" see Jone, soon they are seeing him as well. We try to calm them down but cannot dismiss the reality of their experience, for we also feel Jone's presence. It seems that all of us in Tovu have become part of his frightening legacy.

And then there are the dreams (*tadra*), those giving clues about Jone's whereabouts and desires, and those that are most tantalizing, and feared: the ones suggesting the circumstances behind his death. Dreams are seen as descriptions or predictions of events which express the wishes and actions of the characters in the dream. If the dreams predict something bad will happen, the dream is brought to the healer, to help forestall, deflect, or undo that outcome. In the month after Jone's death, Tevita is busy with this aspect of his work.

One of the sixth-grade girls dreams that she sees Jone walking down through Tovu in his usual clothes. He is walking toward the beach, to the place where workmen from Suva are building the new nursing station. Jone asks the girl to tell the workmen that the proposed building isn't in the right place; it should be moved closer to the ocean. He also speaks directly to one of the workmen, whose ancestral home, like his own, is Momoto. Jone says to this man, "I won't be going back to Momoto. I'm a Tovu villager now."

People agree on the meaning of this dream: Jone will be with us in Tovu, at least until the circumstances surrounding his death are cleared up. A few privately add a further interpretation: at least until those guilty of causing his death are found.

Alipate, one of Tevita's two helpers in Tovu, also has a dream about Jone. Seeing him walking on the school's playing field, Alipate asks, "What is the cause of your death?" At that moment a tall, fierce-looking man, his face shrouded in darkness, jumps forward menacingly and demands of Alipate, "Who are you to ask such a question?" Alipate takes a spear and tries to kill the dark man. Then he wakes up.

Alipate's dream is widely discussed in Tovu. The tall man has appeared in other people's dreams; all stress the darkness of his countenance. Alipate's dream is taken as evidence that it will not be easy to learn the conditions of Jone's death, and that the matter will not be cleared up soon. There are "dark," evil forces at work, one old man says. He doesn't say where these forces reside, but Tovu, along with Ogo and Momoto, are clearly implied.

161

But it's another series of dreams which set Tovu closer to the sharp edge of *rere*. These dreams are all brought to Tevita, sometimes from other parts of Kali, and with the *yaqona* that accompanies them, each person requests that Tevita prevent the dream from unfolding into reality. All these dreams predict further trouble for Tovu, very serious trouble.

One morning, Tevita and I are sitting in his house, preparing for a fishing trip later that afternoon when the tide comes in. Tevita's younger brother comes in with two *yaqona* and a letter. He is a messenger from Vairusi, who lives in a village on the other side of Kali Island from Tovu, and whose son goes to the Tovu school and used to work for Jone. Vairusi and Jone were good friends as well as relatives.

Tevita's brother offers the *yaqona* on Vairusi's behalf, as family matters have kept Vairusi occupied at home. One *yaqona* is for Vairusi's son, who attends school in Suva; Vairusi wishes Tevita to bless his school year. The second *yaqona* is for a dream Vairusi had, which he wants Tevita to interpret and if necessary prevent being realized.

Tevita accepts both *yaqona*, and as is his custom, simply puts them on the shelf behind him. No *yaqona* is mixed, but by accepting them, Tevita agrees to do his healing work as requested — either silently now or perhaps at some later time.

Tevita reads the letter from Vairusi in which he tells his dream.

"Damn," Tevita blurts out. "Lots of dreams, lots of problems. Lots of things from the devil. And lots of cases!"

He turns to me. "I'm planning to go to Suva soon, but with all these cases coming to me, I don't know what to do…. When I'm away, I'm going to have people start coming to you." Tevita is smiling, but only half joking. He watches me, looking for my reaction. I feel unsure. I'm not ready to help in that way — or am I? But if Tevita does want me to help in that way, he'll ask me again. Then I'll see.

Tevita reads Vairusi's letter once more, then hands it to me. "What do you think?" he asks. "I think you can know the meaning of this dream."

Does he really want my opinion? What do I know about the Fijian interpretation of dreams? But I read the letter.

"I dreamed that I was riding in a boat with Jone," the letter begins.

"We are going down a stream, one that has trees on both sides. It is getting narrower. Jone is driving and I am sitting in the front, facing him. He turns up the power and we are going fast, then faster and faster. I get up to tell him to slow down, and an overhanging branch knocks me in the head, throwing me violently into the stream, where I drown." The letter ends, "Could you tell me the meaning of this dream?"

"Well, what do you think, Rusi?"

"I don't know what to say. I'm not even sure I understand all the Fijian words."

"It's hard for you, I know," Tevita agrees, "but I'd just like to know your opinion."

"I'm not sure what to say…I mean, I know something about the Western interpretation of dreams, but dreams in Fiji…"

I look down, trying to avoid Tevita's request, but his unyielding silence shapes it even louder. I can't evade it.

"Well…it's hard to speak about the details of this dream, but it certainly gives a general message of trouble. There is a foreboding in the air, as the stream gets narrower and narrower, and the boat goes faster and faster. Then something disastrous happens — something sudden and disastrous. And all because things aren't being done properly; the boat shouldn't be going so fast in that narrow, tree-lined stream."

"Yes, Rusi, you're right. The dream certainly spells trouble. It's a real problem. It's a terrible problem because it is just like the three dreams I heard about last night. Each dream means the same thing: there will be another death in Tovu."

"You see, Rusi, in each of these dreams there is a death, and in each the death comes suddenly, as if with a bang. Like in the dream my helper Eroni brought here last night. Eroni dreamed Jone was walking across the bridge to the school, and he suddenly falls off and drowns. Eroni is walking behind him, and as he crosses the bridge the same thing happens to him."

"It's a really serious problem…very serious," Tevita repeats. He's preoccupied now, talking as much to himself as to me.

"Why must there be a third death here in Tovu?"

"Rusi, there are lots of things of the devil here."

163

Tevita goes no further. Suliana calls out that the children have come home from school for lunch. "Come eat, please eat with us." Thanking him, I excuse myself, as I want to eat with our children back home. "Then come back after lunch," he says, "and we can continue our talk then."

After lunch, plans have changed. Tevita is going to Ogo for a healing session. An old man there had a dream he wants Tevita to interpret.

"I'll go there alone," he says. "Eroni will stay here in Tovu because a very sick man is coming today from the other side of Kali Island for treatment, and Eroni must do the healing work here. Rusi, I wish that you'd be able to drink *yaqona* with Eroni today. Keep the *yaqona* going in my house until I return from Ogo, sometime during the night."

"I will...I will." I'm grateful that Tevita has asked for my help; I'm now learning what it is I can do.

It is past midnight when Tevita returns. The *yaqona* has been alive in his absence. We sit and visit for one more *tanoa* with him, and then the *yaqona* is over. It's late. We're all tired. The healing work is shut down for the night.

Two days later I go to Tevita's house to see him before he leaves for Suva. I'm beginning to feel this idea of a third death in Tovu as a concrete fear, and now Tevita is leaving — Tevita who is our protection. I go to Tevita's to say goodbye, but like others, I also go to him for some understanding of events, some help with my fears. I fear for my family and myself, for our very lives. I take a *yaqona* to ask for help.

"What can we do?" I ask him. "What can we do about this third death?"

Hearing myself form that question, I realize how scared I am. A part of me struggles to keep a distance; this stuff about people killing each other through *vakatevoro* is Fijian stuff, I can still rationalize. But there is no depth to that assurance. I'm vulnerable, my family is vulnerable, all of us here in Tovu are vulnerable. Even though part of me says it isn't "real," that isn't my stronger side. It isn't me, Rusiate. My rational view of things, the linchpin of my Western socialization, is something I now only carry, not what I am. At the same time, I'm not hysterical or chaotic; I know at my center that I can be strong and work for my protection.

"But what can we do about this third death?" I ask again, as Tevita has slipped into his own world of thoughts.

Tevita replies calmly: "You don't have to worry, Rusi, because you are a Westerner (*kai valagi*)."

"But I don't feel like a Westerner; I feel Fijian (*kai viti*)…that's how I feel," I immediately reply, absorbing the depth of the threat I now face through being Fijian.

"Yes, I know what you're saying is true." Tevita nods. "I know that is true, my friend. And so, Rusi, you'll just have to do what all of us Fijians must do. Stay close to the *yaqona,* and be straight in your behavior. That will protect you and your family."

CHAPTER 13

Conversations with Ratu Noa (Suva)

"Something is wrong with all of Ogo."

Going to Suva brings some relief from the intensity of the events in Tovu during the last two months. Though the rhythms of everyday life have resumed, the tensions and fears associated with Jone's death form an undercurrent, periodically disrupting the flow of events. People are particularly edgy because of the now commonly held assumption that there will be a third death in Tovu. The dreams predict it. We all wonder whether the work of Tevita will be able to prevent it.

I report the latest news about Tovu to Ratu Noa, describing the dreams that were brought to Tevita and his interpretation.

"What can we do about these dreams?" I wonder.

"This is a difficult situation, Rusiate. Tevita is right in his interpretation; the dreams predict another death. But whether that will actually happen or not is a complex matter."

"How can we know whether or not it will happen?" I stop short, suddenly aware of the implication of my question. "I guess it's not reasonable to be told what the future will bring...." My voice trails off.

"Yes, Rusiate, you're right about that," Ratu Noa replies. "What will happen depends on many things."

"But what can we do to influence the way things develop?"

"On that matter, Tevita is right again. It's simply as we have always said: be straight and stay close to the *yaqona*. That is your defense, your protection. It is not a guarantee…but it is all we humans can do. The rest is up to the *Vu*."

Ratu Noa sits back in his silence. There is no more to be said. As he always emphasizes, to say more than we know is not right.

We drink another round of *yaqona*, comfortable in the quietness.

Then Ratu Noa leans forward, anticipating talk. Stillness. He waits several moments, then teases me: "If you come all the way to Suva just to sit silently, what am I to say? I can only talk when I can see what it is you want or need to know. So fire away — ask me questions so I can continue on. Otherwise we'll sit here and people will think we're just stupid."

Ratu Noa and I often sit quietly, communicating through silence. That is how he teaches. But I know he also wants to convey certain knowledge in words, and that is the direction he now wants to pursue.

"I can't bear to have others think we're stupid — especially me, with all my advanced degrees," I say. "So here goes."

"Now that's what I like to hear!" he retorts playfully.

"Could you tell me more about the dreams that patients bring to you?" My question is real, and honest, but the special intensity of our initial discussion — where immediate personal survival was the issue — has loosened its grip.

"Some patients come with dreams that are completely unconnected to their sickness; other patients come with dreams connected to their sickness," Ratu Noa declares. "And there are two kinds of dreams connected to sickness. One kind is a bad dream or a dream that comes from the bad side, where the cause of their sickness is *vakatevoro*. In this bad dream the cause of their sickness will be revealed in opposite form. The second kind is a good dream, where the cause of the sickness is not *vakatevoro*. In this good dream, the cure for the sickness will be revealed in a straight manner. And I can tell the difference between all these kinds of dreams."

Ratu Noa stresses this last point. Knowledge is useless unless one knows what to do with it; only then does it become wisdom.

"I'll give you an example," he continues. "If it's a bad dream, where the cause of the sickness is from *vakatevoro*, the patient might dream that he shouldn't go to a healer, but just take such and such an herb, mixing it in this way or that. If the patient follows what his dream tells him, he will get worse. But if the patient goes to a healer and the healer knows his work, the healer will right away know it's a dream from the bad side, and will do just the opposite of what the dream says in order to help that patient. If it's a good dream, the patient will dream of me and come straight to me for help, and I'll give him the proper herb.

"That's the difference, Rusiate, and it's a big difference. Because these bad things come on very quickly and very easily into your mind, but the good things usually come on very slowly." Ratu Noa leans toward me. "And that's why *you* must know this difference." He sits back.

"And I'll tell you another difference. Some dreams are true, some are false. Some patients you can't cure, and you wonder what to do. You might drink *yaqona,* then fall asleep and dream the correct treatment, and then wake up in five minutes. This is a true dream — truly connected to the case. The false dream might occur after you eat a lot and you just sleep and sleep...and dream a lot.

"Rusiate, prepare the *yaqona,* and as you drink the *bilo,* ask [*kerekere*] the *Vu* about the cause of the illness or death. Then later in a dream you'll be told the cause and what to do. Rusiate, you try this.

"All of this takes practice — practice and experience. Through long experience you can distinguish between the true and false dream. And it is very important for you to tell which is which.

"We healers work in different ways," he continues. "In junior-grade work, the treatment and other things come to healers in their dreams. But in the more senior-grade work, healers communicate directly with the *Vu;* they don't have to go through dreams. These higher-level healers actually hear the words of the *Vu* and see what others can't see about treatments and healing and other things. Rusiate, this junior-grade healing is an apprenticeship period, but you'll come up to the senior grade if you're true and honest and follow the straight path. The straight and honest person can enter the everlasting life of *Kalou.*

"Like right now, as I talk with you, Rusiate, I actually hear from the

Vu words telling me what is your desire and what is the purpose of your research. Rusiate, truth and honesty are very important. Your work is difficult, but it becomes easy as you follow the straight path, acting true and honest in it, and as your faith deepens."

The word *dina*, "truth," keeps arising in our talks. *Dodonu*, "straight," as well as *vakabauta*, "faith" or "belief," also come up repeatedly. I feel discouraged; I know what must be done yet am not always able to do it. "It takes practice, practice and long experience," Ratu Noa keeps telling me, and his words are reassuring. But I can't escape the idea that what is necessary is something I already know — though more with my head than my heart.

"I don't know, Ratu Noa, but tonight I have only a few questions. When we first talked I had lots of questions — but I think that was because I didn't know much then."

"I want you to know a lot more, Rusiate, a lot more."

"That's also what I want. But I'm still very young in this teaching."

"You're right. But it's coming on. Remember, this work comes on slowly."

"I'm not sure how to ask you this..." I hesitate, searching for the right words. "Maybe I'll just put it generally. Could you tell me more about Jone's death? And where does Ogo fit into the picture? Tovu people keep accusing them of wrongdoing."

Ratu Noa straightens up; he has a lot to say about Ogo. Over the years, long before the development of the fishing scheme, the Ogo people have often turned to him for healing help. Not only do they respect him greatly as a healer, but they are also related to him.

"There must be something behind the Ogo fishing business," Ratu Noa begins; "something bad that Tevita doesn't know about. Maybe that's why Ogo people are being suspected in this Jone case. There are three ancient burial sites (*sava*) in Ogo. While the fishing scheme mangers are taking *yaqona* to Tevita, requesting help in their business venture, something else is going on back in Ogo; someone is serving other *Vu* for evil purposes at one of those sacred sites. We'll test out this idea. Tevita will stop accepting *yaqona* from those Ogo fishing boat people and we'll see what happens.

169

"You know, everyone in Ogo is supposed to be part of that fishing project, even though that group of younger men is most active, and has actually taken control. And something is wrong with all of Ogo in regard to this Jone affair, not just with the fishing venture. Something is wrong with the whole community structure. And it's an old problem. Ogo people are in the same lineage group (*yavusa*) as the people of the island to the north, and the leader of both islands should be the chief living in that northern island. But the Ogo people always want to be separate, and not led by that northern chief. That's not the way it should be.

"And now added to this old problem is a new one: Ogo itself is split in two. Even though the fishing business should be for all of Ogo, one faction runs it. And the younger people in that faction don't fully respect the traditional village structure. The older people want the business run through the traditional structure. They want the old chief to be in charge. It's this second faction of older people, cut out from the fishing business, who are serving the *Vu* badly in order to undercut that business.

"It's not a good situation, Rusiate. The Ogo people are inflicting wounds among themselves. And they will get hurt if they overstep the authority of a chief."

I sit and listen...and listen. Here is a detailed explanation of the events at Tovu which have frightened so many of us.

Ratu Noa barely pauses as a round of *yaqona* is served, drumming his fingers on the floor, not nervously, but as if to keep his engine running.

"People who serve the *Vu* for evil purposes are very clever. They're hard to locate. They mix with others and drink *yaqona* just like ordinary people. Or so it seems. Because these evil people do little things to turn the *yaqona* to their evil purposes. They may hold the *bilo* so that one or two of their fingers go into the *yaqona*, or they may pick at some of the little pieces of *yaqona* which settle to the bottom of the *bilo*, so that some of the *yaqona* dribbles off their fingers before they drink the *bilo*. When their fingers touch the *yaqona* before they drink it, then their *Vu* are drinking the *yaqona* before they are. That's how these people can serve their *Vu* to help them realize their bad intentions."

Now I feel nervous. Though I want to hear the details of how this

170

vakatevoro is done, even the names of the evildoers in Ogo, like others in Tovu, I'm also afraid of what I may hear. As Eroni put it, "We all want to know who's responsible for the deaths, but — I don't know....What would we do if we knew? What do you say to someone who may be accused but is one of your relatives?"

"And this is what happened at Ogo." Ratu Noa pushes on, not rushing, but not leaving space between his words either. "That faction of older people performed a ceremonial thanksgiving to thank the *Vu* for helping them do *vakatevoro*. In a thanksgiving to the *Vu*, someone must die — that is what you give in return for the *Vu*'s enabling you to do *vakatevoro*. That older faction purposely chose the celebration of the launching of the boat as the time to do the thanksgiving ceremony. They wanted to confuse people into thinking the two deaths were because of the new boat and its launching. Actually the deaths were a thanksgiving. And these deaths strengthen the power of that evildoing *Vu*.

"The people who do this *vakatevoro* stuff are smart. They work at cross-purposes to the rest of the people, without the others even knowing it. And that's what happened in Ogo, the night they were drinking *yaqona* and Jone died, and the night they were drinking *yaqona* and Jone's sister died. When everyone's drunk, that's when evil can best be done.

"But there are other factors at work, Rusiate. The leaders of the Ogo fishing scheme went to my mother before they launched their boat. They asked her for a card reading so they could see what the future would bring. That card reading showed a death had already been sealed for Ogo. That means all the preparatory work had been completed in Ogo by evildoers. When those fishing business leaders learned of the impending death, and learned it was to be closely connected with their boat, they requested that my mother ask the *Vu* to deflect the death from them and their boat. They actually requested that the death be stopped, perhaps not realizing that once a death is sealed it can only be deflected to another. That request contributed to one of those Jone deaths.

"Now there will be a new plan. Only one Ogo person at a time will be allowed to take *yaqona* to Tevita and ask for his help. That person will be Tevita's helper who lives in Ogo. When those business leaders come to

Tevita in a group with their request for help, in Fijian custom, Tevita must respect them all. He is ashamed to tell off any one of them who may be coming for a bad or improper purpose. It's easier for a person to direct the *yaqona* for an evil purpose when he is part of a group; the evil is then hidden. But Tevita will not be embarrassed to tell his Ogo helper whether a particular request for help is proper or not.

"Tevita is too generous in not telling people outright what they should or shouldn't do." Ratu Noa seems almost sad. "Tevita doesn't realize how much trouble and pain his generosity will cause. He doesn't even know what's behind all the *yaqona* that's being offered to him on behalf of the Ogo fishing business.

"I know those Ogo people better," Ratu Noa continues, with added intensity. "Yes, I know them. I know about an older case of *vakatevoro* in Ogo, where someone died, and I know about lots of other things that explain the present case of Jone's death. For example, years ago, four men were sailing in a traditional Fijian canoe from Tovu to Ogo. They capsized and are still missing. Tovu and Ogo have never been straight since then."

Unfolding the different aspects of the circumstances surrounding the deaths, Ratu Noa creates a many-layered density of understanding. Though part of me is trying to fit the pieces together, perhaps omitting contradictory evidence, I resist. The question "Who is responsible for the deaths?" is being reshaped. The actors in the events mock unity as they each seem to call out his or her own explanation, all the while denying the validity of other interpretations. Ogo's communal violation of tradition by breaking away from the neighboring northern island, the *vakatevoro* of the older Ogo faction, the fishing group's request to Ratu Noa's mother to deflect the predetermined death, the improper acts of some of the fishing group itself, the ill-fated canoe trip and "lots of other things": all form an elusive package whose elements constantly realign to offer another perspective. But everything points to Ogo. Now there is a new ingredient of concern. Tevita's generosity is exposed as his vulnerability — which makes all of us in Tovu more vulnerable. Ogo seems suddenly, even dangerously close to Tovu.

It's as if Ratu Noa reads my mind. "I can shut down the effects of all that *yaqona* the Ogo people bring to Tevita right here from Suva," he

172

affirms, "and that will be the end of that whole Ogo fishing scheme. I know the *Vu* of Ogo very well, and that *Vu* is under control from here.

"Tevita will see only his Ogo helper and will stop the *yaqona* if he has to — and the persons responsible for the evildoing will suffer. It's Tevita's good powers that provide the balance in this situation.

"These changes must begin right away." Ratu Noa seems pressured. "Can we make a tape to Tevita for you to take him when you return to Tovu tomorrow? On that tape I will explain to him, in detail, about the new plan."

We put a blank tape into my recorder. Ratu Noa talks for more than ten minutes to Tevita, facing the tape recorder as if it actually is Tevita. The message completed, I put the tape in my pocket.

"Now, Rusiate, tell me what else is happening in Tovu. How are you and your family getting along?"

I describe what our days are like, how I'm combining living in the village, including daily activities like fishing, with my research and practice. "The parts all blend together," I observe. "But I do wonder sometimes how healing and ordinary life mix?"

"It's not hard...once you get the knack." Ratu Noa's tone is encouraging, not at all patronizing. "Your healing work might take only fifteen minutes. You set a time and keep to that schedule. When the time is up, you're finished.

"I understand you want to know things, Rusiate, and sometimes to know just by asking questions. But there are two sides to your research — asking questions, and practice. You must go ahead and practice, and then you'll be told by the *Vu*, 'Do this,' or 'Do that'; 'That's wrong,' or 'Do it this way.' If you're good at this healing work, you'll hear the actual words spoken into your ears. Once you can follow these words properly, everything will be easy for you. Our *Vu* dislike every form of dirty play (*dukadukali*). All the *Vu* want you to do is be straight. Your progress, Rusiate, is in the right direction."

The knowledge Ratu Noa conveys, and the directions he gives, are compelling. As I learn how to travel the straight path, I no longer wonder as much how far I've come. Part of me, of course, still wants to know if I'm "doing well." But I see the path more clearly now, and with the events in Tovu, that vision is necessary.

"And now I want to tell you an old story about *yaqona* and its origins." Ratu Noa alters the mood without diluting it. "Actually there are three stories. One says *yaqona* originated in Tonga; a second, that it came from the grave of an old chief in Vanua Levu, here in Fiji. But it is the third story that's the true one.

"*Yaqona* actually came to us with our *Vu* when they first came to Fiji. There was then just one type of people in the world, known as the Manu. These people were the first to know *Kalou*. These Manu people lived on high mountains. Whenever they wanted to speak with *Kalou*, they would go to the mountain, pull the *yaqona* root, and mix it as we do now as a means of communicating with *Kalou*. You can read about the Manu people in a book called *The Law of the Manu*, which also contains all the details about *yaqona*. But today — today such people are hard to find.

"In the time of Noah, the earth was covered with floodwaters. When he searched for land, he sent a dove out three times. The first time the dove flew and came back with nothing. The second time the dove brought a small branch. The third time the dove left for good, showing Noah there was land." Ratu Noa seamlessly joins Fijian and biblical material, moving us easily across different segments of traditional history. "So it is in the traditional chiefly *yaqona*: there are three *tanoa*, three rounds of *yaqona*. The *tanoa* in which we serve our *yaqona* was actually first made by Noah: *ta-Noah, tanoa*. Traditionally the first and second *tanoa*, the first two rounds of *yaqona* served, are solely for the chiefs. That is the *yaqona* used to communicate with the *Vu*. Just like in the days of the Manu, the *yaqona* was only for *Kalou*. The third *tanoa*, the third round of *yaqona*, is for everybody."

It's late; less than an hour remains before the last bus back into town. It's too far to walk, and as usual, there's no room for me to stay at Ratu Noa's. There are a few things left to discuss. We're in no hurry, but we know our talk is ending.

"Ratu Noa, before I go back to Tovu, do you have any new instructions for me?"

174

"Do you feel things are going well since the last time we talked?"

"Yes."

"Good. There'll come a time, Rusiate, when you're feeling good and you want to drink *yaqona* — then you must drink it. You must drink it right away! If you're in the middle of your work, leave it aside, and join some who are already drinking or ask someone to drink with you. Whenever you feel thirsty for *yaqona* you must drink it. Because the one who is behind the healing work is the one who is making you crave that *yaqona;* that is the one who will drink with you. And that one is going to teach you better than an instructor like me. This *yaqona* is the missing link between us and *Kalou.* That's why I tell you to study this *yaqona* carefully. This is my advice to you at this stage."

I know the "one" he refers to. His *Vu,* he insists, is the real teacher.

"Rusiate, you're here for only two years, unlike us who train for many years. Since you're here for only a short time, you must work hard. So by the time you've finished here, you'll be well equipped on your return to America with the answer to your research about mental illness.

"Carry on the research you're doing, Rusiate. Interview as many healers as you can — though with some you'll just be wasting your time."

"I know what you mean. I know some of the healers I visited aren't real. Some are just fooling people, and some are doing bad things. But I thought that maybe by talking to those who no longer have the power, I could find out how healers lose their power."

"But you'll be wasting your time." Ratu Noa repeats. "Why ask someone about healing who doesn't know how to heal?"

He makes sense, and I've already revised my original research design of talking to "good" and "bad" healers, effective and ineffective ones. Moreover, I've already visited enough of the ineffective ones, and the practice part of my work focuses on the ones who are effective.

"You probably see many of these false healers here in Suva, Rusiate. Lots of them are coming up, but they don't last. Their spouses are unemployed and they do the healing work because of financial pressures. These false healers too quickly say that every illness they see is caused by *vaka-tevoro.* Even though the patients themselves may be to blame for their sickness because they violated a taboo, these false healers relate the problem to someone else's jealousy. When they say it's *vakatevoro*, they ensure patients will need their help, and they demand money from patients.

"Rusiate, you cannot demand money in this work. But money will come to you when you practice in the right way. There is that kind of return. But it is taboo to ask where the money comes from. When you need it, it will be there."

Ratu Noa changes direction, while still in motion: "Rusiate, two months ago when you were here in Suva, I met you just before you went back to Tovu. You were walking along the harbor, coming from the hill in the north, going toward City Hall. I spoke to you...but you didn't hear me or answer me."

I've never seen Ratu this way. He's playing with me, testing me.

"I guess I didn't see you," I reply innocently and a bit ashamed. It would have been terribly disrespectful not to respond to his greeting.

"You were wearing shorts and a sports shirt and had a pack on your back," he continues, enjoying my befuddled look. "I met you just as you were turning into the City Hall grounds."

"Where were you?" I ask, hoping there is some explanation that can justify this missed meeting.

"I was somewhere! In something! In a car — or a bus — or an airplane — or just plain walking around. What's the difference? I met you, Rusiate, just as you were turning into the City Hall grounds."

Looking at me as I squirm toward understanding, Ratu Noa only smiles. "I've told you that we healers travel in many ways. We don't need to touch the earth, either." We both start to laugh. It's okay. I haven't yet learned to see him when he travels in the spiritual realm, or when he sees me in a vision.

"The time will come when we can have that conversation you never picked up on." Ratu Noa's tone is confident: "The time will come."

It is time for me to leave. Ratu Noa sends me away with a few final words. "Rusiate, you need patience and courage in your work. There is a Fijian saying: a submerged reef is the most dangerous because it is there that the boat can go aground. In this work we are very limited in time.

But I dare not open the door for you continually. Too many deep things too quickly, and you won't truly understand anything — that can sink you. Even though our time is limited, we must take time. Proceed carefully. Step by step. As you see things more clearly, I'll give you more to see."

CHAPTER 14

Monday Night Healing
(Tovu)

As December meets the new year and January emerges, *yaqona* continues to offer its challenges. After six months of living in Tovu, it has become my guide.

Drinking *yaqona* is easy; nearly every night in Tovu there are one, sometimes two houses in which *yaqona* is being served. Known as the person who wants to learn about *mana*, I become an object of humor. As the evening of drinking wears on and people are mellowed with the effects of the *yaqona*, someone might call out to me after finishing his *bilo*, "Rusi, come here. Just look into my eyes. That's where you'll see plenty of *mana*." Or another might comment after I finish a *bilo*, "That's the way, Rusi. *That's* the way. If you really want to find the *mana*, Rusi, just keep drinking and you'll become drunk with *mana*."

This is the kind of *yaqona* drinking that Ratu Noa said is "ordinary." It is a time to visit, and that's what I do, night after night, entering further into the texture of village life. It helps that through these nightly sessions my Fijian is continually improving. "You're a real Fijian," others say, seeing me sit easily in the proper Fijian manner hour after hour. Usually Westerners struggle even with sitting on the floor, let alone in the cross-legged position. My sitting in the Fijian way is a statement of connectedness. "That's the only way one should sit," I have taken to responding, feigning utmost seriousness. "So why should I be excused? I don't want to be driven out of Tovu!"

178

In teasing me, people are taking me in. Being the butt of a joke is a way of giving and receiving, valued as much as the telling of the joke. After my initial discomfort, I'm glad to be able to exchange in this way.

I reach a new stage in this exchange when they try to pull off my *sulu*. As the *yaqona* drinking moves toward evening and people are feeling more relaxed, the joking increases. A standard ploy among the men is to reach over unexpectedly and try to pull the *sulu* from another man who is getting up to leave, usually to relieve himself outside. I always laughed when this happened, especially at the contortions people would make to keep their *sulu* on while pretending that nothing was happening. But as I feel my own *sulu* being tugged off, I don't laugh; I'm too busy holding it in place. Once having arisen successfully with *sulu* intact, I laugh, catching up to the others. Now that my *sulu* too is regarded as fair game, I resolve to be sure to wear shorts under it, as some others do. I may feel more and more like a Fijian, but I still don't trust my ability to tie my *sulu* in an unfailingly nonslip manner, as most others seem to.

Everyone in Tovu knows about *mana,* though with the exception of people like Tevita, most experience its effects rarely, and work with it even less frequently. Their joking about *mana* and being drunk seems to be a way of acknowledging my serious interest in *mana* while keeping some distance from it. But the joking never goes too far, for fear that *mana* itself will be spoken of disrespectfully. People are careful to maintain me as the butt of the joke, never the *mana.*

Ordinary *yaqona* drinking is easy. "Staying close to the *yaqona,*" that is, using *yaqona* to open up the potential for healing, is more elusive. Tevita's Monday night healing sessions continue to be irregular. Other matters often take precedence: an important village ceremony, an unexpected visitor, a fishing expedition, or simply the fact that Tevita is too tired. But increasingly I understand another thing Ratu Noa spoke of: the important aspect of the healing work is the healer's attitude toward *yaqona* rather than the particular ceremonies performed; it is the way the healer lives, the degree to which he or she is *dodonu.*

Soon after I arrive back in Tovu, I meet with Tevita and play for him Ratu Noa's taped message. Though he understands the message, Tevita seems disturbed. "This new plan won't be easy," he reflects.

Tevita is able to keep the healing work alive whether or not he performs a healing ceremony. The high regard in which he is held in Tovu stems as much from his being an honest and kind person as from his knowledge, making his healing work all the more appreciated. Whenever there is a medical crisis, Tevita is always available. "We'd all be sick if it wasn't for him," says Asenati,

Today is Monday. Floating near the top of the sky, the sun drips heat over our bodies like an overturned can of thick orange paint. Most of the men and some of the women are working at the Tovu pine scheme. We're up on the ridge, putting pine seeds into the little black plastic bags where they will germinate into seedlings, ready for transplanting. In his characteristic way, Tevita leads not so much by telling people what to do as by doing himself and setting an example. Working in one area, he stays with a single task, rather than moving from one to another. As a result, he doesn't directly supervise many of the workers.

People are rising from their kneeling positions next to the seedlings; the lunch break will be any time now. Toward midafternoon, after the sun's brutal shine has faded, we'll come back to work several more hours. And already I know that tonight, Monday night, there will be no "regular" healing ceremony at Tevita's. By the end of the long workday, his energy will be gone.

Monday night healing ceremonies. I keep remembering how Ratu Noa emphasized their importance. We celebrate these ceremonies in an amazing variety of ways, rarely having them in Tevita's house, and even more rarely performing the full ceremony. But Monday night remains special, the time to mark my commitment to the practice. The words of Ratu Noa and Tevita guide me: the first two *bilo* of *yaqona*, anywhere, anytime, can be "your ceremony."

"Rusi, I'm pretty tired tonight," Tevita begins that evening when I arrive at his house. I know what will follow next. "I don't think we'll have a ceremony here. But let's go over to Luke's to drink some *yaqona*. Let's have our *yaqona* there. Just a *bilo* or two. Then we can leave."

"Sure...sure. Sounds good to me."

"Sure! Sure!" Suliana joins in. She knows her husband well. She knows Tevita's healing work; she also knows how he relates to the *yaqona*.

"Sure — sure," she continues, enjoying Tevita's sheepishness. "Just a *bilo* or two...or two...or two! When did you ever see Tevita leave after two *bilo*?" she asks me, looking teasingly at her husband.

Suliana is right. Tevita is not one to stop; in fact, he is one of the biggest *yaqona* drinkers in Tovu. I often think about this. According to what Ratu Noa says, Tevita does a lot of drinking just to socialize, unrelated to his healing work. I know at times Tevita seems to me to drink *yaqona* to excess. In that he's quite ordinary — just another Tovu man. But then, who am I to judge? Do I know what is happening when Tevita drinks *yaqona*? Tevita is a very sociable man in his quiet way; he enjoys the company of others and is well liked in the village because he never puts on airs. Drinking *yaqona* is the Tovu way of socializing.

The *yaqona* has already begun at Luke's. A round is served after Tevita and I arrive. Seated next to me, Tevita is served before I am. I feel the intensity of his drinking, and that helps bring intensity to my *bilo*. We are praying together for each other's strength, each in his own way, silently, within ourselves, to the *Vu* behind the healing work.

The talk is animated. People are relaxing after the day of hot, hard work. Tevita laughs with the others; so do I.

Without a ripple of motion, I'm yanked out of the conversation as another round of *yaqona* is served, the second *bilo* for Tevita and me. Drawn back to Tevita as he takes the *yaqona*, I pray with him and through him for the work. Now the *yaqona* comes to me; it's my turn. Praying, deep inside, while just drinking *yaqona*. And it's over. We loosen our invisible bond and stretch out into the room, rejoining the flow of conversation. The "ceremony" is over.

But not the drinking. People are thirsty; the third round comes soon after. Then the fourth, and fifth. And on into the evening.

Tevita and I are spending more time with one another. I generally know where he is and what he's doing. By keeping in contact, we can work together more. When he goes fishing or I want to go, we usually end up going together. If I'm not around, he'll send a message to me. But for the healing work it is often different. If I want to help him with that work, I have to be there, close to him, knowing without his saying so, that it's time to work. It's my responsibility to be "at hand" as a healer's helper, a *liga ni wai*, literally "the hand of medicine."

We work together on Nanise, the daughter of Tevita's older brother. Nanise is nearly thirty. Her husband, Vili, is a stocky man with strong, bony features. They have three children; their youngest, nearly two, suffers from a birth defect in his lower body.

Nanise has had a history of anxiety attacks since she was a little girl. A thin, frail woman, fear has determined the shape and lines of her face. When she smiles, she no longer looks like herself. Often too weak to haul water or wood, she spends day after day at home, doing light cooking outside or staying within, closing out the day with shut windows. There Nanise cares for her afflicted child, who lies on the floor throughout the day, his withered pelvis and legs anchoring him to the ground. Sliding him gently along the mats that cover the floor, she holds his shoulders in her hands. She is convinced his immobility is but another sign of her own condition. "I'm sick, and as long as I can remember it's been this way.... I guess I'm just meant to suffer."

Nanise's father has asked for my help. He knows that my training in the United States is in treating persons with mental disturbances. It's been difficult to explain to people in Tovu that I'm not a "doctor" in their sense of the word, that is, a medical doctor. I say that my specialty is the mind, not the body, realizing this distinction must sound absurd to them. But I don't want people to think I can treat things like cuts and wounds.

When I reach Nanise's house, though it is barely midafternoon, the door is closed. Not the Fijian way — where only at night do you close the door, and then not to keep people out, but as protection against all the things the night can bring.

Once inside I'm swallowed by the darkness. Nanise lies on the bed, hidden in mosquito netting. Her father calls to her to tell her I'm here. She turns over on her side, then slowly, painfully emerges from inside the netting, dropping one foot over the bed, then the other. She sits on the edge of the bed a long time, then finally, wearily, lifts herself onto the floor. She moves like an old woman tired by time.

"I can't move these days. I just don't want to move." Nanise's voice is so low that the words barely crack the surface of hearing. With my Fijian still not totally fluent, I stretch toward her, seeking understanding while trying not to crowd into her delicately bounded space.

"I'm just afraid of going out. What might happen. You know, people here in Tovu can't be trusted." She pauses, sucking in air in what seems a fruitless effort to pump up her lungs. "And I can't breathe right. Sometimes I stop breathing…like I'm going to die. Just like I'm ready to die. I don't want to take a full breath because it might kill me."

The words come out in a stunted rhythm, as Nanise works to give voice to her feelings. She repeats herself again and again, not for emphasis, but because she is so preoccupied with her fears.

I begin slowly, choosing my words carefully so that I can accurately convey what I feel. Inoke isn't in Tovu to help with translating, and school is still in session, so the teachers are also unavailable. Nanise's oldest child, one of the best students in Tovu, knows a little English; but she's not here. I'm on my own. Perhaps it's just as well. What I want to say to Nanise is as much a message from my heart as it is clinical or psychological advice.

I talk to Nanise about her symptoms, affirming their reality, their devastating pain, the terror she feels. Then I ask her whether she is seeing Tevita. "Yes," she responds, her voice still barely audible.

"Well, Tevita and I, we work together. I'm really glad he's helping you. Anything I suggest to you should be done in cooperation with what he tells you. Tevita gives me guidance — I work under him."

I make certain that Nanise understands this basic point, that I'm working under Tevita's guidance. Only then can I offer her anything that comes from my own training. I can't undermine or put aside Tevita's work. I value it too much.

I continue talking with Nanise about her fears, beginning to examine with her the places, situations, and persons in Tovu which set them off. As we talk together, Nanise becomes less withdrawn; her mood lightens and she releases some of her tension, feeling more confident. "Maybe I can overcome this," she offers, "maybe…but I'm so afraid I might die. Sometimes at night I can't breathe. Where is my breath? It's hardly there…and I panic." Nanise repeats her earlier concerns, but now her voice is more measured, her tone more reflective. Her demons are in retreat.

Before I leave I show Nanise how to breathe deeply and gently, demonstrating with calm, deep breaths, indicating how my rib cage moves. She understands. I also show Vili, who came in several minutes ago, how he can massage her to help her relax and support her normal breathing. "These are breaths of life," I say. "With that you will not die. You will not die."

For the first time, Nanise smiles. "I'll try it…I'll try it." Her face relaxes into a calm stillness, unclasping the protective rigidity of her body.

"And keep going to Tevita," I remind her. "Keep going there, because I'm working under him."

Later, when I visit with Tevita, he nods his agreement throughout as I report on how I worked with Nanise. "That mental illness," he says, "it's not easy to fix. And with Nanise it's especially hard. For a long time she has suffered…from when she was a young girl and was hit by a car. She never recovered. She's been weak and fearful since then. All we can do is keep trying…but it's hard to fix.

"Rusi," he continues, "I want to ask you for some help. I'll be away next Monday. There's a meeting of pine scheme managers in Delana. I want to ask you to be my helper, to be with my other helpers Monday night at my place to run the healing ceremony."

Tevita's request is not entirely clear. Who does he want to "run" the session? I wonder. I don't feel prepared to do that. But I leave aside any questions. "Sure, Tevita, I'll try to help. I'll do the best I can."

That Monday I gather with Alipate and Eroni, and we perform the healing ceremony. No one is in charge. Eroni mixes the *yaqona*, and we all drink it. There are no ritual prayers offered of the kind Tevita makes when he has the more formal ceremony. But we are all praying, each in his own way. We are working together. When the healing *yaqona* is finished, we mix another *tanoa* and visit. When that *tanoa* is empty, we take our leave of each other. We've done our job — helping Tevita keep the healing *yaqona* alive for the week.

CHAPTER 15

Telephone to the *Vu*
(Delana)

Research with other healers throughout Bitu is easier now that Inoke has finished our boat, a sixteen-foot craft he designed and built himself. It is sturdy and fast, and Inoke is rightfully proud of his handiwork. Using a minimum of modern tools, he perpetuates the ancient skills of Fijian boat building.

As I travel I learn. Inoke is a demanding teacher. The first time we take our boat out on the open water, Inoke and Nasi accompany Lora, Eliki, Mere, and me. We're off to Delana to see Tomasi, the old healer who communicates explicitly with his *Vu*. The plan is that Inoke will drive our boat while Nasi, taking Mere, runs theirs. As she is warming up the motor, he comes aboard our boat, starts the engine, pulls up the anchor — then leaps over into his own boat, takes the steering wheel from Nasi, and he's off! Out of the bay, streaking toward the open ocean that lies between Tovu and Delana.

At first I'm too surprised to think; then my mind races into gear. Is this a joke? Is Inoke testing my reaction? No. He keeps going — and it's obvious he's not coming back. Soon his lead will be hard to follow. If I want to get to Delana, I've got to go with someone who knows the way around the reefs that lie ahead.

Now we too are off. It's my first time steering a boat...and I'm scared. My passengers are my two children, one of whom is only seven years old and can't swim well, and a young Fijian woman who says she can't swim at all.

But there's no time to be frightened; I've got to catch up to Inoke and follow in his wake. Something else takes over, and around the hidden reefs we swerve, into the open ocean, cutting through the waves at an angle that "calms" rather than "angers" them.

When we arrive at Delana, I'm mad at Inoke for leaving me — but also exhilarated. "Still," I mutter to myself, "that's no way to teach someone how to drive a boat. The risk was too great." And then I let Inoke know what I think.

He smiles. "It's okay, Rusi. I wouldn't have left you alone if I didn't think you could handle it. I saw you were doing all right."

Did he? I wonder.

The next day Inoke and I go along the coast over to Tomasi's, an elder, whose *mana* is considered very powerful. We anchor a ways down the shoreline from his village. Inoke takes the lead, scampering over a stretch of boulders strewn precariously along the shore, while I cautiously pick my way along the rocks. Boulders that shudder momentarily at Inoke's quick step threaten to dislodge as, ever over-careful, I try to find sure footing. Soon he's far ahead. Turning back, he yells out, "If you keep up that way you'll never make it. Don't be so cautious. Just move along. Move along so the rocks don't have a chance to really shake."

That makes sense on one level, but my mind continues to keep my body in check, and still I move too cautiously. The distance between me and Inoke lengthens. Then my body takes over. Soon I too am scampering over the rocks; just as each begins to teeter, I'm off it and on to the next.

Later that day, as I think back on this sprint with Inoke, I'm reminded of what Ratu Noa said: "On the straight path, you can't be double-minded. Once you see how something must be done, do it. Just do it — without turning back, without hesitation." Just do it; move right along.

We talk with Tomasi that afternoon. A small, nimble man, even in his late seventies Tomasi is one of the more vigorous and enterprising persons in his village. He maintains two planting areas, to which he must travel long distances over difficult paths, at times returning loaded with a heavy sack of crops. "Now that's a strong old man," people say of him admiringly. Tomasi also plays an important role in his village as the oldest man and a primary source of information about ritual and tradition. Though at times distant, he is gentle, fulfilling his grandfatherly part with special warmth. A grin softens his usually serious, sometimes fiercely inward expression.

It is in his healing work that Tomasi is more controversial. Unlike other rural healers, he can be heard communicating with his *Vu*. "It's my telephone to the *Vu*," he says, "my *mana*-wireless." Tomasi asks questions of the *Vu* aloud and seeks their advice, cocking his head as he listens, nodding his understanding, or looking confused when the message is unclear. He talks to the *Vu* as they talk to him — but you can hear only his side of the conversation.

In our first meeting he checks out the appropriateness of my research with his *Vu*. "This is Tomasi here. Can you hear me?" he calls out.

He pauses, his ear tilted toward some invisible sound receiver, then smiles. He's reached the *Vu*. "Just wanted to check out with you about helping on this research project here. Is it something good? Should I tell this man here about our healing work?"

A longer pause. Tomasi's brow wrinkles, and his face begins to show enough consternation to make me worry that our talk will not continue. Then he smiles again.

"Well, you'll be glad to hear," Tomasi announces, "that my *Vu* has thought carefully about the research and says it's good. So we can proceed."

Rural Fijians in areas like Bitu distrust this kind of open communication with the *Vu*. Such displays are common in the city, where healers are thought by village dwellers to put on a show and "exaggerate their powers." Any claims of explicit communication are considered boastful, pretentiously asserting that one's contact with the *Vu* is so strong and intimate that one will actually speak with the *Vu* in a public context. There is fear as well, fear of that implied power.

This is not the case with Tomasi. Those who know him well believe his communication is real. Ratu Noa agrees: "He knows how to talk with the *Vu*. That's what happens when you get experienced. But talking to the *Vu* aloud, as he does, demands great discipline. Tomasi is dealing with a lot of power, and because the *mana* he works with is so powerful, it's also dangerous. The more power you have, the more you're tempted to abuse that power. That's when the straight path gets very, very difficult. That's what Tomasi is struggling with."

I stay several days with Tomasi, talking with him, learning from him. Our affection grows. When a question is too difficult for him or he can't remember something he wants to say, he checks back with his *Vu*.

One afternoon Tomasi offers some opinions on Jone's death. He picks up on an idea that has been mentioned only in passing by a few old men of Tovu, that there was some earlier trouble in Jone's home village in Momoto.

"It's Jone's father," Tomasi says, "yes, his father. That man was a preacher. But even though he was a preacher, he acted improperly. And people were afraid to say anything. But eventually they spoke up, accusing him. And that man, Jone's father, stood up in church, at the pulpit from which he preached, and denied the accusations. 'If you are right in your accusations,' he said, 'let my descendants suffer.' He made that statement — from his church. If you speak that way publicly, and you are lying, you will pay. If you speak publicly about being straight and you don't struggle to actually be that way, you must face the consequences. You'll pay, just as if you asked for it — and Jone's father paid the price with his son's death."

Something about Tomasi's tone drives this explanation of Jone's death into my thoughts, precluding any questions. I am only left to ponder on it.

After supper on the fourth day, Inoke leaves to make the trip back to Delana. I spend the night alone with Tomasi.

We go to bed before midnight. In the early morning darkness, I hear the wooden floor squeak and open my eyes to see Tomasi, head bowed, slowly, lightly pacing across the room, illuminated periodically in a shaft of moonlight. He occasionally glances out the window onto the bay. For more than an hour he continues his journey.

With dawn, we both awaken. I'm not sure what I witnessed during the night. Was it a dream? Did it happen? The difference seems unimportant as the intensity of that quiet time remains.

We talk briefly over breakfast.

"Were you up last night?" I inquire.

"Yes, I get up these nights." Tomasi sighs. "When you're old, you know, it's sometimes hard to sleep. When I wake up I realize it's a good time to pray — and so I pray...and pray...and pray. Then when I'm tired, I lie down again."

The straight path, I learn, winds through the far aloneness of early morning darkness.

When I arrive back in Tovu, I ask Tevita about what Tomasi told me. He too has heard that Jone's father violated the trust of the people and the sanctity of the church to lie about his misdeeds. "I can't say what it was that he did wrong in the first place. But when he denied that wrongdoing in the church he was defying the *Vu*. And the *Vu* took up his dare and carried out the punishment, claiming the life of his son."

Stated outright like this, Tomasi's explanation is chilling.

"Rusi, are you going to Suva with me to see Ratu Noa?" Tevita suddenly asks.

This is the first I have heard about a proposed trip. My initial response is ambivalent; it seems like too much of an effort to make such a long trip, and there's so much work to do here in Tovu. Then I am jolted into awareness. How could I not go? Again I remember Ratu Noa's caution against being "double-minded."

Tevita and I will travel to Suva the next day. We'll catch a ride with the government boat anchored in Tovu Harbor which is returning to Viti Levu in the morning.

189

CHAPTER 16

Conversations
with Ratu Noa
(Suva)

*"Within every good thing there is an enemy;
in the bad things, there is no enemy."*

Tevita and I sit with Ratu Noa, drinking *yaqona*. A round is just finishing as Tevita completes his account of the recent happenings in Tovu. The Ogo fishing scheme group, Tevita explains, is not satisfied with Ratu Noa's plan to funnel all requests for Tevita's help through one person, Tevita's helper in Ogo. Specifically, it is Tevita's explanation of the plan they object to. Not wanting to hurt the feelings of others, Tevita finds it difficult to be as firm with the fishing group as Ratu Noa intended. It's especially hard to outline the reasons for the plan, which impute possible wrongdoing on the part of people living in Ogo. The fishing project managers want to talk directly with Ratu Noa for clarification. And Tevita will be present during that meeting.

Ratu Noa points to the *tanoa* that sits in front of him. "The true way to drink *yaqona* is just to have two *tanoa*. That's how it was done in the past. After the two *tanoa*, one more for telling stories [*veitalanoa*]. Then it's over. The stories were timed to last until this third *tanoa* was finished. But now people drink to excess, only to get drunk."

When I talk with Ratu Noa, we certainly drink a lot of *yaqona* — I've never kept count, but sometimes it seems like more than three *tanoa*. But though we drink a lot, we don't drink to get drunk. No matter how many *tanoa* we mix, we seem to talk about important things. The talk and the *yaqona* are intimately paired. The *yaqona* stimulates good talk, and good talk demands that we keep drinking *yaqona*. Maybe like the Monday night healing ceremonies, the ideal number of three *tanoa* can sometimes be more symbolic than literal. As long as we drink *yaqona* to stimulate an important exchange, it's as though we haven't drunk any more than three *tanoa*.

Ratu Noa is extremely careful around the *yaqona*. He encircles us within the dance of his service, the movement of the *bilo*, the flow of the *yaqona*. This is not like the drinking in Tovu. It is a form of worship.

"You know the saying 'Slow water runs deep'?" Ratu Noa asks, his words breaking into my silence.

"Yes."

"Well, it's like that with a good healer. You go slowly in this work; that's how you become powerful. You don't reveal everything to the people. Go slowly — tell them just what they should know, and don't multiply the truth.

"I know a lot about all the healers in Fiji, about their work and power. I know how many are in each area. And who is strong, and who is weak. I'll tell you this. The strong ones don't depend on the strength of their *Vu*. If a healer has a weak or little *Vu* behind his work, yet is faithful to that *Vu* and straight, he is more powerful than the healer who has a big *Vu* behind his work but isn't faithful to that *Vu* and deviates from the straight path. That latter healer becomes useless!"

Ratu Noa is talking more softly now, yet his voice is stronger. "Whenever you zigzag, your healing power is cut. Zigzag again, it's further cut. Zigzag continually, your power is lost. And when your power is lost, you should stop your work. If you insist on going on you'll kill someone, because the *mana* has left you. Only *mana* can heal.

"And I also know about those famous healers of the past, people like Apolosi and Navosa."

"Was Apolosi a good person or a bad one?" As soon as I ask that question I wish I could withdraw it. It is too direct, going against the Fijian value of not speaking against others in public.

"A *little* bit…" Ratu Noa hesitates, then completes his statement. "A little bit good."

"I'm sorry I asked such a Western-sounding question."

"That's okay, Rusiate; you're still learning. Now, Navosa was unique. He did real miracles. He resurrected people, just like Christ. Navosa was straight from the beginning until he died. But Apolosi was a little bad."

"A little bad?"

"He was very bad!" Ratu Noa's bluntness is surprising, but he is now speaking in the intimacy of his home. "Yes, that Apolosi was very bad. He wished to get rid of the British in Fiji, but he misused his power and followed the wrong path. If he had been straight, he could have gotten the British out.

"You know, Rusiate, even though I have the power (*kaukauwa*), my way is to conceal it. My wife and children don't even know what I'm telling you. If it hadn't been for your research and my desire to preserve knowledge for future generations, I wouldn't have revealed things to you. And above all, now that I'm telling you things, I must tell the truth. I don't want future generations to blame me for telling lies. Instead, they'll be proud to hear my words because they are words of truth.

"Rusiate, what remains for you to learn is how to call the *Vu* when you drink *yaqona*. And to know which *Vu* to call. Because wherever you are, in whatever part of the world, that *Vu* will be there after you call him.

"Let me explain more. The *yaqona* must be served in different ways to call different *Vu*; different *Vu* like *yaqona* prepared in different ways. I have my own way of serving the *Vu*. When I dip my *bilo* in the *tanoa*, it looks normal…but I do something special. That is my special way of calling the *Vu*. Special but always inconspicuous.

"When we call the *Vu*, Rusiate, it's like dialing a telephone. Automatically, the number rings on the other side."

Tevita nods his agreement. We exchange easy smiles. "Ratu Noa, could you talk about the tape you made for Tevita explaining how he should serve the Ogo people? When I arrived back in Tovu, I played it

for Tevita, but Inoke and I didn't fully understand your message."
Tevita's smile widens.

"It's just like a doctor writing a prescription; the common man doesn't understand its meaning. It's the same with that tape. Tevita knew its meaning while you and Inoke missed it at first.

"I told Tevita in my tape that the Ogo fishing project people shouldn't go to him as a group because their visit shouldn't be conspicuous. All of Kali already suspects they have done something evil that caused Jone's death, and if they go as a group, that will only raise further suspicions. Then, in the part you understood, I also told Tevita that if he sees them in a group, it becomes easier for one of them to hide bad intentions.

"You understand that message better now, Rusiate. But at first it remained beyond you and Inoke.

"And now I'll tell you the facts about Jone's death. The cause of Jone's death was Jone's father. The father was a minister but didn't truly serve *Kalou* — he switched to the other side. I wanted to tell you this on your last visit because it seemed everyone else was laying the blame on the Ogo people. The people in Jone's home village caught his father dancing for the devil at night [*meke ni vula*], and that shows he was worshiping the devil. In the morning, the villagers confronted Jone's father with what they saw. But he denied it. And then he made a special church service and prayed to *Kalou,* saying that if it was true that he was doing evil, he and all his children would face the consequences. 'May *Kalou* punish me and my children,' he said. And, as we see, that is what happened. Jone's father died. Last year two of his children died. This year, as you saw in Ogo, two more died.

"But for their part, the Ogo fishing scheme managers were very unrealistic. They shouldn't have invited people to come and celebrate the very day their new boat arrived in Ogo from Suva. And they must take responsibility for inviting Jone to the celebration. The invitation should have been for a later day, because when everyone is drunk, like at that celebration, that's when the *Vu* will do evil."

Here is a comprehensive explanation of the death of Jone and his sister, a full version of what Tomasi first broached and others in Tovu earlier

193

suggested. The Ogo group is criticized not for evil intentions but for bad judgment. Ratu Noa's explanation balances psychological issues with spiritual ones.

I realize that I don't even question the details regarding Jone's father's transgression and how Ratu Noa knows them. Perhaps the information was "given" to him from the "other side." As he keeps saying, knowledge is to be passed on, not exaggerated or questioned. Whatever the source, the explanation has solidity.

"I've helped the Ogo business venture from the very beginning," Ratu Noa says. "But I'll help only if it's a good cause. Because if I help a bad cause, I'll end up in the sea itself — I'll come to a bad end. Just like with your research, Rusiate — I help there because it too is a good cause."

A knock is heard at the door. "Come in...come in," Nawame calls from the other room. Four men from the Ogo fishing scheme enter, led once again by Jese. Jese presents their *sevusevu*, which Ratu Noa accepts in an unusually short and direct manner. He has been expecting them and wants to get to the point immediately.

Without any introductory pleasantries, Ratu Noa repeats to the new arrivals the story about how the taped message he sent Tevita was completely understood only by Tevita. "And what I told you last night, Jese, is what I already told Tevita in that taped message." Evidently Jese came to see Ratu Noa alone last night.

"But I didn't want to be the only one to know about these changes," Jese interjects. "I wanted the other fishing scheme people to hear it. That's why I brought these three with me."

"I've always wanted you to be the spokesman for the Ogo people when talking with me," Ratu Noa affirms, "but it's okay to have these other men here tonight."

Ratu Noa reiterates the changes he is instituting but avoids explicitly mentioning the delicate issue he raised with Tevita and me — that the group visit could mask the evil intentions of one member.

"We come here tonight, Ratu Noa, to assure you that we're still faithful," Jese affirms. Though he raises his voice, it's not harsh. "We remain faithful. We don't go to any other healers."

"Yes, the suspicion of all Kali lies on you Ogo people," observes Ratu Noa. "But you'll be blessed, because you aren't responsible for the deaths. It's common for us Fijians to point a jealous finger at others who do well, who take a step ahead, because we all want to stay on the same level.

"Don't worry, Jese, I haven't changed. I'm one hard person to change from my policy. I'm sticking with our previous agreement to help with your business." Ratu Noa stops briefly, looking down at the floor. Jese only nods; there is nothing he can add.

"I must tell you straight, Jese, that Tevita will remain close by because he and I are now directly responsible for the success of your business.

"Now if the Ogo people pay off their government loan on the fishing boat," Ratu Noa continues, "then the government will think well of you and give you a bigger loan, and you can get a bigger and better boat. And then we'll all celebrate…but first we'll stop off in Yabu Island."

"Oh, no…unh-uh!" Jese is shaking his head. "Unh-uh — not me!" Ratu Noa has caught him; no one from Ogo dares to go to Yabu, an uninhabited island nearby where a powerful and not always benevolent *Vu* lives. The serious talk sets the trap for the joke on Jese, and the room explodes with laughter, which Jese soon joins in.

Ratu Noa gets back to the subject. "Jese, the government has one eye on your business now. Take one more step and the government will open two eyes. Try to be even faster than before with your loan repayments; then you pay less interest to the bank. The next step will be to take on passengers. That will help you speed up your payments. But before you take this next step, concentrate on using the boat for fishing. When you get a bigger boat, then take passengers too. The quicker you save and drink the *yaqona*, the better and faster your business will grow.

"It's like cassava — you plant it and then you enjoy watching it grow. So it is with me; I helped start your business, and I enjoy watching it thrive and grow."

"Don't fear that anything will adversely affect your business, Jese. But remember, in village life, you can thrive only if you unite. If you want to go independent, you shouldn't stay in the village."

Jese gets back to his concerns about the suspicions directed at Ogo.

"We heard that most everyone in Kali blames us for Jone's death. It's reached a stage where I tell people who come to Ogo that we are lucky to be blamed for something we know nothing about."

"But things like Jone's death happen when we're all drunk," Ratu Noa observes, gently countering Jese's claim that the Ogo people knew nothing. "Even if someone dies, we just let him lie there if we're drunk. We don't even know what's happening." The discussion of drunkenness and irresponsibility remain general, but the message is heard.

"And I want you, Jese, to understand why only one person must see Tevita. It's because I want only one version, a correct one, of what Tevita says to go from him to your group. If several of you go to Tevita, there could be several different versions of what he says."

Ratu Noa offers yet another reason for his change of plans in Tevita's work. Or is it another variation alluding to the suspicions surrounding the Ogo group?

"I'll tell you a story. A member of the Fijian Public Works Department crew was stationed in Kali Island. He was a powerful seer, very famous. When he came back to Suva, he came to my house, and offered me a full pound of *yaqona*. 'What's this for?' I asked. 'I want to do my *sevusevu*,' he said. After doing the *sevusevu*, he related this story: 'When I was in Tovu, visiting there, I tried to see who this Tevita was. I looked him over in my *bilo* — checking him out — to see how powerful he was and how well he was doing. But I couldn't get an answer to my question. The *Vu* I asked, the one I worship, vanished all of a sudden. I realized then that there is a *Vu* in Tevita more powerful than I ever thought, more powerful than the one that I serve.'

"You see, Jese," Ratu Noa almost lectures, "that's what I've been telling you. Even if you bring ten *tabua* to me, I still can't advise you. You must first go to Tevita, for I can only take what he says. In the future, take Tevita's advice as if it comes directly from me. For as you can see, the *Vu* I serve is with Tevita also.

"Because sometimes you come here bluffing. I ask you if you've already been to Tevita, and you haven't but you say yes. Well, little do you know that the answers I then give to your requests are also bluffing

— you get a bluff right back! In this work, you must talk straight. As the Bible says, if you are true and honest in even the smallest things, you can enter heaven."

Ratu Noa then turns to Tevita to instruct him, though he still looks at both Jese and me, making sure we listen carefully. "You must be faithful to *Kalou* and this *yaqona*, Tevita — they must go together. At the highest level is *Kalou*; the others, the *Vu*, are below this *Kalou*. But you must serve these *Vu* first before you serve *Kalou*. If you serve the *Vu* faithfully, you'll be able to reach the top of the highest. Many wrongly interpret this verse of the Bible: 'Seek ye first the kingdom of God…and all these things shall be added unto you.' Yes, *Kalou* is King of kings and Lord of lords. But if you can't find the *Vu* — the *Kalou Vu* — that's a big problem. Our link in this world to *Kalou* is through these *Kalou Vu*. If you can't recognize the link, you'll just be in a whirlwind.

"Jese, tell the Ogo people they must recognize the *Vu* to find the link. Keep to the links; that will keep you working together.

"I see, Rusiate, that you are getting to understand Fijian terms." Ratu Noa's comment surprises me; I was concentrating on understanding what he was saying. This discussion about *Kalou* and the *Vu* is hard to follow, especially since the word *Kalou* is used to refer both to God and to the *Vu*, that is the *Kalou Vu*. But I'm getting the drift, anticipating Inoke's translation, which of course adds refinement and details. "I can see that on hearing a story, you're beginning to see the true and the false.

"If Rusiate wants an interpreter, he must have a good one, like Inoke here. And Rusiate, you must stay with Tevita and get to know his words and their meaning. Study the process of Tevita's words and meanings. Remember, some translators will miss the point. For example, they'll translate *cina*, which means 'light,' to mean only 'lamp.'

"I'll give you another example." Ratu Noa's manner is almost scholarly. "There are lots of Fijian diseases we know only by their Fijian names; we can't translate them into English. In those cases, we should use only the Fijian names. And once you make the true diagnosis of an illness in Fijian, you will find a Fijian herb to treat it. And we pick these Fijian herbs fresh, then administer them fresh. With Western medicines, they are already old when you take them — sometimes even the expiration date has passed. And sometimes, like with aspirin, you take them and you still have a headache."

Tevita joins in. "In this kind of work, we keep our meanings hidden. We can't jump right to the conclusion even though that would be short-er. For example, if Rusi asks a question, he might want a short answer; but we may give him a long response, and by the time we've finished, he might understand it. Whereas if we give a short answer, he'll get it too fast — and miss it. Our responses start from afar, far away from the point of his question, and we go round and round. By the time we get to the end, Rusi will doubt whether the answer speaks to his question, but that 'end' really is the end to his quest. It's very hard for a Fijian to give a short, precise answer to a question, like a simple yes or no."

"Tevita, try to help Rusiate," Ratu Noa says, imploring as much as instructing. "Work closely with him. Speak slower to him; he under-stands a lot of Bitu dialect words, and you can now show him things, slowly, as you progress along."

"Oh, I can't do that," Tevita jokes. "He's not that smart. To do what you ask would be too...*too* hard." Tevita's frown is almost menacing.

"Well, I'll help out," I jump in. "I'll ask my kids to translate for me." Lora and Eliki's fluent Fijian puts me and my calcified learning processes to shame.

"Now we're getting somewhere," Tevita beams, and we grasp hands, marking the fun of the exchange.

Ratu Noa continues his advice to Tevita. "When you speak to Rusiate, speak in proper Fijian, not in a colloquial manner, so he can understand better. And try to have someone rephrase what you're saying in Fijian, slowly, again into Fijian rather than into English. That way Rusiate will understand things in the Fijian sense of the words."

Now Jese changes the subject. "Can a person announce the *yaqona* to a *Vu* or the *tevoro* (devil) while we're all drinking in a normal session without us noticing it?" he asks. Ratu Noa and I have discussed this topic before; it's something I thought all Fijians would know. But then Ratu Noa adds details that are new for me also.

"Yes, the people who do evil are very smart," he begins. "They can announce the *yaqona* to themselves, in a low voice, and direct it to the *tevoro* before it's been drunk. But let's be very clear. The *Vu* don't cause harm; it's the people who worship bones or skulls, those worshiping the *tevoro*, who cause harm. These *tevoro* are just loafing around and can be called and served in any old way. But the *Vu* are different. They are special and must be served in a special way.

"And the *Vu* don't accept any foolishness. When you want something evil from the *Vu* — say, to kill another person — you must be prepared to give something in return which will be a big loss for you, like the life of your son or wife. The *Vu* offers this to you: either you take this deal or you lose your chance. The *Vu* intentionally make the price dear, in order to stop people from wanting evil. But if people are greedy, they accept the offer — and then you lose your child or wife. That's the offering of a life."

Ratu Noa turns to Jese. "The *Vu* want you Ogo people to work together. Everything depends on your unity, because our aim is to go up and up, higher and higher. And this fishing business is only a minor part of the picture. There's a bigger thing yet to come.... You'll see it when the time is right. But you won't just achieve this thing all of a sudden. It will take hard work — long, hard work. We Fijians don't hold on to a thing hard and long enough — we keep changing. When our faith is put to the test, or we don't see immediate results of our faith, we surrender. There must be a will to go on, to go — go — go.

"Do you know the meaning of the name Ogo?" Ratu Noa asks abruptly.

"No," Jese replies.

"And what your sacred animal is?"

"No."

"And your sacred tree?"

"No."

Ratu Noa seems almost annoyed. "You must know these things," he says, firmly. "You must know about your place. How come I know these things and I'm not even from Ogo?"

He goes on at length, teaching Jese and the three other Ogo men about their sacred traditions. He tells them, for example, "When the

199

Ogo *Vu* goes for a sea bath and his footprints have ashes in them, you know a house in the village will burn because that *Vu* wants to come back from the sea to warm himself up."

Tevita smiles at Jese. "That's never happened to you, has it Jese?" Jese winces. Tevita whispers to me that Jese's house burned recently. They had seen footprints with ashes in them on the beach of Ogo.

Ratu Noa continues. "Some people are from the sea (*kai wai*), some from the land (*kai vanua*). In relation to Tovu, Ogo people are from the water, and in relation to Ogo, Tovu people are from the land. And close by is your *Vu* who binds the water and land people together. If you work hard and unite, this *Vu* will give you *mana*. Consider the Bible verse where it says that what is bound together on earth is surely bound in heaven. Bound by who on earth? Surely, bound by the *Vu*.

"You Ogo people have the power, but you need advice on how to tap into it. And don't believe too much; just listen." Ratu Noa enjoys the bewildered look that shoots across Jese's face. "That's right, don't believe everything we say, because sometimes, after lots and lots of *yaqona*, we become drunk and only lie."

Now Jese is really confused. Certainly we've had lots of *yaqona* tonight, enough to make all of us drunk. But I remember what Ratu Noa told me: "It takes a lot of *yaqona* to really get me going; others may get drunk, but that *yaqona* just makes it easier for me to say what I must say, though I never compromise the truth." I wonder if Jese knows that Ratu Noa has been playing with his credulity.

The mood eases as Jese regains his bearings.

Tevita is reflective — now he returns to an earlier topic, as if picking a passing idea out of the air.

"The problem is that when Inoke translates my Fijian words into English for Rusi, since I don't know English, it's hard for me to judge if the translation is correct."

"Oh, wait a minute," I object. "I've heard you...I know your English is good. Why, just the other day I snuck by your house, and there you were, you and Suliana, just going at it, talking and talking, and all in English!"

Tevita collapses in laughter. He can't defend himself.

Ratu Noa returns to his instruction. "Within every good thing, there is an enemy; in the bad things, there is no enemy. To do good is difficult, but to compete in doing evil is easy. Some healers are just like preachers; they try to interpret verses of the Bible, and each has a different interpretation.

"Rusiate," he continues, "when you write your book later on, stress the more useful and important things (*ka bibi*). It's up to you to deduce the truth of the stories you hear from healers. One will tell you one thing, another something slightly different. And it's up to us to tell you the true story. Once we say one true thing, you'll be able to distinguish when another time we say something false.

"Here's an example. A person came to a healer, offering a *yaqona* and requested the healer to help find the person's lost pig. The healer said: 'Don't worry. I know exactly where your pig is. She's safe and sound, and lucky you — she's just given birth to twelve piglets.' 'Damn,' the person responded, 'my pig is a male.' 'Damn to you,' replied the healer. 'Why didn't you tell me in the first place it was a boar!' This story is like a joke, Rusi, but it shows how much certain healers lack seriousness and honesty in their work.

"Before you came to Fiji, Rusiate, you already knew how this healing works in a general way, but you didn't know the exact details here in Fiji. That's what you're learning now.

"There is only a small place where the *mana* is. If you hold on and persist, it's easy to find."

Another round of *yaqona* is served. It must be past midnight. Very little conversation seems left in the group. Silences expand.

"You people must keep asking questions and telling stories so that I can keep talking," Ratu Noa chides. Inoke has told me that Ratu Noa often leaves things unfinished or unclear in his stories, and that he needs to be prodded into completing his thoughts. "Ratu Noa feels odd just giving a lecture," Inoke said. "He always wants more of an exchange in these talks, with others participating, asking questions, telling stories."

"Once I stop," Ratu Noa warns, "that's the end. There is a different kind of power behind my answering. I'm like a tap that you must keep running. Once that tap stops flowing, it becomes clogged, and then it stops once and for all."

"I have a question." It is Jese who comes to the rescue. "Tevita says that whenever we take the fishing boat from Ogo to Suva or come back from Suva, we should perform the *yaqona* and drink two *bilo* before we set out. But suppose there are only two of us there?"

"That's okay. If there are only two of you there, just do it."

"But it's hard to do that kind of *yaqona* when we leave from Suva because there are always lots of people hanging around already drinking *yaqona* in the ordinary way."

"Well, you just close off the regular *yaqona* and announce the special *yaqona* for the trip you're about to make. Then you drink your two special *bilo*."

"But we're a little embarrassed to do it that way. Can we just think about the two *bilo* while we continue to drink the ordinary way?"

"No, Jese." Ratu Noa is insistent. "No, you must close down the ordinary *yaqona*. And don't encourage drinking *yaqona* in the boat before you depart."

"But people who come aboard our boat drink *yaqona*, not us."

"Jese, the intention of the special *yaqona* must be known," Ratu Noa replies, his patience tested. "You can announce this special *yaqona* with other people there, but it is better if only the Ogo boat people are there when you do it. This thing I speak of is like playing cards. When you try to play your trump card, if there are people out to get you, they will try to do you one better — they will try to subvert your special *yaqona* with their own evil purposes."

"Can only two of us do the special *yaqona* in Ogo, before we leave for Suva?"

"No. In Ogo there should be more of you because everyone in Ogo should know the purpose of this special *yaqona*.

"With me," Ratu Noa continues, "when it's time to do my special *yaqona*, never mind if there are lots of people around; I just carry on. I'm not shy because I know this *yaqona* is useful to me. I'm only shy if I know it's useless."

The evening is slowly dying. Ratu Noa and Jese talk more about the traditional clan network of Ogo, and about the *Vu* that rules Ogo. Each time

Ratu Noa asks Jese if he knows about a certain tradition, Jese says no, and each time Ratu Noa explains it to him. It's quite a lesson in history and tradition, in what it means to be a Fijian, and in particular a Fijian born in Ogo.

"It's coming now," Ratu Noa observes. "Keep asking questions, because if I stop, that's the end — and if I keep talking without your questions, I'll just be multiplying the truth. Keep the questions coming; that way the knowledge comes from a higher source."

But we are all running down; the tap is almost dry.

"After this *tanoa* is empty, is the *yaqona* to be over?" Ratu Noa asks. "Or should we mix one more?"

We all want to leave; we're tired and full of *yaqona* — too full. But at the same time we want to stay. We've been together for nearly eight hours, and it would seem strange to break apart.

"Well, let's mix a little more, just to put a bit more *yaqona* in the *tanoa*."

Ratu Noa has some final words to share. He tells Tevita that his work in Tovu should now have two departments, one for healing, one for business. And he again tells Jese that people in Ogo must work together. "It's like a bundle of wood," he says. "Tied together, it's strong, but if you cut the tie, it all falls apart."

Then he turns his attention to Tevita and me. "Rusiate, be careful of explanations that muddle up your mind. You should be given only the truth because your time in Fiji is growing short. In the remaining time, I want you and Tevita to be in close contact. That will make your research worthwhile. And Tevita, when Rusiate is ready to go back to America, give him a medicine (*wai*). Then if Rusiate must go, he will come back!"

I was feeling sad about this evening's end, and the eventual end of my stay in Fiji. Ratu Noa now changes my mood.

"Rusiate," he says, "when you get back to America, what you want to happen will happen. And even in America, it will be easy for you to find Fijian herbs. But if people are sick, you can also just massage their heads and they'll get better.

"One thing to remember, Rusiate. Once you reach your aim and learn what you've come to learn, it will be difficult to explain it to others. They won't know what you're talking about.

"And now I want to leave you Ogo people with this. I can only believe a message if it comes from Tevita because only he can understand my messages."

The last round of *yaqona* is served slowly; though there is no room, we drink our last *bilo*. The night, now early morning, is ending.

CHAPTER 17

A Third Death
(Ogo/Tovu)

Ratu Noa is clear about what lay behind Jone's and his sister's death; others remain confused, and many of their suspicions still focus on Ogo. Even Ratu Noa leaves open the possibility of some wrongdoing in Ogo; perhaps a taboo was violated in the past, or perhaps there will be some misdeed still to come.

Their concern mounting over continuing suspicions both within their own village and from neighboring villages such as Tovu, the old guard in Ogo invites Reverend Jemesa to come from Suva to "clean matters up." He arrives in the middle of February.

The old guard is intent on proving that it is innocent in the matter of Jone's death. Though its members state their request to Reverend Jemesa in general terms, what they want is that he should point up the wrongdoing of the fishing scheme managers: their disrespect for tradition, their conflict with the chief, and by implication, their involvement in Jone's death. The fishing project managers go along with the request for Reverend Jemesa's visit, believing that, since they too are not at fault, he can only establish that for all to see. Those few in Ogo who are not firmly in one of the two camps are relieved that someone of Reverend Jemesa's stature will come to lay at rest the continual rumors and accusations that have disrupted the island community.

Reverend Jemesa is a man of great reputation. An Indigenous Fijian who is barely forty years old, he is known throughout Fiji for bringing evangelical Christianity to areas where wrongdoing is suspected and removing what he sees as the source of the problem: a "superstitious attachment to old ways." "These old Fijian customs," he thunders in his sermons, "are the tools of the devil. The devil enters into that healing *yaqona*, the devil enters into those Fijian medicines — and then leaps out to those who use these things, and seizes their soul. You cannot come to Christ if you go to that *yaqona*, if you go to those Fijian medicines." His demeanor becomes more threatening. "Lay down the tools of the devil and come to Jesus!" he implores, now shaking his fists. As people filter forward, mostly hesitant, a few striding boldly, and bring their small bottles of Fijian medicine or other traditional sacred objects, Reverend Jemesa's voice barely softens: "Lay down your works of the devil and come to our Lord Jesus...and come, my children, to our Lord Jesus." In his church in Suva where he is stationed — a cavernous, imposing space — the walls are lined with these "tools of the devil," old sacred objects, now hanging limply, lifeless symbols of Reverend Jemesa's crusade for the "victory of Jesus."

Ogo and Tovu people are Methodist, as are most Indigenous Fijians. Though their focus is not evangelical, not being preoccupied with the devil and the devil-like ways of Fijian traditions, the Ogo and Tovu people are devoted Christians and deeply religious. With the fervor of his evangelical, charismatic brand of Methodist faith, Reverend Jemesa comes to "liberate" what he sees as the still "untapped reservoirs" of their faith.

Most everyone in Ogo attends Reverend Jemesa's services. A large contingent of Tovu people also attends part of the time. They too seek a cleansing, for accusations also linger in Tovu, as well as rumors of a widely predicted third death.

The people coming to Reverend Jemesa's services to worship in their accustomed way unknowingly become part of his "victory crusade." Turning from prayer to pursuit, they are urged to ferret out the evildoers and bring them back into the fold. Their *Kalou* of love and forgiveness becomes an avenging *Kalou*, and the fires of hell "lick at the toes" of those who have betrayed the Christian faith.

Reverend Jemesa conducts services in Ogo over several days. He keeps asking people to write their sins on a piece of paper and bring the paper to him so he can tear it up, wiping away their guilt for their transgressions — if they promise to put aside their "superstitious ways."

At first his request goes unanswered. He ups the ante. "This is your last chance. If you love the Lord, you can give up your evil, old-fashioned ways. It's only a little piece of paper, and no one will see what you write, not even me. But the Lord will see, and you'll be forgiven — you'll be saved."

Most people are intimidated by Reverend Jemesa's challenge, and they don't come forward out of fear. "What will Jesus think of all the bad things I've done? And those Fijian medicines I use all the time?" one old lady laments, confused as well as apprehensive. Eventually several people bring up their sheets of paper. Reverend Jemesa rips them up with hands thrust into the sky, throwing the pieces into a fire.

But not all accept the Reverend's views; they doubt that just because something is traditionally Fijian it is necessarily an obstacle to salvation. Two of the visitors from Tovu resist this implication: Tevita's helper Alipate rejects Reverend Jemesa's wholesale condemnation of traditional ways, whereas the acting chief, Luke, is still withholding judgment.

Alipate, who is in his late fifties, is a thin, frail man, neat to the point of fastidiousness; his almost translucent skin looks as though it might tear if it is scratched too roughly. He does not carry the weight in village affairs that his age would normally bestow. People do solicit Alipate's advice, but he doesn't mix with others as frequently as most, spending more time at home with his wife than drinking *yaqona* with the men in the evenings. At ceremonies, however, he is a constant fixture as one of the village elders.

Alipate was born into the clan of priests (*bete*). But as elsewhere in Fiji, traditional priestly functions, such as advising chiefs and healing, are no longer necessarily or exclusively performed by members of the priestly clan in Tovu. Alipate is not considered any closer to the *Vu* just because he was born into the priestly clan; it is more because he is one of Tevita's helpers that people think he might perhaps have some special relationship with the *Vu*.

Several years ago, Alipate became very sick and traveled to Suva, where he was healed by Ratu Noa. Then Ratu Noa gave him the power to help Tevita, a responsibility Alipate sought after he recovered his health. For the past several years he has served Tevita loyally.

As Reverend Jemesa pleads once more with the people to bring forth their sins written on pieces of paper, Alipate turns to his friend Luke. "I have an idea. Could you write my sins with yours on your piece of paper? That way we can save paper!" Alipate's joke makes Luke uncomfortable; is this blasphemy? he wonders. Alipate seems unconcerned.

One week after Reverend Jemesa has left Ogo, Alipate is coming back from the bush outside Tovu village, carrying a load of firewood. At just beyond midday, it is too hot to be carrying such a large weight. Alipate crosses the stream, the water sliding along his calves as the tide begins to come in. On the other side of the creek, he collapses. Within seconds he is dead.

The third death has arrived in Tovu. Again, people seek physical explanations for Alipate's death, trying to see it as the result of ordinary sickness (*tauvimate dina*). Alipate's health was "not good;" he seemed "much older than his age." The exertion of carrying the wood from the bush was probably "too much for him," and his "heart must have stopped."

But a heart attack is not a sufficient explanation. Simultaneously other explanations link Alipate's death to the earlier ones. Several dreams are reported in which Alipate and Jone are the central characters and are talking with each other. This joining of the two in dreams is said to connect their deaths. Stories about how Alipate ridiculed Reverend Jemesa during his visit are offered as evidence that Alipate tempted fate. His joke about saving paper is often repeated. But now no one laughs.

Many people believe that Alipate was involved in *vakatevoro*, which at least in part must have contributed to his death. But Alipate's immediate family, including his wife, Ateca, and her sister and her husband, does not harbor these suspicions. Allegations about *vakatevoro*, like most such allegations, are made in the privacy of homes, never in the hearing of Alipate's wife or family.

Two weeks after Alipate's death, the initial funeral ceremonies having

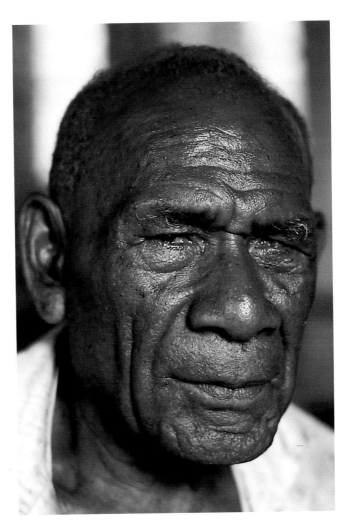

Respected elder and healer

Village bathing area

Woman sleeping inside a traditional thatched house (bure)

Tending the crops

Bringing a dugout canoe (bavelo) *to shore*

Carving a dugout canoe deep in the forest

Woman preparing the leaves (voivoi) *for weaving mats* (ibe)

Young man dressed to perform in the sacred dance (meke)

Mixing yaqona *during an informal gathering*

Evening of informal yaqona *drinking*

Presenting the material wealth (yau) *in ceremonial exchange:
mats, cloth, and sacred whale's teeth* (tabua)

Serving yaqona *at a formal chiefly ceremony*

Healers at work:
yaqona *having been exchanged,*
a massage is given

been completed, I visit Ateca, bringing with me a photograph of Alipate that I took six months earlier. Alipate looks directly, closely into the camera, his face naively open yet revealing nothing. He looks the innocent — a status so many others are unwilling to grant him. I give the photo to Ateca, thinking she will appreciate it as a remembrance (*vakananumi*).

"O my *Kalou*...O — O my *Kalou*. Thank you, Ratu Rusiate...thank you...thank you so very much." Ateca sighs from deep inside and begins to weep. "My husband...my husband...here he is." She lovingly presses the photo to her breast, then holds it out at arm's length to view it, then again caresses it.

Though Ateca does not believe her husband practiced *vakatevoro*, thoughts about the accusations that have been made weigh heavily on her mind. She weeps more over the photo, then finally becomes quiet. Drying her eyes with the hem of her *sulu*, she begins to speak, her tone intimate.

"I want to tell you about my son. He had an automobile accident several months ago — he was hit by a car while he was waiting for the bus. He was only a little drunk. The bus was coming, ready to stop at the bus stop, and suddenly a car came out in front of it. My son felt himself pushed from behind, though there was no one there behind him that he could see. The car hit him, breaking one leg and giving him other injuries. He was in the hospital for a month. Now he's recovering, but the cast is still on his leg. I believe my son's accident is because of *vakatevoro*."

"Why?" I ask.

"Verani, the healer from Kali who now lives in Suva, came in on his case and said it was *vakatevoro*."

Ateca pauses, then leans toward me.

"I also had a dream that tells me my son's accident was from *vakatevoro*. I was lying down in a *bure*. Above me, near the ceiling of the *bure*, lying across one of the beams, was the devil. Its body was very, very small, like the body of a little doll, with very little arms. Its skin was white. I couldn't see what kind of clothes it wore. I only saw its body. And I was very afraid. From above, the hands of that doll reached down toward me, along a road that came down to me from the ceiling, and the hands reached along that road and tried to grab me. I was very, very

209

frightened, and I yelled for help: 'My son! My son!' The doll answered back, 'Your son is with me...and I am in your son.' Then the road came closer and closer to being inside me, and the doll's hands reached farther down, closer to grabbing me. I yelled again, for my fear was great. I yelled out. Then I awoke.

"The *Vu* of our place is the snake," Ateca confides, "but sometimes it changes its form and appears as a Westerner, like that white-skinned doll. At other times, it appears as a grasshopper. Ratu Noa told Alipate he had a Westerner following him, but Alipate said he never saw or knew a Westerner was following him."

I know the meaning of Ratu Noa's words; he felt Alipate had deviated from the straight path, that Alipate had served the *Vu* for the wrong purposes. Representing the *Vu*, the Westerner following Alipate signified improper involvement with the *Vu*. Ratu Noa's observation could be an explanation for Alipate's death, I think. Evidently Ateca is thinking along with me.

"Alipate never served the *Vu* improperly — he never did *vakatevoro*," she says vehemently. "Once he saw a grasshopper in the house and immediately killed it; he wanted no part of the *Vu*. I slept with him, I saw him day and night, and he never served the *Vu* improperly."

Ateca's unusual frankness in talking about *vakatevoro* has been spurred by the rumors she knows are being spread about Alipate. She wants to deny them; she also wants to deny that Alipate was in any way responsible for their son's accident.

"The True God [*Kalou Dina*] is the master of us all. He knows everything that is happening and we must get our strength and help from him."

I take her words in, realizing their honesty. Ateca is respected in Tovu for the depth of her prayer and belief. Alipate was from the priestly clan — he was born to serve the *Vu* with knowledge and dedication, and in that service to help people. Where is the straight path now? I wonder...while already knowing. Ratu Noa warned me that members of the priestly clan could no longer be relied on to follow the straight path merely because of their birth; they no longer enjoyed special access to healing knowledge, having violated the trust of their relationship with the *Vu*. Healers now had to work to become healers. Was Alipate any less vulnerable to deviation because he was a priest? or because his wife was so devout?

A third sudden and "unexplained" death. But this third death confirms what was to happen — Tevita had said there would be a third death — rather than initiates a new loss of meaning. Alipate's death becomes another piece in a picture whose outlines are already drawn. Yet uncertainty and fear linger with us. Though another death is not predicted, as long as the evildoer or doers are not identified, we all feel vulnerable.

CHAPTER 18

The Dance to the Moon (Tovu)

The story spreads through Tovu carefully, yet inevitably. It so full of danger that people tell it, even listen to it, only with hesitation. People want to tell, must tell, but can't. People wish to hear, strain to hear, but fear to. In fragments tucked into the corners of conversations, told with confused disbelief or quiet satisfaction, and always in hushed tones and elliptical language, the story emerges.

On the night of Alipate's death, a man was seen doing a "dance to the moon" (*meke ni vula*). Alone and naked on the Tovu beach, thinking he was unseen, he danced wildly, even feverishly, looking up at the moon, bowing down to it. Everyone understands the meaning of the dance: it is a traditional expression of thanksgiving to the *Vu* for answering one's wish to have another person killed. It is the ceremonial conclusion to an act of wrongdoing. The man who danced to the moon had practiced *vakatevoro*; he was offering thanks to the *Vu* for the death he had requested.

The dance was performed near the homes of Solomone and Pita. Suspicion shifts automatically to these two; one of them is now assumed to be responsible for the recent Tovu deaths. Both are likely suspects, since each has already been thought to be guilty of wrongdoing.

Solomone, it is said, has often been involved in dubious matters. "He must be partners with the devil," says one old man. Besides being engaged in an ongoing dispute with his older brother, whom he should respect,

212

Solomone is also accused by some of having diverted village resources for his own use. His recent illness is seen as proof that he is doing *vakatevoro*.

For his part, Pita has been an object of mistrust ever since he moved to Tovu to marry twenty years ago. He is said to have brought with him a *rewa*, a specially prepared oil that facilitates communication with the *Vu*. Though others have their own *rewa* used for protection and health, people didn't know what Pita's *rewa* was for — and more than a few assumed it was for *vakatevoro*. It was easy to generate suspicions about Pita because he was an outsider. Then, soon after he came to Tovu, he "farmed in the wrong place," crossing the boundary into another's traditional field without permission. As mistrust turned to anger and dislike, initial suspicions were strengthened. The anger has subsided now that Pita has become a part of Tovu life, but the mistrust remains.

The dance to the moon was seen by two different people, but not clearly. Neither can firmly identify which of the two suspects it was: clouds were draped around the moon that night, dimming its light, and the dense coconut trees that march irregularly along the beach obstructed the view. But perhaps the inability to identify one or the other suspect stems more from fearful reluctance than poor viewing conditions.

Despite the efforts of people to pry information from the witnesses, singly or together, the scenario remains vague. As soon as a rumor nearly completes the rounds, another one breaks forth to supplant it. Speculations move in dizzying circles that go nowhere.

Both Solomone and Pita are prime suspects — except to their families. Staunchly supportive of the heads of their respective households, the families join the talk about the other suspect, but never, at least to those outside the family, acknowledge the accusations leveled against their own. No one in Tovu speaks about the dance to the moon in the presence of either the suspects or their families. It's a strange situation, as if the incoming tide left two patches of sandy beach dry under the rush of an ever-deepening ocean.

Sometimes people's desire to know, and their fear of knowing makes them foolish. One night a group of us men are drinking *yaqona*. Pita is among us. It is late, close to the end of the evening. One old man interrupts the quiet. "It was probably you, you old goat," he says, looking at

213

Pita. We are stunned, expecting the worst, but then the old man turns his words into a joke. "Yeah, it was probably you, Pita, because only you could dance so wildly — we all know about your secret dancing lessons."

Later that night I talk briefly with Tevita, who like me was alarmed at first at the old man's accusation, frightened that something would happen, that a direct confrontation would take place. I ask Tevita what would occur if it became definitely known that one of the men performed the dance to the moon and was in some way responsible for the earlier deaths.

"That wouldn't be easy," Tevita replies. "We may feel very angry with such a person for using the *Vu* for killing. And we may want to kick him out of the village. But when we come into a house and see him, face to face, we realize we can't do that. We can't punish him with our eyes. Feeling our relationship to that person, we feel more kindly. We can't expel one of our own relatives from the village. How could we do such a thing?"

With this latest story, Tevita's healing practice intensifies. The dreams that are brought to him carry some insight into recent events. People come seeking advice and understanding. Tevita does not propagate his opinions and is always conservative in how he discusses the problems of Tovu. He rarely makes specific accusations, preferring to address the need to restore a sense of balance in the village. "We must try to balance these forces of killing with the healing power," he says. "We can't expel anyone from our midst. No. But we must make the healing power stronger than anyone trying to do evil acts."

We in Tovu are now backed into our own home. The stories about the role of Ogo people and Jone's father in the deaths seem distant, their outlines fuzzy. The atmosphere in Tovu is charged, like that surrounding a broken electrical wire, buzzing, sparking, threatening to burn.

214

CHAPTER 19

"Everything Is Hard to Explain" (Tovu)

While the tension created by the dance to the moon penetrates the collective awareness of Tovu, it does not disrupt the flow of daily activities. Subsistence must come before solving the terrible riddle of the deaths. People fish and garden, haul water and wood, eat and sleep.

Ceremonial life continues unabated as well, celebrating the arrival of visitors, the exchange of obligations, and occasional special events. Today three important government officials have come to Tovu to discuss the pine scheme. They are accompanied by four high chiefs.

For nearly a week now, Tovu has been preparing for this auspicious visit. Food has been gathered for the *magiti*, *yau* has been collected to make a gift of respectably large proportions, and the *meke* that will be danced in the visitors' honor has been practiced. To mark the special significance of the visit, one more ritual has been planned: a formal, chiefly *yaqona* ceremony.

As the honoring of our visitors begins, the five participants in the *yaqona* ceremony emerge gracefully from Luke's *bure* onto the large, open stretch of grass, which has been covered with coconut fronds to shield it from the sun, where the celebration is taking place. As is the custom, they are all men; it is considered a man's job to mix and serve the chiefly *yaqona*. These men, two still young, are adorned in green coconut leaf skirts, overlaid with large and beautiful pieces of *masi* ("ceremonial bark

215

cloth"), their upper arms wrapped in garlands of strikingly colored flowers. Their bodies glisten with the oil used only for special occasions.

The men slide into their sitting positions: one behind the *tanoa*, mixing the *yaqona*; one next to him, announcing phases of the ceremony; one on each side of the *tanoa*, guarding the *yaqona*; and one several feet in front of the *tanoa*, ready to serve the *yaqona*. Those gathered for the ceremony are hushed. Small children either sit quietly at a respectful distance from the ceremonial ground or, with their younger siblings, stay inside the surrounding houses, perched near the open door to peer at the proceedings.

There is a whispering elegance to the movements, gestures, and expressions of those performing the ceremony. The mixer raises the mixing *bilo* high in the air, and the *yaqona* cascades brightly into the *tanoa*, splashing and settling, splashing and settling. The two guarding the *yaqona* sit upright, motionless. Meanwhile, several of the Tovu elders sing a chant, formally accompanying the mixing. When the *yaqona* is fully mixed, the chant ceases — its end seems in fact to make the mixing complete. Now the server rises, imperceptibly, then walks toward the *tanoa*, kneels to take the filled *bilo,* and proceeds slowly to the most important guest of honor, a high chief from the main island of Viti Levu. After pouring the *yaqona* into the chief's *bilo,* the server sits down carefully and makes a deep-sounding *cobo* ("ritual clap") to mark the drinking of the *yaqona*.

The ritual unfolds again as the remaining six honored guests are each served a *bilo,* followed by Luke, representing Tovu. The order of serving, a subject exhaustively discussed by the Tovu elders, is delicately orchestrated to correspond to the guests' status.

The first round completed, the second one begins. Though the movements and sequence are identical, the stately pace of the ceremony makes each motion a fresh experience. We all sit, intensely still, transfixed.

The second round is finished; the *yaqona* consumed. The mixer wipes the *tanoa* dry. Then it is announced, "*A! Maca!*" — the *tanoa* is "empty" or "dry" of *yaqona*. The ceremony is completed.

Ratu Noa has talked about the special significance of these first two rounds, and it is very impressive to see the *yaqona* end after that. The formal *yaqona* sheds light on the traditional healing ceremony, with its deep respect for *yaqona* as the "drink of the *Vu*."

The Tovu people feel good — we have correctly honored the visitors. With a sense of relief, even relaxation, the *tanoa* is now filled again with *yaqona,* and others at the ceremonial grounds are served. The *yaqona* has shifted into a less formal mode.

For some time now I've wanted to discuss more fully Alipate's death and the stories about the dance to the moon with Tevita. Like others in Tovu, I'm concerned about the atmosphere of evil that now hovers over the village. I know what I must do to protect my family and myself: stay close to Tevita's healing *yaqona* and follow the straight path. But also like others, I'm driven to know what I fear knowing — who actually did the evil, and most important, who is still doing it.

Though I've tried to find Tevita when he is free, he is taken up by his obligations to the pine scheme, his visiting, and most recently, his own sickness. For the past two days, Tevita has been resting in his house. I've heard he cannot sleep well at night because his breathing is "blocked."

This afternoon I go to Tevita's house to inquire about his health. When Inoke and I arrive he is sitting up and looking fit.

"How are you feeling today?"

"Better. Much better."

"What is your sickness?"

"*Yatebalavu*," Tevita responds. "I have difficulty breathing freely. One old woman from the other side of Kali who is staying here in Tovu worked on me. Her specialty is this *yatebalavu*. She massages me around my back and chest. My illness is the same as the one Inoke's daughter has, but a little different."

"What is her sickness?" I ask. I know that Inoke's daughter, an active ten-year-old, has been home from school most of the week, lying in bed and wheezing deeply.

"That girl is suffering from a type of cough," Tevita responds.

"Is her illness an ordinary illness or one caused by *vakatevoro*?" This is what people ask when trying to understand a sickness. One must know the "why" or "how" of sicknesses, and the two alternatives may act singly or together, simultaneously or sequentially.

217

"It wasn't caused by *vakatevoro*, because I gave her herbs for *vakatevoro* when she first came to me. Four days later, her sickness was not cured. It came back. Somewhere else in her body, in her shoulder or chest, there's an old injury to the bones or a fracture that's causing today's sickness. She needed a woman to massage her. After she got that massage she hasn't come back to me."

"What about Vilisoni, the old man here in Tovu?"

"Vilisoni had two illnesses. His first one was a sinus, a small hole discharging pus, on his hip. That one was caused by *vakatevoro* because it healed right away on my giving him the herbs. The second one was an abscess under his arm. I also gave him my *vakatevoro* herbs for that. It should have burst after that if it was my specialty, if it was something I could treat. But it didn't. Therefore I knew that abscess was a case for the nurse, so I told him to go there for treatment."

Tevita is firm about not treating something that is "not his" — as firm as he is about treating anything that is his specialty, or "truly my own sickness" (*noqu mate dina*). Ratu Noa has mentioned this as one sign of a straight healer; and I've observed its presence or absence in the various healers I've interviewed.

Later I discover that Nasi, at Inoke's urging, sent Vilisoni to the hospital for the sinus, fearing it signaled a reactivation of the tuberculosis he had many years earlier. But when Vilisoni got to the hospital the sinus was gone, and he was just treated for his ordinary abscess — certainly not a complaint worthy of a hospital visit. "I looked rather foolish!" Inoke tells me. "But I didn't know Tevita had given Vilisoni an herb for that sinus."

The discussion about *vakatevoro* opens the door for other questions. I sense Tevita is willing to talk about Alipate's death — though about the dance to the moon, I'm not sure.

"People say the deaths of Alipate and Jone are connected. Is that true?"

"There are lots of stories about this." Tevita straightens his back and draws in a full breath. "Alipate and Jone died in a similar way, of a similar cause. In both cases, death was sudden, and help came late.

"Alipate was very hot from walking a long distance with a heavy load of firewood. Then he crossed that cold stream at high tide. No more than ten yards from that stream, he collapsed. We know he had high blood pressure. He took pills for that from the clinic here. But all this doesn't tell us everything that happened.

"Everything is hard to explain," Tevita continues. "There are lots of meanings — in both Fijian and English. Lots of entanglements. It's like a jigsaw puzzle. It could be that Alipate died of both *vakatevoro* and a straightforward illness."

There's been another period of active dreaming around the time of Alipate's death and the rumors about the dance to the moon. Some of these dreams I've heard in their entirety, others only in bits and pieces. Though all are seen as related to the recent events, a few are singled out as especially relevant. In the case of each of these few the dreamer brought *yaqona* to Tevita, asking him to interpret the dream and help prevent the occurrence of any bad consequences.

"Tevita, I know people have been bringing their dreams to you."

"Yes, it's another of those busy times. Lots of problems."

"What about Laniana's dream?" I ask. Laniana, Luke's wife, dreamed that Jone and Alipate are walking around Tovu. Then they come to her and ask, "Where is the road to New Zealand?" She shows them the way to New Zealand on a map she has. "What's the meaning of that dream?"

The dream I ask about was already told to me by Laniana, so I am not breaking a confidence. In fact, dreams of importance are usually discussed with others so that they too can have the benefit of the dream's message. Relating a dream becomes sensitive only when the dream contains an accusation against someone, or the suggestion of wrongdoing, as in these dreams. Our talk isn't meant for the ears of the accused, or their families.

"There could be many meanings," Tevita suggests. "One is that the road could represent the way to heaven. They're asking for the way to heaven, but...they're just wandering around Tovu. Any dead person surely knows all the roads, but these two are still seeking the road to New Zealand. I would say they're after the road to heaven — which they can't find! That shows there is something wrong with them. They aren't pure (*savasava*) in the eyes of *Kalou*."

"Are Alipate and Jone connected in any other way?" I wonder.

"Every night Jone came to Alipate in Alipate's dreams," Tevita responds, to my surprise. I never heard this before. "Every night," Tevita continues, "and Alipate was getting afraid. He told Ateca, 'We should sleep in our big house instead of our usual sleeping hut, because every night Jone is bothering me.' After that Alipate died."

"What does it mean that Jone would come that way every night?"

"The deaths of Alipate and Jone originate from a common point, because when Alipate died, he and Jone are both seen together in Laniana's dream. And after Alipate's death, Jone and Alipate are always together in dreams.

"Who else saw them together?"

"Only Laniana," Tevita says, emphasizing the importance of her dream. "And how quickly those two men are found going together!" The directness of Tevita's judgment startles me.

"Is there a connection between what others have said caused Jone's death — the prior wrongdoing of his father — and what caused Alipate's death?" I ask. Everything seems less clear as it is made clear.

"Yes. The Momoto part with Jone's father is one end of the story. But now we come to understand that there's another end from this side, here in Tovu. There are two sides."

I feel uncomfortable. "This talk is getting more difficult. Should we continue?" Tevita nods.

Inoke leans over when Tevita leaves the house for a short break. "It's okay, Rusi," he whispers. "You've seen that people have been joking about these things during *yaqona* sessions, that some even joke about Tovu being the *only* problem."

"But that's in jest," I counter. "You don't have to stand behind your joke — you can erase its meaning. But now we're talking without jokes. This is a different matter."

"Well, I still think you can go on," Inoke says. "Tevita has given you the go-ahead."

Tevita returns and sits down. He looks toward me expectantly.

My voice as I ask my question is cautious. "What about the dance to the moon?" Tevita raises his eyebrows, not from surprise but from inner struggle. He digs in…then replies in an intimate tone, "My younger brother saw both men naked at a time of night when no one is supposed to be awake. But he was afraid and ran away. So he didn't see the dance."

Pita *and* Solomone were seen! Here is yet another version of the story.

"The deaths of Alipate and Jone are of a similar type — both were sudden. Originally we blamed Jone's death on the evil works of his father in Momoto. But then, why did Alipate die? Alipate comes from Tovu; he has no connection with Momoto. No power from Momoto affected his death. So there must be a connection in the two deaths — which is that they both originate in some way from here. That's what the dreams have been telling us."

Tevita's words express some doubt; it is unclear whether he is saying the deaths "originate" or "originate in part" from Tovu.

"Tevita, do you mean the two deaths originate only from something in Tovu or in part from something here?"

He repeats what he said before. The ambiguity remains.

"Is there any connection between the dance and Alipate's death?"

"We Fijians can die because someone performs a dance to the moon or does other kinds of *vakatevoro*. You never know. It could be that because of that dance to the moon both Alipate and Jone died. No one will ever do that dance if he just wants money or employment or something like that. A person does it only if he wants someone to die. When we see this dance, Rusi, we know right away someone has died…or will die."

Tevita's last remark again raises the specter of death. Still I feel secure being with him and his *yaqona*.

"What about Alipate's dream about Jone and Solomone?"

"I can't interpret that dream very well, Rusi, because the dream is described in different ways, each of which carries a different meaning."

"What I heard was that Alipate dreamed that Jone came to him, and told him that Solomone was a great bluffer and liar and a clever speaker, able to talk his way out of anything and talk himself away from the truth."

"Yes, I heard that version too."

"What does it mean?"

"It's not really clear." Tevita pauses. "But it does mean that Solomone is probably the one who did the dance to the moon and therefore is connected with Jone's death, and with Alipate's as well."

"How is that?"

"I'm not sure." Tevita is not defensive, merely perplexed. "Like I said, this version of the dream is not very clear. Nor are the other versions I've heard. And it's even hard for me to remember much about those other versions."

I take Tevita's cue to move on. I now have more appreciation of the convolutions which pursue the explanations of death. Suspected of doing the dance to the moon, Solomone and Pita are therefore thought to be in some way responsible for Alipate's and Jone's deaths; but so too Alipate, through his own possible wrongdoing, is in some way responsible for his own and Jone's death. At least, that's how it now seems.

"What about Vilisoni's dream?" I've heard this dream is the one that most strongly implicates Solomone in Jone's and Alipate's deaths, suggesting that it was Solomone who did the dance to the moon.

"That dream I know. Vilisoni brought it to me. The dream made him afraid, so he brought *yaqona* and asked me to prevent the death in his dream. Vilisoni dreamed that he and Solomone went fishing in Vilisoni's boat. They anchor outside the village. Nearby they see a foreign fishing boat. All the people on that boat are naked. Vilisoni says, 'We should go to that boat and ask for some fish.' He goes to that other boat and brings back some fresh or raw fish. The fish is not yet cleaned or cooked; the blood has yet to run. Vilisoni and Solomone divide the fish between themselves. Vilisoni takes his share to the village, where it's further divided among the villagers. As his share is cut up, the blood begins to flow from the fish. Meanwhile, Solomone has stayed in Vilisoni's boat, now anchored in the harbor. As the blood flows, Vilisoni wakes up.

"Vilisoni's dream is about fish before it's prepared for cooking. If these fish are cut up or for some other reason their blood flows, that means there'll be a sudden death. Without prior sickness or other warning. The blood doesn't even have to actually flow. The meaning would be the same if the blood *could* flow. When Vilisoni dreams about the raw fish in his boat, blood hasn't flowed yet, but it's there, ready to flow. That Solomone remains in the boat with his share of the raw fish means he is connected with the deaths."

"What about Luke's dream?"

"In that dream Alipate comes to Luke and reads a biblical verse, something from the Psalms — something like 'Death startled me and the grave has now taken hold of me.' Then Alipate tells Luke, 'You people in Tovu who are still alive — Be careful!'"

"'Be careful!'...that's also what I heard, and it makes me uneasy. Before I was only doing research, but now I belong to this place. That's what others tell me...and that's what I feel. And so I really listen when I hear these dreams. What should we do? Is there a new problem now because of the dance to the moon? What's in store for us?"

"We all have to protect ourselves. And I know that includes you too, Rusi. Once you believe these things, they start to affect you."

"But if something like a dance to the moon occurs, how do you stop it? Or stop its effects?"

"It's possible to stop those dances."

"How?"

"By bringing *yaqona* to me — just as others in Tovu are now doing. If people feel evil is being cast on them, they bring the *yaqona* and I'll do the healing work. We build a protective shield (*sasabai*) or a fence (*viribai*) around them.

"But you don't have to be afraid, Rusi, if you have strong faith in *Kalou*! The One God is behind all the protection." Like Ratu Noa, Tevita always returns to this foundation.

Yes, I struggle to keep that faith. And later that day, like others in Tovu, I will also take a *yaqona* to Tevita, requesting a "protective shield" for me and my family.

Tevita is starting to look tired. I won't stay much longer.

Recently, Tevita fell from a breadfruit tree outside his house while attempting to reach a ripe fruit. A fall is a sign that something bad might happen and, as Tevita showed, can signal a death. I'm concerned about him.

"What about your fall? Is there any meaning to that?"

"Don't worry, Rusi. Nothing will happen."

"Did your *Vu* protect you?"

"It's not clear to me." Tevita observes traditional Fijian modesty.

"Tevita, there's something else I want to ask you, but I'm not sure about it." Tevita's nod invites me to go on. "I'm starting to see something in my *bilo* when I take those first two servings. I'm not sure what it is. Maybe a face or a head, but it's not clear. More like clouds. What might this be?"

"That's hard to say, Rusi. The *mana* usually doesn't appear like that. *Mana* is like a secret message that comes to you. It's hidden. You can feel it inside yourself, but you can't see it. It's secret advice that comes into and within you [*lako mai loma*]. When you hear those words, you must pay attention to them."

"I don't hear words…but those images appear in the *bilo*."

"Well, Rusi, *mana* comes in different ways. And yes, sometimes it can happen the way you describe. But whatever way, it only comes when you are straight."

"Tevita, would there ever be a meeting or gathering in Tovu where you would accuse a person you suspect of *vakatevoro* and tell that person to stop?"

"It's against the law to blame someone for *vakatevoro* without a good witness." We both think of the vague and reluctant witnesses to the dance to the moon. "Without good witnesses, the accused will surely say, 'I'm not doing anything bad.'"

"But I heard that one time you told someone to stop working because she was doing bad *yaqona*."

Tevita smiles. It's a story he relishes telling.

"That woman was from the city of Suva. She had been in jail for stealing. She came here and wanted to close down my healing work. She came here to cleanse the village. Everyone went to her *yaqona* sessions. But I noticed when she arrived here she didn't even do a traditional *sevu-sevu*. I knew then that her work was not good. It wasn't true work.

"It was five years ago that this happened. She came to Tovu for one day and one night. Tovu people had requested she come here to do her *yaqona*. And she said lots of people in Tovu were worshiping the devil. But when I saw her, I knew she was telling lies.

"I told her, 'You're telling lies. Just lies. Get out of here!' And she left our place and went back to Suva." Tevita talks not with malice but strength.

I'm finding it hard to leave. I allow myself one more question. "Alipate was your helper. Why did he die?"

"We'll never know. If Alipate did something wrong when he was my helper, his death could be a punishment. But only *Kalou* would know that."

With Alipate now gone, only Eroni remains as Tevita's helper in Tovu — and Eroni is irregular. He rarely attends any of the healing ceremonies, which puzzles me.

"Why wasn't Eroni with us when we had our ceremony last Monday?"

"Wasn't he there?"

"No, it was just you and me."

"Oh. Eroni was probably busy somewhere. We just carry on if he's not present. We can't wait for him, because a lot of people want to be helped. We have to begin the work without him."

Then I accept what I have been avoiding. Tevita has at least one regular helper — me — even though I'm not skilled in the specifics of the healing ceremony.

"So there's a problem on this side, here in Tovu?" I ask.

"Yes," Tevita nods. "All the dreams are closely associated with Tovu, so we tend to believe there must be a cause here."

"Maybe it's both," I wonder out loud. "Maybe there's an old cause that lies in the village of Jone's father and a new cause that lies here in Tovu."

"Yes, Rusi; that's what I also think."

"So it's a 'combined soup,'" I joke.

In Tovu there is a joke about "combined soup." It seems almost everything here ends up being cooked into a soup with some cassava, which is the readily available starch. "Combined soup" is the Tovu specialty. It's a mixture of things, and sometimes it's hard to figure out exactly what's in there with the cassava.

"That's what we've got here, Rusi. More combined soup!"

CHAPTER 20

Conversations
with Ratu Noa
(Suva)

"This work is long and hard."

I'm back in Suva again. Five months have passed since my last visit with Ratu Noa.

Ratu Noa asks me for the latest news from Tovu. I tell him about Alipate's death and the different dreams that Tevita says link it with Jone's. I also describe the dance to the moon, and how it focuses suspicions in Tovu on Pita and Solomone. Ratu Noa is neither surprised nor especially interested — he just listens. As I talk, I become aware of how easy it is now to speak of these matters directly. Ratu Noa, it seems, is hearing nothing new. And I have confidence what I say will remain within his home.

"That's the problem with us Fijians," he sighs. "We place too much emphasis on dreams that come *after* the death of a person. Had the dreams come before the death, that would be different. Then the dream could explain the episode. But after the death, those dreams can't really tell us anything true. With me, before anything happens, I can see it in my sleep. I can tell when you're coming here — well before you arrive.

"Alipate was of the priestly clan," Ratu Noa continues, "and those priests of Tovu used to have their own *Vu*. But things did not go well with

226

that *Vu*. And I told Alipate, 'Don't worship the *Vu* of the old priests, for that will be your doomsday.' I told Alipate that instead he should see Tevita. Alipate was Tevita's helper and Tevita works for me. Alipate should have worshiped the *Vu* only through Tevita. The *Vu* that I serve would have given Alipate all the protection he needed. I'm not accusing him of anything bad. But he must have disobeyed my request. When he worshiped his own *Vu,* that was his death.

"Can you understand what I've just said, Rusiate?"

I nod assent — more or less.

"Jesus' era is over," Ratu Noa states. "Now it's the era of the Holy Spirit. It is required that everything you do should be straight and true, not evil-minded. If this other man has plenty of money, and I wish him dead so I can possess all his money — that is evil-mindedness. If you're straight, then *Kalou* will give that money to you anyway.

"If I hear a dream that tells me someone will die, I perform a *yaqona* to stop that death from happening. Because I hate to see a death occur from the evil wish of another person. But if that death results from a decision from above, well, then whatever I do won't matter. This is where we have to use our judgment, and give only the proper and suitable response.

"Remember this, Rusiate. When a *yaqona* comes to you with a request for help, try to see what this request really is. If it's for a good cause — say, wishing for children or a better education or health — that's okay. Do the *yaqona* ceremony. But if it's for a worthless or evil cause — no way.

"Let me explain how this *vakatevoro* occurs. It's difficult to understand, but even though it's a bad thing, it does have its own rules that must be strictly followed. Take, for example the way marriages were once arranged in Europe. If I wish your daughter to be my wife, I would ask you for your approval. If you say yes, then she could be my wife. It all becomes possible. But if you say no, then she cannot be my wife. It becomes impossible. This example also applies to Alipate and Jone. Say I'm doing *vakatevoro* and I want Alipate or Jone to die. It's not only with the *yaqona* that I seek assistance for their deaths. Through that *yaqona*, I also have to ask permission of each man's *Vu*. If their *Vu* agree, then I ask *Kalou*. If *Kalou* says yes, then I can 'touch' Alipate or Jone. Then it's all possible. In these matters, if the answer is yes, then it's yes to the deaths. If the answer is no, then its no to the deaths. That's the procedure.

"Here's another example. Suppose I do something so that Alipate might die. And he is ignorant of this at first, but eventually he finds out. Then he's liable to put me in court — and my *Vu* as well. His *Vu* will take legal action against me and my *Vu* in the eyes of *Kalou*. The punishment given to me will be visited on my sons and grandsons, my daughters and granddaughters. Others may say this *vakatevoro* is all right to do. For it's not easy to tell someone — 'Oh, you're a bad man for doing these things.' But I hate this evil work! And you hate it too! And we must be firm in telling others: we work only on the straight path.

"You know, Rusiate, I get so tired of hearing these accusations about others. It causes so much more trouble." Ratu Noa has become weary, almost testy. "And those dreams about Alipate. They've come too late. Alipate has already died. And furthermore, if there is a connection between Alipate's and Jone's deaths, then why did Jone die at Ogo? Why didn't he die at Tovu, like Alipate?"

That's a new angle. "Then is there a connection between the two deaths?" I wonder.

"It's hard to know," Ratu Noa concedes. "Do you know what Jone's ancestral kin group [*yavusa*] is?"

"No."

"Nor do I. But if we can learn more about Jone's ancestral kin group, then we can know both sides since I already know Alipate's group. When we know both sides, then we can figure out the exact connection. But it would be difficult to ask Jone's people about their ancestral group. There would be all sorts of suspicion, because Jone's wife and children don't want to believe Jone's father is the cause. They, and many others, believe it's *vakatevoro* coming from Ogo. There are lots of things connected with Jone's death. And the deeper you go into this matter, the more there is. But if Jone's family doesn't accept his father's responsibility, there will be another death. There is no point for the Ogo people — among whom

228

are some of Jone's Momoto relatives — to wish for his death. Also, you don't wish a person to die who helps the community like Jone did."

Ratu Noa is making things more complex as he tries to simplify them. Is a person specially chosen as a victim just because he's a good person, as others in Tovu have said, or is Ratu Noa correct in saying that one's good works make one an unlikely victim?

"How can this thing with Jone end?" I ask.

"The remaining members of Jone's family must go back to a minister and get him to pray to *Kalou* for them, asking *Kalou* to spare them, to cancel out Jone's father's original prayer." Ratu Noa speaks with conviction. "They must go to a minister, not a healer."

"A special minister?"

"No, any minister will do. Remember Jone's father's words: 'All my offspring will suffer if I am unfaithful, and telling a lie.' If his family doesn't do what I say, it will go on and on and on. Jone's father was a minister, and he made a promise to *Kalou*. Therefore the family must go to a minister, though both the minister and the healer end up going to the same *Kalou* in their work."

"What about the dance to the moon?"

Ratu Noa pauses. "I cannot say anything about it unless there is evidence. It's like with the laws; you arrest somebody because you actually see he is doing something wrong. You can't accuse someone if you didn't see what he was doing."

"But it appears that two people saw someone do that dance to the moon," I offer.

"Well…if it was like that, then there is the evidence. And Tevita has the power to handle it.

"You know, Rusiate, there is still another aspect to all this." Ratu Noa becomes reflective. "I myself cannot say I am perfect in my ways. The thing I must ask is, What about me? Do I have a clean slate? No blemish? That's why it's so hard to accuse another of wrongdoing."

Ratu Noa is committed to finding out facts and avoiding what he calls "gossip," unsubstantiated rumors or post hoc explanations. His stance complements Tevita's commitment to seeking protection rather than generating accusations.

"I want to be very clear about these deaths," Ratu Noa insists. "I'll only say what I know. Not add anything. Not subtract anything."

Where in Tovu the matter of the deaths is constantly in danger of expanding, if not exploding, with every wisp of speculation, Ratu Noa seeks to contain the matter. And I realize anew, as with Ratu Noa's work, that any further questioning about the deaths has to be done with complete honesty. We must be straight if we ever hope to understand what is not straight.

"And this reminds me about another thing," Ratu Noa begins, switching to a new topic. "Healing and business are two different departments. The service in healing is in the giving. You don't think about getting anything in return."

"But I've heard about a problem some people have," I observe. "I've heard some say that they can't afford to buy the *yaqona* to ask the healer for help. And I know that some healers demand a small fee or some cigarettes before they'll begin."

"Yes, I know about those people." Ratu Noa sighs. "That's wrong. You don't mix healing with business. And about this *yaqona*. *Yaqona* goes before your request for healing help. It isn't the same as a *loloma*, or a 'gift of gratitude,' which can be given after the healing is done. But if you are in a tight corner and have no *yaqona*, or cash to buy some, it does not matter. If you truly need healing you can approach the healer directly for help — just tell him you have no *yaqona*. But even a little twig of the *yaqona* would be enough, a twig that someone else might throw away or overlook. Because it's your wish that counts, not your money. And don't promise you'll have something to give soon. What is most important is being straightforward, telling the facts: 'nothing is nothing.' Do not try to tread on both sides, being a bit this way and a bit that way.

"These are the things I've been taught, Rusiate. That's the way I learned about healing."

Ratu Noa's statement creates the opportunity for a discussion that seems long overdue.

"Ratu Noa, could you tell me about your years growing up and how the healing power came to you?"

Ratu Noa relaxes and smiles. "You know, Ratu Rusiate, that's a story that speaks of great difficulties...but I'll tell you." He lingers on that last phrase.

"In my young days I didn't often go in association with other children. I lived sort of a loner's life. I spent most of my time with the elders: I served them in their *yaqona* sessions and listened to their conversations. When the elders called for the *yaqona* to be prepared, I attended to it right away. If I overheard the elders calling another boy to help prepare the *yaqona*, I would go in his place. If another boy refused to go when called, I would go instead. I would carry out the elders' request willingly, without saying a word. I didn't start drinking *yaqona* until I was about fifteen or sixteen, and when I started, there was none around who could drink more than me.

"As far as I can recollect, this power was with me from the time I was very young. I could just feel it. After I was married — and my wife can testify to this — the *Vu* appeared to me when I was sleeping on my bed. He came to me and said, 'You take this. It is for you.' And I said, 'No, I don't want it.' He lifted me from the bed and threw me to the door. He threw me three times! But I said, 'I don't want it. This healing work is not for me. I'm not the one meant for that work.' He said, 'I'm going to give it to you whether you want it or not.' Three times he asked me and three times I said no. 'You will take it whether you like it or not,' he said. That is how the gift was first given to me.

"I kept this gift to myself. I kept it inside me. I was afraid to treat anyone; I was afraid I might give a herb that would poison instead of heal. I knew when the power came, but I didn't want to say much about it. I couldn't go around and tell the people that I had the power. When I first had the power, I hid it.

"I was staying at home all the time with this power I had. Then one day I went to drink *yaqona* in a house where a boy lived who was sick. A sickness had appeared on the boy's hand. He had injections and an operation at the hospital but remained sick. He was crying day and night...day and night...and couldn't sleep. I felt pity when I saw him suffering. A man at the house asked me if I would treat that boy. I knew I had this power but I wasn't sure if it would be effective...because this was the first time I would actually use it for healing.

231

"Soon after that request I felt the power come into me. I told the man, 'Let's go.' We went to the northern section of town, then on to the road, down below to the foot of the bay, to the flat land. Then I said, 'We must go slowly…walk slowly.' We came to a mangrove swamp, and there I looked at the leaves. Some were shining, as if a source of light came from them. I told him, 'Wait, we'll go down there.'

"Pointing to the shining leaves, I said, 'Get those leaves.' Then we returned, carrying those leaves, which were the healing herb.

"We returned to the house. The sick boy was lying on the bed. As soon as I put my foot on the front steps, that boy fell asleep — even before I gave him the herb! And he had pain no more.

"This work is long…and hard," Ratu Noa reflects. "There are steps to be followed. Three steps. When you've passed them all, the knowledge will come to you automatically."

Ratu Noa turns his gaze intently on me, though his demeanor remains casual. "Rusiate, you are now on your way to the second step. You are aware that this healing work is very special."

I don't know what Ratu Noa is referring to.

"Yes, Rusiate, you've passed the first step, the test of the healing work on Monday evenings. And there are two more. Try hard to pass steps two and three. If you follow the right and proper channel, you'll achieve your objective. And remember, avoid shortcuts! One day I might question you: 'What is in between here and there?' You might have to answer, 'I don't know,' because you left that part out. You should always know things in detail on your way through. You go step by step, each step in its time."

Remember all the details, I repeat in my mind. Ratu Noa is talking about respect for the proper way, not an obsession with trivia.

"That's how this healing work unfolds. Go slowly. Don't jump around. Don't jump over any steps. At the end of the steps, when you are questioned, right on that spot the correct answer will come. I'll give you an example. Say you're working in America and you find that there's a patient you don't know how to help — you don't know what herb to give. Well, you can't come back here to Fiji for advice. Instead, you must trust yourself. Go into the bush to find the herb. Ask the first tree for help. If help doesn't come, then ask the second tree. If it's not there, then the third. Okay — help is here. This tree will give me the medicine. But don't skip over any of the trees. If you do, your effort will be of no use."

Slowly, step by step — in the correct manner, with no shortcuts, I think. And then — the answers come, right on the spot. It's that last part, when the answers come, that I'm still struggling with. It seems too automatic. But then, if I really walk the straight path, who knows what could be possible! I smile, almost laughing.

"You know what I mean, Rusiate." It feels like Ratu Noa is reading my mind. "Rusiate, I want you to pass the two remaining tests."

"When I go back to Tovu, what is my task? Do I still try to do the healing work with Tevita every Monday, even if he's busy? And is there anything else you wish me to do?"

"Keep to those Monday nights. That is the first step. You're standing on that first step now, ready to reach for the second step. The second test is another part of the healing work that Tevita hasn't opened up to you yet. This is a most difficult and important part of his work. The first part of his *yaqona* work, the Monday night sessions, is for healing; this second part is for research and education. All kinds of research. And all kinds of learning. This second step is the work of the *daurairai* or *daukilakila*."

A *daurairai* is one who sees deeply, spiritually; a *daukilakila* is one who knows truly, in a spiritual sense, who can see into and through people and into the future. Now the path is becoming clearer — and more intimidating. But I feel there is no turning back — or even around.

"Rusiate, have things firmly in grasp. And don't copy words from others. Say what you think is right, and you yourself will know when what you have said is wrong. I'm not advising you to go beyond this. The door is there. If you open it, you can enter. If you don't, you won't. Once inside the work, you'll see the difference between the three steps."

I know not to ask about the third step. Our talk shifts to the healing of mental illness as I relate the work I did in Tovu with Nanise.

"Do you know about this Nanise?" I ask. "Do you know the cause of her sickness?"

"Nanise's case is very complicated," Ratu Noa says. "But the problem is with her woman's organ, the womb where the child is reared."

Ratu Noa looks at me, slightly quizzical. "You're the doctor who specializes in these mental problems, Rusiate. I'm only telling you what I see, what I know."

"That's good enough for me! My training in mental health has definite limitations."

"I saw Nanise when she was a young woman, while she was attending school here in Suva."

"How old was she?"

"About fourteen. And at that time her body was physically very weak."

"Nanise's father told me she had a car accident at that time, and that accident made her sick for a long time and weakened her body. Did you see that?"

"That may be one of the causes of her condition. But her condition is complex. This mental illness is complex. We can't be definite about its cause. Nanise also overworked her body when she was young, and part of her nervous system may have been twisted or displaced or even snapped. Only women who have given birth can get this condition where part of the nervous system snaps. We call that condition *cavuka*. If this *cavuka* comes after giving birth and the right medicine for *cavuka* is not given, then other symptoms can occur. The hair can fall out, one can become deaf, there can be swellings in the body. And when this *cavuka* reaches the brain, it causes an unbalanced condition and the person becomes a nonstop talker and tends to stare off uncaringly into space.

"How is Nanise now, Rusiate? Is she mentally ill?"

We are two doctors working together. "She's very nervous now," I comment. "Very scared of being alone or going outside. And like you say, she stares off into space."

"Yes, this *cavuka* makes one very tense. Women suffering from this disease tend to be scared. They also suffer from lack of sleep because of the disturbance to their nervous systems. They're afraid, and feel they have to stay up all night to protect themselves from anything happening without their knowing it."

"Nanise is afraid all night," I report, "and she has shortness of breath."

"That shortness of breath is caused by the fear, which rises up from one side and blocks the other," Ratu Noa explains.

I report to Ratu Noa how I told Nanise just what he now says, that fear caused her shortness of breath, and how I taught her to breathe deeply and taught her husband to massage her to help her breathe. Ratu Noa nods, smiling. "Yes," he murmurs. "Yes...that's the way to work with her."

"Nanise also thinks she's going to die," I add, "and I told her she needs to breathe in life, to relax and not let fear choke her."

"Yes, it's good to tell her that. You'll excuse me, Rusiate, for telling you all these things, because you're the doctor in these matters. But I'm only telling you what I know to be true."

"Your advice really helps. Yes, in one sense, my training is to help the mentally ill. But in another sense — a very important sense — I know very little."

"There are not many people who understand the real facts about this mental illness as you and I now talk of them," Ratu Noa says. "What we can see, others cannot comprehend. They see mental illness only as a sign of being possessed by the devil. Others will say that you, Ratu Rusiate, are coming to Tovu to search for devils. But they have very little knowledge of the unknown. In your search you are working toward healing people. In your university, you've studied the human brain as much as you could but still you believed there is something more you can understand which can help heal mental illness. So you must seek. You are seeking! That's your assignment here in Fiji.

"Rusiate, you were a chosen child when you were born in America. *Kalou* has chosen you for the job of being a doctor of the mind. There are many people to cure. If you fail to comply with that job, there will be trouble.

"*Kalou* has given some people the gift to seek." Ratu Noa becomes more passionate, though his voice remains soft. "Others just sit around and wait, wasting time. *Kalou* has given these people the belief that they will just stay where they are. With us — you and I — we go deeply into the search...but we don't sing a song about it! We can tell stories to each other freely, but not to others.

235

"This search you are on, Rusiate, is not only for white people; it also applies to us Fijians. If there is another person like myself, then there can be communication. Never mind what part of the world we're in — there's a common link between us. The electric current [*livaliva*] that is in you is the same as the one I have in me...and that current passes between us."

"Yes — I know that electricity. I feel it." Our affirmation goes beyond mutual recognition, to simple joy.

"That's good, Rusiate; we're talking the same language. But the trouble is that time is short for you to gain the necessary wisdom, and also we are both busy. When you are paid like you are to do research on healing, you don't feel the full pressure of the healing work. But if you have no job, and you engage yourself fully in the healing work, then you would see how difficult and important this thing really is.

"In this work you must be patient and responsible. We healers are also given punishments for failing to meet our assignments, our commitments to our clients. Once when I was still learning I wasn't there at the exact time I was supposed to work on a client. My punishment was to prepare five *tanoa* of *yaqona* and drink them. I almost burst my stomach, but I carried on and drank each *tanoa* because I didn't want to dishonor a promise and responsibility I was given. If you're supposed to come at six o'clock to meet your *Vu*, you must knock off your ordinary job, take your bath, prepare yourself, and wait. You must tell even your best friend, 'Wait for me until I'm free.' After you've accomplished the meeting with your *Vu*, then you can attend to other business."

Before I leave his house, Ratu Noa speaks to me in an unfamiliar tone, one I remember only in our first talks, when it was not clear the next one would even occur.

"*Kalou* hides the real, true things and we have to search for them. If you don't seek, Ratu Rusiate, you cannot find them. But don't worry that the time left for your research is getting short. I know that worries you. The time left is very, very short. And I worked on this learning for nearly fifteen years. But don't worry. I want you to pass the steps. And what is not accomplished here in Fiji will continue on your return to America. When the time is due, the work will be done.

236

"Your approach, Rusiate, is correct. You have come and searched; that is why I tell you as much as I know. But I am not an easy man to handle. As you can see, you and I are working fine together now. But there will be a time when I divorce myself from you, when you will try to find me and you cannot. Nothing will draw me back. Then you must remember what I told you."

CHAPTER 21

Reverend Jemesa Comes to Tovu (Tovu)

Back in Tovu, mistrust regarding the tragedies continues to hover around Pita and Solomone. Because the identity of whoever performed the dance to the moon is not definitely established, the fascination with those two men feeds on itself. In Ogo, the old chief and his supporters are still convinced that the fishing project managers are connected with the evil-doing, while the project managers themselves still feel desperate to escape the stain of suspicion.

Under the pressure of this collective guilt, the Ogo people invite Reverend Jemesa to return. "Ogo is not yet clean (*savasava*)," says the old chief. "We need help to get rid of the dirty things still going on here."

I'm reminded of something Ratu Noa said: "People of today don't understand the real meaning of words. Like *savasava*. It doesn't just mean 'clean,' or 'having no evil'. *Savasava* is more than that. It is the way we are supposed to be. Clean, yes. But also 'pure' and 'honest' and 'respectful.' *Savasava* goes very deep. It is the way our ancestors told us to be."

Reverend Jemesa returns to Ogo, his message unchanged; if anything, his fervor screams higher. His first visit did not remove the cancer, and now he attacks more fiercely; determined to rip out the disease. Sweeping aside conventional respect, he doesn't merely call for people to give up their "primitive and pagan ways," or label "traditional Fijian things," like Fijian medicine, "tools of the devil." This general condemnation is, however, effective. Several people in Ogo surrender their traditional objects and *rewa*, medicines they keep for their health or protection. "Killers," the Reverend calls these medicines.

But Reverend Jemesa wants to go further to clean out the sickness. Now, by implication, he also confronts individuals involved in the practice of traditional Fijian religion.

We first hear about Reverend Jemesa's public intrusions on people's personal lives when we learn that Tevita's trusted helper on Ogo, the man Ratu Noa empowered to carry all of Ogo's messages to Tevita, has given up his *rewa*. This *rewa*, given him by Tevita, is the symbol of his allegiance to Tevita, Ratu Noa, and through them the *Vu* behind all the healing work. Tevita's Ogo helper withers when faced by Reverend Jemesa's accusation to the assembled: "If any of you carry one of those *rewa*, you're doing the devil's work. Deny the devil, or the devil will crush you. Give up that *rewa* and come to Jesus." Tevita's helper's *rewa* will now join the other so-called "primitive" objects that "house the devil" and crowd the Reverend's "rooms of purity."

After several of the Tovu people attend the Reverend Jemesa's services in Ogo, they invite him to expand his "cleansing" work to Tovu itself.

At high tide, the moment when the ocean seems suspended, Reverend Jemesa lands on the Tovu beach, brought by a relative of the Ogo chief in an old boat, its paint peeling. Jemesa looks as though he is still in Suva; wearing a crisp, formal *sulu* and a stiff, immaculate long-sleeved white shirt, his urban dress connotes cleanliness, propriety, and power. Stepping onto Tovu land, he seems to ignore the ocean water and sand that swirls around his ankles and strides forward, bringing Suva with him into the waiting village.

Jemesa is indeed imposing. Tall, strong, and forceful, his expression is almost fierce; rarely does he smile, and he hardly ever jokes. He offers his *yaqona* for a *sevusevu* to the village elders, but it is a clearly perfunctory performance. He does not insult the *yaqona* ceremony, but neither does he treat it with the customary care and respect.

After the *sevusevu* is over, Jamesa stays awhile drinking *yaqona*, visiting but mostly describing his evangelical work of "cleansing." He is close to boasting, but others don't seem to mind. They are enraptured by the magnitude of his stories, the number of people he is said to have "saved," and especially how he has rescued so many people from lives destined for tragedy and death.

When he is finished, Reverend Jemesa retires to the house of Ropate, the Tovu man officially responsible for the local church. It is there that he'll stay and conduct his service. Jemesa thereby conveys his lack of interest in the traditional chiefly structure of Tovu as well as its mainstream religious institution, the Methodist church.

Word spreads through Tovu that Jemesa will hold his service in the late afternoon. People are more unclear about what they are going to wear than whether they will go. Will his service be a regular church service, or a healing service, or an evangelical revival meeting? Should we wear formal *sulu* like we do when attending church on Sunday? Or everyday *sulu*? Many people already know the answers, having been to Jemesa's services in Ogo — his services combine all three. The questions are more a measure of people's anxiety about what is to come than true confusion.

People arrive in Ropate's house quickly, and soon the house becomes too small. People are standing around outside, looking in the door and the windows. Referring to how people stepping outside the church during a long Sunday service will take off their "church faces" and return to ordinary joking, one young man who is forced to stand outside jokes about not knowing where he is: "Is this part of the church, or can I act normal since I'm outside?" But this afternoon the young man's attempt at humor feels lonely in the prevailing serious, even somber atmosphere.

Unlike the ordinary Tovu church services with their shared responsibilities, the service begins with Jemesa clearly in charge. He chooses the hymns and "directs" them with his strong, articulate singing, his voice traveling over the heads of others and out the door, resonating through the village. The hymns are sung loudly, yet it is quiet inside; anticipation ushers people into silence.

Another young man outside the house, turns to his friend and says, "Those hymns are so loud inside I can't hear myself pray." He too means to lighten the mood, but his friend only looks at him without expression. The memory of Alipate intervenes, his joking with Luke about writing their sins down on the same piece of paper stilling them both.

Jemesa is beginning his sermon, his voice booming as though to drown out any dissenting thoughts. "Give up these old Fijian things, these things of the devil, and come — come…come to Jesus." The *rewa*, he says, is "the sly tool of the devil. The devil makes us think the *rewa* is an oil for healing, a medicine, but it is really his way to our hearts. We rub that on ourselves not to protect ourselves, but to invite him into our souls." All those who have a *rewa* are targeted, in particular Tevita, Eroni, and Pita.

Jemesa doesn't mention anyone by name, however, and no one that afternoon admits guilt or asks for atonement. Yet the silence of the room, and the way people look away from those known to have *rewa*, condemn. The tension within that packed house prevails. After the service is over, Eroni seems strangely alone. The next day he delivers his *rewa* to Reverend Jemesa.

Tevita is reflective as he leaves the service, though he converses casually with his family. Reverend Jemesa has stopped short of confronting him. It's as if Jemesa acknowledges the respect that envelopes Tevita and his work in Tovu. But Jemesa visits him the morning after his sermon. With careful indirection, he asks, "Are you involved in what we call traditional Fijian religion?" Tevita evades more than responds, but when Reverend Jemesa departs to return to Suva, he is perhaps convinced his work is done.

The poison works slowly. Tevita is deeply troubled by the fact that many have given up their *rewa*, which he gave them for healing and protection, not killing. The fact that both his Ogo helper and Eroni gave up theirs is too much to comprehend. "Isn't our healing work for the good?" he asks, repeating the words in a daze, seeking strength from a question created in doubt, and each time it's asked, filling up more with confusion.

A week after Reverend Jemesa has left Tovu, the zeal he unleashed still vibrates, and several homes have become centers for continual prayer meetings. A negativity has formed against traditional Fijian worship,

241

and especially healing, though it remains tentative. Because Tevita and the other Tovu healers are each "one of us" — relatives, long-trusted companions — the criticism is not expressed openly.

But the atmosphere in Tovu has shifted. At the Tovu nursing station, Nasi has gone on a month-long vacation; her temporary replacement is a nurse without her respect for the work of Tevita and the Fijian way of healing. "If we let people go to those traditional healers," the substitute nurse says, "they could become sicker. They should come right away to the clinic." She does not speak badly of Tevita personally, but her commitment to the "modern way," to "scientific medicine" sows doubt that interferes with Tevita's work.

I pass Tevita's house on my way to the beach. People are still in their houses, drinking their morning tea, breakfasting on their morning cassava. Tevita is sitting outside, absentmindedly cutting shavings from the edge of a coconut husk.

We greet each other. Preoccupied, he remains committed, in a distracted way, to his whittling. He invites me to join him. We sit for several minutes, though it seems longer. Tevita seems to be in pain. Then he turns to me, his soft voice hiding the force of the feelings that now tumble out.

"I've been thinking a lot about what Reverend Jemesa said about 'all things Fijian.' I'm confused...I'm just confused." Tevita returns to his whittling, then speaks again.

"I don't know if I can continue the healing work. It seems that others now doubt its power. People don't come to me anymore. They doubt whether the work is for the good."

Tevita is no longer holding back, but his words still struggle for form. It is hard for him to name what he dreads to do.

"I'm not sure I can go on with this work if everyone else doubts it, and especially if that man of *Kalou* says I must give it up. I didn't turn in my *rewa* when he asked everyone to do that. I couldn't do that...because that *rewa* isn't mine to give away. It was given to me by Ratu Noa; it is for him to decide. But I just don't know what to do. I think — I think I'm going to have to stop the healing work.... I think I'm going to have to retire [*vakacegu*]."

I knew Reverend Jemesa's visit greatly troubled Tevita, but his conclusion still shocks me. How could such a good man, one doing such good work, be on the verge of ending his healing practice? I can't find the answer; and I don't give myself time to probe further.

"But you can't give up the work," I implore, touching Tevita's arm. "We all need your healing." I'm surprised by the force of my words; they don't seem to originate with me. Tevita returns the touch — and then we hold each other.

"Tevita, if you talk with others in their homes, as I've done, I know they'll tell you that your work must continue."

Although there are many reasons for Tevita to reconsider his decision, I feel uncomfortable; I know how seriously he has thought about it.

"I can tell you that the medicines and herbs you use are often greatly valued by doctors in the West. They wish to study these kinds of herbs and want to learn how to use them." I'm not sure whether this argument carries weight with Tevita, but I am marshaling all the forces at hand to establish the value of his work.

"And besides," I add, "this Reverend Jemesa may not be entirely correct. He may not know all there is to know about Fijian healing. After all, he's just one person, with just one person's point of view. And he doesn't know Fijian healing from actually practicing it — as you know it."

Even as I say this, I acknowledge the doubts raised in Tovu by the authority of Reverend Jemesa now that the village is in the middle of a religious revival. Do my words about Jemesa appear to be anti-Christian? I can't put Alipate out of my mind. Was his anti-Christian attitude, his flippant joking about Reverend Jemesa's sin papers, the cause of his death? But while I'm certain that my criticism of Reverend Jemesa is not anti-Christian, I feel how crippling the fear of being labeled un-Christian can be.

"Rusiate, I agree with what you say. I agree. But I'll tell you this. It's easier for me to say that when it's just you and me, talking like this, in private."

Tevita draws up from what has turned into idle picking at the coconut husk. "I agree with you, Rusiate. But I still remain unsure. And since I'm unsure, I think it's best that I discontinue the work."

243

"It'll be hard for all of us with you not working, but you must do what you feel is right." I respect Tevita's wish, but my mind is still trying to find some other outcome.

"Here's another idea," I offer. "I'm going to Suva soon. Suppose you give me a message to take to Ratu Noa about all this and see what advice he may have. Perhaps he can understand this mission of Reverend Jemesa better than we can. I can make a tape of your message if you like — just like the taped message he sent you. That way he can hear your thoughts and worries exactly. Maybe he can help you decide what to do."

"That's good, Rusiate. A tape like that will be good.... It was really helpful when I got Ratu Noa's tape about my healing work with Ogo. Until I get some answer back from him, I'll let people know that I'm retired from the healing work."

Four days later, Tevita asks me to bring the tape recorder to his house. When I arrive and have set up the machine, he begins his message to Ratu Noa. Largely ignoring the tape recorder itself, he reaches out to his teacher.

"Greetings to you, Ratu Noa. I am giving this message to Ratu Rusiate to bring to you as I'm unable to accompany him to Suva. I'm too busy here in Tovu.

"There is a big problem here in our area with the church's evangelical missionary work. For example, both my helper here and my helper in Ogo have surrendered their *rewa,* and so have many others. It's all happening because of the coming of Reverend Jemesa, the one who does the evangelical missionary work for the big church in Suva. Because of his work, people have surrendered all their objects that are used in traditional Fijian religion.

"I could see and feel that I was embarrassed with the coming of this missionary work to Tovu. Now I can also see that after Reverend Jemesa left, people here no longer come to me for help with their sicknesses.

"What I want to know is whether this traditional Fijian religion that we practice is in conflict with the aim of that missionary work. To me, I believe that we aren't serving the heathen version of religion. I believe we are doing healing work that is good and essential. But I'm not sure.

"Reverend Jemesa came to my house one day and asked me about the problems that are common here in Tovu. Then he questioned me whether I'm involved in the work we call Fijian religion. I found that I could not frankly state an answer to his question until I made contact with you.

"The problem is this: the evangelical missionary work is coming on strong here, and it seems to fight against our traditional Fijian religion.

"I need your help. A decision must be made. Do I hold on fast to our work? Or is there another alternative?

"I hope I've given you a clear picture of what is happening here so that I can have a clear picture back from you. I'm eager to hear your advice when Rusiate brings your speech back to Tovu. Until then, I'll be retired from the work."

Finishing his message to Ratu Noa, Tevita says goodbye as if they were face to face, unaware that the machine has been turned off. He is already anxiously awaiting Ratu Noa's response.

CHAPTER 22

The Weight of Suspicion (Tovu)

The winter settles on Tovu in July with relatively low evening temperatures of fifty degrees bringing a penetrating chill to the air. At night many people forsake their regular visiting, preferring to cover up early in blankets on their sleeping mats.

While Tevita waits for his response from Ratu Noa, he remains "retired." He has not entirely abandoned his healing work. The Monday night healing ceremonies have ceased for now, and the number of persons requesting his help has diminished; yet he is always available for healing emergencies. But his withdrawal from formal healing ceremonies seems to be part of a more general change of outlook. Not only has Reverend Jemesa "cleansed" Tovu of traditional Fijian religion, but also he has left an active evangelical group in his wake.

Suspicions still focus on the two suspected of doing the dance to the moon. Recently both men have been sick. Solomone became violently ill while in Suva, experiencing severe headaches and nearly losing consciousness. He was rushed to the hospital, where he recovered, but doctors could find no cause for his sickness. A traditional Fijian healer is said to have given him protection from another person who was doing *vakatevoro* on him. As for Pita, he has had a swollen and painful neck for the past several weeks. He first became sick toward the end of May, and at the time of Reverend Jemesa's visit in June, his condition grew worse.

Tevita has treated Pita several times in the last two weeks but cannot understand the cause of his problems.

The sicknesses of these two men, many believe, are a further sign of their connection to the earlier deaths. Both sicknesses, with their "mysterious" causes, show that these two men are "living close to the devil."

Any theory about the deaths which creates a satisfactory explanation draws people in with predictable fascination. Everyone tries to piece together fragments of information to make a coherent whole. It's as if many of us are working on a giant communal puzzle.

One evening when Inoke and I are visiting at Tevita's house, Inoke repeats a story he heard about Pita. Immediately our conversation becomes more hushed.

"Did you hear about Pita's visit to Reverend Jemesa?" he asks.

We nod, but encourage Inoke to continue.

"It seems he went to Ogo when Reverend Jemesa was there for his second visit, and I hear he went to confess his sins. He went personally to see the Reverend after the service was over."

"And I hear Pita may have confessed his role in the deaths here in Tovu," Inoke adds, almost innocently.

Tevita and I, who have been listening intently, sit back a bit at Inoke's last remark, as if to dissociate ourselves from the tale. Then we again lean toward Inoke, entranced by the prospect of new, maybe even definitive, information.

Inoke steams ahead. "I heard that Pita's wife and that woman who is my cousin accompanied him."

We wait, anticipating the logical next step.

"And maybe I can ask…" Inoke begins tentatively, "maybe I can ask that cousin of mine about what happened there in Ogo with Pita and Reverend Jemesa…. Maybe she'll tell me what he confessed about."

Yes, maybe, we say without words.

The next night the three of us are again gathered, this time at Inoke's. Without any plan, we're here. We talk and visit, as though without urgency, just enjoying each other's company.

"I spoke with my cousin," Inoke says, not interrupting our conversation, but slipping his announcement into a waiting space of silence.

"And she was willing to tell me what happened there at Ogo between Pita and Reverend Jemesa." Inoke's voice tells us that this accomplishment was not easy. We know how hard it would be to ask someone to describe a confession that definitely implicated a person. Inoke becomes distracted, then regains his focus to continue.

"My cousin, she was there, right there in Ogo with Pita and his wife. Pita said he wanted to see Reverend Jemesa, and he and the two women went over to the place where the Reverend was staying. At the door of that house, Pita turned to the two women and said, 'I'll go in alone.' That was all. He just said, 'I'll go in alone.' And that's all my cousin can report. Pita was in there alone, and only he and Reverend Jemesa know what he said."

We are more relieved than disappointed. Soon we are joking about our pursuit of information, how answers keep eluding us.

"Well," I add, "a confession is really between oneself and *Kalou*. No reason why we *should* be party to that communication."

Tevita and Inoke both agree.

"Tomorrow I've got to see Pita," I remark. "I have some cloth I want to give him, and I've been meaning to do it for almost a week. It won't be easy going over to his place. Especially given the way we're talking about him tonight."

"Don't worry, Rusiate," Inoke assures me in a joking tone. "Don't you worry. Now you can find out what happened that day in Ogo. Just ask Pita! 'What did you confess about?' You can just ask him!"

Inoke is teasing me — and isn't. This makes me uncomfortable.

"Inoke's right," Tevita joins in, he too both teasing and not teasing. "Tomorrow's the time. When you see Pita, you can ask him."

I don't have a good feeling when I leave Inoke's. Part of me agrees with them; I too would like to know what really happened.

In the morning I am reluctant about visiting Pita. Nor have I decided what I'll do there.

I enter Pita's house. His wife greets me.

"Pita's been a little tired these days," she says. "That sickness of his doesn't want to leave him.

"I'll go wake him," she offers, and before I can say 'it's okay, I'll come back later,' she has gone behind the curtain to rouse him.

Pita comes out to the center of the room and sits down next to me. We greet each other, then talk a little about the weather, and especially the cold nights.

As I look into Pita's eyes, I see just another human being, tiredness still controlling his face...that's all. Confessions, suspicions all seem irrelevant. Suddenly, I feel a flash of deep sadness that this man has been brought into all these damning scenarios. With shame, I remember my own curiosity.

We talk some more, just visiting. Then I give him the cloth and take my leave.

CHAPTER 23

"There Is Sickness in the Land" (Tovu)

During all of July and much of August, someone is seriously ill in at least one of the fourteen households in Tovu. For several weeks, four houses smell like hospitals, each with a sick person lying in bed and people visiting quietly throughout the day and on into the night. Early morning brings the only respite, as the families prepare for the new day's visitors; tending to the sick ones, refreshing them, comforting them. Then the air is still, and the rest of the village falls gratefully into normal routines. Soon enough those who are well will be visiting one or more of the sick people, and the depression that surrounds illness will return.

In addition to Pita's swollen neck, Solomone's condition remains troubling. He no longer has headaches, but his fatigue has deepened into a melancholy lethargy. The sharp winter sun cannot penetrate his mood, and the shutters of his house stay tightly sealed. One of the old women in Tovu has also weakened suddenly. An exceptionally active woman, whose strength has always been admired, she now only wants to lie in bed during the day. There is delicate talk of her advanced age, but people don't see that as an explanation. "Not that woman," her niece says. "Why, just the other day she was carrying her usual load of firewood." And this old woman carries among the largest loads in all of Tovu.

The most serious sickness involves Luke and Lariana's son Joeli, an unmarried man of about twenty, still very much an adolescent. He slipped while carrying coconuts in from the bush, and what started as a bruised back has turned into a numbness from the waist down. He lies in bed all day, unable to walk. Though not working on him intensively, Tevita accepts *yaqona* in order to perform a healing for Joeli and gives him massages and herbal remedies. "I will not ignore someone who is suffering like Joeli," Tevita says, "even though I cannot fully resume my healing work."

Nasi has returned from vacation, but still sickness does not yield. A phrase is often heard in Tovu: "There is sickness in the land." A few go a step further. As a woman elder puts it: "Ever since Tevita stopped his practice, sickness has taken over."

However, there is another response to the sickness: that of people who take part in the revival movement that sprang up after Reverend Jemesa's visit to Tovu. Evening prayer services are conducted by Nanise's husband, Vili, the leader of the movement, in his home. Usually three or four people gather to read the Bible and pray. At one point Nanise's sickness flares up, and a healing service is held at her bedside.

At times this group visits one of the other sick people in Tovu and Vili performs a healing service, praying over the sick person while he lays on "healing hands." These healing services attract a wide audience: some come in order to participate in the service, but most attend from a curiosity to witness this new and still strange event.

Vili's healing efforts are dramatically different from the private, understated nature of traditional healing practiced by Tevita. Vili prays intensely, in a loud voice amplified by his rising emotions. He can be heard several houses away, with the murmurs, sighs, and amens of others punctuating his rhythmic prayers. He gestures grandly, waving his arms over and around the head and body of the sick person. As the service proceeds and people's emotions accelerate, he begins to sway, and the others hover around him, ready to catch him in the swoon that never happens.

One night when I'm out walking with Luke, we pass a house where Vili is performing a healing service. I ask Luke about Vili's evangelical work. He replies matter-of-factly: "We've all known Vili since he was a little boy. He grew up in this village. You don't suddenly become a healer if there was nothing before in your life to give you that power. You have to develop that power and work at strengthening it. What Vili does

251

is all right. It probably helps people. But we don't take it as serious healing. For we know Vili very well...he's one of us. And he's not special in his knowledge and practice of healing. As long as he does only what he's really able to do — and no more — then I think what he does is all right."

The sickness is not confined to individual illnesses. Tovu's collective life also seems to be threatened as a new road is planned which will penetrate the boundaries of Tovu's sacred space.

As part of the national program of rural development, the road is to be built between Tovu and a village on the other side of Kali Island, replacing a footpath that in some places is difficult to negotiate. The initial planning for the road has been completed largely within the central government. Local involvement increases as the planners come to Tovu to look at the site and to solicit volunteer labor to assist government workers. The project precipitates a moral crisis when it becomes clear that the planned road will pass through a sacred area where the *Vu* are said to reside.

The elders of Tovu are deeply troubled. "The road threatens our sacred space; it will drive us from our traditional way," they lament.

"We have always been taught to respect those sacred places," says Asenati. "We never, ever enter them except for certain special ceremonies." Asenati looks down as she speaks, her demeanor underlining the seriousness of her concerns. "We always walk clear of them, staying away. Because the *Vu* live there and we respect the boundaries of their residence."

The attitudes of some adolescents toward the *Vu* are more lighthearted. "Yes, we stay clear...we don't want to meet any of those things in the bush — especially in the dark!" Though joking, these young people are showing their respect, fearing even to name the *Vu* other than by calling them "those things."

For a majority of people in both villages, however, especially the young adults, the road represents "progress." It is also an occasion for rural Kali to "get even" — to receive some of the government's largesse, which they believe is directed disproportionately to the urban area.

The elders speak to the head of the government road crew, which is now stationed in Tovu, to have the road redirected. He wants to accommodate them but the projected roadway cannot be made to bypass the

252

sacred area completely; the road will still touch on what the elders consider an outlying part of the area.

Members of the government road crew, themselves rooted in traditional rural values, are uneasy with this partial solution. "I can't go on with this without some kind of *yaqona* offering," says the crew head. Though he doesn't know what kind of ceremony is needed, he is not alone among the crew in his awareness of *rere,* the uncontrollable fear that comes over those who stumble on a sacred place in the bush.

Our local elders intervene and try to resolve the escalating dilemma. They make a ceremonial offering to the *Vu.* Encouraged by a group of progress-minded villagers, those in charge of the ceremony seek a compromise, asking the permission of the *Vu* to allow the road to contact the outskirts of the sacred area. But some elders, worrying that tradition is violated in the way the ceremony itself is conducted, privately voice their doubts. "You can't bargain with the *Vu,*" warns one old man. "Those who ran the ceremony want that road so bad they left out parts. You can't throw away respect for the *Vu* just for a road!" An old woman adds her view: "And did you hear what they said? Is that the proper way to offer *yaqona*? Were those the proper words of prayer?"

At the end of the ceremony, those in charge pronounce that the road project can continue along the redirected route without violating the sacred space or showing disrespect for the *Vu.* Yet a number of elders remain unconvinced. "You don't compromise your sacred obligations," one woman insists. Her husband nods in agreement. In their view the ceremony has not settled the issue; in fact, it has made the dilemma more difficult. Tradition, embodied in the ceremony, has been misused, which makes the issue of the road even more threatening. "How can we be straight if our road is crooked?" asks one elder.

The compromise is not a permanent solution. For some, Tovu is no longer "sick in its heart"; but for others, it is still not well.

Individual sicknesses in Tovu also seem to resolve only in part. There is no clear understanding of why so many became sick or what their sicknesses mean, but those who were ill during July and August generally recover.

Except for Joeli. His sickness continues...and gets worse.

253

CHAPTER 24

Joeli's Sickness (Tovu)

"How did it come to this?" Laniana asks Inoke and me. "How did my boy Joeli become so sick?"

Laniana's pained look does not accuse. It only seeks the comfort of some explanation she can understand. We are seeking the same comfort.

For the past two weeks Joeli's condition has unaccountably worsened. Only Joeli can know when his illness began, so insidiously did it start. Joeli has recited the history of his illness several times, with the corroboration and addition of certain details from Nasi and his parents. His story is now common knowledge.

Three weeks ago, Joeli noticed a sore spot on his heel. It didn't bother him. He remembered it only two days later, when he slipped on a dew-drenched tree root while carrying a heavy bag of cassava back from his family's garden. Falling hard on a bulge in the root, Joeli hit the small of his back and almost passed out. He felt an intense shooting pain at the moment of impact, but afterward only a throbbing persisted. He got up after resting a minute or two, then carried the cassava into the village.

For the next five days, Joeli tried to go about his normal activities, thinking nothing of the fall. But a throbbing continued, now centered again in his heel, which limited his movement. By the seventh day the pain was too much, and Joeli went to the nursing station. Nasi gave him an injection of penicillin, and another the next day. She diagnosed the pain as caused by an infected bruise on his heel.

254

Joeli felt no improvement after having the shots. In fact, the pain grew worse, and was now focused in his lower back. The next day, Joeli's parents called for his grandmother, Asenati, to come and massage him. Joeli's pain lessened, and for the next four days, he moved about more, trying to exercise his legs and back. He was able to walk, though only with a certain stiffness. At times the pain returned, and he was forced to rest.

Four days ago, a new symptom appeared — a numbness in his right leg. Walking then became difficult for Joeli, and he began to spend most of his time in bed. The next day, a numbness appeared in his left leg. And then he walked only when he had to relieve himself.

The day numbness began to occupy both his legs, Joeli received help from three different sources. The family asked Lilieta, one of the other traditional healers in Tovu, to see him. She massaged Joeli, focusing her thrusting movements along his thighs and legs while rubbing his feet very gently, almost without touching them.

Later that day, the medical doctor stationed in Delana, who was in Tovu on his triannual rounds, made a house visit to examine Joeli. Nasi, worried about the persistence of Joeli's pain and the recent deterioration of his condition, had asked the doctor to see him.

People in the village are uncomfortable around this doctor. His attitude of superiority makes them feel stupid, as if they are to blame for their sicknesses. When the doctor visited, Joeli became withdrawn, giving minimal responses to his questions. Joeli talked only about the pain in his back, omitting entirely the numbness in his legs. The doctor's diagnosis: muscular backache. His prescription: aspirin and rest.

That evening, the family finally sent for Tevita. Though officially retired, Tevita never rejects requests for help. The family needed Tevita because Joeli's illness had taken on a new, disturbing symptom — his stomach had started to swell, and painful gases gurgled inside. Most important, Tevita was needed because Joeli's sickness defied the help he had received thus far.

Speaking to Inoke and me, Laniana put it this way: "This sickness of Joeli's must be from *vakatevoro*, because it keeps moving from place to place after different help from different people. When Joeli's grandmother massaged him, the pain moved from his leg to his back; and when Lilieta massaged him, the pain left the back and the stomach started to swell. The devil is running away from each healer, reappearing in another place."

"There are a lot of devils in Tovu," added Luke. "And now our boy is their victim."

This supposition of *vakatevoro* did not come casually. Most sicknesses are recognized as stemming from natural causes; the numerous aches, pains, cuts, and infections people have are usually treated at the clinic, and many more serious conditions such as high blood pressure, fatigue and loss of appetite, anxiety and loss of sleep are also seen as *tauvimate dina*, whether they are treated at the clinic or by Tevita, or both. But illnesses attributed to *vakatevoro* grab an inordinate amount of attention and concern. They suggest something "out of control." "That *vakatevoro* is dangerous," said Luke, "because we don't know where it comes from and when it will strike." Whenever there is a major unexplained element in a sickness — for example, if the illness persists long after it should, or if it "moves around" — *vakatevoro* is one explanation.

In Joeli's case, no one mentioned the failure of the Western medical help given by Nasi and the doctor; it was understood. What was on people's minds was *vakatevoro* — and curing that is Tevita's specialty.

Tevita examined Joeli, carefully touching his distended stomach. He leaned over the boy, asking a few questions. "It's his bowels," Tevita said. "He hasn't moved his bowels for a while. That's why his stomach swells up." Tevita massaged Joeli's stomach, both hands almost caressing his bulging flesh. Then he brought over a medicine for Joeli to drink.

"This *wai* will tell us what is involved," Tevita said to Laniana and Luke. "Depending on how he responds, we'll know whether there's *vakatevoro* involved or not."

Less than two hours later, Joeli threw up. He said he felt better, but was still weak. "I just have to lie here for a while," he said, then fell asleep.

Tevita had his diagnosis. The medicine he gave Joeli was meant to make him vomit, to get rid of the wastes accumulating inside him. When the boy responded as intended, Tevita knew that *vakatevoro* was indeed involved. The next day Tevita gave Joeli another medicine for *vakatevoro* and massaged him on three different visits.

But Joeli's pain worsened, now becoming more localized in his spine. He lay in bed all day, only sitting up on occasion. He could no longer walk, or even stand, unassisted.

At night, Tevita gave Joeli another medicine for *vakatevoro,* and again he threw up. His stomach lost its ugly bulging, and the pain left that area.

But Joeli became very cold as evening came on. He complained especially about his legs and feet. "They're so cold," he moaned, his whole body shivering. Laniana and Luke applied steaming hot towels to his legs, asking, "Is it any better now? Do you feel the warmth?" And Joeli kept saying: "No — no…it's still too cold." More and hotter towels were applied until finally the boy fell asleep.

In the morning, the skin on Joeli's legs and feet was badly burned, the damage horrifying all who viewed it. The numbness in Joeli's legs was more serious than anyone had thought: he hadn't felt the warmth of the towels, even when they carried extreme heat.

Inoke and I now sit in the growing afternoon shadow at Joeli's bedside. Laniana smothers her weeping in a towel as she looks at her son. Luke wipes the sweat from the boy's forehead. From his calves down to his feet, Joeli's legs are covered with raw skin and bulging white blisters. A shiny surface of oil highlights the ravaged skin. He doesn't say much, but his soft, half-sounds cry out his pain.

Joeli's parents are deeply confused. Though the chronology and symptoms of the illness are clear, the illness itself remains hidden. "Why Joeli?" "Why do his pains keep shifting from place to place?" "Why doesn't he get better?" The members of Joeli's family keep asking these questions of each other and the friends who visit. From his expression, these questions no doubt trouble Joeli as well. The whys of his sickness yield no answers. Now even the family's own efforts to help seem destructive.

I've talked with Joeli and his parents throughout the course of the sickness, listening to their fears and confusion and offering whatever help I can. Today is especially hard; both Laniana and Luke feel terribly guilty about Joeli's burns. We talk about how their feelings of being responsible for their son's pain can be understood and accepted, and the stranglehold on their emotions seems to loosen. I've been working closely with Tevita during his visits to Joeli, helping him administer medicines, holding Joeli while Tevita massages him, massaging him myself. And most important, though the Monday night healing ceremonies have ceased, Tevita and I continue to drink *yaqona* in our special way during ordinary *yaqona* sessions at other houses. Tevita has also held a healing ceremony at Joeli's bedside, where we were joined by Laniana and Luke.

Joeli's withdrawal has become foreboding. A quiet, almost shy young man, he is now encased in silence. For the past four days there has been a constant stream of visitors. In the Fijian custom of *veisiko*, when someone is sick groups of people — whole families, friends, church clubs, people from the nursing station — bring gifts and spend time with the sick person and the family. Some people in Tovu visit numerous times as members of various groups. But Joeli lies quietly amid the animated conversation that usually accompanies these visitations — except when the young men of the village come as a group to visit. For his "buddies" he manages to joke a bit, though his smile is weak, almost pathetic. It makes his family weep to think about it.

Laniana and Luke are determined to find the root of Joeli's sickness. With Tevita's diagnosis of *vakatevoro*, they turn their attention to the questions of who might be responsible, and how it was done. "Once we know that," Luke speculates, "then we can do something about the sickness."

Luke again goes to Tevita for help, this time taking with him a dream. Believing he already knows the dream's meaning, Luke seeks Tevita's confirmation. As he relates the dream, the inevitable attribution of blame for Joeli's illness emerges.

"I come over to my *bure*," Luke begins. "And once inside I see, near the left side door, that a man is playing around with an outboard engine that rests on a wooden stand." Luke unwraps his dream more slowly now. "It is inside my *bure*. And a group of men is sitting around that engine. That man who was playing with the engine pulls the cord to start it. And as he does, sparks begin to jump out. Sparks come flying out of the engine, leaping about. I rush over to the engine with my jacket and cover it, trying to put out the sparks." Luke pauses to take a breath. "I think they are all put out…but then some of the sparks leap up…to the roof of the *bure*. I don't know this man who was playing with the engine, but I know a bad thing is about to happen. Then the sparks flying up to the *bure*'s roof burst into flames, and the roof catches on fire. I climb up the center pole, then over the cross poles, and then quickly reach up for the roof. I have a blanket with me, and I race to different sections of the roof, putting out the flames, which are starting to spread."

Tevita is silent for a moment. "Fire inside a house," he says, "is a very bad thing. It is such a great danger. It's the work of *vakatevoro*."

Tevita doesn't identify the man who started the engine, causing the sparks to leap out. But Luke, without mentioning his name, clearly thinks Pita is "that man" in his dream; by extension, Pita is the one causing the danger right now in Luke's own house.

"He's the one, isn't he? He's the one doing that *vakatevoro*," Luke announces as much as asks. Still not mentioning Pita's name, he describes how "that man" was looking out of his house the other day in a very suspicious way, looking toward Luke's, where the sick Joeli lay, "as if he was checking to see the results of his work." And Luke has more evidence: "Also," he adds, "'that man' didn't come to visit Joeli until almost everyone else had come, and then he only sat in the back, didn't say anything, and left after only a short time. What kind of visit was that? He was too guilty to stay for a proper visit! It's those things he does that show he's guilty."

Luke rests his case. Tevita doesn't explicitly agree, but by not disagreeing, he reinforces Luke's suspicion.

By coming to Tevita, Luke has strengthened his resolve to fight the *vakatevoro*. "I must put out that fire in my house," he asserts. At the same time, he has become more convinced of the strength of his opponent. "Now I see how that *vakatevoro* can come at you from all sides."

Luke now decides to offer a *bulubulu,* a ceremonial apology and request for forgiveness to the village of Tovu. For several years, Luke has acted as chief in Tovu, assuming that role until a new hereditary chief can be selected to replace the one who died. He wants to clear the air of all misunderstandings or wrongdoings he may have committed in this role.

"I want to be sure my actions haven't offended the *vanua* and the *Vu,* and as a result brought misfortune to my family — and to my Joeli."

Luke offers his *bulubulu* to the assembled elders of Tovu, apologizing for his past errors: for at times speaking too harshly and without respect, for not always fairly distributing the *yau* that came into the village. He asks for forgiveness and promises to correct his mistakes.

On behalf of the *vanua,* and speaking for the elders, Solomone accepts Luke's *bulubulu* and declares him clean. "If you did something wrong, all is now forgiven."

After the ceremony is over, Luke tells me he acted improperly because he was in error. "So many things have been occupying my mind," he says, "including now the sickness of my son, that I've forgotten my proper behavior. I do that *bulubulu* to apologize for my mistakes in the proper way, so that I can cancel out the anger people may feel toward me, and then Joeli can become better."

But though the *bulubulu* is over and the apology accepted, questions linger…and multiply.

"I didn't advise Luke to do the *bulubulu,*" Tevita comments. "After he came to me with the fire dream, he was the one who proposed doing it. We have to wait and see if the *bulubulu* is sincere or not. It was accepted by the elders, yes, that's true. But some who accepted it actually felt inside that they weren't sure. They want to wait and see for themselves if Luke actually changes his behavior. And since Joeli is still sick after the ceremony is over, that's further reason to believe the *bulubulu* may not have completely cleared the air."

Another elder has a slightly different opinion. "Since Joeli didn't recover right away after the *bulubulu,* I believe there were no prior bad actions on Luke's part in regard to the *vanua.* Because if there were, then since his apology was accepted, right away Joeli should have improved since the cause of his illness was now removed."

Inoke has yet another interpretation. "Since that *bulubulu* was accepted," he says, "Luke is clean of whatever problem he had with the *vanua.* He has atoned. But since Joeli hasn't recovered, *vakatevoro* remains the logical cause. And there's further evidence of this *vaka-*

tevoro. Joeli's sickness doesn't proceed in one simple, straight line. It keeps shifting and changing its course. First it's his heel, then his back, then his legs, then the swelling stomach, now the numbness. His sickness keeps jumping from place to place."

Joeli is in fact getting sicker. Now he cannot lift his legs. They lie there, the burn blisters still wet, seemingly disconnected from his body. He is numb from the waist down. Tevita returns to massage him again. In the evening, Vili brings his prayer group to the house and they perform a healing service, though this time they are more subdued than usual.

For a while now, I have felt that Joeli should be sent to the Suva hospital. Whatever the cause of Joeli's condition, the hospital can add an element of treatment that could be significant. As I've learned, good healers take advantage of any treatment that might help and, when appropriate, make referrals themselves to the hospital. Tevita is such a healer, and he and I have already discussed the necessity of moving Joeli to Suva.

Inoke and Nasi are also convinced that Joeli should be transferred to the hospital. Both have been closely involved over the course of Joeli's sickness. And because of Joeli's numbness, Inoke says there is pressure on the spinal cord, thereby discarding his earlier diagnosis of infection. So just to be ready, Nasi wires for a ship from Suva to pick Joeli up.

But others in Tovu, and especially Joeli, his family, and his friends, have an intense fear of the hospital; they do not want to talk about sending him there. "It's not a place for our boy," Luke laments. "How could he live in such a place?"

The family's wishes must be respected; we can't steamroll over them. Laniana's and Luke's confusion and fear must subside before they can make a decision. It is Tevita who guides them through their fears. At this point, he is in charge of Joeli's case; he must discharge his patient to the hospital before the family can act.

"My part of Joeli's treatment is now completed," he says. "I've cleared away anything that may be due to problems in the spirit world. I've also done what I can to clear up what is due to natural causes. But sickness still remains. So I think he should go to a Western doctor. I've cleared the path for Western medicine to work, but I can go no further. I've reached the limits of my work. Now we should send Joeli to the hospital in Suva."

Reluctantly, the family agrees. Joeli is silent; he is too terrified to voice an opinion.

But the way is still not clear. Because the ships that make the trip between Bitu and Suva are undergoing unexpected repairs, we must wait another four days.

It is now twenty-two days since Joeli first noticed the sore spot on his heel. Today he is a very sick young man. In a private conversation he and I have, he expresses his fear at what is happening to him, and his dread of what is to come. "The hospital in Suva," he murmurs, "that hospital…it's a place where people die." I hold his hand as his fears tumble out. He becomes a little calmer.

Three days later the ship arrives. Joeli is carried out to the small boat that ferries him to the ship, which is anchored in the bay. The improvised stretcher of several blankets draped over two long poles cradles his now frail body. Four of the strongest young men carry him delicately, battling the incoming tide and wind-swept waves with the lower halves of their bodies.

Joeli is frozen in panic. Wide with fear, his eyes look like those of a wild animal skewered by the hunter's searchlight. But, there is no fight left in him, not even the ability to move. No one wants to pose the thought clearly, but many see Joeli, sunk into a blanket-coffin, as if he were already dead.

CHAPTER 25

Conversations with Ratu Noa (Suva)

*"Long before they came to our land,
we knew of* Kalou — *the One Living God."*

The ship that takes Joeli to Suva also takes me to Ratu Noa. It's been nearly two months since Tevita retired from the healing work, a victim of Reverend Jemesa's cleansing mission. Since then, because no ships were available sooner, I've held Tevita's tape asking Ratu Noa for advice on how to proceed. Now, in mid-August, I'm finally in the city.

But the visit is overshadowed by Joeli's sickness. When we arrive, he is carried off the boat in Suva on a hospital stretcher by two nurses. Luke and I, the only two people known to him, must trail behind, forced away by the waiting ambulance crew.

Joeli looks sick, and also scared — very scared. Modern medical equipment frightens him and his father. Rolled briskly from the ship and slid into the ambulance, his body is stiff. His eyes search chaotically for some familiar comfort. The very professionalism of his care — the whiteness of the nurses' uniforms, the polished gleam of the metal bed, the unyielding red flashing from the ambulance roof, and the hurtful scream of the siren — only throws him deeper into fear's corner, so far inside we can no longer communicate with him.

Once in the hospital, it's only a little better. He feels each new hospital procedure — none ever really explained to him — as an invasion. His fear goes on alert, and the wildness returns. Draped in white, Joeli looks wrapped for death. With only his father and me to visit him, and then only during the brief visiting hours, he is alone, adrift in a strange and frightening world. Occasionally, he enjoys a joke or two, but mostly he is still...and confused. There is not yet a clear indication of what is wrong with him. Western medicine is also stumped by his case, but less willing to admit it.

Death has also preceded my visit to Ratu Noa. Arriving in Suva, I learn that his son, who was approaching his twenty-eighth birthday, died nearly four weeks ago. Partying with a group of friends late into the night, the drinking turned sour and a fight broke out. Knives flashed. People screamed. Ratu Noa's son was brutally beaten about the head and stabbed several times in the stomach. Struggling to get home, trying to stop the blood, he made it as far as a deserted road less than one-half mile away. There, in the cold of the early winter morning, unable to generate the strength for another step, he lay down and died.

Ratu Noa and his family are devastated. The boy had such a bright future, everyone says; his death was so unnecessary. Nawame is also angry: "Why did it have to be that boy?" she demands. She wonders if she and Ratu Noa did enough as parents. "Did we teach him the right way?" she asks. "Did we teach him about alcohol? Did we teach him it can kill you?" Her questions judge her husband as much as herself.

The initial ceremonies commemorating the death are over. Grief is now part of the family's life, a permanent fact after the original disbelief and horror.

Tonight I go to Ratu Noa's with a *tabua*, my contribution to the family to honor their loss. I'm not sure whether to deliver Tevita's message. It depends on the *tabua* ceremony and, more important, how the family feels.

The house looks the same. Activities continue as usual. While Ratu Noa prepares to sit down for our conversation, Nawame gets her nurse's uniform ready; she is working the night shift. Their daughter is putting her two children to bed. Everything looks the same, but the atmosphere is muted.

I present the *tabua*, which Ratu Noa receives on behalf of the family. Nawame and their daughter are seated around him on the floor. Only a few words are said, expressing my sadness and sympathy, the family's sadness and acceptance.

"And with all this we go on," Nawame says, rising to continue her preparations for going out and bringing the *tabua* presentation to an end. "We go on...and you two, you and Ratu Noa, should carry on with your work. It's important work. Please — now, carry on."

I look toward Ratu Noa. "Whatever you wish. I can come back another night for our talk. That's no problem.... I can just come back another night."

"Rusiate, you're here...and I'm glad you've come. We're glad you can share in our grief. And my wife is right. Our work must go on. Tonight we talk. So — tell me the news from Tovu."

I tell him about Reverend Jemesa's cleansing mission in Tovu, the giving up of the *rewa*, and Tevita's decision to retire. Then I play the tape with Tevita's message. It's sad to hear again Tevita's description of how Reverend Jemesa has collected the people's *rewa* and other objects of traditional Fijian religion, how people in Tovu are no longer coming to him, how doubt has penetrated into his resolve to continue the healing work. I'm sad, and angry that Tevita has been made to give up his work in this way.

"Would you like to hear it again?"

"No, Rusiate. Once is enough. I understand Tevita's dilemma. The trouble is that many people are taking advantage of him, especially the people of the village. It's not like people from other villages. When there's a problem or sickness, they come straight to him. But I would say the people of Tovu have lessened their trust in Tevita."

"Yes. There is a lessening of trust in Tovu."

"In this work, Rusiate, faith is the key. If there's faith, all is possible. Without faith, sometimes it works...and sometimes not."

A sadness has come into Ratu Noa's voice, but he carries on. Soon he resumes his usual calm, authoritative tone. "*Kalou* gives each people their own form of worship, and each is different. It took a long time for me to extract myself from the way white people worship, and that cleared the path for the Fijian way. But most Fijians are unstable. We have a tendency to be swayed too easily from our own way and to rush to follow other teachings. The reason is that we lack truth and honesty."

"What will become of Tevita's task?" I ask.

"Tevita's duty is to heal people at all times. But Reverend Jemesa comes to preach in Tovu — and then he returns to his home here in Suva," Ratu Noa says with uncharacteristic sarcasm. "We're all different, and we have different ideas about *Kalou*. And that's okay. But remember, there is only one *Kalou*. And there are still some people who are ignorant of *Kalou*, the One Supreme Living God. That is the cause of the problem.

"Reverend Jemesa was mistaken in saying that it is wrong to use traditional Fijian rituals these days. The only thing wrong about these rituals is if you do not perform them in the proper manner; that's when you'll get the bad end of the deal.

"Yet most Fijians today want to do away with the Fijian way of life. That's Reverend Jemesa's one aim: to abolish all traditional Fijian rituals. But these traditions, these rituals, are given by *Kalou* for us to use, and to use wisely, without abusing them."

Ratu Noa's anger has subsided. "Most people today are ignorant of these traditions and their meaning. It was the same when Jesus came. Look at what happened when Jesus first came to the Temple. The priests did not believe he was Jesus. They reacted with fear: fear that secrets would be exposed, especially those about healing. The priests hated Jesus because he was healing the sick. Nothing more! Simply the fear that he would become known all over the land for his healing work. So they said Jesus was not the son of *Kalou*. But Jesus worked with *mana*. And now we know the priests were wrong: Jesus is the son of *Kalou*."

"We Fijians must practice our traditional ways without fearing they are weak or wrong. But there are quite a few among us who don't really understand the inner part of these traditional rituals and ways of living. For example, I don't think many Christian preachers realize they did not bring *Kalou* to us. Long before they came to our land, when we first arrived here as a people, we already knew of the One Supreme Power.

266

We knew of *Kalou*, what we call the One Living God, the God who rules among all our Fijian gods."

"What about Reverend Jemesa's asking the Tovu people to turn in their healing *rewa* as a sign of giving up their evil ways?" I ask. "I can't believe that's right. I said that to Tevita, but it's hard to speak out against the church."

Ratu Noa understands the difficulties Tevita faces in Tovu. He, however, is not held back in the same way.

"What Reverend Jemesa is doing is not in accordance with the will of *Kalou*. It comes from his own desire to build himself up so he can become a big shot. He does not realize what he is doing. He is killing the very foundations of our way of life, destroying the very core of Fijian tradition and social structure. It is not enough for Reverend Jemesa to go to Tovu, pray a little, and then go back to Suva. If he wants to achieve something worthwhile, he must be with the Tovu people, live and work with them, help solve problems that arise in day-to-day activities.

"I know what I am saying. I am deep within the inner circle of our traditions and the traditional religion. I have gone right up to the uppermost limit...where I see *Kalou*. I hate it when a person speaks like Reverend Jemesa, telling me rubbish when I am well acquainted with the real nature of the universe. Most people have not seen and do not know the true facts; they do not know the differences between *Kalou*, the *Vu*, and the *tevoro*.

Ratu Noa's words are vivid with emotion. We do not speak right away.

"I told Tevita he should carry on with his work," I finally say — "that he shouldn't be scared, because his work is true and just. He agreed that his work might have some truth, but he still would like to discuss things with you."

"One who knows and has reached the highest level of attainment can see the real and true facts," Ratu Noa responds. "The person who is only halfway doesn't fully grasp the facts. If we know the real facts about Tevita's healing work, we know that he isn't here to kill people; his role is to heal the sick. But as I've already said, the priests in the era of Jesus hated him simply because they feared he would become a famous healer.

"Rusiate, there are those who know about *Kalou*...and I am one of those. In the realm of *Kalou* and the *Vu*, this is where my work has been concentrated. Because I've already seen *Kalou*...and therefore I know. And I also read the Bible and study what it says.

"What's so sad, Rusiate, is that Christian people ignorantly changed our traditional religion so that now it's considered to be worshiping devils. Yet the Christian version of religion only makes our life more difficult — it's full of loopholes, and in places it's false."

Ratu Noa takes a deep breath. His manner is intensely sincere.

"The truth that binds the Fijian healer is that his assignment is healing...and nothing more. It is that truth he must face. There's no other place to go. But it all depends on whether we wish to continue the practice — or give it up. If we wish to give it up, it clearly shows a weakness on our part."

As Ratu Noa serves another round, *yaqona* sounds absorb our voices.

For several moments there is no conversation. Then Ratu Noa speaks.

"There's also another way of looking at this," he begins. "I cannot say that I am perfect. I cannot just say that someone performed *vakatevoro* and that is why my son died. The thing is...the thing is — what about me? Am I clean? No stains? It's wrong just to accuse someone else for my son's death. We must also realize it's the will of *Kalou*. His will must be done, and so it is done.

"A minister came here to my house after my son's stabbing and prayed. I knew that that minister didn't know what he was doing, because what I can see, he cannot. What is needed is a straight heart. I must not be angry with others. And I must pray...really pray. If I pray with my tongue, but my soul is far away, that is only lip service.

"If we cannot hear *Kalou* speaking to us, Rusiate, it is because our approach to him is incorrect; we are on the wrong path. Read the Bible. When *Kalou* spoke, the Israelites heard him. The Christianity brought into Fiji by the white people has ruined our traditional way of life. We were not heathens when the white people came here! We had our own religion and we were worshiping God Almighty through our *Vu* — and *yaqona* was the medium."

268

Now intimate, Ratu Noa's tone conveys the strength of his convictions. "My children know that I have seen *Kalou* six times. In my sleep I saw him, right here. Here where I sat, I saw him. That Reverend Jemesa has not seen *Kalou*. And why me? I am not a reverend or even a churchgoer. If one does not go to church in Fiji, one is considered a heathen, even when there is no good reason to go.

"What *Kalou* wants is for the people to have straight and clean hearts. There should be no evil thoughts inside your house. If there are, you must change."

Our talk is ending as the last *yaqona* empties from the *tanoa*. "I do not drink liquor, Rusiate, only *yaqona*. *Yaqona* opens up my mind so that I can think properly. There are great dangers to drinking liquor. Like with my son who was just killed. He died through the abuse of liquor. He went and got drunk and got hurt. People wanted to borrow money from him, but he said he had none. Then someone beat him up and he died. Had he been sober he would have come directly home.

"Rusiate, Westerners may say they drink liquor moderately, or for their health. But…well, I know when Fijians take liquor they often reach a stage of helplessness, where they cannot control themselves. Also, they spend too much money on liquor, neglecting their families. And though they don't talk about it, I believe Westerners have these same problems."

Ratu Noa stops our talk without his usual closing remarks. Clearly, his son's death still plagues him.

Before I go, Ratu Noa records a brief message to Tevita for me to take back to Tovu. It's the advice Tevita's been waiting for.

"I'll play it for Tevita as soon as I arrive back in Tovu, when just the two of us can find a time and place to be alone."

"That's how he should listen to it," Ratu Noa agrees. "So he can hear properly."

CHAPTER 26

Ratu Noa's Message to Tevita

"Greetings to you, Tevita. I have received your message about the visit of Reverend Jemesa to Tovu and how you've decided to retire from the work. I've listened to that message, for which I want to thank you very much.

"You ask me for advice. You wonder what to do. Now I wish to show you the facts in regard to your questions.

"Everything on this earth is given by *Kalou* — there is nothing created by man. The healing work you and I are doing is a gift from *Kalou*. No human being, Reverend Jemesa or anyone else, from the church or from any other place, can take that healing work away from you.

"It's the folly of men that creates problems because we don't know the will of *Kalou*. Our Fijian way of worshiping and of serving *Kalou* is given to us, and it is for us to lose — not to be taken from us. There is only one enemy among us, whom you understand and know as the devil — every other thing is nothing. That's all you need to know as a basis for deciding about the healing work.

"Think of the priests in the time of Jesus. Jesus performed healing miracles. That's why those priests accused Jesus, saying he wasn't the son of *Kalou,* but instead was possessed with devils. They accused him because they themselves couldn't do what he was doing.

"Tevita, I'm giving you the foundation to work from. And don't be led astray by Reverend Jemesa's preachings. Remember, if someone comes to you in trouble, and Reverend Jemesa is preaching right next door, it's up to you to decide whether or not you serve that patient and heal him. If you believe this healing talent is given to you by *Kalou,* then serve that patient.

"And don't worry if the people are not coming to you for help. That's their way of deciding. It may be a good time for you to have a rest. But they will come again — and then you'll have to serve them. You must always think deeply about the part you play in serving the *vanua.*

"Tevita, do not lose hope. *Kalou* will show the truth. Don't be discouraged by the harsh words and gossip that goes around Tovu. And should Reverend Jemesa want to run you down, let him do so. And then tell the people, and tell him, that the Bible says some people are nearer to *Kalou,* not through words that come only from the mouth, but through words that come from the heart.

"Let me repeat. No person can take the healing work away from you. Only if you're no longer on the straight path, no longer even struggling to stay on that path, will the healing work end — and then *it* leaves *you.*

"I tell you this, Tevita. Don't be disheartened. These things I speak of are facts. If it so happens that we are doing the wrong work, that our service is unjust, then we *should* be afraid! But you are involved in healing, and you should be grateful for that.

"Tevita — carry out the duties that *Kalou* gave you.

"That is all I have to say. And thank you for listening."

CHAPTER 27

Tevita is No Longer Retired (Tovu)

Tevita and I sit in my house during a rare moment alone in the middle of the afternoon. I play the tape containing the message from Ratu Noa. Tevita cranes his neck toward the recorder and cups his ear; the sound level, though low, is adequate.

Ratu Noa's message, recorded in strength, conveys strength; offering hope, gives it; demanding truth, expects it; and bowing before *Kalou*, prays to *Kalou*.

Tevita asks to hear the tape again, and again he leans toward the recorder, entering into its sound-space.

"I'd like to hear that message again, a little later. Is that possible?" he asks.

"Sure. You can have the tape…and use this tape recorder."

I give Tevita a quick lesson in using the recorder. One of his sons, who has worked in Suva for several years, is also familiar with these machines, so I know he will be fine replaying the tape.

Several days later, Tevita has a healing session. It's a brief ceremony, and only the two of us are there. It is a Monday night in August, almost three months since Tevita decided to retire. With this ceremony he announces he is resuming the healing work. The work never entirely stopped, of course, since he was always available if needed. But as he now tells those who ask, "I'm no longer retired."

The next day Tevita and I discuss Ratu Noa's message.

"On hearing that message, I find that Ratu Noa is right," Tevita says firmly. "Reverend Jemesa did not behave properly. He was showing off. When Reverend Jemesa came, he did a lot of things that frightened us. He is doing more harm than good, and harassing people. But this message from Ratu Noa is perfect, perfectly to the point. Ratu Noa's words have given me confidence. He said that the *rewa* he gave me is from *Kalou*. And that Reverend Jemesa's version of things — working through prayer — is also *Kalou*'s gift. There is nothing created by man."

I agree. "The medicines, the serving of others, everything."

"And that preaching and Bible lessons that Reverend Jemesa was doing," Tevita adds, "those too are things originally from *Kalou*.

"You know, Rusiate, one of the men came to me with a *yaqona* to atone for his mistake in giving up his *rewa* that I'd given him earlier. I asked him where the *rewa* was, and he said that Reverend Jemesa had taken it away. And that man came with another *yaqona*, requesting that I help him to retrieve the *rewa*."

"What did you do?"

"I gave him a massage, and another *rewa*. He came to me in the right way with his request. Now he can start again, and the *rewa* will give him protection."

"But another man came with a *yaqona* asking for a new *rewa*," Tevita adds, "and I turned it down."

"Turned it down?" This is the first time I've heard of Tevita's doing such a thing.

"I turned it down because he must first present an atonement for having given up his *rewa* to Reverend Jemesa, and he didn't. Surrendering their *rewa* the way they did showed a dislike for me and this work."

"I think people will start using the healing work again, Tevita. That's what Ratu Noa said."

"I think so too, Rusiate. But I feel bad about the sickness that has gone on while I was retired. I heard about the death of one old woman in Ogo. If I had been responsible for her care, she wouldn't have died. One of her relatives should've come to me and asked for help.

"And those Ogo fishing boat people, it's the same with them. They used to be with me every Monday with *yaqona* to fortify them in their business. Now they don't come — and they're awaiting a court order charging them with carrying too many passengers on their vessel. If they'd have continued fortifying themselves with the *yaqona,* there'd be no court case."

I think about Joeli, now in Suva hospital. Though he was then retired, Tevita worked on him. We worked together.

"What about Joeli? When I saw him in Suva hospital, he still seemed so sick."

"Joeli's sickness has progressed very fast," Tevita observes. "Though at times he may seem in good shape, that's only a temporary condition. His sickness is a *tauvimate vakavanua,* caused by a violation of one of our sacred traditions. There are things Luke did, connected with his role as acting chief, which caused that illness. Luke didn't get the villagers' consent to use village things for his own use. Only when Luke's *bulubulu* ceremony is finally fully accepted by all can the horror of Joeli's fate be lifted. And since I believe some of the elders and people at the *bulubulu* are 'dirty within their hearts,' not really accepting the *bulubulu* although they speak nicely, then the *bulubulu* is useless.

"Joeli's case is very difficult. It seems his body is okay, but he's still unable to walk. He's like a patient who has been bedridden for six months or a year. Even though Joeli had only been lying down for several days, already he seem to have died. He looked as if he was bitten up! A few days in bed and he couldn't walk! He's still a young man, yet he now looks so old, like an old man who has suffered from years and years of cold and hard work."

"Joeli's sickness has troubled us all," I reflect. "It happened so quickly. None of us was prepared.... Tell me, is there any connection between Joeli's sickness and Jone's death?"

"It appears to be the same sickness. The cause of Joeli's sickness, like Jone's death, is *vakavanua,* a violation of a sacred taboo. These are things dealing with Fijian tradition. And the problem is here at home."

Is *vakavanua* — now used to refer to a violation of the sacred traditions of the land — replacing *vakatevoro* — someone's evil intent to harm another — as the explanation for Tovu's afflictions? The two origins of tragedy can be closely linked, so perhaps a more accurate word might be "encompassing" rather than "replacing."

Whatever the cause, the problem, at least according to Tevita, is still within us.

CHAPTER 28

Continuings
(Tovu, Suva)

There is a very popular Fijian song that is sung with great emotion when visitors leave. *Isalei*, an expression of sadness and yearning, is a basic theme in the song. It is a sadness about the leave-taking and at the same time a yearning for the person's return. After telling how much the visitor will be missed, the song says: "Until you come back again, we'll wait patiently for your return." With that there is a waving of handkerchiefs, expressing not only goodbye but also "Please return, we'll be waiting for you." The song now reflects the Tovu spirit for us.

With the end of the fieldwork near, we prepare to leave. Soon it will be October of our second year in Fiji, and our sixteenth month since we moved to Tovu. Our leaving is of course but one event in the life of Tovu, which has more to do with continuings than leave-taking, and only rarely with endings. Our leave-taking itself becomes a kind of continuing. "Until we come back," we say, and that wish becomes a promise as it is repeated to our Tovu friends, who have become like family.

The focus on Jone's death and the related mysteries and suspicions has by now softened. Distance and the progression of daily events bring comfort, though they offer no final closure.

For some time people will be reminded of the circumstances surrounding Jone's death by the *meke* that has been composed to commemorate these events. With beautifully stylized head, hand, and body motions, this traditional Fijian dance is accompanied by a song that tells a story, for example an episode in the history of a locality. The dance movements and the song lyrics are sacred, coming to the composer (*dau-nivucu*) as a special gift from the *Vu*. The stories recorded in this way have special significance. As one elder says, "These *meke* are our traditional Fijian newspapers."

Each village has *meke* of its own, recounting, preserving, celebrating important aspects of its past. The repertoire changes as some *meke* are forgotten and others are newly fashioned. As the *meke* evolve, a people's history gains life.

A *meke* composer living in a neighboring village is one of the few in northern Bitu who still practice that sacred art. A frequent visitor to Tovu, he was a witness to most of the events connected with Jone's death, and a party to many of the village discussions that related to it. One late night and into the dawn, he sat up and, in a vision, composed a *meke* narrating the story of the Tovu deaths.

That story is not an official version, though because it is embedded in a sacred form it is also more than just another telling. Presenting a bare outline of events, omitting the key "suspicious" events, the *meke* alludes only briefly to explanations and interpretations. The Tovu elders say "this is the way with the *meke*": the real story is usually unspoken, hidden between the lines. They point to the "most revealing" lines in the *meke* about Jone:

> Many are saying, even insisting:
> "His death is not clear."
> But it is taboo for me to pronounce a name.

Though the *meke* composer cannot name names, these lines, the elders suggest, "say it all."

Meke are performed at all major rituals, so the story of Jone's death is likely to be told and retold for some time to come. It will remain, unresolved, as part of Tovu's living history. But whereas, vitalized by this *meke*, the events surrounding Jone's death will live on in people's memories, his family has long since left Tovu. Several weeks after the death ceremony, Jone's wife returned to Suva with her two children. She was tearful on leaving, revealing both her sadness and relief. She could not stay in Tovu, which was not her original home, and now only reminded her of the terrible details of her husband's death. Jone's replacement as headmaster is less outgoing, less connected with village life. The school continues, the awful presence of the dead Jone no longer haunting the far edge of the school playing field.

We say goodbye to people in Tovu, always trying to remember, "until we return." But with the old people it becomes very hard. When we return, will they still be there? And with Tevita and his family, even though we promise to return, our hearts hurt. Theirs and ours.

Part of leaving is a formal leave-taking. Mere and I are expected to give a little talk, our last words to the people. This is customary when special visitors leave. But we feel less like special visitors, and more like ordinary neighbors, members of an extended family. And so our talk, given in the church to the entire village, is especially hard. We struggle to express ourselves, not wanting to say out loud that we feel we are leaving our home. Trying to check the sadness or at least stall its arising, I find my breath choked off. No longer composed, my emotions eat up my thoughts, and my words splinter apart. People sit and wait, waiting for our discomposure to abate, sending us their strength. We are able to finish, though the edges of our words remain blurred as both our tears and theirs no longer hide behind handkerchiefs.

The morning we leave, our friends are on the beach, waving their handkerchiefs, waving goodbye, waving "Come back soon," waving "We'll be waiting here." A few are not there. One I miss terribly. This goodbye is too painful for Tevita.

The trip to Suva stretches out. For a long time I can still see the people on the beach, and then only the waving handkerchiefs, white flutters along the deep green of Tovu Bay. Tovu recedes slowly, very slowly.

In Suva, urban acceleration helps put my sadness to rest. Before our return to the United States, there are many things to do.

I visit Joeli in the hospital. He has undergone surgery on his back, to remove a precancerous tumor that was exerting pressure on his spinal cord. He's at ease, though thin and tired and missing his family and friends. Unlike Tovu, where a constant stream of visitors came to visit him when he was sick, bringing food and staying for *yaqona* and conversation, now the hospital's visiting regulations prevail: no more than two adults at a time, and then only during visiting hours. He feels isolated and lonely.

I talk with Luke, who visits as often as he can.

"I can't understand this hospital," Luke says. "They keep him from the love of his family."

I think about Joeli's operation. Is the tumor the only explanation for his sickness? Like Ratu Noa, I feel that the tumor is as much a vehicle for other forces as a cause in its own right. And like the Tovu people, I may never know exactly what those other forces are.

Suva is much bigger than Tovu. I only know a few of its seventy thousand inhabitants, which makes leaving easier. I'm not constantly confronted with sadness as I complete different errands, shopping in the market, packing things for the trip back to the United States.

But my friendships in Suva still tear at my heart when I have to say goodbye. My relationship with Inoke, though often task-oriented, is intense. Tears overwhelm us both when we shake hands goodbye. Seeing Sitiveni before I leave is almost impossible. But I know I'll see him again, and so we say goodbye, "until I return." And it's with this knowledge that I spend the last days in Suva visiting with Ratu Noa.

CHAPTER 29

Conversations
with Ratu Noa
(Suva)

"When your search is honest, the mana *will come to you."*

With just a little over two weeks left before returning to the United States, I ask Ratu Noa, "Is there anything I might do to intensify our work together in these last few weeks?"

He looks pleased and surprised. "Just come by as much as you can so that you can be close to the *yaqona,*" he says.

We meet for four evenings during the middle of November, mostly sitting quietly, drinking *yaqona,* talking a little. We drink a lot of *yaqona,* which has always been the way Ratu Noa and I have made our talk simple and "straight."

"You know, Rusiate, most of us hear things, but we don't actually listen to what is said. A well-educated person can seriously consider things. But half-educated people are a real problem. It's difficult to convince them of anything. Uneducated people are really much better. Many ministers are in that half-educated group. They're clever with their lips — they argue well — but they don't have real understanding or faith. But I have faith. Faith in the only Fijian religion, the *yaqona.*

"When you drink *yaqona,* it opens up your mind. And *yaqona* is the medium for opening the *mana*-box, so that *mana* will come to you."

Ratu Noa's words about *yaqona* make sense to me, and a different sense than when I first started drinking *yaqona*. As we spend time together, hour after hour, we enter a special space. Truth lives there. The atmosphere encourages our respect; speaking carefully, we bring forth what we know, no more and no less. Of course what we know differs. I do most of the listening and learning. But my listening has to match Ratu Noa's talking. He talks to the degree I listen; he gives to the degree I can receive. His search for the proper words meets my search for understanding.

If truth is not the ground we stand on, the whole enterprise falls apart. It hasn't collapsed yet, because in our talks, centered around the *yaqona*, we join the best in each other. Throughout the night, we seek to exchange what we know. It's that electricity Ratu Noa spoke of before. When we sit down with the *yaqona* and begin to talk, sparks emerge, current passes, and we're fused together. And then only one commitment is possible — to the truth.

Yet I also know that to an outsider, these nightly talks could be seen as merely drinking sessions. The more you drink, the more your consciousness is affected — the more you feel "as if" you're being truthful. To this perception, I now know there is only one answer, which is at the same time no answer. Only when you've experienced drinking *yaqona* with a teacher like Ratu Noa, drinking without getting drunk, can the particular atmosphere of truth which is created be understood.

This is not to say that all is perfect in our talks. We're human. Our conversation is sometimes boring; sometimes it stalls. Ratu Noa doesn't always inspire me with his wisdom, and I know I don't always inspire him with my questions. But as he says, the *yaqona* opens our minds; it "opens the *mana*-box," and *mana* demands truth — otherwise it vanishes.

The first night I visit Ratu Noa, I relate the story of our leave-taking in Tovu, including the parting gifts the people gave us. "Those Tovu people are so generous; they have so little and they gave us so much. Not just things like the mats and the tapa cloth. But they let us live with them and share their lives."

"That's how it should be, Rusiate," Ratu Noa replies. "You gave plenty to them…and they gave plenty to you. Traditionally in Fiji there was always enough. Sharing created plenty.

"Take, for example, our ceremony of the first fruits," he continues. "The ritual offering of the first fruits — the first harvest of fruit, root crops, and fish — was always very important. You give these special foods to your chief. Today people think that by selling all their crops and fish they can get money and get more food. But food production is actually going down, and people now have less to eat. Offering your first fruits to your chief brings more of his blessing, and your field will produce more and better food. The idea of the first offering is to bring *mana* into food production. Without *mana*, the results can be disastrous. Traditionally a very small village could feed many, many people, even when there were lots of visitors. Today, more and more, villages are facing a food scarcity because they believe the traditional system has no place in the modern economy.

"Traditionally, Rusiate, we exchanged things — it was a give-and-take process. When money was introduced, this free exchange was destroyed. Money ruins the sound relationships of blood and family. Money can be used to buy clothing and pay for education, but we don't need it for food. Food is bountiful in our sea, reefs, rivers, and mountains. Money is not for life. Money makes a line between the rich and the poor; but Jesus establishes that we are all equal to him.

"We Fijians are too much under the rule of Western things. Take our houses. We spend lots of money to construct Western-style houses — money for the plans, the materials, the labor. And money for rents. Instead, we should be living in *bure*, built by us, from local materials, without money. A traditional thatched house keeps us warm in the winter and cool in the summer. What about those Western-style houses with their sheet metal roofs? They keep you cold in the winter and warm, sweltering warm in the summer. And we pay for that discomfort!

"Most people don't believe in the traditional way anymore," Ratu Noa states, not sadly, but in a matter-of-fact tone. "It's the work of the devil, they say. But tradition is our strength. Respect. Love for all. Humility. Honesty. Service. These are the things our elders taught us. These are the things that make us straight and guide us in giving.

"Before you can return to these traditional ways, Rusiate, you must know the life history of your own country. In fact, you should know your own *Vu*. And you can't learn about the old ways by studying the present social structure, because the structure of today has no tie with those old ways."

This emphasis on my "own" *Vu* is new; I'm not sure what Ratu Noa is suggesting.

"Are the *Vu* in my country related to the *Vu* here in Fiji?" I ask.

"All the *Vu* know each other," Ratu Noa replies. "The *Vu* in each country are different, but they work together. And you, Rusiate, will work with your own *Vu* under the guidance of our *Vu* here.

"But I can tell you this, Rusiate, if Fijians of today want to return to the old ways, it will be impossible for most. It would be like a swimming contest across the ocean to a distant island. Very few would finish the race. So too there are very few people who know what our future will be because only a few really know our past."

Though Ratu Noa says that traditional exchange is insufficiently valued in Fiji, it is just such an exchange that characterizes our last talks. And that exchange prepares me to leave.

"When I return to America, there'll be no one to talk with about these things. I'll be on my own."

"I find the same exists for me," Ratu Noa affirms. "I always have to find things out for myself. When someone tells me something, I always doubt it. For years and years I press on and on, offering my prayers, and yet I cannot see to whom I am offering them. Just last night I prayed to *Kalou* to show me a sign. I prayed and then went to bed. As I lay in bed I saw the Light coming down from heaven. I cannot believe anything unless I have seen it. It's my way to get the real facts whenever I do anything.

"And that's how it must be, Rusiate, as you work on the next steps. You must find things out for yourself. When your search is honest, the *mana* will come to you. And like the one who sees spiritually, you'll see things — deep into the past, far into the future. And like the one who knows spiritually, you'll know things — way beyond anything you learned at the university. But these things are not for show. They'll strengthen your healing, and they'll strengthen your service to others. Like with me — I can go through a concrete wall if I wish. It's an expression of the *mana* that comes to me. But I don't show that off. And you, Rusiate, you'll have to be extra careful because those Westerners always want proof of your powers."

There is one question that still troubles me. Perhaps it is the last question I can offer.

"When I see faces starting to emerge in my *bilo* of *yaqona,* is that related to what you're talking about?"

"Yes...yes, Rusiate. That could be the beginning of seeing what can happen to people in the future."

"But what do you do with that kind of knowledge? Especially if you see something bad will happen?"

"When you arrive at that point, we'll talk about it. Just remember, your job is to serve others, to heal them — not to build yourself up, or to advertise your powers.

"The *Vu* will grant your requests when your heart and soul are pure and straight, Rusiate. That will guide your work — your healing work, and your work on the book."

The *tanoa* is dry. Our talk is over. "Until you return," Ratu says, a slight smile warming his sparse words. "Until we meet again."

Ratu Noa sends me out, on my own. He has guided me toward the straight path. The only remaining task is to follow it. More than enough of a task for a lifetime.

It's only after I arrive back in my room downtown that I fully cry.

CHAPTER 30

Return to Fiji (Suva)

Though more than six years have passed since I left, Fiji has remained a home. I think a lot about the two years I lived there, remembering in my heart Tevita and others from Tovu, Sitiveni, Inoke, and especially Ratu Noa. But though I have not forgotten Ratu Noa's words of advice, direction, and caution, I haven't devoted myself to their practice. I try to follow the straight path, but my attempts lack an ultimate intensity; they are not a struggle for life — for my life.

I continue my healing work, but haven't fully accepted Ratu Noa's challenge to realize the opportunities created by his teachings and my own training in psychology. My work remains largely within the context of informal, spiritually oriented counseling, with occasional spiritual healing; but I haven't assumed the full responsibility of the healing work in which, as Ratu Noa said, "your life is no longer your own." Though I observe the Monday night healing ceremony as I was instructed by Ratu Noa, these ceremonies are not convincingly regular and, in the other parts of my life I don't always feel the faith that makes up for the gaps.

As the new year of 1985 takes hold, I recognize I have to return, to reconnect to the healing work, to recommit; otherwise I would slide away through neglect. When an invitation comes to deliver several lectures in Australia, all expenses paid, it is an obvious sign. This time I will be going alone; Mere and I are in the process of getting a divorce.

There is another reason for my wish to return. A first draft of the book I am writing about Fijian healing, featuring interviews with Ratu Noa and the story of the deaths in Tovu, is nearly complete. I need to talk again with Ratu Noa, as well as with Sitiveni, and maybe others.

Several months before my scheduled departure for Fiji, I call my friend, Marika, a Fijian elder in Suva who helped with interviews and translations during my earlier visit. Marika has a deep understanding of Fijian tradition and of Fijian healing. He would have been an excellent associate in my interviews with Ratu Noa, but I had committed myself to Inoke. Now Inoke, I heard, is unavailable, living in his home village of Delana in Bitu.

On this return trip, I will be spending most if not all of my time in Suva. Given the unpredictability of transportation, there might not be enough days to visit Tovu.

"Hello...hello. Marika? Marika, is that you?" I can barely hear the voice at the other end, thousands and thousands of miles away in Suva. It has taken me the better part of a week even to complete this call, which is barely a connection.

But between the static and silence and the words that come apart in the middle, I can make out Marika's voice on the other end. And the voice is speaking Fijian!

Marika's initial greeting is no problem; I remember enough Fijian to get through the opening dialogue. It's truly wonderful to hear his voice. I'm overjoyed — and then worried. He keeps talking in Fijian, asking me about how I've been, about my family, my work, and when I'm returning. "We miss you here." Again joy takes over.

"Marika, I'm coming back in June, in several months," I say in English. "Oh, Marika, I'm so sorry I have to speak in English, but I haven't remembered my Fijian that well."

"That's okay," Marika responds in English, and then proceeds, again in Fijian, to ask more questions and share the news about his own family. As he talks, going more into detail, I understand less.

"I'm really glad to hear about your family," I say in English, interrupting before he gets too far. "And I'm really sorry that I can't speak with you in Fijian.... Maybe when I return my Fijian will come back."

"That's right, Rusiate, when you come back you'll be speaking again like you once did, just like us," Marika replies, starting in English but switching to Fijian before he finishes.

Our conversation is not long, but throughout Marika slips automatically into Fijian, as if he is talking to me as he would six years ago. Hesitantly, I say a few words in Fijian. We arrange for Marika to meet my flight, and he agrees to help me in my talks with Ratu Noa.

We make our parting exchanges. This time my Fijian is just fine. I'm relieved at this small experience of success, but I feel uncomfortable. When they see me, people in Fiji will expect what they last remember — a Fijian speaker. And I can no longer speak as fluently as before. Though I know how impractical, if not impossible, it was to maintain that level, the realization of how much I have forgotten still bothers me; it's like a betrayal of trust.

Now that the trip to Fiji is imminent, I wonder why I've waited six years before returning. Was it the expense? Though certainly the trip is not cheap, I know that when we have to do something in our lives we often find a way — or the way finds us. Perhaps only now am I ready to return — ready to admit that I haven't lived up to Ratu Noa's teachings, but ready to take on his responsibility again, if he offers it. The invitation to lecture in Australia wakes me up, making me aware of my yearning.

The flight to Fiji, which takes more than twenty-four hours, gives me time to savor my feelings. There is pure excitement in the idea of seeing friends again, and smelling the land and trees, but also a dense anxiety. Will I fulfill my own and others' expectations? And what if Ratu Noa is not there? Or worse, what if he backs away because the intensity in my work has been lacking.

At shortly before four o'clock in the morning, my plane has just landed and I'm sitting in the coffee shop in the airport at Nadi. Except for an old Fijian woman and me, the shop is empty. The three Fijian women who staff the place are relaxing at a nearby table. They are having fun, joking about this and that — mainly about me, wondering where I'm from and where I'm going with my duffel bags. Looking me over, they launch into a sexually tinged discussion of the next steps they could take to "get" me. Speaking in Fijian, and assuming this Westerner doesn't understand them, they are completely public in plotting their conspiracies, with me just two tables away. But I do understand them. That's a relief! My confidence rises.

Now I'm set to go.

As I leave to get the plane for Suva, I say goodbye to these women and thank them for their compliments — in Fijian. They're embarrassed, but having too much fun to be really disconcerted. "Have a good stay in Fiji," they say. "And remember to come back here. We'll miss you!"

Marika meets me at the Suva airport. We hug. Our words are few, and though my Fijian can handle it, he also makes many allowances, speaking primarily in English. Only gradually over the next few days does Marika switch more and more to Fijian.

Marika tells me he hasn't been able to reach Ratu Noa. Ratu Noa still has no telephone, and Marika doesn't know where he lives. Marika sent several messages to some of his relatives and friends, but no messages have come back.

As we drive away from the airport, I keep trying to remember where Ratu Noa's place is. I know that we'll be passing by it as we head into the center of Suva. I begin to recognize things along the road. I'm sure Ratu Noa's house is somewhere along here. I tense up, hoping to see more landmarks. Suddenly a large building becomes visible beyond a sloping hill. "That's it! That's it! His house is right in off the road there, in a large tract of government housing. I'm sure of it."

The next day, Marika and I look for Ratu Noa. I have obligations to perform on that first visit. With me is a large *yaqona* and a *tabua* to present. In the traditional manner, I need to ask Ratu Noa's forgiveness for the events I've missed during my absence — the births, marriages, and deaths in his family. It's the correct way to be received back into his community. With the *yaqona* and *tabua*, it would not be us talking, but our *Vu* speaking to each other, receiving each other once more in the proper manner. At Marika's urging, I also plan to ask Ratu Noa for continued strength in my writing project, to help me be straight and tell the true story.

We drive back up the main airport road, reach the large building, and turn in. We take several more turns within the housing development, which goes on for block after block, all the houses looking too much the same. I'm trying to reconstruct my many trips to Ratu Noa's house when I was here more than six years ago. Unfortunately, those earlier trips were made in the dark and on foot. But I recall very clearly turning in from the main road at the big building, then taking several turns before coming to an L–shaped bend that brought the road past Ratu Noa's house.

But, though we follow the route I remember, now it's all different. Turning in from the main road, that's the same; take a left, a right, a left, a short right — all that's the same. But then we don't come to the expected bend; instead the road goes winding into new patterns. I don't know where we are.

We go around in circles several times, asking people where the "old road" might be. Nobody knows; they don't even understand what we're talking about. The roads we see are the only ones they know. Getting only shrugs in response to our question "Where does Ratu Noa live?" we soon see how absurd it is to expect an answer in this enormous housing development, with its constant flow of people moving in and out. I begin to wonder whether I'm meant to find Ratu Noa this time.

Finally I remember there was a Hindu temple in the field near the bend in the road. But when we ask, "Where is the temple?" we learn there are several in the vicinity. We go to one, then another. Eventually we're directed to still another, and when I see it, I shout, "This is it! This is the street!"

The vertical line of the L has been extended and is now a through road. We turn off at what we figure is Ratu Noa's street. There are only four houses on it.

"Do you know where Ratu Noa lives?" I ask an Indian man outside one of the houses, near where Ratu Noa's house should be.

"Who?" he says, as if he didn't hear the question. My heart sinks. We're still lost.

"The Fijian man who works in construction."

"Oh, yes, we know him," the man replies. "That's his house." It's the house right next door.

289

We walk up to Ratu Noa's house. His daughter is looking out of the window and sees me. She's exclaiming, "Rusiate?...Rusiate! Rusiate is here! Oh, that's Rusiate!"

We enter the house. It's one of the strongest experiences I've ever had in my life.

"It's been a long time, Rusiate...a long time." Ratu Noa says no more as we shake hands, facing each other without hiding the tears in our eyes. The love we feel on both sides is profound. We sit quietly as I make the formal presentation of the *yaqona* and *tabua*. The ties of recognition are bursting, but first we must have the formal ceremony. With Marika acting as my *mata-ni-vanua*, the *yaqona* is presented in the *sevusevu*, and the *tabua* is offered. Ratu Noa accepts the *yaqona*, then the *tabua*. His demeanor is serious, more than formal. The room is completely still, but its quietness is not heavy.

Now our traditional obligations are fulfilled. Ratu Noa breaks into a wide smile and reaches out again to shake my hand. "It's good that you're back. I've been waiting for you."

We joke and laugh, and laugh some more. It's good to be home again. We exchange news of the last six years, from each side of the ocean. There are changes — births, deaths, marriages, separations — and continuities — the work, always the work.

Now Ratu Noa is ready. This time he doesn't have to tell me "fire away."

"I've brought a copy of the book. It's here," I say, putting the manuscript in front of me. "It's not completed, only a first draft. But I have some questions about it." I describe in some detail the general structure of the book, and how it combines the story of events in Tovu and what he said in our talks.

"Do you think that plan is okay?"

"Yes. It's good. Rusiate, I trust your judgment in these matters. I tell you the true story. You find the correct plan. And now for your other questions."

"Well...there is another question about the events in Tovu — Jone's death and the other two deaths, and especially how people thought that *vakatevoro* was involved. Should I be writing about *vakatevoro*?"

In my own mind, I don't think of "witchcraft," the common translation of *vakatevoro*. Events are attributed to *vakatevoro* through people's attempts to make sense of confusing, anxiety-filled happenings, to forge a deeper, spiritual understanding of things, and to make the community whole again. That's how I present it in the book. Yet I know how easily such matters can be misunderstood.

"Would *vakatevoro* be misunderstood by readers, who would then think of Fijians as 'primitive' or 'backward'? Even though the book emphasizes the straight path, not *vakatevoro*?"

I restate my concerns several times, in different ways, reading parts of the manuscript aloud. Given the Fijian value of respecting another's right to proceed in the manner he or she has chosen, I don't wish Ratu Noa to feel he cannot disagree. But we know each other well. Ratu Noa is aware of how much I value his opinion, whether it is approving or disapproving — and he will give it. I'm putting the book on the line, realizing that without the discussion of *vakatevoro*, it will probably collapse.

"It is important, Rusiate, to write about *vakatevoro* because in the end that will help people see the power of the *Vu*. The strength of *vakatevoro* shows how much stronger the straight path must be, because it is only through the straight path that we can deal with and balance out *vakatevoro*. The two sides of the story must be told if the whole story is to be known.

"Also, your description of *vakatevoro* will show people how one should *not* be as a Fijian. You are describing what some people call 'witchcraft,' which is really when people have strayed from the straight path. You are describing how people are disrespecting and doing things against the *vanua*.

"Let me explain something to you," he continues. "There's an order to these things. If someone wants to kill me, they must first ask my *Vu* for permission. Actually, their *Vu* asks my *Vu*. Then my *Vu*, my ruler, refers the request to *Kalou*, the One Above. And if it's okay from there, then it goes back the same route, back to the *Vu*. Then it's done."

"A child's history is all there when the child is born. The One Above is already aware that at a certain time a request may be made to kill that child in its later years. It's up to the One Above, who from his position sees the whole picture, to decide if that person is good or not good, and then decide if that request will be granted or denied."

"We have a problem here in Fiji. Too often Fijians jump to a conclusion — 'oh, it's *vakatevoro*,' they say, 'something caused by devil worship.' But you always have to consider the finer points, to evaluate things and really see why something has happened. It's also possible to get into trouble because one has strayed from the path of tradition [*vakavanua*]. That can cause a death. And that's what happened with Jone, too. Not *vakatevoro*."

"It all starts, Rusiate, if people are suspicious somebody is doing *vakatevoro* and they don't try to find out the inner meaning of events. They don't really understand why a person dies. They should keep asking: 'Why did this person die?' Was he a troublemaker? Or maybe he was a good person. Then why him? Maybe the one who dies behaves like a good person, but there is something wrong inside. Maybe he violated a taboo of the land, like planting in the sacred area. This violation of sacred tradition can kill. This is a thing of the land, not a thing of the devil. And the two are different!"

My concerns are in retreat. The issues around Jone's death, Ratu Noa is saying, will speak for themselves. And what others mistakenly presume is secondary.

"The land lays out all its rules and laws, Rusiate. We all know beforehand what is right and wrong, what is allowed and what is taboo. Once you disturb this pattern, you've mixed things up — and you'll be punished. You're vulnerable to death.

"There will be no confusion. It all goes back to *Kalou*, the Almighty, who gave the order for the deaths. Jone's father was challenging the Almighty. The book will be a good example of the power of the Almighty.

"There will be three groups of people who will read your book," Ratu Noa elaborates in a deliberate manner. "Each group will respond in its own way. The first group are the Fijian chiefs and others who are familiar with traditional Fijian life. They know of these things you write about and they will understand the book and appreciate it. The second group consists of those who live in the village, whose life it is that you are writing about. Those people live these things you write about. They also will appreciate the book, and will know it's true because it is their life. Then there will be a third group, those who have a little knowledge, and because they have a little knowledge, some of them can be really dangerous. This third group will not understand the book — but we cannot worry about them."

"The only problem is that many readers will likely be from this third group," I say. "Yet I know that some in that group will not misuse their knowledge, but will seek more."

"Yes, that's true. But you cannot modify the book so that those who *will* misuse their knowledge will understand properly," Ratu Noa cautions. "If you do, you will end up in trouble. And eventually even those who misunderstand because of little knowledge will begin to understand.

"Rusiate, we don't need to talk further about the book. There is no problem with it. The only problem that is being raised is the one you're raising with your concerns. But I tell you now, there is no need to worry.

"I want the book published — *vakatevoro* and all!" Ratu Noa's abrupt statement closes the subject.

"Another round," Ratu Noa exclaims, "so we can have more stories and good conversation." The *yaqona* lightens our talk, not detracting from its seriousness, but removing any somber echoes. We're all so glad to see each other again.

"When do you have to leave Fiji, Rusiate?"

"In three weeks."

"Before you go, you'll get the blessing."

I'm not sure of his meaning, and my face shows it.

"Before you go, I'll give a blessing to the book."

This first visit to Ratu Noa is more than full. I am learning from him again. Did I ever stop?

The next day I visit Sitiveni. Our emotions burst forth before we perform the traditional exchange and greeting. I present him with a *yaqona* for my *sevusevu,* and a *tabua* asking forgiveness for missing the funeral ceremonies and other events of importance in his family which took place in the time I was away. And I also ask for his help in the book. Then we visit more, looking each other over with joy at our reunion.

The next day Sitiveni and I talk again — this time in detail about the book. We go through the manuscript and he makes several suggestions about the writing, but he is still wholeheartedly encouraging. With passionate certainty, Sitiveni reaffirms the permission, support, and approval he gave the book seven years ago, when it was merely projected.

"This is a book that must be written for our Fijian people," he asserts. The story is true. Now all that's left is the telling. And it's you who must decide about the form and details of that telling. Make no mistake about it. I know.

"Rusiate, you are doing very difficult work. You are dealing with the seen and the unseen, and you are trying to show people how the two are connected. People do not understand the unseen, which is the reality of our lives; they do not realize its power. They look only at the seen, which is illusion. And that keeps them in darkness, attached to material possessions, to what they can touch. You are seeking a way to show people the reality of the unseen. This is a very difficult job...but one that must be done!"

I know Sitiveni's words speak more to what I wish to become than what I am. The straight path is a constant challenge; just as one becomes content that one is on the path, one wakes up — off it.

"You must show the world that the unseen power is here, Rusiate, right here in Fiji. People look all over the world for this unseen power. They look in the heavens and in other places. They don't believe that the power is right here in Fiji. Your book will help them see that."

Sitiveni blesses the book. Several times I ask him about visiting Tovu in order to talk to people there about the book, to get their further suggestions. But he assures me there is no more to do.

"I want you to follow our traditional ways," Sitiveni says. "I speak for the people of Tovu in the matter of the book, and I have given their complete approval and support. Because I've already discussed the book with the elders there, I speak now for the *vanua*. What I say goes — and if my decision is wrong, I must pay for it.

"The way we do things in Fiji, the correct and traditional way of our land, is just how you've done it — you should come to me just as you have. No need to speak again with other Tovu people."

As it turns out, a trip to Tovu is impossible. The schedule of ships going there is such that no sooner would I get off the boat once it arrived in Tovu than I would have to reboard and leave. I'm sad that I won't see Tevita and the other Tovu people. So sad, all I can think is…"another time."

Four days after my visit to Ratu Noa, I return for a second conversation. He talks about our sporadic talks when we first met, now more than eight years ago.

"For the first two months I avoided you, Rusiate. I was testing you to see what your intentions were. Then I realized you fitted an old prediction, and I had to work with you."

"Yes…I had such trouble finding you," I respond, "and then I often thought our meetings wouldn't continue. It was lucky your wife took pity on me. There was one night when it was raining, and I came to your house for our appointment — and you weren't there. She asked me in, let me dry off, and encouraged me to come back. 'Oh it's too bad you've come from such a long distance,' she said. 'I'm sorry Ratu Noa isn't here, but I'm sure he wants to see you.' I really needed that encouragement!

"And I remember how at the end of one of our early talks you said to me, 'Rusiate, you may never see me again. I can't guarantee you'll ever see me again.' I really thought it was all over — just when it seemed so wonderful that we had finally started." We laugh together, although that moment in the past was only painful. We clasp hands, knowing that all along we have been connected.

I've been waiting to ask one question. "How is Tevita? How is his work?"

"Tevita is fine — but he's given up the work," Ratu Noa replies in a matter-of-fact manner.

"He's stopped the work?" I can't hide my shock.

"Yes, Tevita has left the work. He was double-minded about it, and I believe he lacked the necessary understanding to carry it on."

"How did it happen that he gave it up?" I ask, unwilling to believe.

"It was that church movement. You know, the one that Reverend Jemesa brought to Tovu when you were there."

"But Tevita decided to resume his healing after you sent him that message — remember, you told him not to waver because the work came from *Kalou* — and no man, not even a preacher, could take it away from him." In describing the tape, I'm almost trying to ensure its continued influence. "And then Tevita started healing again. What could have happened?"

"Well, about a year later, there was another visit to Tovu by Reverend Jemesa and his group." Ratu Noa's voice now holds a hint of sadness. "And most everybody lined up with the church and against the healing work. People even tried to convert Tevita. And he found himself alone. That was the problem — when he saw himself alone, he felt weak. His spirit wasn't firm and he lost his power. Then he had to give up the work.

"But Tevita didn't come to me directly before he stopped the work," Ratu Noa continues, a swift disappointment streaking through his voice. "The work came from the *Vu*, through me, and the only proper way was for me to take Tevita's request to stop back to the *Vu* who first gave him the power. Instead Tevita sent me a message saying that he wanted to give up the work so he could devote himself more fully to the church. He was planning to become a deacon. I sent a message back to Tevita saying it was okay to stop but that he shouldn't come back to me later for help.

"Tevita should have understood that this work is only from *Kalou*. The healer must be filled with love so that all who come for help can be helped. You love all who come, whoever they are, whether they come in the middle of the night, whatever. This healing work is religious work, true religious work because we aren't paid. Not like ministers. You know I just heard that when ministers go to live and preach in the village they get paid at least seventy dollars a month. They get paid to pray and help people!"

I know Ratu Noa feels that the matter is closed. If a person doesn't desire and deserve the work, it's not for him or her. But still — it's Tevita we're talking about. Yes, Ratu Noa has settled the matter for himself. His sadness has healed.

Ratu Noa turns his attention more directly to the issue of money and the healing work. "You know, in the work, we cannot charge any fees. At one point in my work, a hundred dollars in cash kept appearing each morning. My wife was very suspicious. She wondered if I'd been stealing the money or getting it in some illegal way. She experienced a great conflict. But I told her, 'No, this money doesn't come to me illegally. If you would like to see where this money comes from, I'll take you to my special room where I pray and prepare for the healing work. In that room I can request the *Vu* to make the money cease.' And so we went to my special room and I made that request. The *Vu* responded, 'I only gave you this money because you never charge for your work and you have to have some form of support. It was a gift. But since you requested that it stop, we will stop it.' My wife then realized the money was coming from the *Vu* — but the request to have it stopped still held.

"Ratu Rusiate, you don't have to worry about money because you'll be taken care of. People will give you things as gifts, gifts of appreciation. The straight path teaches us three things: *dina,* which means to be truthful and loyal; *savasava,* which means to be clean and pure; and *dodonu,* which means to be straight or correct. If you follow the straight path, money will never be a worry for you.

"Any more questions, Rusiate? If you have anything else to ask, now's the time. If not, that's okay."

"Almost all the questions I have were already answered by you when I was here six years ago. I've thought a lot about what you said then…but I wasn't always ready to put your advice into practice. I remember you told me I was very fortunate to have been trained in psychology and to live in America where there is so much. After my work here in Fiji, you said I had to repay that good fortune by doing work that would serve people. I've been trying, and now I'm ready to do more."

"Yes, America is a lucky place to be," Ratu Noa reflects. "There they pay you to serve people, but here, in our healing work, we serve without pay. The question is this: How can you change the way it's done in

America so it's like the way it's done in Fiji?"

"It can be done," I answer confidently. "In America, I get paid to teach; and on my own time, I also do some counseling as part of that job. That counseling is related to the healing work, but now I'm ready to do more of the healing work you've taught me. And to do that work without pay will be very unusual in America."

"Rusiate, I have one request to make of you. From your question and from the way you speak, I know there is something you want. Therefore, it's better to tell me now what that is."

Ratu Noa's directness takes me by surprise. I can't escape, yet I still can't say exactly what it is I want.

"It's not easy to describe. Everything I would need you've already spoken of during my first visit six years ago."

"Yes. I try to say things only once," Ratu Noa agrees. "That's all that has to be said. If I were to say it twice, it could turn into a lie.

"You know, Rusiate, it was promised that you would come back to Fiji as you have. And I know you've been training since you left…and you've made some progress."

"Only a little," I protest, and now there is no false modesty.

"That's true," Ratu Noa responds, "but you must keep trying. What you're aiming for is to work with the *mana*, to work with it and prove it. *Mana* will come to you, but we must build it up bit by bit. I can't give you the *mana* all at once."

Ratu Noa has put my feelings into words. "That's the way I want to work," I nearly burst out, "…and take on the next phase of the training."

"There will be a contract made for a three-year period," Ratu Noa says, "and during that time you'll try to become even more acquainted with my work. You'll start on a small scale and gradually pick up, meeting more and more serious tests. When I get the message that you've passed those tests, at that point I'll increase the power that's available to you. Yes…in three years, you'll begin to feel the effects of this in your work with the *mana*. And this *mana* will pass on to your children. Rusiate, I can tell you that once you undergo all the tests and pass, you'll reach the state where the One who is giving the blessing will bless you.

But for this to happen you must always stick to the straight path.

"Yes, Rusiate, your work with the *mana* will be very important in America. It will be a new thing, because you'll serve without charging. And always remember that patients will give you something to express their appreciation when you heal them. But it's a gift, a gift from the heart — not a payment. And if you follow the principle of receiving only such gifts, more power will be given to you."

"But Ratu Noa, is it possible to work in America without mixing the *yaqona*? Because it's difficult to get *yaqona* there."

"It's possible to work without the *yaqona*," he assures me. "On the final day of your visit here in Fiji, I'll give you the details of how to work back in America. And remember, there are *Vu* in every nation, and they are sent to various places to be in charge of different functions. The way to find the *Vu* in your place is just as it says in the Bible: one must look for the kingdom of *Kalou*. The *Vu* of the world gather together, and after they meet they go back to their own places. The *Vu* reflect the power of the places in which they reside. *Mana* is given to nations sparingly and carefully so that it isn't abused. That's what happened with Germany in the two world wars. They seized *mana* and abused it.

"And Rusiate, never exaggerate in your work."

"That won't be easy," I joke. "America is the land of exaggeration. It seems as though everyone exaggerates — Americans are all trying to sell something."

"That's what I've heard," Ratu Noa says, shaking his head. "But if you stay with the truth, you'll go right to the center. You'll penetrate to the very soul. And only speak to the client who comes to you. 'Yes,' you might say, 'I'll try to take care of your case.' No more. Your patients who are helped will spread the word about your work.

"Rusiate, we'll fix a special time before you go, because I have certain things to tell you. You know, it's not really a question of which herbs to use, or even the *yaqona*. It's more a question of your faith. With that faith, the *mana* will be with you, and you'll be shown the trees to use for herbs — and they'll be trees in your area. You'll be shown what leaves to use, what branches, what bark. And you can just mix them in water to make a medicine. I'll show you the basic elements, and then with faith — with belief coming from your heart and soul — the rest will come. If you aim to help people, it will all be shown to you."

As soon as I return for my third visit, Ratu Noa begins.

"You'll be coming back to Fiji, Rusiate?"

"I want to…I really want to."

"Next time you come, come straight to this house. And maybe someday I'll travel to America and visit you there.

"Yes, your land, Rusiate, sounds like a beautiful place. Maybe I'll visit you there, and then you'll come back here to Fiji. Because we don't want you to be very far from us."

With our slightly sad smiles, we grasp the moment together.

"You know, Rusiate, the Fijian people of today don't understand their own traditions," Ratu Noa says quietly. "According to our tradition, when a child is born, there is a series of feasts [*magiti*] paying tribute to the *Vu* for giving the family that child. The same thing is done at the time of a person's death: the feast thanks the *Vu* for taking that person back.

"The soul of the dead person stays with us on earth and helps us in our ways." Ratu Noa is condensing a lot of information, without rushing his words. "But the missionaries came and taught us that the soul goes up to heaven after a person dies. And Fijians today believe that, forgetting their own ways. Also, many Fijians today do these various feasts blindly, without even knowing the meaning of the ceremonies they perform.

"Take the feast of the fourth night. That's the most important feast in any ceremony. Like in the Bible you have the number four — the forty days and nights and things of that nature."

"During the years I was away from Fiji," I remark, "I always tried to respect the number four, celebrating markers like the fourth day after an event."

"Rusiate, I'm glad. That number four is very important. There's also the fourth night after we first give a medicine, when we examine the patient again to see if the medicine is working. And we look to the four cardinal directions — north, south, east, and west. Power comes to us from each of these directions, and that makes the fourth night a time of power."

"These four directions are important with other people as well, like Indigenous people in North America," I mention.

"Oh, that's good to know." Ratu Noa is more affirmed in his own understanding than surprised by new information.

"Let me tell you more about these numbers," he continues. "You start off in this healing work with building a foundation. You do your first-grade work on the number four. Everything you do has to do with that number four. Then, when you learn something and you're ready to proceed further in your work, you can work with any number — any number you wish. And each healer has a number, which establishes the nature and degree of his or her power. That number is like a master key, opening all the doors. And since I know the meaning of those numbers, I can see into the nature of another healer's work.

"Now, Rusiate, you're going to use all that you've learned over your lifetime, and combine it with the new power you have from Fiji, and use it all together. And if you're honest in your work, you'll see results.

"And you must be firm. Too many of us are double-minded, not knowing which way to go and unable to make up our minds. Should I...or shouldn't I? Once you become double-minded, the One responsible for these healing things will leave you."

"I know what you mean. It's taken me six years since I left Fiji to come to where I am now — wanting definitely to put what you've taught me into practice."

Ratu Noa smiles broadly.

"That's good, Rusiate...that's good. Your faith, that's what has taken you through this. And your patience. Now you can practice this work every day — Monday, Tuesday, Wednesday, Thursday, Friday, Saturday, and Sunday. Especially Sunday — that's a good day for prayer, a day when the gate is open, when the road is clear.

"And every time you finish performing your work, Rusiate, you come back and express appreciation to the Source of the work, the One above.

"The hidden wave will bring whatever you need for your healing work as long as your work remains straight. That wave will come to you from all directions. When the key is with you, the waves will keep coming to you, and then you'll have to monitor them and look inside to understand them. And as you do this work, you'll have the gift of sight, and you'll know and see things before they happen.

"Rusiate, you've paid for this knowledge over the past six years — and you've earned it. I've never told these things to other people who've worked for me."

"Here, Ratu Rusiate — here, drink your *yaqona*." Ratu Noa offers me the first *bilo* in a new round of *yaqona*. It is not my place to drink before him, out of regard for his status as a chief and as the one who is teaching me. And so I demur. But he insists, at first playfully, then firmly though always respectfully. "Drink now, Rusiate. You drink and I'll follow you." Again I try to decline, but again he insists. "Yes, you drink. That is my wish." I take the *bilo* and drink; he follows me in drinking.

The round of *yaqona* is finished. Already it has merged into the many rounds that came before, and will surely follow, as the evening comes into its own.

"The problem with most Fijians," Ratu Noa says, "is that when they seek help, they overlook the fact that we must always give thanks to the One Above for that help. When most people come in contact with *mana*, they try to hold on to it, hoarding it, and boasting about it. But they must realize this *mana* is a gift to them. It's not theirs to own. And since *mana* is a gift, you can't demand payment for the work that *mana* does. This *mana* is all over the world — in America as well. But only here in Fiji do we know the right path that will release *mana* into the work." Ratu Noa is not boasting — just stating facts. He now waits for another question.

Earlier I learned from Sitiveni that Luke has become Ratu Noa's helper. "When did Luke begin to help you in the work?" I ask.

"Well, you remember that Luke brought Joeli here to the hospital in Suva. During that time Luke also brought Joeli to my house, and I saw what was wrong with that boy. And I gave Luke some beads from my necklace to show him that the power of the *mana* was now with him."

"And Luke now works in Tovu?"

"Yes, he's doing the work there."

302

"On Monday nights?"

"Yes. Monday is the night doctors all over the world do their service work [*veiqaravi*].

"You know, Tevita had too many helpers," Ratu Noa muses, not addressing Marika or me. "I told him to lessen his number of helpers. I didn't know those helpers; I knew only Tevita. The connection with Tevita was direct. It came to him after I healed him. He was the source of power down in the Tovu area, and that power came from here. Those helpers of his — that was another story. They were people of his own choosing. I told Tevita that he alone was supposed to go and work on sick people, not to send his helpers. Because those other helpers he chose — well, they often treated the work as a joke."

"But what about Alipate?" After he had been cured by Ratu Noa, Alipate was supposedly empowered by Ratu Noa himself to help Tevita.

"Alipate didn't take his work seriously. He kept trying to contact his own *Vu*."

"And Eroni?"

"He died."

"Died! From what?"

"From diabetes. His death was from natural causes."

"And Tevita's helper who lives in Ogo?"

"He's no longer in the work. As with Tevita, he's given up his *rewa*."

I reflect more on Tevita. No longer working: that's still hard to accept. And then I think about how he chose his helpers. He probably had a hard time saying no if they asked him. I know he wanted help in administering the many requests he received; he didn't like traveling all the time. And maybe he didn't have full confidence in himself, confidence enough to believe that only he should heal people. Ratu Noa suggests this lack of complete confidence — or faith. Then I realize afresh that Ratu Noa selected me to work with Tevita. I was Tevita's helper, but also worked directly under Ratu Noa. In that I was different from Tevita's other helpers.

Ratu Noa leans into the space between us. "I'm going to give you my blessing, Rusiate. But please remember, if you violate that trust, that blessing, if you yield to temptation, it will come back to me and the One above. Try to think of me before you're tempted to stray. Because if you stray, I will suffer."

"Rusiate, what we talk about these days are the laws and principles of the work. I'm instructing you in these principles because you're already on the path."

Ratu Noa has concluded. We need only to arrange our next meeting.

"When do you leave Fiji?" he asks.

"In a week."

"Two days before you leave, please come back here for our last meeting. And we'll have another *yaqona*, a good *yaqona*. We'll drink together, and talk — and talk. And when you come I'll tell you what to do when you arrive back in America. How you are to offer thanks for all that happened to you in Fiji, all the blessings you received. And then after that, you can do whatever you want."

I arrive earlier than usual for our last meeting. Night still waits in the east.

Carefully, I present my *sevusevu*. With his own quiet care, Ratu Noa accepts it and proceeds to mix the *yaqona*. Ratu Noa's actions around the *yaqona* release a magnetic field. Now irresistibly together, we are praying to the power behind the healing work.

After the first round of *yaqona*, Ratu Noa begins giving me instructions about what to do in the first two days after I return to America, and how generally to conduct the healing work. He goes into great detail, and several times I have to ask him to repeat his instructions.

"Don't worry, Rusiate," he assures me. "If you have faith, you'll remember what to do. That faith, and being straight, are more important than any of the *particular* things I'm telling you to do.

"Now I've given you all the suggestions I can. After you leave Fiji and go back to your place, I'll follow you. But really, it's up to you.

"So we carry on, Rusiate." Though he speaks of the future, Ratu Noa's voice dips, taking on the tone of endings. "While there's still *yaqona* left in this *tanoa*, we can continue to talk. Ask questions if you have them. Then when this *tanoa* is finished, we will mix the final *tanoa* of *yaqona*.

During that last *tanoa,* no talk, no stories. We'll just drink *yaqona.* When that last *tanoa* is empty, and the end has come, we will shake hands. With that handshake I will be blessing the book...and passing the power on to you. We'll shake hands — and then you'll leave."

My feelings sink. The inevitable end to our talks is coming too soon. I try to stay with Ratu Noa and "carry on," now finding there are still a few questions seeking voice.

"How do I keep in touch with you about progress that I'm making and difficulties I might be encountering? Because I don't think I'm going to be able to come back again — at least soon."

"In whatever way you wish, Rusiate. You can communicate by letter...or by telepathy. Perhaps you can use both. It's up to you.

"And remember, if you're trying to help someone, and you become doubtful, the One that is with you will retreat. But don't be discouraged; the One who is behind you is very, very ancient, and has great power."

Ratu Noa motions with his eyes toward me, through me, and above me. I know that language. The "One who is behind me" is behind me right now, in this room.

"Yes, that One has been keeping a close watch on you," Ratu Noa comments, without surprise or drama.

We sit quietly for a moment, aware of the immediate presence of power.

"Rusiate," Ratu Noa advises, "bear in mind what Jesus said: that he came to serve, not to be served.

"And you don't have to use *yaqona* in your healing service," he reemphasizes. "Just using water is okay."

"Any more things you'd like to talk about?" As ever, Ratu Noa keeps us on track. "Any more questions? Remember, Rusiate, that after tonight, we will not meet again. So now is the time to ask."

One remaining question rises to the surface. "Should I take a *bilo* with me?"

"Definitely. I'll give you one. In fact, take two *bilo:* one for serving and one that you'll drink from."

He rises and goes to a small cabinet with glass doors which stands

305

against the back wall. Arranged carefully on the shelves I can see a *tabua* and some old tapa cloth that is folded up. He opens the doors and removes two *bilo,* one nesting inside the other. Returning, he wipes them off, caressing them more than cleaning them. Then he hands them to me, holding on as I take them; for a moment the *bilo* bind us together. And then he moves the *bilo* into my hands, pressing them into my work, sending them into my life.

Everything now seems imbued with extra meaning. Though I don't analyze each meaning, I feel its weight.

There is not much *yaqona* left in the *tanoa.* Our last round is waiting for us. I hear fresh *yaqona* being pounded outside; we won't be using the factory-ground *yaqona* we always have, but fresh. In the city, that signifies a special *yaqona.*

"Rusiate, you're ready to return. You have your own field of study as a psychologist, and you've learned that well. And now you've come to Fiji to study this work. The combination of these two kinds of work is very powerful indeed. And your teaching is in the same line as this healing work. So you can say that when you're teaching, you're also doing this work.

"You were well aware of the principles and laws of this healing work before you returned this time. You knew them from your first visit. This time we're just underlining some things, and passing on the power.

"As you progress in this healing work, others who may be up to no good will try to find out where your power comes from. At that time, just relax and let things take their course. Then others won't be able to dig into you for knowledge. Never tell others the details about where the power comes from.

"We're at the end, Rusiate. But you'll be back. This healing work operates like a battery. If the battery isn't charged, there is no work, no power. And so — in one form or another — you'll come back to Fiji. To check your battery, and recharge it."

The *tanoa* is empty. Ratu Noa dries it thoroughly. And now the freshly pounded *yaqona* is mixed. Our final *yaqona* is ready.

One round. We drink, almost without gestures. No talk. We look down; only occasionally do we allow our eyes to meet. A second round. The *tanoa* is empty. Ratu Noa dries it, wiping every edge. It's dry. And clean. He leans forward and shakes my hand.

PART THREE

THE STRAIGHT PATH

CHAPTER 31

A Way of Living

"The meaning of our traditions can come only to those who live them," Ratu Noa says, "but to live them we must know those meanings." Experience and reflection are inseparable aspects of human functioning. The story I have related of Fijian healing emphasizes experiences; in the following chapters I reflect on those experiences, offering some interpretations and suggesting some implications.

There is a fundamental continuity between the story and the reflections which follow. The Fijian people I worked with remain my guide; it is their story which will educate us. Indeed, it is out of respect for the *experience* of Fijian healing that the book, stressing interviews and narrative, tries to *describe* and *document* that experience more than to *interpret* it, and avoids placing the experience in the context of existing psychological or anthropological theories.

The "straight path" permeates this book because it describes the way healers, as well as Fijians in general, are supposed to live. The straight path is a way of healing which is in essence a way of living. While pursued most loyally and respected most intensely by healers, that path represents a dynamic ideal for all.

◢ THE NATURE OF THE PATH

The straight path is a journey through life which one discovers to the degree one searches for it honestly and with faith. Its nature and stages unfold as one walks it, and it becomes more difficult as it goes along. The path is never straight because it is traveled by human beings who struggle constantly to stay on course but inevitably, and often unpredictably, fall off. But though the path itself is not straight, the attitudes and the state of being one cultivates must be.

The struggle then becomes one of remaining straight as one journeys through the deviously contorted pathways of life. In being straight, one must strive to tell and live the truth, have love for all, and practice proper and correct behavior. One must exhibit humility, respect, single-mindedness, and service to others. This list is not inclusive; the straight path is an ideal way of being, but it is not authoritatively held out as a fully articulated model. It unfolds as one travels it.

To follow the straight path is to search for the "unknown," the "beyond," the "spiritual." It is to search for *mana*. *Mana* is what makes healing possible, *mana* from the *Vu*, who are behind the healing. Yet it is the faith of the healer which allows *mana* actually to enter the healing interaction. As Ratu Noa says, "If one's *Vu* is strong but one's faith is weak, the healing power available will also be weak; if one's *Vu* is weak but one's faith is strong, healing strength can come to the patient."

Though its power comes from *mana*, the nature of the straight path is determined by the character and actions of healers and of students seeking to become healers. What is important for learners remains relevant to practitioners, who should always be learning. Whether and how the *mana* enters the healing interaction is largely determined by whether and how healers act. It is critical to be dedicated to the search for *mana* and to use *mana* to serve people. If healers lose their dedication, if they "zigzag" in their faith, their power will weaken or abandon them. The straight path demands consistent, constant hard work.

Yet seekers on the path cannot be given too much too soon — too much knowledge, power, *mana*. Ratu Noa gives students *mana* only "bit

311

by bit." The student's character must grow in order to be able to handle increasingly strong *mana*; strength of character is the soil for *mana*, and at the same time it is enriched by *mana*. One must go slowly, gradually, carefully in learning about and traveling the straight path. To rush prematurely into contact with too strong *mana* can be harmful to both the healer and the patient. There are no shortcuts to the path; it is taken step by step, and as Ratu Noa insists, through knowing each step.

The straight path is silent, humble work. Healers are not to brag or even talk too much about their work. One's patients can do all the talking, spreading the word. Healers should not reveal everything to people about how they work, their power, and especially the source of that power. They may be tempted to reveal more than they should, especially to impress prospective clients, but the source of their power remains for them alone to know, along with perhaps a few of their trusted students. Conversely, healers are required to tell only what they know — no more and no less. Multiplying the truth destroys it, Ratu Noa warns.

Though the straight path may seem burdened with "shoulds" and "oughts," it is formed by healers' strengths — their honesty and faith. But certain attitudes and actions must be avoided; otherwise honesty and faith can become contaminated and the *mana* diluted. Two of the most severe prohibitions are asking for, or accepting payment for, the healing work and using the power of the work to manipulate clients sexually. It is appropriate to accept gifts of appreciation from patients, including gifts of money, but they must be gifts, given as tokens of thanks, not payments for services rendered. Though the prohibition about sex is commonly directed at the male healer who might be tempted to take advantage of his power to trick or manipulate a female client, the prohibition is gender-free and covers all forms of manipulation, intimidation, and abuse. Whenever payments are demanded or sex is engaged in during healing work, the healing power is gone. Such healers may continue to practice, but their work now becomes harmful because they are off the straight path.

Healers undertake a difficult struggle to find and follow the straight path, which requires them to live up to demanding ideals and develop purity of character. But there are characteristics of the path itself which

Healer

ease or at least enhance the struggle, forces that attract, captivate, ener-gize, and even engulf the healer. *Yaqona*, the key to *mana*, is said to act like a magnet, drawing the healer to it. Ratu Noa speaks of the "wave" that washes over the learner, bringing with it power and knowledge, and the "electricity" that animates the relationship between teacher and stu-dent and between coworkers on the path. These forces become irre-sistible, provided the seeker is honest and faithful. They are like forces of nature, like ocean waves and lightning, and therefore can be dangerous unless one works hard to stay on the path.

VISIONS ON THE PATH

Traveling the straight path is initiated by a first healing vision. Sometimes there is one dramatic dreamlike experience; sometimes a series of more subtle visions, less clearly demarcated experiences that are enmeshed in the practicalities of everyday life. The first healing vision calls a person to the healing work, introducing the possibility of a new way of being, a new way of working with the *Vu*. The process by which this new way of being unfolds, and the actual healer and healing work emerges, can be called "envisioning." Envisioning takes place when the first healing vision works itself into a person's life, when the vision becomes real and healing results.

Loti, a healer from southern Bitu who at the time I lived in Fiji was nearing sixty-five, had a first healing vision of the more dramatic type. He told the story of his first vision with some of the surprise, even shock he experienced when it came to him nearly twenty years before:

> I was sleeping or maybe just resting a bit. The *Vu* of our vil-lage appeared to me as a woman. She told me to go to the cliff by the shore and jump onto the ancient Fijian sailing canoe that lay in the bay. I went to the cliff. The boat lay beneath, far below. I was afraid to jump...very afraid...but jumped, landing on the deck. The canoe sailed out to sea. Suddenly a sea snake appeared, and around its neck, hanging by a gold

chain, was the *mana*-box. The *Vu* told me to take the box. She said it was for me. But I was afraid, afraid the snake would bite. I approached carefully, using a long pole from the sail to try to lift the *mana*-box off the snake's neck. I hesitated more than once, and moved cautiously. I reached out with the pole…and failed. I was undecided about continuing on. A second time I reached out with the pole…and again failed to get the box. The *Vu* said that I must return to the village. "The *mana* is not for you today," she said. The next day she appeared again. "You have one more chance. Leap onto the canoe and take the canoe and the *mana*-box." Again I went to the shore, leaped onto the canoe, and soon found myself facing the sea snake with the *mana*-box around its neck. This time I did not hesitate. I slipped the *mana*-box off its neck and didn't even need the pole. The *Vu* told me that I was now to use that *mana* for healing, that I was to begin the healing work. The next morning I awoke somewhat confused. How could I begin to heal, I wondered, since I did not know how to perform the healing ceremony? The *Vu* spoke to me again: "Do not worry. You have the *mana* with you. Use the *mana* for healing and the ways of healing will come to you." (Katz, 1981, p. 68)

The *Vu* who wishes to provide *mana* for the healing work appears during the first vision, requesting that the person engage in healing work on his or her behalf. In offering the straight path, the *Vu* makes clear what is needed to follow the straight path. Loti learned, for example, about the importance of being single-minded. The first vision calls for a commitment to use the power of *mana* only for healing.

These healing visions, which are enhanced states of consciousness, vary in detail and in intensity. For some the vision occurs in a dream state, at times moving into or out of a waking state; for others the vision occurs while the person is awake, and most often alone. Frequently the person sees the *Vu*, and usually they converse. In many cases the healer reports leaving his or her body and traveling (often flying) away to the

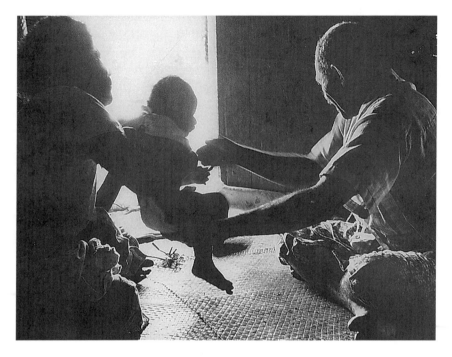

A mother handing her sick child to a healer

Vu or to see something the *Vu* wants to show, such as the traditional canoe in Loti's trip.

The first vision lays the foundation for the healing work, the connection with the *Vu* who will be the source of power. But envisioning goes beyond carrying out the intent of the first healing vision or visions. Envisioning involves advice and instruction from a teacher, if there is one; subsequent visions; lessons learned from one's patients; and most of all the continual practice of healing in one's community. In other words, becoming a healer is accomplished through recreating one's initial vision and subsequent visions in daily life. The visions offer guidance for everyday behavior, which in turn helps reshape the visions into guides of the possible. The core transformational experience necessary to become a healer is thereby enacted and reaffirmed in daily life.

The first vision calls forth the healer's emotional commitment to the healing work rather than presenting information about healing technique. Healers must affirm their belief in *mana* without knowing precisely how to conduct a healing ceremony; they agree to begin the healing work, trusting that specific healing techniques will come as the work is done. The call is felt as an agonizing challenge, a necessary responsibility, since Fijians do not seek the healing power. One must try to refuse the *Vu*'s request, acceding only when the *Vu* insists. Feeling humble and unworthy of the responsibility of power, one also intuits the pain and difficulty of the healing work, a life filled with temptations, tests, and the suffering of others.

First visions commonly occur in mature adulthood, but can occur during adolescence or early adulthood. Many, especially those not yet adults, do not take up the healing work immediately after the first vision. Weeks, months, even years may pass. The vision may be reconsidered, its consequences reevaluated. Another strong emotional experience often precipitates the practice, perhaps an unexplained request for healing from a sick person.

VAKATEVORO

Just as the straight path is defined by what it *is* in its unfolding, it can also be defined by what it *is not*. In this book the straight path is constantly juxtaposed with *vakatevoro*, but this is not a simple dichotomy. As complicated as the straight path is, so too is *vakatevoro*.

The number of crises Tovu experienced during my time there was relatively unusual in Fijian villages. But the story of Fijian healing I have related accurately portrays the dynamics of *vakatevoro*.

Why the *Vu* would honor a request to harm or kill someone, and the details of how *vakatevoro* is performed, are subjects never discussed at length by most people, partly out of fear that any knowledge they reveal will be taken as evidence that they themselves practice these rituals. But such subjects remain intensely interesting. By gleaning bits and pieces, one can begin to understand the workings of *vakatevoro*, which subverts the normal healing *yaqona* ceremony in order to ask the *Vu* to bring harm to others. The ways of subversion are many and subtle, often occurring during a regular *yaqona* ceremony, but sometimes also consisting of a special ceremony done just for purposes of *vakatevoro*.

The question of "why" is even more intriguing. Any request that accompanies an offering of *yaqona* has great force, regardless of its intent. Moreover, some *Vu* are said to be unreliable. As one elder put it: "You can perform this *vakatevoro* because some of the *Vu* are not entirely trustworthy." But imputing evil intentions to the *Vu* is a risky business. Other interpretations explain how the *Vu* can be persuaded to cause harm. It is said that, because the *Vu* live at a different level from that of human beings, what may seem to be a harmful outcome from the limited human perspective is seen in another light by the *Vu*. Others also say that the *Vu* may get a certain pleasure out of seeing people behave in ways that harm others, a pleasure people cannot understand. In a perverse way, human frailties — indeed, human evil — is "the entertainment of the *Vu*."

These explanations of *vakatevoro* coexist with the basic function of the *Vu*, which is to protect and guide human beings and, when they violate a sacred tradition, to redirect or punish them. The *Vu* are fundamentally allies. In a common Fijian saying, "They are our old people, our ancestors, and wish us well."

The enormous danger of *vakatevoro* is a testimony to the strength of the straight path. Followers of both ways call on the *Vu* for assistance, though the nature of their request divides them. The straight path and *vakatevoro* are theoretically at opposite poles; one is the denial of the other. But in practice the two intermingle, causing a few healers to lose their power, and others to lose their way. All are at times tempted to stray off the path. As one travels along the straight path, along with the increasing power come increasing temptations to abuse that power.

I have spoken only of *vakatevoro*, which more precisely means using *yaqona* to request the *Vu* to harm or kill another. It is making a sacred pact with the *Vu*, but because it uses *mana* to harm, it is a pact with the devil. It is "devil work," or work of a devilish nature. There is also *vaka-vanua*, which, when used in a particular context, refers to the violation of sacred traditions, a dishonoring of the *Vu* by disrespectful behavior toward customs.

Vakatevoro and *vakavanua* both involve the *Vu,* and certainly the practice of *vakatevoro* violates sacred traditions. When, for example, people speak of spiritually caused sickness (*tauvimate vakatevoro*), as opposed to sickness from natural causes (*tauvimate dina*), they often don't distinguish between the two causes of the spiritual sickness — *vakatevoro* and *vakavanua*. And the one word *vakatevoro* is commonly used to refer to both causes.

Vakatevoro, as mentioned earlier, is usually translated in English as "witchcraft," but I prefer not to reduce it to that category. In spite of many attempts to explore the complexity of witchcraft and to distinguish it from sorcery (see, for example, Amoah, 1986; Ehrenreich and Dierdre, 1973; Evans-Pritchard, 1937; Kuhn, 1990; Luhrmann, 1989; Middleton, 1967; Taussig, 1987; Whiting, 1953), in common usage witchcraft remains a distinctly pejorative and therefore shallow concept. In contrast, the practice of *vakatevoro,* and the search for the practitioner, release essential processes of meaning-making, attempts to understand the world and to affect events based on that understanding.

In Tovu, a central feature of the peoples' reaction to the deaths was their need to know — and their simultaneous fear of knowing — whether *vakatavoro* was involved. The constant making and unmaking of hypotheses kept events from being definitely resolved. By preserving ambiguity, a dynamic balance between the forces of healing and *vaka-tevoro* could be maintained. Finally, identifying the evildoer would require confronting and perhaps even expelling that person, who might be a relative. Instead, the aim was a correct balance between conflicting forces, not the destruction of the side responsible for wrongdoing.

Whenever problems of *vakatevoro* or *vakavanua* arose, the counsel of Ratu Noa and Tevita delineated the straight path. "Be straight," they would say; "Keep your faith strong" and "stay close to the *yaqona,*" praying to and honoring the *Vu.* The emphasis was always on what positive things one could do to fortify oneself and to check the forces of wrong-doing — never on directly fighting against the evildoers. As for all human activities, there are rules and procedures for *vakatevoro,* but following the straight path does not mean using these rules to subvert the practitioner of *vakatevoro.* One's own spiritual strength is the best, and the only correct protection. The rules of *vakatevoro,* its unpredictable mystery, serve to establish the formidable nature of the opponent — outside oneself and within.

The straight path thus cannot be reduced to a battle against the devil, or to a response to deaths assumed to be caused by evildoing, or simply to a way to avoid violating the sacred traditions of the land. It is an intricate and enduring human experience grounded in opposing forces within the person and the culture, moral dilemmas that must be lived through in all their unknown complexity.

▲ YAQONA

Though *yaqona,* the primary vehicle for communication with the *Vu,* is essential to the healing ceremony, its meanings are also many and varied. *Yaqona* can be presented in several forms — fresh, dried, pounded, ground — and the offering itself can be mixed or not, served or not in the ceremony. How the *yaqona* is presented, prepared, mixed, and served can become significant, determining the potency of the ceremony.

But *yaqona* is more than the plant *Piper methysticum,* as Ratu Noa suggested when he talked about what was needed for a healing ceremony. A little twig of *yaqona* is enough if that is all one can afford and one really needs help. Or, as he advised me, *yaqona* doesn't always have to be presented. Ratu Noa and others are never precise when they say *yaqona* is more than the plant, but the drift of their understanding is clear. *Yaqona* represents a way of being, a deep attitude that the healer brings to the work, and that the patient brings to the healer. Both are requesting help, and the necessary attitude is that of one following the straight path.

Yaqona is this way of being, not merely a symbol of it. Ratu Noa often talks about "living the *yaqona.*" Moreover, this way of being is essential

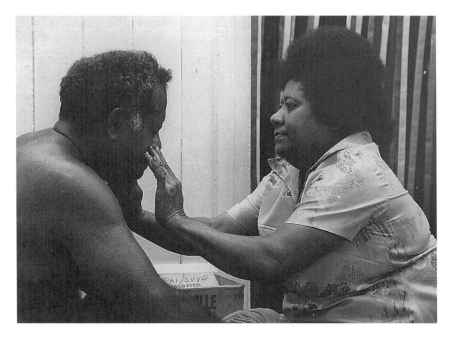

Yaqona *having been exchanged, the healer massages her client*

not just for performing the ceremony, but for making the healing work itself effective. It is the way of correct daily living. As the "food of the *Vu*," *yaqona* reminds humanity of its place in the universe, demanding the honesty and humility that must precede any granting of power. As with any gift, *yaqona* can be abused. Instead of using *yaqona* with respect, drinking, as Ratu Noa says, "for the *Vu*," Fijians often consider it the poor man's alcohol. When *yaqona* is used properly, however, it supports the journey along the straight path, especially at times intensity and crisis.

◢ A PATH OF LIFE

The straight path as an ideal way of being is not an unusual phenomenon. The concept of a path in life, or "a path of life," is common to cultures throughout the world, as is the requirement that the path be "straight" or approached with "straightness." In Buddhism, for example, the Eightfold Path leads to *nirvana,* the state transcending the limitations of earthly experience and self-seeking (see, for example, Burt, 1955); the Diné (Navajo) path of life stresses harmony and balance with all of nature (Beck, Walters, and Francisco, 1992); and in the Christian tradition, the path of asceticism, contemplation, and affirmation followed by the fourth-century Desert Fathers is the source of Western monasticism (Merton, 1970). Among the Lakota, life is seen as a choice between the Red Road, which offers the challenge of correct living, and the Black Road (Lame Deer and Erdoes, 1972; Neihardt, 1972); and the Seven Fires of Life celebrate successive stages or levels that mark a proper transition through life for Anishinabe (Saulteaux) people (Musqua, 1991a).

Sometimes the values and personal characteristics necessary for right living have been distilled and written down to encourage and guide the people. Such is the case with the list of Inupiaq values offered to the Inupiat people of Kotzebue, Alaska, by their elders (Craig, 1988); as well as the set of values based on the meanings of each of the fifteen poles used to construct the tipi, which has been articulated by Cree elders in Saskatchewan (The Tipi, 1988). These values are said to describe what it means to be a truly respectful and respected member of the culture; they describe the terrain of the culture's spiritual journey.

These manifestations are not reducible to a single pattern, but they do share important features. The paths evolve from a relationship with a higher power or spiritual force. They are described and presented to the people by elders, those who have learned about the path from experience, and who are committed to passing on their own life experience and, most important, the ancient truths they have themselves been taught.

The English writer Aldous Huxley (1944) has called the idea of the path of proper living the "perennial philosophy"; the American Huston Smith (1977) calls it the "primordial tradition." An important feature of the path is that it is a spiritual discipline, and following it involves hard work as well as devotion. The straight path requires "discipline" and "work." As Ratu Noa says, the straight path is "long and hard," demanding constant vigilance and effort in the struggle to be honest. For

Indigenous peoples, the path is simply the traditional way of life which defines what it means to be truly human; it is a series of simple and very practical truths, not abstract philosophical ideas.

Traveling along the path requires constant struggle and vigilance. It is not a clear and linear process but rather is filled with ambiguity, confusion, and temptation, leading to wrong turns on the way to understanding. Specific behaviors may be necessary in staying on the path, and one may pass through specific stages along it. But since the path presents a way of being, it is not so much an exact prescription or chronology as a guide for the way life should be lived. Critical to this way of being are certain fundamental values and attitudes needed to find and stay on the path, such as respect, humility, love, sharing, and service.

Though the path may be practiced most faithfully only by a certain segment of the society, such as healers, it is a cultural ideal for all. In Fiji, for example, healers represent the ideal others strive for, and they guide others' travel on their own paths. Usually, teaching about the path remains in the oral tradition, the traditional mode of discourse. When the path is described in writing, there is the additional attempt to speak more directly to the young generation which relies more heavily on the written word. The essence of the teaching — and the real learning — remains, however, in the oral tradition, in the lived experience.

Finally, the concept of being "straight" has particular relevance to patterns of decision making and conflict resolution (Watson-Gegeo and White, 1989). One who is straight is correct, right, and truthful; such a person learns how to "straighten things out" and to "make things right" — that is, to resolve conflict according to certain moral principles.

The straight path of the traditional Fijian healer presented in this book is unique, but it is also archetypal, shared with cultures around the world. As such it can offer valuable insights into healing practices and ways of being in the West.

CHAPTER 32

A Transformational Approach to Healing, Development, and Social Change

Fijian healing lives through exchange. If the story of Fijian healing in this book is to thrive, we must continue initiating exchanges. "As that story educates your people in our ancient ways," Ratu Noa says, "it will help us appreciate more who we are and who we must remain." In this chapter I will focus on the implications of the straight path for Western health and healing, individual development, and social change. My special task is to speak to my own people about these "ancient ways."

Simply "learning from" Fijians is not enough. We must follow the principles of the straight path as we learn about it — the learning must emerge from a respectful relationship, and must be put into practice in order to serve the people.

But bringing the straight path into our lives is only part of this exchange. As Ratu Noa says, this book must also help Fijians "appreciate" their own present and future identities. For that part of the exchange, I rely on my Fijian teachers. The truth of the story, they assure me, will speak to the Fijian people — in its own time, in its own way.

One of my reasons for writing this book is that, along with so many others, I believe that humanity is in a precarious state, its survival threatened. In my own areas of experience — health and development — I can see the lines of deterioration clearly. They have progressed most fully in industrialized societies. In the West, we are searching for ways to change our situation, or at least to deflect those lines of destruction or slow down their pace. As a way of healing and a way of being, the straight path offers hope in that effort.

Many consider the core of Western culture, its spiritual foundation, to be missing, perhaps dead. The straight path can lead us to rediscover the freshness of our own spiritual traditions from within the dry materialism of our world. We in the West must connect with our own spiritual life — with our own *Vu*, as Ratu Noa puts it. Only then can we begin to realize the spiritual reality that connects us all. In that, I am convinced, lies the straight path to our survival.

An elder and her granddaughter

The straight path is important for four interrelated aspects of human growth and development: ways of being, healing, individual development, and social change. I start with a consideration of the straight path as the way healers are educated, which is also a way of being for all people. This introduces a transformational model that can then be applied to healing, individual development, and social change. Moreover, the process of healing itself is central to individual and social change, which are in themselves intricately linked. It is in its expression of this transformational model that the straight path offers certain valuable possibilities of change for the West.

The implications of the straight path are rich, as is the case with any such intensely lived experience. To preserve that richness, I want to stay close to the words of Fijian healers and their interpretations, not using their words merely as evidence to prove or disprove Western anthropological or psychological theories.

325

I also want to stay close to the heart of the straight path. I went to Fiji expecting complex healing rituals, since Fijian culture is noted for its pervasive and delicate elaboration of ceremonial life (for example, Ravuvu, 1983; J. W. Turner, 1986a, 1987). There are indeed many complex rituals for healing, which emphasize the precise performance of specific activities. But the essence of healing is in the straight path, a simple set of attributes to live by. The heart of Fijian healing lies exposed, recognizable yet at the same time fiercely elusive.

⊿ THE EDUCATION OF A HEALER: A WAY OF BEING

The straight path, in its most literal sense, describes the way healers are educated; but as it unfolds, the process of becoming a healer also offers a model for the way all people should ideally live. To highlight the characteristics of the straight path, I contrast the traditional process of becoming a Fijian healer with the education of the "health care professional" in the West, in particular in the United States. I focus on medical and mental health providers, including physicians, psychotherapists, social workers, psychiatrists, and psychologists. The differences are sharply drawn because Fijian healers, especially in the rural areas, function more closely to their ideals; the overlap that already exists in the two ways of practice would be even greater if I compared the ideals of practice in both cultures.

In drawing contrasts, I emphasize central tendencies, although of course there are among Fijian healers those who deviate from the straight path, just as there are among Western health care professionals those who struggle to find a similar path. Here in the West we see an increasing effort, in a variety of contexts, to oppose or at least balance the mechanistic tendencies of the prevailing biomedical model of care. The discipline of family practice plays a leading role in this movement in medicine; and various therapeutic approaches based on mind-body interactions play the same role throughout the health care professions (Goleman and Gurin, 1993). There are numerous programs and practices in which the humanistic aspects of care and the spiritual dimensions of

326

healing are emphasized. Marie Balter, for example, tells of the humanistic and spiritual nature of her recovery from mental illness (Balter and Katz, 1991); Kabat-Zinn and associates describe how meditation can reduce stress and anxiety (Kabat-Zinn, 1991; Kabat-Zinn et al., 1992); Byrd (1988) documents the positive effect of prayer on recovery from heart attack; and Remen (1990) investigates the importance of transpersonal counseling in the treatment of cancer.

Specialization and professionalism prevent an exact comparison between Western and Fijian healers, but the community psychiatrist, for example, offers a reasonable parallel (R. Katz, 1981). Community psychiatrists assume medical, social, and psychological responsibilities; they are often called "priests of the new science" or "scientists of the new religion." Though community psychiatrists make up only a small specialty within psychiatry, their influence is broader than their number because their discipline shapes the teaching and practice of other professions such as clinical psychology and social work.

To become a Fijian healer is to connect to and work from within a spiritual dimension. It is the *mana* that heals; the *mana* comes from the *Vu*. The healer's first healing vision establishes that connection, initiating a lifelong process of reconnecting and recreating, or "envisioning." Spiritual transformation becomes the dynamic of the straight path. As Ratu Noa stresses, no other human being can take healing power away; one can only lose it by breaking the connection. The straight path is a journey into the beyond, where the *Vu* reside, and where the forces of good and evil are not abstractions but lived spiritual principles.

In contrast, becoming a health care professional in the West is more of a "scientific" process, explicitly antispiritual. What can be known with the five senses is what is real; the "beyond" or the "unknown" is dismissed as "speculation" or "error factor." When asked what it is that heals, health care professionals typically point to medical technology or some professional skill or technique.

Becoming connected to the spiritual dimension demands commitment to a healing power beyond the self, and entails humility about one's own contribution to the healing. The Fijian healer does not claim personal ownership of *mana,* or take personal credit for its healing effects. In contrast, the Western physician is more likely to claim control over, if not ownership of, the ability to cure or heal. Competence — knowing what to do, or at least not revealing that one doesn't know — is stressed over natural human vulnerability.

Furthermore, the Fijian healer respects the sacredness of the spiritual dimension, of the healing power. Indirect language is used to refer to the *Vu,* out of respect for their power. Truths are revealed, but never sacred secrets. Health care professionals are instead taught to "demystify" the process of healing. Though they may make known the "ancient and unknown" sources of some techniques, they usually lack the profound respect for these sources so characteristic of the Fijian healer.

For the Fijian healer, healing is a way of living — the straight path, the path of life. But for Western health care professionals, healing is more of a job, separate from their personal life.

Healing for the Fijian is a way of dealing with fundamental life tasks, a "moral exploration," an attempt to make meanings and construct realities. Sickness has its own meanings that must be understood; for example, it can tell a story of *vakatevoro* or the violation of a sacred norm. The aim is to understand sickness in order to heal it, to work with it in order to understand it. Therefore, sickness or *vakatevoro* is not attacked directly. One prays, one stays close to the *yaqona,* one strengthens positive forces in order to remain well. Faith heals by balancing out negative forces and rendering them powerless.

In contrast, battle metaphors dominate the work of health care professionals in this country. Symptoms must be "conquered" or "eradicated." A physician is a warrior in the fight against disease, with hardly any time left to learn. Success is measured by symptoms removed, not balance achieved.

Becoming a Fijian healer is a journey into unknown territory, through cultural mysteries. The healer knows the straight path by traveling it, and the path itself is full of the unexpected and unexplained. Faith is critical. The health care specialist, on the other hand, is bombarded with "cookbook" approaches to care which lay out the stages of training, including the speed at which one should progress.

An elder telling his story

In the Fijian healer's journey of learning and practice, character precedes and lays the foundation for learning healing techniques. It is the commitment to values such as truth, love, respect, and humility which gives techniques their healing power. Being straight is the issue; *yaqona* is a way of being. Internal transitions are valued rather than particular states achieved. The health care professional's journey is more often marked by external labels that legitimize progress or certify a level of skill. Framed diplomas adorn the practitioner's office, their number sometimes inversely proportional to competence. Furthermore, there is a fascination with technique, sometimes at the expense of character. Expertise in healing techniques often becomes a measure of power or success, and the newer or rarer the technique the better.

The very idea of progress is alien to the Fijian healer's learning. The straight path is not linear. The further one is along the path, the more difficult it becomes — vulnerability is the intimate partner of power. The Western notion of progress, in which one goes higher and higher, advancing in a straight line through preset stages, gaining more and more control, is just the opposite. This neatly rewarding idea of progress plays a larger role in the motivation of the health care professional.

The straight path is long, slow, and painful; it is hard, it is a struggle, it is work. No shortcuts are allowed. Step-by-step, bit-by-bit, not too much nor too soon. In the West, the process of becoming a healer often mimics the general culture's infatuation with mechanized efficiency. Social workers, psychologists, and psychiatrists are besieged with skill-training workshops — "intensives" — that in a brief time give the practitioner yet another stamp of approval. If learning to be a healer is not quick, at least the stages are laid out in advance. Patience is not emphasized, as it is in the straight path.

The straight path is silent, humble work. One keeps to the truth, saying only what one knows, "no more, and no less." There is no self-promotion, only the quiet talk of satisfied patients. Finally, the straight path is service work; Fijian healers are the community's servants. Through their commitment to serve, their time is no longer their own. No economic rewards can be expected, though gifts of appreciation can be received. And that, says Ratu Noa, will always be enough.

These last two characteristics of the straight path — silence and service — represent the difficulty or struggle many Western health care professionals wish to avoid. Socialized in a culture based on individual self-promotion, which makes all things, including healing, into commodities to be sold, which values people according to how much money they earn, and which places individual and personal achievement at the pinnacle of success, it is nearly impossible to remain silent and simply serve.

▲ HEALING AS TRANSFORMATION

The transformational model presented here has been deduced from my field data on Fijian healing. The model was originally suggested by my earlier fieldwork in 1968 among the Zhu/twasi (!Kung) in Botswana (R. Katz, 1982a), supplemented by the research of other field workers (see, for example, Lee, 1979, 1984; Marshall, 1969). The model was reconfirmed and refined by my second period of work among the Zhu/twasi in 1989, and fieldwork among traditional Inupiaq healers in Alaska (Katz and Craig, 1987, 1988) and Lakota (Sioux) medicine men, as well as the research of others with various Indigenous and non-Indigenous peoples in different parts of the world (Katz and Seth, 1993).

The Fijian and Zhu/twasi approaches to transformation, though different in some respects, share fundamental similarities (R. Katz, 1981). Also, the model of transformation appears to have a more widespread relevance, especially among non-Western cultures. For example, "education as transformation" has been shown to characterize healer education among: hunter-gatherers (Hahn and Katz, 1985); traditional Puerto Rican *espiritistas* (spiritual healers) (Nuñez-Molina, 1987); and practitioners of the sweat lodge (Hampton, 1984). Transformation as a theme can be found also among some Western approaches to helping, such as with community psychologists (Cheever, 1991), within self-help groups (Katz and Seth, 1986), and in the self-directed teaching of counseling skills (Simonis, 1984).

The straight path implies a concept of healing which is a search for meaning, balance, connectedness, and wholeness; in short, a process of transformation (R. Katz, 1973, 1981, 1982a, 1986). One expression of this transformation is a dramatically enhanced state of consciousness, but the transformational experience can also take place in more subtle shifts in ordinary consciousness. Whether the context is dramatic or ordinary, transformation brings on an experience of reality in which the boundaries of self and social organization become more permeable to contact with a spiritual realm. Accessing the enhanced state of consciousness, and applying its effects within the community, combine to constitute the transformational experience.

The transformational nature of healing has been approached from a variety of perspectives, including those emphasizing the power of the language of transformation (Csordas, 1983) or the mental imagery of transformation (Noll, 1985; Skultans, 1987). Yet a transformation of consciousness remains the essential experience.

"Healing as transformation" is increasingly recognized as a necessary antidote to the notion of "curing," of the removing of symptoms (Berg and Lipken, 1982; R. Katz, 1990; Katz and Craig, 1988; Kleinman, 1979). This concept, however, is an elusive one, as it does not allow for the sort of satisfaction that comes from a focus on observable criteria such as test results or measurable symptoms.

Individuals and communities that seek such healing are often in the midst of crises, confusion, or a search for fulfillment. In their vulnerability and openness to change, they reveal their fears and hopes. These in turn are the context for the healing transition as well as their resolution or fulfillment, the aim of that transition. Healing can be not only a source of insight about human nature but also a means of actualizing human potential (Alexander and Langer, 1989; Bourguignon, 1973; R. Katz, 1982a; Katz and Wexler, 1990; Lévi-Strauss, 1963; McGuire, 1983; Van Gennep, 1960). Focusing as it does on vulnerability, healing deals with critical turning points in community and individual development. This concept of healing is not merely confined to curing sick people. It involves central tasks of psychological development as well, such as defining reality and making meaning.

Western systems of health care are characterized by assumptions about health and illness which contrast sharply with this transformational model. For example, in the West there is an emphasis on technological intervention to cure illness, breaking the process down into isolated categories, such as the "change agent" and the "target population." Indigenous people, on the other hand, focus more on the emotional and spiritual context in healing the individual and the community, which are seen as inextricably interconnected.

The expert technical skills of service providers in the West are emphasized over their character. Being experts, they are by definition a scarce resource. The provider "intervenes" in a situation to "isolate" the problem and "remove" or "excise" it. The recipient of services in the Western medical system is usually described as a person or group "with a problem" — and the problem or illness is seen as being discrete from the person or group. In many medical settings, the ideal patient follows "doctor's orders." Submitting passively to an expert, patients let the doctor "fix them up," trying not get in the expert's way. Because the number of experts is limited, and because the client and the community are cut off from rather than enlisted in the treatment effort, Western health care remains a scarce and costly resource.

In contrast, the traditional Fijian approach to health focuses more on healing resources that expand and replenish themselves and are therefore available to all members of the community (R. Katz, 1983/84). Endowed with special healing skills and responsibilities, traditional Fijian healers pray to the *Vu* to give them accurate perception and to make them sensitive to the body's ills so that they can successfully treat the patient. Fijian healing thus becomes an expression of spiritual work. Since the spiritual source of power is infinite, there is no limit to the healing available.

Through its spiritual basis, traditional Fijian healing is embedded in a web of interrelated elements. Spiritual power infuses all elements of the healing process: the patient, his or her family and community, the healer, the healing act, and healing power. As these parts become sources of healing, they support and transform each other, continually creating new and expanding capacities for healing.

The work of traditional Fijian healers thus becomes an intrinsic part of the self-healing efforts of the patient and the community. Healers cannot work without community support; they need the prayers of the people to give them strength. As healers heal members of the community, so the community heals the healers. The community as healer enables the healers to give help.

Tevita's eventually leaving the healing work was deeply influenced by the evaporation of community support in Tovu. Reverend Jemesa's missionary zeal helped ferment people's abandonment of Tevita's work in Tovu and Ogo by labeling it as against Christianity and from the devil. This pattern of attempting to destroy an Indigenous culture through the destruction of its spiritual and healing traditions is, of course, common throughout the world and throughout history, and is still being recounted by elders today (for example, Musqua, 1991b; Skin, 1988).

Fijians view the healing work of the family and the community as a reinforcement of the healing power of *mana,* an aid in helping to remove obstacles in the patient that prevent health from returning. In this way the patient's self-healing powers are strengthened. Through the intervention of *mana,* the healthful forces are released both within the person and the community. Health thus becomes an expression of the Fijian way of life.

PSYCHO-SPIRITUAL DEVELOPMENT

From this transformational model of healing among Fijians we can extrapolate models of psycho-spiritual development and social change. In fact, there appears to be a single transformational model originally derived from spiritual development. Though in contemporary Western culture healing and spiritual development are each usually considered as separate dimensions, in Fijian tradition both are inseparable from other aspects of life.

Traveling the straight path is fueled by enhanced states of consciousness during which healers experience a sense of connectedness that joins them and their communities with spiritual healing power. This enhanced state of consciousness is firmly rooted in the context of ordinary life and is only part of the transformational experience.

Chief and his grandson

The envisioning process, during which the experience of enhanced consciousness is continually reenacted and affirmed in the healer's daily life, requires that the healer's vision offer direction for everyday behavior. Through this envisioning process the healer rediscovers direction, and bonding to the community is renewed. The straight path charts a developmental course, a trajectory toward cultural ideals. It offers both a normative and an actual model, describing both the life toward which people aspire, and the continual reaching and falling back from these ideals which is the actual condition of people's lives.

The transformational model of individual development suggested by the straight path distinguishes itself in several ways: in its focus on a spiritual dimension; in its movement back and forth through transitions; in its flexible, nonlinear sequence of development; in its association of power and vulnerability; and in the inseparability of individual and sociocultural development.

Perhaps an effective way to understand the implications of the straight path for concepts of individual development is to compare the journey along the path with Piaget's model of development. Jean Piaget (1952, 1970) has articulated one of the most commonly accepted theories of developmental psychology in the West. The contrasts between his model of development and the transformational model implied in the straight path are striking.

THE SPIRITUAL DIMENSION

The contribution of the spiritual dimension to development is fundamental to the transformational model. In Piaget's work, cognitive aspects of development are central; spiritual aspects receive scant attention, and affective aspects are merely correlates of the structural, cognitive side. Fijian spirituality, however, is not spiritual in the sense of a distant or abstract dimension. The dualism inherent in much Western thinking between the spiritual and other dimensions — the material or the human or the psychological dimension — is not present in Fijian society.

The straight path means learning to live in harmony with spiritual principles. The distinction between secular and spiritual tasks is minimized. The power to heal in the form of *mana* comes originally from this spiritual dimension. *Mana* "makes things happen" in all aspects of life; it is said to make not only healers but also politicians and athletes powerful. Though it represents a realm beyond the community in Fijian culture, this spiritual dimension is also close at hand. This closeness does not lead to a disrespect or diminution of its power. Instead, familiarity, even an intimacy with the spiritual dimension, prevents it from being considered as separate from ordinary life. Fijian healers do not find the actual experience of spiritual power surprising, nor does it make them feel "different."

Other developmental theories often isolate or focus on particular aspects of development. Apart from theories of cognitive development, for example, are theories which emphasize affective development (Hesse and Cicchetti, 1982; Izard, 1982; Izard and Malatesta, 1987) or moral development (Gilligan, 1982, 1988; Kohlberg, 1984, 1986; Turiel, 1983). Many theories also attempt to integrate several aspects of development: social and cognitive factors (Lewis and Brooks-Gunn, 1979; Selman, 1980), social and emotional factors (Sroufe, 1990), emotional and cognitive factors (Cowan, 1982; Kagan, 1978, 1988), and moral and affective factors (Hoffman, 1978, 1980). Others have acknowledged the role of spirituality in development but have tended to discuss spirituality in terms of "faith," seeing it as a more separate area of development (Fowler, 1981). But the transformational model we have seen in Fijian healing integrates social, cognitive, affective, and moral elements, infusing all with the spiritual dimension. Some Western developmental theorists are working toward such an integrative model (Alexander and Langer, 1989).

Optimal human functioning for Fijians means living in the spiritual dimension, which requires that the human capabilities labeled in the West "emotion" and "cognition" be guided by spirituality. The Fijian *Vu* not only represent the most complete expression of the spiritual dimension but also exhibit the full range of emotion and cognition: jealousy as well as love, and trickery as well as honesty.

The spiritual dimension constantly directs the individual toward interaction with the community. Healers merit respect as participants in the healing ceremony, but this does not set them apart from the community or give them special status. Fijian healers are expected to fulfill everyday duties as members of their communities; healing is an additional responsibility. The elder's description of the healer Tevita bears repeating: "Tevita is one of us, just like the rest of us." Healers differ from other community members in internal psychological qualities predisposing them to work at healing, but not in measures of everyday status or functioning.

The Fijian healer is not focused entirely on a spiritual reality, nor inward on the individual self. The *Vu* penetrate the healer's consciousness through a vision and send the healer to his or her immediate community to serve. For example, when Reverend Jemesa tried to convince

Tevita that his healing work was harming the community, Tevita was extremely disheartened and believed he should give up healing. The fruits of his transformed consciousness — his healing — amounted to little if it did not benefit the community. Healers are not seeking to extricate themselves from a secular realm, to replace it with a spiritual dimension. They seek to remain within the community, meeting their daily responsibilities while exhibiting changed behavior through a transformed state of consciousness.

TRANSITIONS

From the perspective of the transformational model of development, movement along the straight path is characterized by moving through transitions. In contrast to Piaget's model, this movement is neither unidirectional nor the basis for permanent developmental gains. One moves toward increasing clarity and commitment, and deeper or more powerful visions, but also away from them. Life history is enlivened by the recurring process of movement and transition. Healers who are active in moral exploration alternate between clarity and ambiguity of comprehension. After receiving Ratu Noa's taped message, Tevita moved from ambiguity to clarity in his understanding regarding the Christian church versus Indigenous healing practices.

Similarly, transitions characterize the envisioning process as healers move between their visions, altering their daily context as a result of those visions, and experiencing new visions that result from their own changed behavior and sociocultural environment. Develement occurs through a continual series of transitions rather than a linear (or even spiral) progression over the life course which culminates in an end state or stage. Life history in the transformational model becomes a continuous pattern of meeting and being overwhelmed by developmental crises; in each crisis the recurring challenge is to transcend the self in order to channel healing resources to the community.

In Piaget's theory, despite his emphasis on oscillations around key transition points, developmental processes are unidirectional, toward increasing generalizations and differentiation. In the transformational model, movement in both directions is constant. One moves both toward and away from meaning, balance, connectedness, and wholeness. There is a continued struggle around these issues, and each movement, regardless of direction, is considered important and part of human development.

NONLINEARITY

The transformational model of development is not characterized by hierarchical stages. Moving through a transition does not guarantee "success" in the next transitional challenge or assume "success" in the previous one. Experience does not follow a universal and irreversible order. No more than half of the healers begin their work as apprentices. All healers have initial healing visions, but their visions differ in intensity, detail, and in the state of consciousness experienced. No set ages or developmental stages can be specified that apply to the development of healers. The common element is contact with *mana*. From the perspective of a linear, teleological concept of development, these life histories might be seen as stalled in an endless dialectical movement. Moving into and out of states of consciousness, and regulating healing power, are the developmental tasks for Fijian healers rather than progressing toward possession of power.

For Fijian healers, the boundaries between stages are open. The sequence of stages is flexible, and there is no one articulated end point toward which the stages progress or culminate. Achieving a certain stage is not cause for celebration, nor does it bring status or other rewards. Remaining at a stage is a dynamic task that can easily be undone. Instead, traveling the straight path means developing a correct or "straight" attitude and motivation and maintaining it through continual challenges.

POWER AND VULNERABILITY

In the transformational model, power and vulnerability are associated. Again, we can contrast this with Piaget's model, which implies a steady progression away from vulnerability. As the healer meets increasingly difficult challenges along the straight path, he or she has access to greater power. But that power cannot be used to make the healer invulnerable. Though access to power generally does increase with experience, it continually fluctuates. The goal is to relate with integrity to power and to regulate it with care and wisdom, not to possess it. The most powerful Fijian healers are the most vulnerable to abusing their power, and thus completely losing the power. Merely having access to greater power does not guarantee a successful outcome. Healers are constantly forced to reassess their relationship to the healing power. They continually reestablish the quality and basis of that power in their lives. Healers move between their fear of the transforming experience and their desire to heal others, their search for increased healing power and the difficulty of working with it.

Each transition is a risk, exposing the integrity and continuity of the self. The terror that accompanies the transitions is no less because the healer experiences numerous such transitions in a lifetime. Knowledge of how to make a transition must always be relearned; at times it is unavailable, even to the experienced healer. The process is accompanied by a basic sense of vulnerability, both more frightening and liberating than the feelings that accompany developmental transitions in Piaget's framework. Though the use of power for healing rather than harm may be the pattern, that pattern is constantly tested through temptations for misuse. The moments when the relationship to power is in flux are points of vulnerability, but also opportunities for change.

INDIVIDUAL AND COMMUNITY DEVELOPMENT

In the transformational model we have been examining, an individual's development is inseparable from his or her sociocultural context. Individual and community development merge through their reciprocal influence on each other; healers experience transformation in order to serve the community as the community experiences transformation in order to serve the individual. As a result, both individual and community benefit beyond what was possible for each alone. This pattern of mutual benefits has been described as a "synergistic community" (R. Katz, 1983/84; Katz and Seth, 1986).

The Fijian conception of the self-embedded-in-community contrasts with the Western value of individualism with its idea of the self as separate and separating from others (LeVine, 1982; Shweder, 1991). The embedded conception of self is much closer to the connected self described by Gilligan and others in their work on female development (for example, Gilligan, 1982, 1988). Developmental psychology has been moving toward a broader model, one that includes, for instance, the development of social systems (Bronfenbrenner, 1979; Kilner, 1986; Lerner and Spanier, 1978), an interactional perspective (Maccoby and Martin, 1983), and attention to development in family systems (Minuchin, 1984). These expansions of the conventional models of development introduce notions of bi- and multidirectionality as well as reciprocity and mutuality to the process of development (Kilner, 1986).

In Fiji, self is defined by one's place in the network constituting the community; it is experienced contextually. Creativity emerges in connection with others. For example, the beauty of the sacred dance songs (*meke*) performed by the community resides in the delicate interrelationships among the performers and between performers and audience.

The Western assumption that the individual is often inherently in conflict with her or his community, with the needs of one often pitted against the other (Meza, 1988; Triandis, 1989), does not dominate Fijian thought and behavior. When Fijians visit another village, they are received as representatives of their own village. After expressing this representative function, they can emphasize their idiosyncratic personal characteristics. Personal meaning-making is encouraged, but as a resource to be shared with the community, not as a means to accumulate personal prestige or distinguish oneself from the community. A movement toward separation as well as connectedness certainly exists, generating a tension between individual and community aims, but Fijian values of self and community assume an extensive interrelationship that alleviates some of the tension.

While connecting the healer to healing resources beyond the self, transformation commits the healer to serve the community. The concept of transformation involves the individual and the society simultaneously. As the individual is transformed, so is the society, and vice versa.

The understanding of the healer as a "moral explorer" clarifies the links between individual and sociocultural development. Healers are faced with the task of defining reality, and thus imparting meaning, in their interactions with cultural mysteries. In doing so, they make judgments about morality. None of these activities is predetermined. Though the straight path existed for many before them, all healers must find and travel the path for themselves. The community sends healers on a journey to new territories of experience to answer new questions of reality, meaning, and morality.

This merging of individual and social development again offers a sharp contrast to the more individualistic emphasis in Piaget's model. Piaget views development as an innate and unchangeable process. His theory describes inner processes that occur naturally as the individual interacts with the environment. One can argue that education based on Piaget's principles can speed up the cognitive development of individuals who may, in turn, positively affect the community, but the individual may develop while the community does not. In contrast, in the transformational model development is a shared enterprise, a joining of self and community with unexpected benefits to both. The community offers support as the individual faces difficulties during transitions, and the benefits the individual gains in those transitions are distributed to the community.

The applicability of the transformational model of development in Western cultures may be limited due to the enormous differences between Western and Fijian cultures and their respective economic situations. The model is most relevant in the West to those concerned with healing and spirituality.

But there is much evidence of the destructive effects in the West of splitting the spiritual dimension off from general developmental concerns (Jung, 1952; Wilber, Engler, and Brown, 1989). Perhaps we should expand our definition of healers to include all those involved in the human quest for meaning, balance, connectedness, and wholeness. Thus we could define as "healers" various roles in the human service professions, including teaching (Katz and St. Denis, 1991). This seems a worthy goal in light of existing evidence of the negative effects of limiting the healing function to medical and medically dominated professions (Albee, Joffe, and

Dusenbury, 1988; deVries, Berg, and Lipkin, 1982; Ehrenreich and English, 1979; Light, 1980). The straight path may indeed suggest developmental tasks and patterns of general relevance in a variety of professions.

▲ SYNERGISTIC COMMUNITY AND SOCIAL CHANGE

In a "synergistic community," valued resources are renewable, expanding, and accessible (R. Katz, 1983/84). Shared equitably with all members of the community, the whole of these resources becomes greater than the sum of the parts and what is good for one member becomes good for all.

The term synergistic community has been used to describe various phenomena (Katz and Seth, 1993), such as community discourse among women in Gujarat state, India (Seth, 1987), the spirit of collaboration in a grass-roots labor organization in the Dominican Republic (Reichmann, 1985), the learning exchange between a Puerto Rican teacher and her class of Puerto Rican children (Gonzalez-Ortega, 1991), and the functioning of a consensus-based action group (Kreisberg, 1992).

There is evidence in our story of contemporary Fijian healing in urban areas, which seemingly contradicts the concept of synergistic community. Some healers compete with each other and at times limit people's access to the valued resource of *mana*. But those specially charged with following the straight path, whether chiefs or healers, ideally focus their efforts not on competition but on giving access to *mana* to all who need it, thereby enhancing the entire community. Ratu Noa's talks build on and elaborate this traditional way of social organization.

Synergy and scarcity represent two ends of a continuum which in actual situations exist in combination (R. Katz, 1983/84). What might be called a scarcity paradigm dominates Western thinking about the existence and distribution of a wide variety of resources. Also known as the zero-sum game, this paradigm assumes that valued resources are limited, and the degree of scarcity determines value. It further assumes that individuals or communities must compete with each other to gain access to

343

these resources, struggling to accumulate their own supply and resisting pressures to share.

The relation of actual scarcity of particular resources to cooperation or competition may differ according to the resource in question as well as the social structure governing access to and control of the resource. Water is a scarce and valued resource for the Zhu/twa people of the Kalahari Desert, while building materials are a plentiful and valued resource. Both resources are shared among the !Kung (Lee, 1979).

An alternative paradigm is based on synergy. The word "synergy" describes a pattern of relationships, including how people relate to each other and other phenomena (Fuller, 1963; Maslow, 1971; Maslow and Honigmann, 1970). In a synergistic pattern a new and greater whole is created from disparate, seemingly conflicting parts. In the pattern, phenomena exist in harmony with each other, maximizing each other's potential. Within a synergistic paradigm, a resource like healing can become renewable and accessible yet still remain valuable (R. Katz, 1983/84). Individuals and communities activate resources. They function as guardians, not possessors, of resources, and allow resources to be shared by all members of the community. Greater amounts of the resource become available when collaboration rather than competition is encouraged. Paradoxically, the more the resource is used, the more there is available.

It can be argued that resources created at least in part by human activity and intention, such as healing, are intrinsically expanding and renewable. Yet the scarcity paradigm can dominate the generation and distribution of these human resources. In most Western biomedical and psychotherapeutic systems, healing is seen as existing in scarce supply. Value, expressed in varying fee schedules, becomes entrained to scarcity. People are forced to compete with each other for their share of healing. Scarcity seems more a function of ideology than of necessity.

Although most communities in industrialized societies function primarily within the scarcity paradigm, they nevertheless require moments of synergy in order to remain intact. Synergistic community refers both to the phase of synergy which is intrinsic to community and to particular communities in which there is relatively more synergy.

344

Synergy and transformation function together. For example, *mana* is a most highly valued resource for the Fijians. It is meant for the people, to be shared freely by healers with those in need. Transformation activates that resource to the community in the form of healing, making it accessible to all. In turn, when *mana* is released in the process of healing, it stimulates developmental processes so that further access to *mana* is facilitated. The community shares in the healer's movement back and forth through transitions. As one healer gains access to *mana*, it becomes more likely that another will; it is not a zero-sum game, but a situation of renewable and expanding resources. In synergistic fashion, effects are produced which are far beyond what is possible from separate actions.

The striking contrast of this transformational model with Western ones deserves further comment. An important source for concepts of community in contemporary Western culture, as well as for strategies of introducing community change, is the discipline of community psychology (Joffe, and Dusenbury, 1988; Heller, 1989; Heller et al., 1984; J. Rappaport, 1987). As an outgrowth of social science, community psychology operates primarily within a scarcity paradigm, assuming an inherent conflict between the individual and the community because resources are insufficient to satisfy both; often one is satisfied at the expense of the other. The difficulty found by community psychology in bringing about individual and community change may be due in part to its commitment to the scarcity paradigm.

The necessity of sharing, as well as of other features of the transformational model, for the survival of the human community is increasingly evident (Argyle, 1991; Jung, 1952; R. Katz, 1982a; Kohn, 1986, Lee, 1979; Maslow, 1971; Sarason, 1977; Schmookler, 1984). The linear, competitive model of functioning, which parallels the ideology of Western free enterprise, at times threatens the survival of the human community more than it promotes it (Berger, Berger, and Kellner, 1973; Eagleton, 1985; McLean, 1986).

Establishing a synergistic community in Western society would require a paradigm shift, a major shift in the way people experience meaning and interpret data. Accepting a sense of vulnerability would create the possibility for such a shift (Katz, Argyris, and Lapore, 1986). Experiencing the self-in-community as desirable along with the sense of the separate and separating self, might be one result. If lasting change is to occur, our sociopolitical structures must initiate new ways of making sense of experience. Roy Rappaport (1978) suggests that rituals in which we experience a transpersonal bonding are essential for the survival of humanity. Only through participating in such rituals can we overcome our separateness as individuals and become able to accomplish the tasks essential to communal survival. In industralized societies, individualism fragments communal efforts. The transformational model offers an alternative to this fragmentation, stressing a transpersonal bonding within in a supportive sociocultural context.

Change initiated by and rationalized according to political and economic principles alone has not yielded desirable results (Goulet, 1985; Schmookler, 1984; Trainer, 1989). The straight path offers the additional ingredient of a set of spiritual principles which help to articulate concrete human needs and to allow envisioning of proper human aims. With that guidance, economic and political goals can be put in perspective. The call for spiritual guidance of human development has been particularly eloquent among Indigenous peoples, who strive for the continuing life of their own traditions in today's world (Berger, 1985; Craig, 1988; Hampton, 1984; Katz, Biesele, and St. Denis, in press; Lame Deer and Erdoes, 1972; Little Bear, Boldt, and Long, 1984; Moody, 1988).

The introduction of the spiritual dimension into the processs of social change involves a "renewed tradition" or change guided by sacred traditions applied to contemporary issues and problems (Katz and St. Denis, 1991). This is not a new concept. There is a long history of changes initiated by religious, if not spiritual, principles. What the straight path suggests, however, is a kind of spiritual guidance, that, in demanding truth of its practitioners, also demands they love others, thus eliminating intolerance of others, which often escalates to violence in the name of religious purity.

The straight path is a dynamic healing system that can bring about effective social change, building on the foundation of traditional knowledge and practice in a creative rather than reactionary manner.

346

Going Out: Responsibility and Exchange

In the beginning of this book, I traveled from the present back to 1985, when I made my return visit to Fiji. In this section I travel back again from 1985 up to now. Though the narrative of events in Tovu may suggest a linear chronology, the beginning and end of the story flow toward each other. As the straight path is not traveling along a *straight* path, but *traveling straight* on a winding path, so time also circles back on itself.

Since 1985, the exchange initiated through this book has become clearer and the accompanying responsibilities more challenging as they go beyond what has become obvious. It is now finally recognized as intolerable for a visiting anthropologist to mine the riches of foreign cultures. It is unforgivable to bring back stories that have not been properly given to one, to describe a people's way of life while ignoring their wishes about what to include or exclude — even in the interest of "science" or "truth." These unidirectional actions, often taken to build one's own academic career, leave nothing but unfulfilled expectations and broken promises in the place where the stories began. The sense of loss and betrayal in the community is lasting.

"Academic imperialism," which purloins traditional knowledge and stories and disguises them in elegant wraps of theory, must constantly be challenged. The lack of exchange with the peoples whose stories have fed this theorizing has been exposed. Equally absurd is any notion that someone foreign to a place can *simply* "speak for" that place, no matter how empathic the intention to "give voice to the people."

Though the book is now finished, I still struggle with these traps of irresponsibility, knowing I am not immune to their lure. To understand the necessary exchange and deepening responsibility, I keep returning to Ratu Noa's words.

Ratu Noa's precondition for my writing this book was first to learn enough about the straight path to write about it, truthfully and honestly, to the best of my ability. To solidify and expand that learning, he gave me the task of practicing what I've been taught. Knowing what to say entails knowing what to do. In the years since 1985, my practice has developed — slowly, silently — as I risk activating what has been given to me. But that practice is not, on the surface, recognizably Fijian. Though I am dissatisfied with the devaluation of the spiritual dimension and community context in conventional Western therapies, I know that Fijian healing, or for that matter any other non-Western approach, cannot be literally applied in North America. Healing traditions are not "import goods" that can be easily transplanted in another setting.

Instead, the idea of the hearty country soup which cooks over time in a simmering pot is the model for my practice. Into the pot go many ingredients — my life experiences — and through the simmering process, no one ingredient predominates. Instead the soup becomes its own special blend, further enhanced with subsequent cooking. The ingredients are not destroyed but become essential parts of the whole. I have had a number of experiences with traditional healing systems in different parts of the world. They are part of the soup. But the source of my present work remains in Fiji, where Ratu Noa energizes it.

Critical to understanding the Fijian way is the commitment to learn from the people who speak through the book. Though this commitment could be a mere refinement of the earlier crude mining operations of anthropologists, hiding exploitation at a more insidious level, it can also be of mutual benefit. We indeed learn from Fijians about healing, about ways of being and thereby improve our own understanding and practice. But that is only the beginning. Such lessons are only the first step in creating a better awareness of how, to the extent of our learning, we can directly and concretely support our teachers, the people who gave us these lessons. Like healing, learning is an exchange.

This exchange could be a model for a broader exchange between industrial nation-states and Indigenous peoples throughout the world. It must be a true exchange, without the veneer that covers the continuing exploitation of these peoples. Because from them we learn that the offer of foreign aid can mask a move to control local resources, including raw material and cheap labor; the support of "democratization" or "modernization" can be a form of cultural imperialism, aimed at opening new markets of consumers; "development" can mean seizing "unused" land for generating profits, disrupting sustainable small-scale or labor-intensive uses of land; and even the call for "self-determination" can conceal another agenda, forming a loyal elite among these Indigenous people who partake — to a limited extent — in the profits.

But understanding the necessary exchange at the global level does not make the question of how and what to give in a true exchange any less difficult. It remains a personal question and demands a personal response. Guided by the thoughts of Fijians, I believe the exchange back to them must be specific and direct, supporting their land and culture, the soil that nurtures their teachings. But I cannot offer particular suggestions on what or how to give. It is up to Fijians to tell us — and up to us to listen first, then act. The healing can then begin.

"This healing work is hard," says Ratu Noa. "It goes slowly…step by step. But the straight path is there to guide us along the way."

APPENDIX A

Respect and Vulnerability in Research

Patience, a willingness to travel into unknown spaces, and above all respect were essential to my research. I remember the hours at the beginning of my fieldwork I spent sitting in the evenings, night after night, visiting with people, struggling to keep listening to conversations in a language I could not understand. Only through patient listening did sense gradually emerge. I remember attending healing ceremonies at the beginning of my fieldwork, unprepared and inexperienced in the way healers interact with the *Vu*, yet wanting to yield to the unexpected and be in the presence of the unknown. Only through a willingness to explore what I did not know did acceptance gradually develop.

Respect makes such research possible. Deep respect for the people, the ceremonies, and the land instilled in me the necessary patience and allowed me to take risks.

A VERSION OF THE STORY

"Tell our story" — I made Ratu Noa's simple yet difficult request unnecessarily more difficult through my preoccupation with the form of the telling. Did Ratu Noa, along with the others who made that request, understand the vagaries of Western commercial publishing? I wondered. Fortunately they broke through these preoccupations with their constant emphasis on the story and its truthfulness. It was up to me to select a way of telling which honored that story rather than diluting or misconstructing it.

Ratu Noa and others further released me from potentially dominating conventions of social science by not requesting me to tell *the* story, but only that part of it I understood. They also emphasized that any story has many parts and many sides, depending on the teller and the listener. Though originally trained in the positivistic social science of the 1950s, where the task of research was to analyze, categorize, and organize field data so that the researcher could interpret "*the* meaning" of the experiences or events studied, I could not practice it. That method of research strove to manipulate or, as some put it, "massage" the data into an ordered reality. Ratu Noa's teachings affirmed the direction my research had actually taken over the past thirty years, as my own understanding of how to understand supported an alternative to researcher-derived or theory-driven interpretations.

There have been numerous discussions of methodological alternatives to the position of positivistic social science (Bredo and Feinberg, 1982; Clifford and Marcus, 1986; Hollway, 1989; R. Katz, 1987; Katz and Nuñez-Molina, 1986; Patton, 1990; Reason and Rowan, 1981; Reinharz, 1982; St. Denis, 1989). Many have skillfully offered a detailed discussion of basic questions in the philosophy of science, including the conception and perception of meaning and reality. My intention in this appendix is just to describe my method briefly.

Working in a culture other than my own, I obviously needed a research method adapted to culturally diverse communities and cultural diversity within communities. The still dominant method of field research based on logical positivism is the expression of one particular worldview. It is a way of knowing, a way of generating and distributing knowledge carried out in certain locales at a particular point in history. It is labeled as a "method of science" or simply "science."

A monocultural approach to research presumes that phenomena that may be distinctly different are in fact similar to phenomena already studied. The positivist approach often reduces distinctly different phenomena to its own grid of understanding to make them more familiar. (For an empirical critique of this reductionism see, for example, Menary, 1987; Nuñez-Molina, 1986; Seth, 1987.)

Community-based participatory research is but one example of an alternative approach that is sensitive to cultural diversity (St. Denis, 1989). There are in fact a variety of research methods that are both culturally sensitive and scientific, empirical, and objective — three adjectives that have heretofore been appropriated by the logical positivists to describe their method alone.

If research is to be sensitive to cultural diversity, it must respect each community's own culture, going beyond variations in demography and behavior to an appreciation of variations in experiences of reality. Genuine research strives toward understanding and perhaps dares to help elucidate the reality experienced by other peoples.

WHEN SEARCH AND RESEARCH ARE ONE

Because of my previous fieldwork, I reached Fiji with certain attitudes about people, events, and experiences, and about how these data are and become the meaning of reality. I did not, however, have a fixed set of research and data-gathering techniques or interaction patterns guiding my ongoing work. Method for me is not a focus, but an evolving process for understanding. Nevertheless, any method affects the eventual nature of that understanding. For this reason I will try here to describe how I worked.

Ratu Noa used a single word, *cakacaka,* "work," to refer to three apparently distinct phenomena: the healing work in Fiji, my particular research project, and my search to learn about healing, which became an effort to become a healer. He used the word *cakacaka* to refer to healing because it is a respectful way of naming something too powerful and sacred to name directly. Sometimes Ratu Noa would simply refer to the healing as "it" or "that," since only those who knew what he meant would understand the reference. At the start, Ratu Noa referred to my research as *vakadidiki,* translated literally as "research." But increasingly as our relationship evolved, he insisted that my research and my search had become one, and properly so — and that one thing was the "work," *cakacaka*. It is not that he was confusing the two, for he did see how each also had its own contribution to make. In his view, to attain any semblance of truth, the research could not exist independently of the search.

When research and search are joined, research becomes another form of the search for truth. My research method then was at one with my personal search, which became fused with the Fijian healing approach. From Ratu Noa's perspective, the research search, like the healing it sought to understand, was a sacred activity, bound by rules of truth and honesty. My research and search became another manifestation of the struggle to find and follow the straight path.

"Re-searching" is a way of describing this three-part process, emphasizing as it does a "going back" and "finding within" to establish truth in the world. A first principle I kept trying to remember was my focus on Fijian healing, specifically on the teachings of Ratu Noa and the events in Tovu, and how they explicated each other. Sometimes researchers using one of the "newer" reflexive methods fill us with details about themselves, as if that were the focus of the research. We may hear about the researchers' reflections on their reflections on the adequacy of their research. Where are the people the researchers spent time with?

While risking the descent into solipsism which a careless use of reflexivity entails, the inclusion of the researcher in the story is necessary. Yet I know that I did not totally avoid that risk — even when using great care. Ratu Noa's and Tevita's teachings are the focus, but those teachings are best understood in context; thus I show myself being taught by Ratu Noa and Tevita, and Tevita being taught by Ratu Noa. The teachings are not abstract monologues about the structure and principles of healing. For Ratu Noa, that type of monologue would in fact be impossible. "I can only talk about what I feel you want to and should know," he often said. "Unless you ask questions, I'll have to stop. So, Rusiate, fire away."

My method of re-searching also emphasized three other commitments: to engage in respectful inquiry, to recognize and value experiences of vulnerability, and to activate an exchange, giving something meaningful back to those with whom I worked.

RESPECTFUL INQUIRY

"Respect is our most basic principle," Ratu Noa said. "We respect each other, always, because we are all creatures of *Kalou* (God), just as we respect our traditions and our land, for they too come from *Kalou*." It was respect in the Fijian sense — what might be called "radical respect" from a Western perspective — that came to guide my research.

Only to the degree that a researcher respects the people or community with whom he or she is doing research can the researcher truly begin to understand the experienced reality, the actual life of that person or community. Research becomes respectful inquiry — "research with" or "within," rather than "research on." Persons and communities become partners in the research process, not objects of study. Seeing the value and significance of an event or experience from within the world of the participants helps avoid reductionism, ridicule, and other defenses of arrogance as well as the denial of confusion. Respectful inquiry demands we suspend our own judgments, which often serve primarily to reduce confusion, and let the experiences speak to us.

Respectful inquiry functions like traditional discourse, expressing the way elders in many traditional cultures communicate (Apassingok, Walunga, and Tennard, 1985; Knight, 1990; MumShirl, 1981; Vatu, 1977). Each person is given the opportunity to speak his or her mind and heart. Time and space are made available for all. Therefore all can fully listen to what others are saying, not having to worry about whether they must interrupt to be sure their own viewpoints are heard. Also, the emphasis is on patient and careful listening to what is said because that is all the speaker is willing or prepared to share. To say any more would violate the truth and the speaker's own standards of responsible behavior. Elders wish to share their knowledge, but only when they meet someone who really wants to know and is able to listen. The hallmark of conventional social science research — a series of questions formulated by the researcher to gather, even pry out, information — becomes inappropriate. The rationale that the researcher sometimes must uncover things the other doesn't know is insufficient.

This is not to say that questions are inappropriate. Ratu Noa insists that they are the life-blood of teaching. When researchers ask something they really need to know and are sensitive when the other does not wish to respond, that inquiry can be respectful. It is the persistent research-driven questioning, which is so characteristic of the positivist paradigm that is inherently disrespectful, striving explicitly to confirm or refute the researcher's own preconceptions or hypotheses rather than to find out what the other is actually saying.

In presenting material I try to make a distinction between "truth" and "secrets." Ratu Noa spoke about issues of truth and secrecy:

> I have the power but conceal it. If it hadn't been for your research and the purpose of keeping the knowledge for future generations, all that I'm telling you about myself, my work and healing, would not be revealed to you. When future genera-tions hear what I'm telling you now, I don't want them to blame me for telling lies. Instead, they will be proud to hear my words, because they are words of truth.

Truth demands that one report what actually happened, not covering over mistakes in data collection or exaggerating one's own importance — magnifying one's role in the story, elaborating on what one actually knows, or pushing the elegance of a theoretical interpretation at the expense of the data.

In deciding what material to report, what "truth" one tells, further dis-tinctions between truth and secrets are required. Healing systems contain many secrets, that are appropriately kept within the oral tradition of the culture. Sometimes these are culture-specific techniques necessary for an effective healing performance — the specifics of preparing herbs, for example, or calling the *Vu*. Sometimes these secrets are keys to the use, and abuse, of spiritual power. Truths deal with essential principles in the healing work which, though common knowledge, are difficult to practice. Since they are common knowledge, they are not sacrificed when reported in a research study. The "straight path" describes such principles.

I believe the aim of research is to report such truths, not to reveal secrets. Unfortunately, field work often reveals, sometimes unknowingly, too many secrets, and does not tell enough of the truth. The hunger for secrets encourages this tendency. I remember the first time I lectured on Fijian healing in the United States. Someone from the audience came up afterward and asked, "Where can I find a workshop that teaches how to *do* this Fijian healing?" That the person wanted to add Fijian techniques to his clinical practice was implicit in his question. Such an acquisitive approach to secrets can discourage serious reporting of field work on healing, as well as cooperation from those who have the knowledge.

▲ VULNERABILITY

Any method of research into the experienced realities of another culture must first emphasize Indigenous descriptions, eschewing a comparative framework until the phenomena being studied are clearly understood. This means that researchers must give up their worldviews and allow others to express their own, whether directly or through the help of the researchers (R. Katz, 1987). Researchers must become vulnerable, letting go of their accustomed sense of self to let that of others be known.

By *vulnerability* I mean a radical questioning of one's worldview. One must give up the comfortable protection of assumptions as to what is "valid," "correct," "obvious," and "common practice." Only then does understanding the world from within another culture become possible. Vulnerability resides in all aspects of the process of existing, even for a moment, between or without worldviews; experiencing the multiplicity of valid worldviews is deeply unsettling. However, being inside another culture, exposed to its risks, touched by its joys, one can tell a richer and more accurate story. Because it is a story from within the culture as well as from without, it can be the telling of "our story to your people."

The experience of vulnerability is a source of fear, even at times terror. John Welwood (1983) writes about the vulnerability that accompanies "moments of world collapse." These moments occur "when the meanings on which we've been building our lives unexpectedly collapse.

When an old structure falls away and we don't have a new one to replace it, we usually feel a certain inner rawness. That kind of tenderness and nakedness is one of the most essential qualities of our humanness, one which we are usually masking" (pp. 148–49).

Jules Henry (1972) discusses vulnerability, what he calls the "susceptibility to destruction and defeat," as a characteristic of our human nature. He suggests that for society to function it must educate its members to understand and accept their own vulnerability.

Painful as it is, the experience of vulnerability can open the door to special knowledge, in part through opening the door to self-knowledge. Instead of being dismissed as subjective, self-knowledge can become an important source of valid data, helping to erase the distinction between subjective and objective validity. K"au Dwa, a powerful Zhu/twa healer who was blind said, "When the healing begins you can really see, you see the insides of people and all that troubles them. At other times, you can look but you do not see" (R. Katz, 1968, field notes). Like so many other healers in all parts of the world, K"au Dwa, distinguished between forms of seeing, emphasizing the importance of seeing from the inside.

Field work demands vulnerability if it is to allow one to enter into another culture (Dwyer, 1982; R. Katz, 1982a; Katz, Argyris, and Lapore, 1986; Luhrmann, 1989; Rabinow, 1977; Stoller and Olkes, 1987). Vulnerability, though often ignored or denied, is both a methodological asset and an experiential component of participant observation.

During my work in Fiji, I experienced the contribution of vulnerability to field research many times. Early in the field work, I interviewed a healer known to become possessed in her healing work. I went to the healer's place of healing with my friend Inoke, who served as my research associate and translator.

"Could we talk with you about your healing?" we asked.

She responded in a matter-of-fact tone, "It all depends on what the *Vu* (ancestral god), who is the source of my power, says."

A reasonable response, we thought. Then immediately the signs of her possession began, with the twitching, the sweating, the grimacing, and the exaggerated angularity of her movements. Soon she began chain-smoking, and her face assumed a terrible expression, overpowering in its anguish.

The healer now spoke in a new voice, low and grunting, her rasping breath drawing out the noises she made from within, which were sounds more than words at first. Then in a dialect different from the Fijian we were using, different almost to the point of intelligibility, the healer — the *Vu*? — addressed us: "What is it you want to learn from me?"

Rapt within our fear, we stopped thinking. We could not answer.

The *Vu* spoke again, now more urgently: "I am waiting here for your answer!"

I looked at Inoke; he was already looking at me. I saw in him what I myself felt: I did not know what to say because I did not know where I was.

I whispered to him, "What do we do now? Who are we talking to? The *Vu*? The healer? The *Vu* through the healer? Is this real?"

"I don't know! I'm lost too!" he replied in a strained whisper. "I've seen many healers at work, but this has never happened before."

Then he added, "You're on your own here. Just do what you think you should."

As my sense of place and time returned, my sense of what to do became clearer. I realized I was possibly in the presence of a *Vu* and felt the deep respect and privilege such a visit traditionally meant for Fijians. I would attempt to talk to the *Vu* because that was possibly who was talking to me. A conversation began, my fear transmuting into respect. The *Vu* spoke of many things. Eventually the *Vu* said he must go and formally took leave of us. The healer returned to her ordinary state, going through the same changes in tone and body expression, now in the reverse order. With a sudden last wrench of her entire frame, she slumped over, exhausted.

After a minute or two, posture again upright, the healer resumed talking with us again. We continued to discuss her healing work but not the prior conversation with her *Vu*. With unquestionable finality, she said, "I don't remember what went on then because the *Vu* took over, so there is nothing I can say, nor will I add anything to what he said. You heard it all."

Walking away from the healer's house, Inoke and I almost simultaneously asked each other the same question: "What happened? What *really* happened?" We agreed we did not know. Would a *Vu* have conversed with us? Were we deserving of such a visit? It could have been the *Vu* we spoke with, but maybe it was just a dramatic performance by the healer meant to impress prospective clients. Or maybe the *Vu* was speaking and the healer was exaggerating her own role as the vehicle. We considered all these possibilities — and dismissed none. But we knew that whatever had happened, our attitude and behavior of respect was correct. If the *Vu* had come, that was the only way to be.

To this day, my understanding of my apparent conversation with the healer's *Vu* is no clearer. But it is clear that by suspending disbelief that particular conversation, and the understanding of Fijian healing and the *Vu* which it stimulated, became possible. It would have been more comforting to dismiss the healer's possession as only a dramatic act. But believing as a Fijian that the *Vu* was there, while at the moments when my Western mind intruded, believing it was not, kept me not only in a state of intense uncertainty but also open to unexpected learning. I was not acting as though I believed in order to get "good data," but suspending my own beliefs to allow new beliefs to enter on their own terms.

To tell a story we must experience it to the best of our ability. The radical questioning brought on by vulnerability allows us to live inside a story, even to the point of risk which can threaten our lives. We are then better able to tell that story.

Throughout this book, I try to describe the varying ways and degrees to which I felt "connected to," "inside," or "at one with" another culture. The phrases I use — for example, "as a Fijian," or "I feel Fijian" — are inadequate to convey the subtlety and complexity of those experiences of connectedness. These experiences were neither unreflectively naive nor intentionally manipulative, "trying on for size" the idea of being inside a culture in order to learn about it. Yet I remained in some deeply existential sense "myself" when inside Fijian culture. There remains an enormous difference between growing up as a member of a culture and being a part of the culture through participating in day-to-day activities and exposing oneself to moments of vulnerability.

The experience of vulnerability need not come within dramatic events or psychological upheavals. Often during those two years in Fiji, in situations unrelated to healing, I would realize both the safety my home culture's assumptions provided and the fact that these assumptions were not operative and therefore unavailable. For example, during a village ceremony in which gifts were to be given by each family, we could not excuse ourselves from the delicate deliberations Fijian families must undergo to decide which were the proper gifts. Adopting a Western approach to gift giving, with the attendant excuse that we didn't know any better since we were Westerners, was not acceptable. The feeling of vulnerability came as we realized we were Fijian in that situation, exposed to all the complexities and risks of offense inherent in the local situation. We began to understand the Fijian exchange of gifts — both the difficulties in deciding about what gifts to give to whom, as well as the rewards of giving — simply by exchanging gifts as members of that culture.

These ordinary experiences of vulnerability are harder to describe; they are more subtle, without clear boundaries. But since they occurred more frequently and more within the ongoing context of daily life, they had more enduring and significant effects on us.

In research on traditional healing systems, the contribution of vulnerability is particularly evident. As repositories of central cultural mysteries, traditional healing systems do not yield inner meanings easily to outside questioners. An oppressive and demanding research program or a too-willing and usually marginal informant will yield only distortions. It has been my experience that only when I am truly interested in living inside a healing system will its inner meaning be revealed — whether I am a nonjudgmental observer, a client in actual need, a student, an assisting practitioner, or most likely some combination of these.

The experience of vulnerability also allows one to appreciate transitions and transformation, which I believe are fundamental to the process of healing. I define healing as a series of transitions toward meaning, balance, connectedness, and wholeness, both within individuals and between individuals and their environments (R. Katz, 1982a).

Vulnerability itself is characterized by transitions and transformation. It exists largely "betwixt and between," with the fear that comes from moving between states. The experience of vulnerability, when accepted, can become a healing experience. As my fieldwork on healing unfolded, the transformation of healing evoked personal transformation and the vulnerability inherent in the healing process supported my own acceptance of vulnerability.

Traveling the straight path requires that one constantly meet and accept one's vulnerability. That challenge has informed and sensitized other aspects of my research. Ratu Noa guided me in this direction. In the many talks we had, he suggested priorities: "You must begin to participate in the healing — to practice. Only then will your understanding deepen."

Ratu Noa's advice made eminent sense. I sought more direct participation, though again with inevitable naïveté. Only after several months did I realize that learning about the straight path had more to do with daily living than with healing rituals. Getting to know Ratu Noa and his student Tevita, seeing how they struggled to follow the straight path in the ordinary events of daily life, and through our friendship, beginning to walk with them on the straight path — these things put the actual healing sessions in perspective. Healing sessions in Tovu village were infrequent, my talks with Tevita about healing even more infrequent. But Tevita was continually teaching; his living exemplified how one must meet the challenges of the straight path. With this necessary focus on ordinary life issues, participation became more subtle and demanding than simply attending healing ceremonies, and therefore more likely to involve experiences of vulnerability.

Early in the field work, the two sudden and unexpected deaths connected to Tovu created a level of tension and confusion that was intense and palpable. During the following months a number of dreams came to people which portended a third death in Tovu. Like others, I was frightened and went to Tevita for some understanding of events, some help with my fears. I feared for my family and myself, for our very lives. "What can we do?" I asked him. Tevita replied, "You don't have to worry, Rusi, because you are a Westerner." "But I don't feel like a Westerner. I feel Fijian." "Yes, I know what you're saying is true. And so, Rusi, you'll just have to do what all of us Fijians must do: stay close to the *yaqona*, and be straight in behavior. That will protect you and your family." From that point on, I was "inside" in a new way, and the fieldwork changed radically.

If we grant the contribution of vulnerability to fieldwork, why does it remain a suspect and rarely used tool? For one thing, it is assumed that accepting, let alone encouraging, vulnerability destroys the objectivity, the "real" validity, of the data. Nothing less than the debate between objectivity and subjectivity is at issue here. But, as Polanyi (1958) has argued, all knowledge, including that of science, is a fusion of subjectivity and objectivity. He establishes an alternative ideal of knowledge: "[There is] personal participation of the knower in all acts of understanding but this does not make our understanding subjective.... Such knowing is indeed objective in the sense of establishing contact with a hidden reality...." (pp. vii–viii). Disciplined subjectivity can be a source of valid data (Hollway, 1989; Reinharz, 1982).

Experiences of vulnerability also correct the erroneous dichotomy between Western science and traditional spiritual disciplines. One can see systematic empiricism in traditional healing systems (Tambiah, 1973), just as one can recognize illogical, wishful thinking in contemporary Western medicine (Shweder, 1977). There are "scientists" and "magicians" in both Western and traditional systems. By now it is obvious that traditional healing systems are not "primitive," but neither are they pre- or pseudoscientific.

The interview process provides one example of how, through accepting one's vulnerability as a researcher, "mistakes" in method can lead to understanding. Reports of fieldwork rarely include accounts of mistakes. In my own work, I purposely present interviews with mistakes included — the naive and ethnocentric questions, the times I push too hard for certain answers. These mistakes belong in the field report because they are an aspect of interviewing, intrinsic to the trial and error that characterizes in-depth interviews (Mishler, 1986). These mistakes can provide opportunities to improve the interview. For instance, when I realize I've lost contact with the person I'm speaking with, I regain the possibility of connecting with the person in perhaps a more meaningful way and again interviewing with sensitivity.

Vulnerability is seen by some as a source of bias. Moments of confusion reported in an interview, for example, can be misunderstood as a sign that material is being missed or distorted. But if the characteristics of the researcher as the vehicle for the story are described carefully and modestly — his or her preferences, presuppositions, and intentions — their influence on the story-telling process becomes clearer, and the story itself can become more accurate. My responsibility in this book is not to call attention to myself but to describe myself so that the Fijian material is better explicated. Ratu Noa and Tevita insisted that the focus remain on the healing work. "One never calls attention to oneself, one never promotes oneself as a healer," they constantly warned.

Some social scientists strive to avoid vulnerability because of the presumed limits of emotional and cognitive flexibility. Carl Jung (1969) pinpointed an important reason vulnerability is not cultivated in Western field research: the ultimate interpretive and controlling powers of the Western self. Writing about the Tibetan Buddhist concept of "one mind" or "at-one-ment," he says, "But we [Westerners] are never able to imagine how such a realization ('at-one-ment') could ever be complete in any human individual. There must always be somebody or something left over to experience the realization, to say 'I know "at-one-ment," I know there is a distinction'" (pp. 504–505).

Whereas Jung held that one could go up to the edge of ego loss, he cautioned about going over the edge, which could result in unconsciousness, madness, or death. But this caution may not be appropriate when it prevents one from going over the edge into another reality that is not madness but something "other," from which it is still possible to return to one's "home" reality. Jung surely acknowledged such experiences. Typically, their own culture is so fully and finely imprinted in researchers that they can find the way back home even after going over the edge, and can indeed travel back and forth — if they accept their vulnerability.

If the risk of losing oneself can be faced, one can live within another culture, respecting the validity of that culture's reality. Unfamiliar patterns of thinking, forms of belief, or rituals of action become settings for learning rather than barriers, signals for fearful retreat or occasions for pejorative labeling. Rather than inhibiting the researcher or creating bias in method, the experience of vulnerability can thus lead to deeper understanding,

△ WHERE IS THE EXCHANGE?
THE POLITICS OF RESEARCH

The history of field research — characteristically done by Western social scientists on Indigenous peoples with less power — is not a proud one. Instances of exploitation are rampant (G. Campbell, 1987; Huizer, 1978; La Framboise and Plake, 1983). The appropriation of a people's sacred texts, rituals, and knowledge as part of an outsider's academic study or research project is but one example (Churchill, 1988). This exploitation reflects a more general situation of manipulation and oppression experienced by most Indigenous peoples as their land and resources are increasingly undercut, producing debilitating stress on their culture (Adams, 1989; Benjamin, 1987; Burgos-Debray, 1984; M. Campbell, 1973; Churchill, 1989; Fanon, 1963; Gray, 1989; Memmi, 1965; Ngugi, 1986).

Even when field research claims to give "voice" to a people, that seemingly well-intentioned motivation usually falls short, failing to give voice to what that group sees as important in its life. Another seemingly well-intentioned motivation is to present the "true" picture of a people, in spite of the fact they do not want some of these truths to be reported. This motivation, ostensibly in the service of "scientific truth," is more subtly fallacious, assuming there is just one true picture rather than realizing truth comes from a multiplicity of sources and perspectives. Furthermore, it discounts the inherent validity of a people's own contribution to their cultural identity, and ignores the fundamental truths that emerge from telling one's own story. In fact, the history of field research is all the more exploitative in that its proffered rationale often has such apparently "good" intentions, concealing the continued exertion of power over the people being "researched."

The Brazilian educator and activist Paulo Freire, who developed methods for teaching literacy as a means of sociopolitical liberation (Freire, 1968, 1985), was once asked to comment on the political aspects of education. His reply was uncomplicated: "All education is political." I believe, likewise, that all research is political. The topics we decide to research, and not to research; the methods we use to collect data; to whom and how we present our findings — all these are political decisions, with political consequences. The conduct of research has very much to do with issues of power and control. Who has control over the topic chosen, the method used, the format selected? The researcher? The persons being researched? The community of the researcher? Of those being researched? Some combination of the above?

The people who share their lives to make research possible must exercise that power and control in these areas. It is up to them to make known their wishes in regard to the uses and goals of that research. As a precondition to hearing their agenda, we must insist that the one-way, "coercive" process of research change into a two-way process that is entered into freely. We can then commit ourselves to devoting as much energy to giving as historically has been devoted to taking — and more.

APPENDIX B

Research Structure

I did fieldwork in Fiji from January 1977 through November 1978, and for the month of June 1985. Approximately fourteen of these twenty-four months were spent in the village of Tovu; much of the rest of the time was spent in the city of Suva.

Though it is now 1993, I describe the story of those years in Fiji in the present tense, what in anthropology is called the "ethnographic present." The present tense reflects my continuing connection to the experiences in the story. As I listen to the tapes of interviews with healers, read my field notes, and look at slides, I reconnect to my work in Fiji. It is from that connection that I always try to write.

My research during 1977 and 1978 was part of a team project with my then wife, Mary Maxwell Katz, whose Fijian name became Mere. As with any team effort, we had endless discussions, helping to inform each other of new information and to counterbalance each other's biases and blind spots. We also supported each other in practical ways, from setting up our home, to traveling to other villages for interviews, to participating as a family in ceremonies. Her sensitive observations of socialization patterns, her ability to interpret data from both a psychological and anthropological perspective, and her deep involvement with the women of our village were invaluable contributions to my understanding. Her skills and insights were especially helpful because she was working with many of the same people I worked with, and a fuller picture emerged as a result.

A fuller picture also emerged from an unexpected source — our children. When we arrived in Fiji, Laurel, who was called Lora, was nine and Alex, or Eliki, was six. Rapidly becoming fluent in Fijian, the two quickly became an intimate part of our home village, Tovu, blending in easily with their peers. They attended school in Tovu and in their off-time traveled about with other children, fishing, gathering wood, playing. We never "enlisted" them in the research effort, but as they described their daily activities or when their friends came to visit, we learned many things about Tovu and its people. The view through a child's eyes is truly different from that through an adult's, and fascinatingly valid.

The foundation of the research team was the group of Fijians who worked with us as research collaborators, translators, and teachers. Inoke served as our primary translator and facilitated the research effort in innumerable ways; Marika and Alifereti worked with me as translators in the Suva area. Inoke's wife, Nasi, the Tovu village nurse, was also a valuable research team member. Skilled translating was only a part of their contribution. At different times, each of the three men acted as a *mata-ni-vanua* — taking the traditional role of speaking for me as they led me into interactions with people and advising me about the correct ceremonies of exchange. My contact with Fijian healing, with its carefully concealed insights, required a particularly intimate commitment to traditions. I could not allow myself the excuse of not knowing any better because I was not Fijian. Out of respect for all those I spoke with, I always insisted we follow traditional Fijian custom.

The healers I interviewed were more than sources of information. They guided the research with their willing interest in my work and sound suggestions about its direction. This continues to be the case with Tevita and above all with Ratu Noa.

Participant observation was my fundamental method, and I generated extensive and detailed field notes. By the end of the first year I could understand most of the Fijian I heard and spoke the language well enough to be understood, though I still had difficulty in abstract discussions. After a year and a half I was more fluent in both understanding and speaking, though eloquence came only when my emotions broke

369

through my language and I spoke from the heart. I never mastered the art of the more formal discourse of public ceremonies, but by the second year I was able to conduct interviews by myself.

In the context of my participant observation, I attended forty-four healing ceremonies, twenty-three of them in Tovu and Bitu, the rest in the Suva area. I also conducted 154 in-depth interviews, averaging two to four hours in length. I interviewed thirty-six different healers in a total of eighty-seven interviews; eighteen of those healers lived in Suva, eighteen in rural Bitu. Among the eighteen Suva healers, eleven were women. Their ages ranged from the late twenties to the late fifties; eight of the women and four of the men were under forty. Among the eighteen healers on rural Bitu, all but three were men. Their ages ranged from the early forties to the late seventies, with five of the men and two of the women in their seventies. I believe these demographic data fairly represent the actual picture of healing in Fiji. In Suva, for example, there are more women practicing and they are generally younger than in Bitu.

My sample was generated by the so-called "snowball" method, with colleagues, friends, and healers themselves suggesting healers to visit. With all the frequent moves, interruptions in practice, and secrecy that characterize the work of many urban healers, a random sample would have been impossible — and inappropriate. Suggestions were cross-checked with several sources, and a consensus usually emerged about who was actually or honestly practicing as well as the effectiveness of the healer's work.

Suggestions about other persons said to have traditional or contemporary knowledge were similarly cross-checked, and an even stronger consensus often emerged. Besides the interviews with healers, I spoke with seven chiefs and other Fijian elders who were also especially trained in traditional matters, for a total of twenty-six interviews. Finally, I met with twenty-three persons knowledgeable about particular areas of the research, for a total of forty-one interviews. Included in this last group were government ministers, linguists, museum curators, university researchers, and medical doctors; all but two of them were Fijian.

In addition to interviews, I collected other sets of data, including systematic and detailed observations of behavior, particularly of *yaqona* drinking in Tovu; casebooks filled out by myself and the four Tovu healers documenting clients who came for help, the problems they came for, and the help given; the Health Opinion Survey, measuring people's assessment of their own health, which everyone in Tovu completed; a modified Thematic Apperception Test (T.A.T.); a systematic collection of dreams; a linguistic and phenomenological analysis of the experience of *mana;* and a rating scale establishing characteristics of the "ideal Fijian." Matched samples of healers and nonhealers were constructed for most of the above data sets. Along with my field notes and interviews, these data sets helped establish the background and context for the research.

As the fieldwork progressed, I spent less time collecting these specialized data-sets, and more time interviewing and participating in healing ceremonies. Also, I began to work only with acknowledged and respected healers.

The interviews were more *veitalanoa,* "conversations" or "the telling of stories" than interviews guided strictly by a predetermined schedule of questions. Therefore they follow Fijian rather than Western social science conventions for the exchange of information. Interviews were held in the healers' own homes and at different times, depending on the healer's choice and availability. Often the interviews occurred at night, and invariably around *yaqona* drinking. Again, this reflects traditional Fijian practice, since significant and sacred information — like information about healing — is never exchanged without the ritual exchange of *yaqona.*

All interviews were taped and transcribed. When I worked with a translator, there was on-line translating. But the tapes of all interviews, and especially those I conducted on my own, were subsequently retranslated in order to achieve a more accurate and complete translation. The transcriptions were exhaustively detailed, including various metalinguistic elements. I tried to adhere to Ratu Noa's committed insistence on good translation.

These transcripts appear in the book as interviews with Ratu Noa, Tevita, and others, though not all transcripts are used. Certain editorial changes have been made in the transcripts, including minor revisions to make them read more like they sounded, changes in the sequence of certain topics in several interviews, the removal of unnecessary repetitions, and the omission of detailed discussions about specific Fijian rituals and beliefs, especially those meant to remain in the oral tradition, such as healing prayers.

371

Names
That Make
the Story

All those involved in the story told in this book have given their permission to tell it, personally standing behind the accuracy of their version. As Tomasi, a healer in Delana, put it, "What I tell you has to be the truth, because when my grandchildren and great-grandchildren and great-great-grandchildren hear my story, I want them to hear only the truth."

At the suggestion of those involved in the story, I have used pseudonyms when referring to Fijian places and persons. Their reason was simple: privacy. They had nothing to hide, but there is an advantage in keeping the actual identity of places and people under their own control. A commercially published book reaches many types of reader. Some may wish to see for themselves what is described in the book, and it is best that only those with a serious and sincere motivation be able to do so.

The pseudonyms used are Fijian names, though they do not necessarily occur in the specific locale of the story. In several instances, when the persons and places are very much part of public knowledge, I use the actual names, e.g. the city Suva.

The photographs in this book pose a particular problem. To identify the people pictured with their pseudonyms would not only be confusing but would also defeat the pseudonyms' protective function. Therefore, no personal names are used. This decision should not be confused with the absence of names in many earlier anthropological photographs of Indigenous people, where their identity was being ignored or denied through lack of respect rather than protected out of respect.

It may seem that using pseudonyms precludes certain individuals from gaining the recognition they deserve. But I am guided by the Fijian concept of respect. "It is the Fijian way," said Asenati, an elder in Tovu, "not to boast or brag or even call attention to oneself. We gain respect without putting ourselves forward. And those who *should* know our real names...well, they will know."

In the special case of writing about the *Vu* and other sacred rituals and objects, I have again been guided by my Fijian teachers: I try to speak the truth without revealing sacred secrets. Rather than referring to a *Vu* by a specific name, I speak simply of "the *Vu*." In writing about the most publically known *Vu*, Degei, I do use the Fijian name since so many other stories about his life and exploits have already been recorded. But I keep his "private" names where they said to belong, in the oral tradition, available only to those who need to know them. And instead of describing the details of a particular healing ritual, I give only a general account of its structure and purpose or the atmosphere generated in the ritual.

Fijians' respect for these spiritual and sacred matters is so profound and intense that they commonly allude to them only indirectly, and never casually — for example, one might refer to a particular *Vu* by saying, "We know that one is here"; the phrase "the requirements of the work," refers to the challenges of becoming a healer. I sometimes forsake this more indirect way of speaking, so that readers without the lived context necessary for interpreting an allusion can still understand the general meaning.

I. PLACE NAMES

"Tovu": The village where most of the fieldwork and action described in the book takes place.

"Kali": An island in the northern end of the Bitu chain where Tovu is located.

"Bitu": A chain of outlying rural islands ten hours from Suva by cargo boat.

"Ogo": A small island village several miles from Tovu whose residents are closely linked with Tovu through kinship.

"Delana": A village about ten miles south of Tovu.

"Momoto": The large island hundreds of miles away from Tovu where the head of the Tovu school was born.

Suva: The capital of Fiji and its largest city, with a population of approximately seventy thousand in 1977–78; located on Viti Levu, the largest Fijian island.

II. PEOPLE

"Alifereti": Owner and captain of the boat stationed in Suva which takes passengers and cargo to Tovu. A man in his early forties with a keen interest in traditional healing.

"Alipate": One of two men in Tovu who help Tevita in his healing work. Though in his late fifties, Alipate has just recently become Tevita's helper. A somewhat aloof though gentle man, Alipate is married to Ateca.

"Asenati": An herbalist (*dausoliwai*), who is one of the traditional healers in Tovu. Though she is nearing her eightieth birthday, and is among the oldest women in the village, her energy seems undiminished; she easily takes charge of domestic settings around her home and frequently provides healing herbs and massages to those in need. Asenati is Luke's mother and Joeli's grandmother.

"Ateca": A Tovu woman in her mid-fifties who is an avid churchgoer. She is joyful where her husband, Alipate, is subdued; she is known for joking broadly while he remains quiet, though she too has a reflective side to her nature.

"Bale" : An outgoing, hospitable woman in her late thirties who is a well-known traditional healer (*dauvagunu*) in Suva.

Eliki: The name given to my son Alex; Eliki is six when we move to Fiji.

"Eroni": An introspective and somewhat unpredictable man in his late forties who is one of Tevita's two helpers in his healing work in Tovu.

"Inoke": Raised in a traditional manner and schooled in Western medical practice, a highly educated man who does not hesitate to speak his mind. Approaching his mid-forties, he serves as my primary research collaborator and translator, roles for which he is ideally suited. As a *mata-ni-vanua* whose traditional role it is to speak on behalf of chiefs, Inoke has been trained from birth in the customs of the land — the forms of when and how to enter a village, to initiate and continue a conversation, and to perform ceremonies. His knowledge of sickness and healing draws deeply on both his traditional and Western training, and the network of traditional healers to which he has access is remarkable. Though Inoke comes from Delana, he lives in the village of Tovu with his wife, Nasi, who is the Tovu nurse.

"Jese": An articulate and forceful speaker who is one of the leaders of the government-sponsored fishing scheme in Ogo. Nearing forty, Jese is very involved in the business aspects of the fishing enterprise, which sometimes pushes aside his involvement in the traditional life of his village.

"Joeli": The son of Luke and Laniana, appears shy in public settings, but among his peers is just another fun-loving Tovu adolescent. Joeli will soon turn twenty.

"Jone": A dignified yet outgoing forty-year-old man who is the head schoolteacher in Tovu. Jone is from a chiefly lineage in the distant island of Momoto. He combines a deep reverence for tradition with a commitment to Western styles of education. Like all schoolteachers, Jone is respectfully addressed as "Master Jone," a title he has merited among the villagers of Tovu.

"Laniana": A caring and generous woman in her late thirties who is Luke's wife and Joeli's mother. She holds her household together in a strong yet welcoming manner.

Lora: The name given to my daughter Laurel; Lora is nine when we move to Fiji.

"Luke": A close relative of Sitiveni's who lives in Tovu and serves as its chiefly leader in Sitiveni's absence, though he is not actually in line to be the chief. The husband of Laniana and father of Joeli, Luke is an easygoing man approaching his mid-forties.

"Marika": A warm-hearted, insightful man who was raised in the traditional manner and has developed contemporary research skills, such as interviewing and translating, which complement his traditional knowledge. Approaching his early sixties, Marika is a resident of Suva.

"Meli": A part-time maintenance man at a school in Suva who also practices as a traditional healer (*dauvagunu*). He is in his mid-forties.

Mere: My wife's given name, Mary, in Fijian. In America she goes by the nickname Max. Mere is in her mid-thirties when we begin our fieldwork.

"Nanise": A thin, almost frail Tovu woman in her early thirties who has been troubled for many years with physical and mental problems. The niece of Tevita, she is married to Vili.

"Nasi": The nickname (Fijian for "Nurse") of the knowledgable and generous government nurse stationed in Tovu. Like her husband, Inoke, Nasi was raised in the traditional ways and is also schooled in Western medical practices. With quiet persistence, she seeks to combine the two sources of knowledge in her nursing practice.

"Nawame": A practicing nurse trained in the Western medical model. A woman in her late forties, she and her husband, Ratu Noa, live in Suva. Nawame is not above teasing him about his traditional healing work — but always with love and respect. Her upbringing, like her husband's, was traditional.

"Pita": An energetic farmer who married into Tovu, where he now lives. Approaching his fifties, his generally quiet presence at village functions is punctuated by uninhibited joking and teasing.

"Ratu Noa": A highly respected traditional healer (*dauvagunu*) of chiefly status who lives in Suva and is married to Nawame. In his early fifties, Ratu Noa is regarded as a keeper of sacred traditions. The honorific "Ratu" is used in addressing persons of chiefly status, and Ratu Noa exemplifies chiefly demeanor and presence — dignified but not distant, thoughtful and sensitive to the needs of others. Ratu Noa is my primary teacher and guide, a man of deep wisdom who shares it with care. Tevita, the primary traditional healer in Tovu and my teacher there, is Ratu Noa's student.

"Reverend Jemesa": A captivating speaker who is one of the leading Fijian preachers in the Christian evangelical movement. Working out of Suva, Reverend Jemesa, though not yet forty, has traveled widely throughout Fiji, spreading the word of the Gospel and sparking religious revivalism.

"Ropate": A man in his mid-forties, with a serious, sometimes somber demeanor who is responsible for organizing church activities in Tovu. Though he fills the role of pastor, he remains a man of the village who in addition has undertaken these special tasks.

Rusiate (Rusi): My name, Richard, in Fijian. People sometimes address me as Ratu Rusiate or Ratu Rusi, "Ratu" being used as a term of general respect and not in its more conventional usage as a way of addressing a chief. I am nearly forty when we begin living in Fiji.

"*Sera*": A shy, almost withdrawn young woman in her late twenties who is a traditional healer (*dauvagunu*) in Suva. She regularly becomes possessed during her work.

"*Sitiveni*": A proud man, in the best sense of the word, expressing an inner pride in his people and culture. Though not in line to be the formal chief of our home village of Tovu, Sitiveni is Tovu's acknowledged leader and chiefly representative. He is by birth a *mata-ni-vanua,* one who speaks for the chief, and is thus very knowledgeable about traditions and customs and the performance of ceremonies. He also possesses considerable research and political skills. Sitiveni is in his mid-sixties and has been a longtime resident of Suva, where he is also a respected elder.

"*Solomone*": A man in his early fifties who is one of the most articulate of Tovu's elders. His dignified manner graces the village ceremonies.

"*Suliana*": The wife of the healer Tevita who is originally from outside Tovu. Trained in the preparation and use of traditional healing herbs, she assists her husband in his work. Whereas Tevita is more quiet, she is more outgoing. Approaching her mid-forties, she is the mother of their nine children.

"*Tevita*": Suliana's husband, and Ratu Noa's student, a quiet, soft-spoken man in his mid-forties who is the primary traditional healer (*dauvagunu*) in Tovu and the surrounding area. Tevita's quietness bespeaks an inner strength and sensitivity, and he possesses a scrupulous sense of fairness. He is my Tovu teacher in the ways of Fijian healing; I become a helper in his work. Tevita is my closest friend in the village, and his family is my family's closest link.

"*Tomasi*": A traditional healer (*dauvagunu*) respected for his power who is a prominent elder in the village near Delana. His crusty demeanor overlies a gentle disposition. Though he is almost eighty, he is a vigorous farmer, an active leader in village ceremonies, and the devoted head of a large family of children, grandchildren, great-grandchildren and great-great-grandchildren.

"*Verani*": A vigorous, engaging woman in her mid-thirties who is a popular traditional healer (*dauvagunu*) practicing in Suva. She is originally from Kali Island, where Tovu is located.

"*Vili*": Nanise's thirty-five-year-old husband, a large, soft-spoken man who becomes the leader of the newly emerging Christian revivalist movement in Tovu.

Glossary

This glossary is meant only as that — providing glosses rather than the formal definitions of Fijian words. For more detailed and precise definitions, several Fijian-English dictionaries are available, including Cappel (1973) and the updated government dictionary project nearing completion.

The words listed are those used in the text that relate to the fieldwork; their glosses are likewise derived from that field or colloquial usage. Therefore not all the definitions of a particular word are presented. Specific attention is not given to technical matters, such as the exact form of speech, or whether the words in a term are connected or written separately.

A guide to pronouncing Fijian words follows:

> *b* is pronounced *mb* as in ti*mb*er
> *c* is pronounced *th* as in fa*th*er
> *d* is pronounced *nd* as in ba*nd*
> *g* is pronounced *ng* as in ki*ng*
> *q* is pronounced *nq* as in fi*ng*er

The word *yaqona*, for example, is pronounced as if it were written *yangona*, the word *bilo* as if it were written *mbilo*.

With rare exceptions, Fijian nouns do not change from singular to plural; the context, including modifiers and verbs, indicates number.

bete: traditional priest; member of the traditional priestly clan (*mataqali*)

bibi: important, serious; difficult; heavy

bilo: cup used to drink *yaqona*; made from half of the shell of a coconut, which is then smoothed and sometimes polished

bogi va: the fourth night; a special time marker in traditional ceremonies

bulubulu: a ceremony seeking forgiveness and atonement

bure: traditional thatched Fijian house

cakacaka: work

cakacaka ni yaqona: healing, or healing work; literally, the work of the *yaqona*

cake: up, at the top

cobo: ceremonial clap; a deep-sounding clap used to mark important features of the *yaqona* ceremony; formed by clapping the hands while cupped.

coi: the accompaniment or garnish to the staple starchy foods; usually vegatables, or fish, and served in smaller amounts than the staple starch

curumi: to be entered into, as in becoming possessed

dalo: taro (*colocasia esculenta*); a valued and staple starchy root crop

daukilakila: a type of traditional Fijian practitioner whose powers come from the *Vu*; one who knows in the spiritual sense

daurairai: a seer; one who sees in the spiritual sense

daunivucu: a composer of *meke,* the sacred and ancient form of Fijian dance, accompanied by songs

dausoliwai: an herbalist; one form of traditional Fijian healer; literally, an expert at giving medicines

dauvagunu: a spiritual healer; the traditional Fijian healer whose work is most characterized by the use of *yaqona* in the ceremony and a great reliance on the power of the *Vu*; literally, an expert at drinking (*yaqona*)

dauveibo: a massage specialist; a type of traditional Fijian healer. Literally, an expert at giving massage

Degei: the name of one of the most powerful and publically known *Vu* (ancestor gods). Often assumes the form of a snake

dina: true or truth

dodonu: straight or correct

draunikau: bad medicine, a form of *vakatevoro*; specifically the use of leaves or other materials for evil purposes

e liu: before — in time or place, in the past, in the olden days; the one in charge; sometimes used to refer to the *Vu* in charge of the healing work

era: down, at the bottom

gaunisala dodonu: the straight path; the traditional and ideal Fijian way of being, which is especially practiced by healers

i tovo vinaka: proper behavior or demeanor; behavior which respects tradition

378

ibe: woven mats; made by the women from the *voivoi* (*Pandanus thurstoni*) plant; depending on their quality, used for a variety of ordinary and ceremonial occasions

ka vakaviti: a Fijian thing

kai Viti: Fijian, or from Fiji

kai vanua: an inland person; literally, from the land

kai wai: a coastal person; literally, from the water

kakana dina: the main part of the meal, the starchy root crops; literally, the real or true food

Kalou: God, the Supreme Being; the God, it is said, of all people

Kalou Dina: the true or real God

Kalou Vu: the ancestral gods (cf. *Vu*)

kani: to be possessed (by a *Vu*); literally, eaten (by the *Vu*)

kato ni mana: the *mana* box or chest; where *mana* is said to be stored

kaukauwa: power; spiritual power

lali: wooden drum, made of a hollowed out log (a slit gong); when beaten, its deep sounds summon people to church or other important meetings and occasions

lasu: lie, false

leqa: problem, trouble

liga ni wai: a spiritual healer's helper; literally, the hand of the medicine

loloma: love, generosity; also, a gift of gratitude

lomalomarua: double-minded; literally, going two ways inside

lovo: earth or underground oven; used primarily to cook food for ceremonies or large gatherings. The men are in charge of cooking in the *lovo*

madrali: a ceremonial thanksgiving offering to the *Vu*

magiti: a ceremonial presentation of food; also, a feast

mana: the ultimate spiritual power in Fiji; power that makes all things, including healing, happen

masi: tapa cloth; bark cloth made out of the mulberry tree; worn on ceremonial occasions

mata-ni-vanua: a herald, the one who speaks for the chief; a person belonging to the herald clan; literally, the face of the land

mataqali: clan; more literally, a lineage, a kin-related subclan; part of the larger kin-related clan, called a *yavusa*

mateni: referring to an altered state of consciousness which varies depending on whether it comes as a result of drinking *yaqona* or alcohol, in what way, and how much. When one is *mateni* from drinking alcohol, or from using *yaqona* in an abusive manner, the translation "drunk" is appropriate

meke: a sacred Fijian dance with accompanying lyrics. Performed at formal ceremonies, the lyrics usually tell the story of an event in an area's history.

meke ni vula: dance to the moon; a ritual in which someone who has done *vakatevoro* celebrates their evil-doing

mosi ni ulu: headache

nasi: nurse

qase: old, an elder; a master

rere: an uncanny fear; terror or dread induced by the *Vu*

rewa: an herbal mixture used to preserve health and gain the protection of the *Vu*. Usually prepared by a traditional Fijian healer

sau: spiritual power or *mana;* used to speak of the *mana* belonging to chiefs

sava: sacred burial site or ancient house site; where the *Vu* are said to reside

savasava: clean, pure; also, ritual cleansing

sega na i vukivuki: humility; don't be boastful; literally, don't (show off) by turning around and around

sega ni lomaloma rua: single-mindedness; literally, don't be double-minded

sevusevu: the ceremonial exchange of *yaqona*

tabu: taboo; a sacred prohibition; something or someone sacred that one is prohibited from approaching or touching

tabua: whale's tooth; a specially prized sacred object of exchange

tadra: dream

talatala: minister

tanoa: wooden bowl, in which *yaqona* is mixed, and from which it is served

tauvimate: sickness

tauvimate dina: "true" or "real" sickness, implying the cause is natural or ordinary

tauvimate vakatevoro: spiritual sickness, implying the illness is the result of violating a sacred norm or working in allegiance with the devil; literally sickness from the workings of the devil

tavioka: cassava or tapioca; the starchy root crop which is the most common and widely available staple food

tevoro: the devil

tulou: a word of apology; said when one must violate a canon of respect, such as when one must stand or reach above another, or walk in front of others

turaga: chief; term of respect used to refer to the male members of a kinship group

uto: breadfruit

uvi: yam; a highly prized starchy food

vakabauta: faith, belief

vakacequ: to rest or retire

vakadidike: research

vakadinadina: telling and living the truth

vakarokoroko: respect

vakasama: belief

vakatevoro: evildoing, evil work; harming another by abusing *yaqona* or *mana;* literally, something devil-like, from the work of the devil. Commonly translated as "witchcraft" *vakaturaga:* tradition, traditional, in the traditional manner; literally, according to the way of the chiefs, a chiefly or highly respectable manner or demeanor (cf. *vakavanua*)

vakavanua: tradition, traditional, in the traditional manner; literally, according to the ways of the land or respecting the sacred customs of the land

valagi: Westerner, European; Caucasian

vanua: the land, and its people and traditions

veiqaravi: service; refers to the healing work

veitalanoa: discussion; literally, the telling or sharing of stories

vinaka: good; a way of expressing approval or thanks; goodness

viti: Fiji

voivoi: the pandanus leaves used by women to weave mats

Vu: the ancestral god or gods, ancestors, spirits; the source or basis of things, as in the word for doctor, *vuniwai* (literally, the source of medicine)

vuku vulici: school-based or learned knowledge

vuku soli: knowledge given to one; commonly used to describe knowledge given by the *Vu*

vulagi: guest, visitor

vuniwai: doctor; literally, the source or basis of medicine

vuniwai vakavalagi: Western doctor; a bio-medically oriented doctor

vuniwai vakaviti: Fijian doctor; that is, a traditional healer

wai: medicine; literally, water or other liquid. In its usage in healing, the word refers to the water or oil (*waiwai*) in which herbs are mixed to make medicine. *Wai-ni-mate,* literally water for sickness, is the complete word for medicine. Also refers, for example, to the sea (*waitui* or "salt water"); and to water as a general mixing agent — such as *wai-ni-niu,* coconut milk, made from shredded coconut mixed with water

waqa waqa: a person who becomes possessed by the *Vu*

yaqona: the sacred plant, *Piper methysticum,* used in ceremonial occasions and as an essential part of the spiritual healer's practice. Its roots are dried and pounded, then mixed with water and drunk.

yau: goods, riches; wealth in the form of material goods — especially traditional items like *tabua* and *ibe* — exchanged during ceremonies

yavusa: a kin-determined social grouping, members of which claim descent from a common founding male ancestor

Bibliography

Adams, H. 1989. *Prison of grass: Canada from the Native point of view.* Saskatoon, Saskatchewan: Fifth House.

Ahenakew, F. 1986. Teaching the Cree way. *AWASIS (Journal of the Indian/Native Education Council)*, 4 (3).

Akwesasne Notes 1974. *Voices from Wounded Knee: In the words of the participants.* Roosevelt, N.Y.: Mohawk Nation at Akwesasne.

Albee, G., Joffe, J., and Dusenbury, L., eds. 1988. *Prevention, powerlessness and politics: Readings on social change.* Newbury Park, Calif.: Sage.

Alexander, C., and Langer, E., eds. 1989. *Higher stages of human development.* New York: Oxford University Press.

Amoah, E. 1986. Women, witches and social change in Ghana. In D. Eck and J. Devaki, eds., *Speaking of faith: Cross-cultural perspectives on women, religion and social change.* London: Women's Press.

Anzaldua, G., ed. 1990. *Making face, making soul (Haciendo cara): Creative and critical perspectives by women of color.* San Francisco: Aunt Lute Foundation.

Apassingok, A., Walunga, W., and Tennand, E. 1985. *Lore of St. Lawrence Island: Echoes of our Eskimo elders.* Unalakleet, Alaska: Bering Strait School District.

Argyle, M. 1991. *Cooperation.* New York: Routledge & Kegan Paul.

Arno, A. 1976. Ritual of reconciliation and village conflict management in Fiji. *Oceania* 47 (1):49–65.

———. 1980. Fijian gossip as adjudication: A communication model of informal social control. *Journal of Anthropological Research* 36 (3):343–60.

———. 1992. *The world is talk: Conflict and communication on a Fijian island.* Norwood, N. J.: Ablex.

382

Barnett, H. G. 1953. *Innovation: The basis of culture change.* New York: McGraw-Hill.

Basow, S. 1984. Ethnic group differences in educational achievement in Fiji. *Journal of Cross-Cultural Psychology* 15 (4):435–51.

———. 1986. Correlates of sex-typing in Fiji. *Psychology of Women Quarterly* 10 (4):429–42.

Bateson, G. 1972. *Steps to an ecology of the mind.* New York: Ballantine.

Beck, P., Walters, A., and Francisco, N. 1992. *The sacred: Ways of knowledge, sources of life.* Tsaile, Ariz.: Navajo Community College Press.

Bellah, R. 1968. Meaning and modernism. *Religious Studies* 4 (1):37–45.

Belshaw, C. 1964. *Under the ivi tree: Society and economic growth in rural Fiji.* Berkeley: University of California Press.

Benjamin, M., ed. and trans. 1987. *Don't be afraid, Gringo: A Honduran woman speaks from the heart: The story of Elvia Alvarado.* San Francisco: Institute for Food and Development Policy.

Berger, P., Berger, B., and Kellner, H. 1973. *The homeless mind: Modernization and consciousness.* New York: Vintage.

Berger, T. 1985. *Village journey.* New York: Hill & Wang.

Berne, E. 1959. Psychiatric epidemiology of the Fiji Islands. *Progress in Psychotherapy* 4: 310–13.

Biesele, M., ed. 1987. *The past and future of !Kung ethnography: Critical reflections and symbolic perspectives.* Hamburg: Buske.

Biesele, M., and Weinberg, P. 1990. *Shaken roots.* Marshalltown, South Africa: Environmental & Development Agency.

Bodley, J. H. 1990. *Victims of progress.* 3rd ed. Mountain View, Calif.: Mayflower.

Bourguignon, E. ed. 1973. *Religion, altered states of consciousness and social change.* Columbus: Ohio State University Press.

Bredo, E., and Feinberg, W. 1982. *Knowledge and values in social and educational research.* Philadelphia: Temple University Press.

Brewster, A. V. 1922. *The hill tribes of Fiji.* Philadelphia: Lippincott. Reprinted by Johnson Reprints.

Briggs, C. 1986. *Learning how to ask: A sociolinguistic appraisal of the role of the interview in social science research.* Cambridge: Cambridge University Press.

Brody, H. 1982. *Maps and dreams.* New York: Pantheon.

Bronfenbrenner, U. 1979. Contexts of child rearing. *American Psychologist* 34 (10):844–50.

Brookfield, H. C. 1988. Fijian farmers, each on his own land. *Journal of Pacific Studies* 23 (1):15–35.

Brosted, J., et al. eds. 1985. *Native power: The quest for autonomy and nationhood of indigenous people.* Bergen, Norway: Universitetsforlaget.

Brown, J. E. 1971. *The sacred pipe: Black Elk's account of the seven rites of the Oglala Sioux.* Harmondsworth, Middlesex: Penguin.

Bullivant, B. 1983. Cultural reproduction in Fiji: Who controls knowledge/power? *Comparative Education Review* 27 (2):227–45.

Burger, J. 1987. *Report from the frontier: The state of the world's Indigenous peoples.* London: Zed.

Burgos-Debray, E., ed. 1984. *I, Rigoberta Menchu: An Indian woman in Guatemala.* London: New Left Books.

Burt, E. A., ed. 1955. *The teachings of the compassionate Buddha: Early discourses, the Dhammapada, and later writings.* New York: New American Library.

Byrd, R. 1988. Positive therapeutic effects of intercessory prayer in a coronary care unit population. *Southern Medical Journal* 81 (7):826–29.

Campbell, G. 1987. Ethics and writing Native American history: A commentary about People of the Sacred Mountain. *American Indian Culture and Research Journal* 11 (1):81–96.

Campbell, M. 1973. *Half-breed.* Halifax, Nova Scotia: Formac Publishing Company.

Capell, A. 1973. *A new Fijian dictionary.* Suva: Government Printer.

Cheever, O. 1993. *The training of community psychiatrists: A test of the model of "education as transformation."* Ph.D. diss., Harvard University.

Churchill, W. 1988. Sam Gill's Mother Earth: Colonialism, genocide and the appropriation of Indigenous spiritual tradition in contemporary academia. *American Indian Culture and Research Journal* 12 (3):49–68.

————, ed. 1989. *Critical issues in Native North America.* Copenhagen: International Work Group for Indigenous Affairs.

Clifford, J. 1988. *The predicament of culture: Twentieth-century ethnography, literature and art.* Cambridge: Harvard University Press.

Clifford, J., and Marcus, G. E., eds. 1986. *Writing culture: The poetics and politics of ethnography.* Berkeley: University of California Press.

Cornish, P. 1991. Defining empowerment: Toward the development of phenomenologically based theory and research methods. M.A. thesis, University of Saskatchewan.

Cowan, P. A. 1982. The relationship between emotional and cognitive development. In D. Cicchetti and P. Hesse, eds., *Emotional Development,* San Francisco: Jossey-Bass.

Craig, R. 1988. NANA Eskimo Spirit movement. Unpublished paper, College of Rural Alaska, University of Alaska, Fairbanks.

Crapanzano, V., and Garrison, V., eds. 1977. *Case studies in spirit possession.* New York: Wiley & Sons.

Crocombe, R. 1987. *The South Pacific.* Auckland, New Zealand: Longman Paul.

————. 1990. Review of C. Browne and D. A. Scott, *Economic development in seven Pacific Island countries. Pacific Affairs* 62 (4):581–82.

Csordas, T. J. 1983. The rhetoric of transformation in ritual healing. *Culture, Medicine and Psychiatry* 7 (4):333–75.

De Mallie, R. J., ed. 1984. *The sixth grandfather: Black Elk's teachings given to John G. Neihardt.* Lincoln: University of Nebraska Press.

Derrick, R. A. 1950. *A history of Fiji.* Suva: Government Printer.

deVries, M., Berg, R. and Lipkin, M., eds. 1982. *The use and abuse of medicine.* New York: Praeger.

Diamond, S. 1974. *In search of the primitive.* New Brunswick, N.J.: Transaction.

Diamond, S. 1990. *Spiritual warfare: The politics of the Christian right.* Montreal: Black Rose.

Donahue, J. M. 1986. Planning for primary health care in Nicaragua: A study in revolutionary process. *Social Science and Medicine* 23 (2):149–57.

Draguns, J. G. 1990. Review of A. Robillard and A. Marsella. *Contemporary issues in mental health research in the Pacific Islands. Contemporary Psychology* 35 (1):83.

Durkheim, E. 1915. *The elementary forms of religious life.* Rpt. New York: Free Press, 1965.

Dwyer, K. 1982. *Moroccan dialogues: Anthropology in question.* Baltimore: Johns Hopkins University Press.

Eagleton, T. 1985. Capitalism, modernism and postmodernism. *New Left Review* 152: 60–73.

Eck, D., and Jain, D., eds. 1986. *Speaking of faith: Cross-cultural perspectives on women, religion and social change.* London: Women's Press.

Ehrenreich, B., and Dierdre, E. 1973. *Witches, midwives, and nurses: A history of women healers.* Old Westbury, N.Y.: Feminist Press.

Ehrenreich, B., and English, D. 1979. *For her own good: One hundred fifty years of the experts' advice to women.* Garden City, N.Y.: Anchor.

Ehrenreich, J. ed. 1973. *The cultural crisis of modern medicine.* New York: Monthly Review Press.

Eliade, M. 1964. *Shamanism: Archaic techniques of ecstasy.* Princeton: Princeton University Press.

———. 1965. *Rites and symbols of initiation.* New York: Harper & Row.

Erikson, E. 1984. Reflections on the last stage—and the first. *Psychoanalytic Study of the Child* 39:155–65.

Evans-Pritchard, E. E. 1937. *Witchcraft, oracles and magic among the Azande.* London: Oxford University Press.

Fanon, F. 1963. *The wretched of the earth.* New York: Grove.

———. 1978, Medicine and colonialism. In J. Ehrenreich, ed., *The cultural crisis of modern medicine.* New York: Monthly Review Press.

Firth, R. 1940. The analysis of "mana": An empirical approach. *Journal of the Polynesian Society* 40:438–510.

Fogelson, R., and Adams, R., eds. 1977. *The anthropology of power.* New York: Academic Press.

Fong, A., and Ravuvu, A. 1976. Sacred and historic sites of Namosi. Paper prepared for AMEX Corporation, Suva, Fiji, June 28.

Fowler, J. 1981. *Stages of faith: Psychology of human development and the quest for meaning*. New York: Harper & Row.

Freire, P. 1968. *The pedagogy of the oppressed*. New York: Seabury.

———. 1985. *The politics of education: Culture, power and liberation*. South Hadley, Mass: Bergin & Garvey.

Fuller, B. 1963. *Ideas and integrities*. New York: Macmillan, Collier.

Garret, J., and Mavor, J. 1973. *Worship the Pacific way*. Suva, Fiji: Lotu Pasifika.

Geertz, C. 1983. *Local knowledge: Further essays in interpretive anthropology*. New York: Basic Books.

Gilligan, C. 1982. *In a different voice*. Cambridge: Harvard University Press.

———. 1988. Two moral orientations: Gender differences and similarities. *Merrill-Palmer Quarterly* 34 (3):223–37.

Giorgi, A. 1985. *Phenomenology and psychological research*. Pittsburgh: Duquesne University Press.

Golde, P. ed. 1980. *Women in the field*. Chicago: Aldine.

Goleman, D., and Gurin, J., eds. 1993. *Mind/body medicine: How to use your mind for better health*. Yonkers, New York: Consumer Reports Books.

Gonzalez-Ortega, C. A. 1991. *Synergy in the classroom: Explorations in "education as transformation" with Puerto Rican children and their teacher*. Ph.D. diss., Harvard University.

Good, B. ed. 1987. Culture-bound syndromes. *Culture, Medicine and Psychiatry* 11 (1):1–2.

Gould, S. 1981. *The mismeasurement of man*. New York: Norton.

Goulet, D. 1985. *The cruel choice: A new concept in the theory of development*. Washington, D. C.: University Press of America.

Government of Fiji Bureau of Statistics. 1976. *Social indicators for Fiji*. Suva: Government Printer.

Gray, A. ed. 1989. *Indigenous self-development in the Americas*. Copenhagen: International Workshop for Indigenous Affairs.

Gregory, D. 1989. Traditional Indian healers in northern Manitoba: An emerging relationship with the health care system. *Native Studies Review* 5 (1):163–74.

Guenon, R. 1962. *Crisis of the modern world*. London: Luzac.

Guenther, M. G. 1986. *The Nharo Bushmen of Botswana: Tradition and change*. Hamburg: Buske.

Hahn, H., and Katz, R. 1985. Education as transformation: A test of the model. Unpublished paper, Harvard Graduate School of Education.

Hampton, E. 1984. The sweat lodge and modern society. Unpublished paper, Harvard Graduate School of Education.

Hansel, 1968. Characterization and physiological activities of some Kava constituents. *Pacific Science* 12.

Harris, G. 1989. Concepts of individual, self and person in description and analysis. *American Anthropologist* 91 (Sept. 1989):599–612.

Harvey, Y. K. 1979. *Six Korean women: The socialization of shamans.* St. Paul: American Ethnological Society.

Heller, K. 1989. Ethical dilemmas in community intervention. *American Journal of Community Psychology* 17 (3):367–78.

Heller, K., et al. 1984. *Psychology and community change.* Homewood, Ill.: Dorsey.

Henry, J. 1972. *On education.* New York: Random House.

Herbert, B. 1982. *Shandaa (in my lifetime).* Fairbanks: Alaska Native Language Center.

Herr, B. 1981. The expressive character of Fijian dream and nightmare experiences. *Ethos* 9 (4):331–52.

Hesse, P., and Cicchetti, D. 1982. Perspectives in an integrated theory of emotional development. In D. Cicchetti & P. Hesse, eds., *Emotional development.* San Francisco: Jossey-Bass.

Hickson, L. 1986. The social context of apology in dispute settlement: A cross-cultural study. *Ethnology,* 25 (4):283–94.

Hobsbawn, E., and Ranger, T. 1984. *The invention of tradition.* Cambridge: Cambridge University Press.

Hocart, A. M. 1929. *Lau Islands, Fiji.* Rpt.: Kraus. 1971.

———. 1952. *The northern states of Fiji. Royal Anthropological Institute Occasional Publication* 11.

Hoffman, M. L. 1978. Toward a theory of empathic arousal and development. In M. Lewis and L. A. Rosenblum, eds., *The development of affect.* New York: Plenum.

———. 1980. Moral development in adolescence. In J. Adelson, ed., *Handbook of adolescent psychology.* New York: Wiley.

Hollway, W. 1989. *Subjectivity and method in psychology: Gender, meaning and science.* Newbury Park, Calif: Sage.

Howard, G. 1991. Culture tales: A narrative approach to thinking, cross-cultural psychology and psychotherapy. *American Psychologist* 46 (3):187–97.

Huizer, G. 1978. Anthropology and multinational power: Some ethical considerations on social research in underdeveloped countries. In Idris-Soven and Vaughn, eds. *The world as a company town.* The Hague: Mouton.

Hurlich, S., and Lee, R. B. 1979. Colonialism, apartheid, and liberation: A Namibian example. In D. Turner and G. Smith, eds., *Challenging anthropology.* Toronto: McGraw-Hill Ryerson.

Huxley, A. 1944. *The perennial philosophy.* New York: Harper & Row.

Illich, I. 1982. *Medical nemesis: The expropriation of health.* New York: Pantheon.

Izard, C. E. 1982. *Measuring emotions in infants and young children.* New York:

Cambridge University Press.

Izard, C. E., and Malatesta, C. Z. 1987. Differential emotions theory of early emotional development. In J. D. Osofsky, ed., *Handbook of infant development.* 2nd ed. New York: Wiley.

Jung, C. G. 1952. *Transformation.* Princeton: Princeton University Press.

————. 1965. *Memories, dreams, reflections.* New York: Vintage.

————. 1969. *Psychology and religion: West and east.* Princeton: Princeton University Press.

Kabat–Zinn, J. 1991. *Full catastrophic living: Using the wisdom of your body and mind to face stress, pain, and illness.* New York: Delacorte.

Kabat-Zinn, J., et al. 1992. Effectiveness of a mediation-based stress reduction program in the treatment of anxiety disorders. *American Journal of Psychiatry* 149:936–43.

Kagan, J. 1978. On emotion and its development: A working paper. In M. Lewis & L. A. Rosenblum, eds., *The development of affect.* New York: Plenum.

————. 1988. The idea of temperament categories. Paper presented at the annual meeting of the American Psychological Association, Atlanta (August).

Kaplan, M. 1988. The coups in Fiji: Colonial contradictions and the post-colonial crisis. *Critique of Anthropology* 8 (3):93–116.

————. 1989. "Luve ni wai" as the British saw it: Constructions of custom and disorder in colonial Fiji. *Ethnohistory* 36 (4):349–71.

Katz, M. M. W. 1981. *"Gaining sense" in the outer Fiji Islands: A cross-cultural study of cognitive development.* Ph.D. diss., Harvard University.

————. 1984. Infant care in a group of outer Fiji islands. *Ecology of Food and Nutrition* 15 (4):323–40.

Katz, R. 1968; 1989. Unpublished field notes, Kalahari Desert.

————. 1973. *Preludes to growth: An experiential approach.* New York: Free Press.

————. 1977–78; 1985. Unpublished field notes, Fiji Islands.

————. 1981. Education as transformation: Becoming a healer among the !Kung and Fijians. *Harvard Educational Review* 51 (1):57–78.

————. 1982a. *Boiling energy: Community healing among the Kalahari Kung.* Cambridge: Harvard University Press.

————. 1982b. Commentary on education as transformation. *Harvard Educational Review* 52 (1):63–66.

————. 1982c. Utilizing traditional healing systems. *American Psychologist* 37 (6):115–16.

————. 1983/84. Empowerment and synergy: Expanding community healing resources. *Prevention in Human Services* 3:201–226.

———. 1986. Healing and transformation: Perspectives on development, education and community. In M. White and S. Pollak, eds., *The cultural transition: Social transformation in the third world and Japan.* London: Routledge & Kegan Paul.

———. 1987. The role of vulnerability in fieldwork. In A. Schenk and H. Kalweit, eds., *The healing of knowledge.* Munich: Goldman.

———. 1990. What is a healing community? *The Community Psychologist* 24(1):13–15.

Katz, R., Argyris, D., and Lapore, S. 1986. The contribution of vulnerability to fieldwork. Unpublished paper, Harvard Graduate School of Education.

Katz, R., Biesele, M., and St. Denis, V. In press. *"Healing makes our hearts happy": Spiritual traditions and social change among the Zhu/twasi.* Rochester, Vt.: Inner Traditions.

Katz, R., and Craig, R. 1987. Community healing: The rich resource of tradition. *The Exchange* 8 (2):4–5.

Katz, R., and Craig, R. 1988. Health is more than not being sick. *The Exchange* 9 (2):6–8.

Katz, R., and Kilner, L. 1987. The straight path: A Fijian perspective on development. In C. Super, ed. *The role of culture in developmental disorder.* New York: Academic Press.

Katz, R., and Lamb, W. 1983. Utilization patterns of "traditional" and "Western" health services: research findings. *Proceedings of Annual Meeting of the National Council on International Health.* Washington, D.C.: National Council on International Health.

Katz, R., and Nuñez-Molina, M. 1986. Researching realities: The contribution of vulnerability to cross-cultural understanding. *Community Psychologist* 19 (3).

Katz, R., and Rolde, E. 1981. Community alternatives to psychotherpy. *Psychotherapy: Therapy, Research and Practice* 18 (3):365–74.

Katz, R., and Seth, N. 1986. Synergy and healing: A perspective on Western health care. *Prevention in Human Services* 5 (1):109–36.

Katz, R., and Seth, N., eds. 1993. *Synergy and healing: Perspectives on development and social change.* Unpublished manuscript, Saskatchewan Indian Federated College.

Katz, R., and St. Denis, V. 1991. Teacher as healer: A renewing tradition. *Journal of Indigenous Studies* (2):23-36.

Katz, R., and Wexler, A. 1990. Healing: A transformational model. In K. Peltzer and P. Edigbe, eds., *Clinical psychology in Africa.* Eschborn, Germany: Fachbuchhandlung für Psychologie.

Keesing, R. 1983. *Elota's story: The life and times of a Solomon Islands big man.* New York: Holt, Rinehart & Winston.

Kelly, J. D. 1988. Fiji Indians and political discourse in Fiji: From the Pacific romance to the coups. *Journal of Historical Sociology.* 1 (4):399–422.

Kilner, L. 1986. The role of family relationships in adolescent development. Unpublished paper, Harvard Graduate School of Education.

Kim, C. S. 1990. The role of the non-Western anthropologist reconsidered: Illusion versus reality. *Current Anthropology* 31 (2):196–201.

Kleinman, A. 1979. *Patients and healers in the context of culture: An exploration of the borderland between anthropology, medicine, and psychiatry*. Berkeley: University of California Press.

———. 1987. Culture and clinical reality: Commentary on "culture-bound" syndromes and international disease classification. *Culture, Medicine and Psychiatry* 11 (1):49–52.

Knapman, B., and Walter, M. 1980. The way of the land and the path of money: The generation of economic inequality in eastern Fiji. *Journal of Developing Areas* 14 (2):201–22.

Knight, H. 1990. The oral tradition and Native story-tellers. Unpublished paper, Prince Albert Tribal Council, Prince Albert, Saskatchewan.

Kohlberg, L. 1984. *Essays on moral development*. San Francisco: Harper & Row.

———. 1986. A current statement on some theoretical issues. In S. Modgil and C. Modgil, eds., *Lawrence Kohlberg*. Philadelphia: Falmer Press.

Kohlberg, L., and Higgins, A. 1987. School democracy and social interaction. In W. M. Kurtines and J. L. Gewirtz, eds., *Moral development through social interaction*. New York: Wiley.

Kohn, A. 1986. *No contest: The case against competition*. Boston: Houghton Mifflin.

Konnor, M. 1982. The tangled wing: Biological constraints on the human spirit. New York: Holt, Rinehart & Winston.

Kreisberg, S. 1992. *Transforming power: Domination, empowerment and education*. Albany: State University of New York Press.

Kuhn, P. 1990. *Soulstealers: The Chinese sorcery scare of 1768*. Cambridge: Harvard University Press.

La Framboise, T. 1988. American Indian mental health policy. *American Psychologist* 43 (5):388–97.

La Framboise, T., and Plake, B. 1983. Toward meeting the research needs of Native Americans. *Harvard Educational Review*, 53 (1):45–51.

Lakoff, G., and Johnson, M. 1980. *Metaphors we live by*. Chicago: University of Chicago Press.

Lame Deer, J., and Erdoes, R. 1972. *Lame Deer: Seeker of visions*. New York: Simon & Schuster.

Lal, V. 1990. *Fiji coups in paradise: Race, politics and military intervention*. London: Zed.

Langer, E. 1989. *Mindfulness*. Reading, Mass.: Addison-Wesley.

Lasaqa, I. 1984. *The Fijian people: Before and after independence*. Canberra: Australian National University Press.

Leacock, E., and Lee, R. B., eds. 1982. *Politics and history in band societies*. Cambridge: Cambridge University Press and Maison des sciences de l'homme.

Lebot, V., Merlin, M., and Lindstrom, L. 1992. *Kava: The Pacific drug*. New Haven: Yale University Press.

Lebra, W. 1972. *Mental health research in Asia and the Pacific*. Honolulu: University of Hawaii Press.

Lee, R. B. 1979. *The !Kung San: Men, women and work in a foraging society*. Cambridge: Cambridge University Press.

———. 1984. *The Dobe !Kung.* New York: Holt, Rinehart & Winston.

———. 1985. Foragers and the state: Government policies toward the San in Namibia and Botswana. *Cultural Survival: Occasional Papers* 18:37–46.

Lee, R. B., and Devore, I., eds. 1968. *Man the hunter.* Chicago: Aldine.

Lerner, R. M., and Spanier, G. B., eds. 1978. *Child influences on marital and family interaction: A life-span perspective.* New York: Academic Press.

LeVine, R. A. 1982. *Culture, behavior and personality.* 2nd ed. Chicago: Aldine.

LeVine, R.A., and White, M. 1986. *Human conditions: The cultural basis of educational development.* New York: Routledge & Kegan Paul.

Lévi-Strauss, C. 1963. *Structural anthropology.* New York: Basic Books.

Levy, R. 1975. *Tahitians.* Chicago: University of Chicago Press.

Lewis, I. M. 1986. *Religion in context: Cults and charisma.* Cambridge: Cambridge University Press.

Lewis, M., and Brooks-Gunn, J. 1979. *Social cognition and the acquisition of the self.* New York: Plenum.

Light, D. 1980. *Becoming psychiatrists: The professional transformation of self.* New York: Norton.

———. 1988. Toward a new sociology of medical education. *Journal of Health and Social Behavior* 29 (4):307–22.

Lincoln, Y. S., and Guba, E. A. 1985. *Naturalistic inquiry.* Newbury Park, Calif.: Sage.

Lindstrom, L. 1991. Kava, cash, and custom in Vanuatu. *Cultural Survival Quarterly* 15 (2):28–31.

Little Bear, L., Boldt, M., and Long, J. 1984. *Pathways to self-determination: Canadian Indians and the Canadian state.* Toronto: University of Toronto Press.

Luhrmann, T. M. 1989. *Persuasions of the witch's craft: Ritual magic in contemporary England.* Cambridge: Harvard University Press.

Maccoby, E. E., and Martin, J. A. 1983. Socialization in the context of the family: Parent-child interaction. In P. H. Mussen, ed., *Handbook of child psychology.* New York: Wiley.

Manson, S. M., ed. 1982. *New directions in prevention among American Indian and Alaska Native communities.* Portland: Oregon Health Sciences University.

Marcus, G. E., and Fischer, M. J. 1986. *Anthropology as cultural critique: An experimental moment in the human sciences.* Chicago: Chicago University Press.

Marshall, L. 1969. The medicine dance of the !Kung Bushmen. *Africa* 39: (4)347–81.

———. 1976. *The !Kung of Nyae Nyae.* Cambridge: Harvard University Press.

Maslow, A. 1971. *The farther reaches of human nature.* New York: Viking.

Maslow, A., and Honigmann, J. 1970. Synergy: Some notes of Ruth Benedict. *American Anthropologist* 72 (2):320–33.

Mavor, J. E. ed. 1977. *Traditional belief and the Christian faith.* Suva, Fiji: Lotu Pasifika.

McGuire, M. 1982. *Pentecostal Catholics: Power, charisma and order in a religious movement.* Philadelphia: Temple University Press.

———. 1983. Words of power: Personal empowerment and healing. *Culture, Medicine and Psychiatry.* 7: 221–40.

McLean, A. 1986. Family therapy workshops in the United States: Potential abuses in the production of therapy in an advanced capitalist society. *Social Science and Medicine* 23 (2): 179–89.

Memmi, A. 1965. *Colonizer and colonized.* Boston: Beacon.

Menary, J. 1987. The amniocentesis and abortion experience: A study in psychological healing. Ph.D. diss., Harvard University.

Merton, T. 1977. *The wisdom of the desert.* New York: New Directions.

Meza, A. 1988. A study of acculturation of Chicano students at Harvard College: Evidence for the collectivist ego. Ph.D. diss., Harvard University.

Middleton, J., ed. 1967. *Magic, witchcraft and curing.* Austin: University of Texas Press.

Minuchin, S. 1984. *Family kaleidoscope: Images of violence and healing.* Cambridge: Harvard University Press.

Mishler, E. 1984. *The discourse of medicine.* Norwood, N.J.: Ablex.

———. 1986. *Research interviewing: Context and narrative.* Cambridge: Harvard University Press.

Moody, R., ed. 1988. *The Indigenous voice: Visions and realities.* Vol. 2. London: Zed.

MumShirl. 1981. *An autobiography.* Richmond, Victoria, Australia: Heinemann.

Musqua, D. 1991a. Traditional Saulteaux human growth and development. Lecture delivered at the Saskatchewan Indian Federated College (March).

———. 1991b, personal communication, April 4.

Navarro, V. 1976. *Medicine under capitalism.* New York: Prodist.

Nayacakalou, R. R. 1975. *Leadership in Fiji.* Melbourne: Oxford University Press.

———. 1978. *Tradition and change in the Fijian village.* Suva, Fiji: South Pacific Social Sciences Association, Institute of Pacific Studies, University of the South Pacific.

Needleman, J. 1983. Psychiatry and the sacred. In J. Welwood, ed., *Awakening the heart.* Boston: New Science Library.

Neihardt, J. 1972. *Black Elk speaks.* New York: Pocket Books.

Newnham, P. 1984. Fijian myths and culture change. Honors thesis, Harvard University.

Ngugi, W. T. 1986. *Decolonising the mind.* London: Currey.

Noll, R. 1985. Mental imagery cultivation as a cultural phenomenon: The role of visions in shamanism. *Current Anthropology* 26 (4):443–51.

Nuñez-Molina, M. 1987. *Desarrollo del Medium* The process of becoming a healer in Puerto Rican *espiritismo.* Ph.D. diss., Harvard University.

Overton, J. 1988. A Fijian peasantry: "Galala" and villagers. *Oceania* 58:193–211.

Parsons, C., ed. 1985. *Healing practices in the South Pacific.* Honolulu: The Institute for Polynesian Studies.

Patton, M. Q. 1990. *Qualitative evaluation and research methods.* Newbury Park, Calif.: Sage.

Peacock, J. 1987. *Rites of modernization: Symbols and social aspects of Indonesian proletarian drama.* Chicago: University of Chicago Press.

Perin, C. 1986. Speaking of tradition and modernity. *Cultural Anthropology* 1 (4).

Phillips, D. C., and Kelly, M. E. 1978. Hierarchical theories of development in education and psychology. In *Stage theories of cognitive and moral development: Criticisms and applications.* Cambridge: Harvard Educational Review.

Piaget, J. 1952. *The origins of intelligence in children.* New York: International Universities Press.

———. 1967. *The child's construction of the world.* Totowa, N.J.: Littlefield, Adams.

———. 1970. *Structuralism.* New York: Basic Books.

Piaget, J., and Inhelder, B. 1948. *The child's conception of space.* Rpt. New York: Norton, 1969.

———. 1969. *The psychology of the child.* New York: Basic Books.

Polanyi, M. 1958. *Personal knowledge: Toward a post-critical philosophy.* Chicago: University of Chicago Press.

Pukui, M., Haertig, E. and Lee, C. 1977. *Nana I Ke Kumu (Look to the source).* Honolulu: Hui Hanai.

Quain, B. 1948. *Fijian village.* Chicago: University of Chicago Press.

Rabinow, P. 1977. *Reflections on fieldwork in Morocco.* Berkeley: University of California Press.

Rabinow, P., and Sullivan, W., eds. 1988. *Interpretive social science: A second look.* Berkeley: University of California Press.

Ralph, D. 1983. *Work and madness: The rise of community psychiatry.* Montreal: Black Rose.

Rappaport, J. 1977. *Community psychology.* New York: Holt, Rinehart & Winston.

———. 1987. Terms of empowerment/exemplars of prevention: Toward a theory of community psychology. *American Journal of Community Psychology* 15 (2):121–48.

Rappaport, R. 1978. Adaptation and the structure of ritual. In N. Blurton-Jones and V. Reynolds, eds., *Human behavior and adaptation.* New York: Halsted.

Ravuvu, A. 1983. *The Fijian way of life.* Suva, Fiji: University of the South Pacific.

———. 1987. *The Fijian ethos.* Suva, Fiji: University of the South Pacific.

Reason, P., and Rowan, J., eds. 1981. *Human inquiry: A sourcebook of new paradigm research.* New York: John Wiley.

Proceedings of the Regional Meeting of Pacific Islands Women's Non-governmental Organizations 1985. Noumea, New Caledonia: South Pacific Commission.

Reichmann, R. 1985. *Consciencia* and development in the Association of Triciceros: A grassroots labor organization in the Dominican Republic. Ph.D. diss., Harvard University.

Reinharz, S. 1982. *On becoming a social scientist.* Rutgers, N.J.: Transaction.

Remen, R. 1990. Living next to cancer. In *How your mind affects your health.* San Francisco: Institute for the Advancement of Health.

Report of the select committee of inquiry into the health services in Fiji. 1979. Parliamentary paper No. 28. Suva: Government Printer.

393

Ritchie, J., and Ritchie, J. 1979. *Growing up in Polynesia.* Sydney: Allen & Unwin.

Rokotuiviwa, P. 1975. *The congregation of the poor.* Suva, Fiji: South Pacific Social Sciences Association.

Roth, G. K. 1953. *Fijian way of life.* London: Oxford University Press.

Rutz, H. J. 1978. Ceremonial exchange and economic development in village Fiji. *Economic Development and Cultural Change* 26 (4):777–805.

Sahlins, M. 1962. *Moala: Culture and nature on a Fijian Island.* Ann Arbor: University of Michigan Press.

————. 1985. *Islands of history.* Chicago: University of Chicago Press.

Sangren, P. S. 1988. Rhetoric and the authority of ethnography: Postmodernism and the social reproduction of texts. *Current Anthropology* 29 (3):405–35.

Sarason, S. 1977. *The psychological sense of community: Prospects for a community psychology.* San Francisco: Jossey-Bass.

Scarr, D. 1984. *Fiji: A short history.* Sydney: Allen & Unwin.

Schmookler, A. 1984. *The parable of the tribes: The problem of power in social evolution.* Berkeley: University of California Press.

Schoun, F. 1975. *Logic and transcendence.* New York: Harper & Row.

Schutz, A., and Komaitai, R. 1971. *Spoken Fijian: Intensive course in Bauan Fijian, with grammatical notes and glossary.* Honolulu: University of Hawaii Press.

Selman, R. 1980. *The growth of interpersonal understanding: Developmental and clinical analysis.* New York: Academic Press.

Seth, N. 1987. *Baira ni vato* (women's talk): A psychological context for exploring fertility options in traditional societies. Ph.D. diss., Harvard University.

Shah, F. S. 1987. Culture and education in community-based psychiatric care: The Fountain House model in New York and Lahore, Pakistan. Ph.D. diss., Harvard University.

Shapiro, M. 1978. *Getting doctored: Critical reflections on becoming a physician.* Kitchener, Ont.: Between the Lines.

Shweder, R. 1977. Likeness and likelihood in everyday thought: Magical thinking in judgments about personality. *Current Anthropology* 18 (Dec.):637–58.

————. 1991. *Thinking through cultures: Expeditions in cultural psychology.* Cambridge: Harvard University Press.

Shweder, R., and LeVine, R., eds. 1984. *Culture theory: Essays on mind, self, and emotion.* Cambridge: Cambridge University Press.

Silman, J. 1987. *Enough is enough: Aboriginal women speak out.* Toronto: Women's Press.

Simonis, J. 1984. Synergy and the education of helpers: A new community psychology approach to counselor training. Ph.D. diss., Harvard University.

Singer, M. 1986. Toward a political economy of alcoholism: The missing link in the anthropology of drinking. *Social Science and Medicine* 23 (2):113–30.

Siwatibau, S. 1981. *Rural energy in Fiji: A survey of domestic rural energy use and potential.* Ottawa: International Development Research Center.

Skin, A. 1988. Personal communication, December 1.

Skultans, V. 1986. On mental imagery and healing. *Current Anthropology* 27 (3):262.

Smith, H. 1977. *Forgotten truth: The primordial tradition*. New York: Harper & Row.

Spencer, D. 1937. Fijian dreams and visions. In D. Davidson, ed., *Twenty–fifth Anniversary Studies of the Philadelphia Anthropological Society*. Philadelphia: Philadelphia Anthropological Society.

———. 1941. *Disease, religion and society in the Fiji Islands*. New York: American Ethnological Society.

Sroufe, L. A. 1990. The role of infant-caregiver attachment in development. In J. Belsky and T. M. Nezworski, eds., *Clinical implications of attachment*. Hillsdale, N.J.: Erlbaum.

St. Denis, V. 1989. A process of community-based participatory research: A case study. M.A. thesis, University of Alaska, Fairbanks.

Starr, P. 1982. *The social transformation of American medicine*. New York: Basic Books.

Stewart, R. 1982a. *Human development in the South Pacific: A book of readings*. Suva, Fiji: University of the South Pacific.

———. 1982b. Us and them: Beliefs about human nature held by young people in the South Pacific. *Social Behavior and Personality* 10 (2):221–26.

———. 1984. Cognitive, socio-cultural and institutional explanations for ethnic differences in academic achievement in Fiji. Paper presented at the Conference on Thinking, Cambridge, Mass. (August).

Stoller, P., and Olkes, C. 1987. *In sorcery's shadow: A memoir of apprenticeship among the Songhay of Niger*. Chicago: University of Chicago Press.

Stull, D., and Schensul, J., eds. 1987. *Collaborative research and social change: Applied anthropology in action*. Boulder, Colo.: Westview.

Super, C., ed. 1987. *The role of culture in developmental disorder*. New York: Academic Press.

Swampy, G. 1982. The role of the native woman in a native society. *Canadian Journal of Native Education* 9 (3):2–20.

Tambiah, S. 1973. Form and meaning of magical arts: A point of view. In R. Horton and Finnegan, eds., *Separate from modes of thought*. London: Farber.

———. 1990. *Magic, science, religion and the scope of rationality*. Cambridge: Cambridge University Press.

Taussig, M. 1987. *Shamanism, colonialism and the wild man: A study in terror and healing*. Chicago: University of Chicago Press.

Taylor, P. 1981. *Border healing woman: The story of Jewel Babb*. Austin, Texas: University of Texas Press.

The Tipi (poster with text). 1988. Saskatchewan: Saskatchewan Indian Cultural Center.

Thompson, B. 1908. The Fijians: *A study in the decay of custom*. London: Heinemann.

Thompson, L. 1940a. *Southern Lau, Fiji: An ethnography*. Honolulu: Bishop Museum.

———. 1940b. *Fijian frontier*. New York: Institute of Pacific Relations.

Tiffany, S. 1975. Giving and receiving: Participation in chiefly redistribution activities in Samoa. *Ethnology* 14 (3):267–86.

Tippet, A. 1968. *Fijian material culture: A study of cultural context, function and change.* Honolulu: Bishop Museum.

Torrey, E. F. 1986. *Witch doctors and psychiatrists: The common roots of psychotherapy and its future.* Norvale, N.J.: Aronson.

Trainer, T. 1989. *Developed to death: Rethinking third world development.* London: Merlin.

Triandis, H. C. 1988. Individualism and collectivism: Cross-cultural perspectives on self-ingroup relationships. *Journal of Personality and Social Psychology* 54 (2):323–38.

———. 1989. The self and social behavior in differing cultural contexts. *Psychological Review* 96 (3):506–20.

Trompf, G., ed. 1977. *Prophets of Melanesia.* Port Moresby: Institute of Papua New Guinea Studies.

Tupouniua, S., Crocombe, R., and Slatter, C., eds. 1975. *The Pacific way: Social issues in national development.* Suva, Fiji: South Pacific Social Sciences Association.

Turiel, E. 1977. A critical analysis of Kohlberg's contributions to the study of moral thought. *Journal of Social Behavior* 7:41–63.

———. 1983. *The development of social thought: Morality and convention.* Cambridge: Cambridge University Press.

Turner, B., ed. 1990. *Theories of modernity and postmodernity.* Newbury Park, Calif.: Sage.

Turner, J. W. 1984. "True food" and first fruits: Rituals of increase in Fiji. *Ethnology* 23 (2):133–42.

———. 1986a. The sins of the father: Rank and succession in a Fijian chiefdom. *Oceania* 57 (2):128–41.

———. 1986b. "The water of life": Kava ritual and the logic of sacrifice. *Ethnology* 25 (3):203–14.

———. 1987. Blessed to give and receive: Ceremonial exchange in Fiji. *Ethnology* 26 (3):209–20.

Turner, V. 1969. *The ritual process.* Chicago: Aldine.

———. 1974. Liminal to liminoid in play, flow and ritual. *Rice University Studies* 60:53–99.

———. 1974. *Dramas, fields and metaphors: Symbolic action in human society.* Ithaca: Cornell University Press.

Valkeapaa, N.-A. 1983. *Greetings from Lapland: The Sami — Europe's forgotten people.* London: Zed.

Van Gennep, A. 1960. *The rites of passage.* Chicago: University of Chicago Press.

Vatu, S. 1977. *Na veitalanoa me baleta na i tukutuku maroroi (Talking about oral traditions).* Suva: Fiji Museum.

Wallace, A. 1956. Revitalization movements. *American Anthropologist* 58 (2):264–81.

Ward, C., ed. 1989. *Altered states of consciousness and mental illness: A cross-cultural perspective.* Newbury Park, Calif.: Sage.

Watson, G. 1987. Make me reflexive—but not yet: Strategies for managing essential reflexivity in ethnographic discourse. *Journal of Anthropological Research* 43 (Spring):29–41.

Watson-Gegeo, K., and White, G., eds. 1989. *Disentangling: Conflict discourse in Pacific societies.* Stanford: Stanford University Press.

Watters, R. F. 1969. *Koro: Economic development and social change in Fiji.* Oxford: Clarendon.

Weiner, M. 1970. Notes on some medicinal plants of Fiji. *Economic Botanist* 24 (3):279–82.

Welwood, J. 1983. Vulnerability and power in the therapeutic process. In J. Welwood, ed., *Awakening the heart.* Boulder, Colo.: New Science Library.

Wengle, J. L. 1983. Anthropological training and the quest for immorality. *Ethos* 12 (3):223–44.

West, M. M. 1988. Parental values and behavior in the outer Fiji Islands. In R. A. Levine, P. M. Miller, and M. M. West, eds., *Parental behavior in diverse societies.* San Francisco: Jossey-Bass.

White, G., and Kirkpatrick, J., eds. 1985. *Person, self and experience: Exploring Pacific ethnopsychologies.* Berkeley: University of California Press.

White, M. I., and Pollak, S., eds. 1986. *The cultural transition: Human experience and social transformation in the Third World and Japan.* Boston: Routledge & Kegan Paul.

Whiting, B. 1953. Paiute sorcery. *Viking Fund Publication in Anthropology.* 15. New York: Wenner-Gren Foundation.

Wilber, K., Engler, J., and Brown, D., eds. 1989. *Transformations of consciousness: Conventional and contemplative perspective on development.* Boston: Shambhala.

Williams, T., and Calvert, J. 1858. *Fiji and the Fijians.* New York: AMS 1977.

Winkelman, M. 1984. *A cross-cultural study of magico-religious practitioners.* Ph.D. diss., University of California, Irvine.

Wolf, E. 1982. *Europe and the people without history.* Berkeley: University of California Press.

Wolfe, A. 1989. *Earth elder stories.* Saskatoon, Saskatchewan: Fifth House.

Young, D., Swartz, L., and Ingram, G. 1989. *Cry of the Eagle: Encounters with a Cree healer.* Toronto: University of Toronto Press.

Index

174; presentation upon return to Fiji, 290; ritual exchange of, 47-54, 57, 73-74, 130-131; social drinking of, 49, 51-54, 138, 178, 179; special versus ordinary, 202; truth and, 200; village ceremonies and, 122; as way of being, 320-321. *See also Bilo; Mana*

Yau, 43. *See also* Gifts
Yavusa, 26-27

Zero-sum game, 343-344
Zhu/twa(si), 4, 21, 331, 344

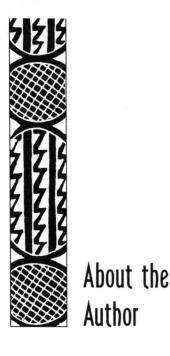

About the Author

Richard Katz, Ph.D.

Dedicated to the repectful exchange of healing wisdom, Richard Katz has worked for twenty-five years with traditional healers and community healing systems throughout the world. After receiving his B.A. from Yale University and his Ph.D. in clinical psychology from Harvard University, he teaches at Saskatchewan Indian Federated College in Saskatoon, Saskatchewan, Canada. He is the author of *Healing Makes Our Hearts Happy, Boiling Energy: Community Healing Among the Kalahari Kung,* and coauthor, with Marie Balter, of *Nobody's Child.*